TOTAL QUALITY

Management, Organization, and Strategy

Second Edition

James R. Evans
University of Cincinnati

James W. Dean, Jr.
University of North Carolina

South-Western College Publishing
Thomson Learning™

Australia • Canada • Denmark • Japan • Mexico • New Zealand • Philippines
Puerto Rico • Singapore • South Africa • Spain • United Kingdom • United States

Total Quality: Management, Organization, and Strategy, 2e, by James R. Evans &
James W. Dean, Jr.

Publisher: Dave Shaut
Acquisitions Editor: Charles McCormick, Jr.
Senior Developmental Editor: Alice C. Denny
Marketing Manager: Joseph A. Sabatino
Production Editor: Elizabeth A. Shipp
Manufacturing Coordinator: Dana Began Schwartz
Cover Design: Jennifer Martin-Lambert
Cover Image: ©1998/PhotoDisc, Inc.
Production House: Trejo Production
Printer: Webcom

Printed in Canada
 5 04

For more information contact South-Western College Publishing, 5191 Natorp Blvd, Mason,
Ohio, 45040 or find us on the Internet at http://www.swcollege.com

For permission to use material from this text or product, contact us by

• telephone: 1-800-730-2214

• fax: 1-800-730-2215

• **web: http://www.thomsonrights.com**

Library of Congress Cataloging-in-Publication Data
Evans, James R. (James Robert)
   Total quality : management, organization, and strategy / James R. Evans, James W. Dean, Jr. —
2nd ed.
    p. cm.
  Dean's name appears first on the earlier edition.
  Includes bibliographical references and index.
  ISBN 0-324-01276-4
  1. Total quality management.   I. Dean, James W., 1956–   II. Title.
  HD62.15 .D4 2000
  658.4'013—dc21

                                                                                      99-33201

CONTENTS

PREFACE

Although the terminology "total quality management" may appear to be a fad that has come and gone, the need for employees to learn and understand the principles of total quality remains vital to the success of business. As the principles of total quality (TQ) have become ingrained in the way many organizations conduct their daily affairs, they are demanding that their new employees understand not only the importance of providing quality products and services to customers, but also the principles and tools of TQ. People starting their working lives unfamiliar with total quality will indeed be one step behind.

It is difficult for readers to learn about TQ on their own, because there are so many different approaches to the topic. Although these approaches are similar, each has its own jargon and acronyms, which makes trying to penetrate the subject for the first time a difficult experience. Furthermore, most books about TQ are not written with the needs and experiences of students in mind.

This book has three objectives:

- to familiarize readers with the basic principles and methods associated with total quality;
- to show readers how these principles and methods have been put into effect in a variety of organizations; and
- to illustrate the relationship between TQ principles and the theories and models studied in management courses.

This book presents the basic principles and tools associated with TQ and provides many cases that can be used as the basis for group discussion. The cases focus on large and small companies in manufacturing and service industries in North and South America, Europe, and Asia.

This book is organized so that it can be used as a supplement to textbooks for courses in management, organization theory, organizational behavior, and/or strategic management. The book can also be used as a freestanding introduction to TQ in an elective course on quality management, or a seminar setting.. Readers who have had the basic courses in management will be familiar with the various theories to which TQ is compared in the book.

Changes in the Second Edition

In preparing the second edition of this book, we added approximately 25 new "boxed" vignettes that illustrate the concepts and themes of TQ in real, and sometimes unusual, circumstances. These are meant to provide an appreciation for the application and universality of the principles of TQ. We also added over a dozen new end-of-chapter cases. In addition to these changes, we brought many discussions up to date with new material or deleted clearly dated material. In particular, we added

- new discussions of TQ and organizational models,
- a more complete and comprehensive discussion of the Baldrige Award and its criteria,
- ISO 9000 frameworks,
- international quality awards,
- statistical thinking,
- process focus,
- quality strategies and results,
- TQ and strategic management theory,
- new examples showing leadership and strategy in action.

Organization of the Book

Unlike most books on TQ, this one is organized according to traditional management topics. This organization helps readers to see the parallels between TQ and management theories in areas such as organizational design and leadership. Total quality is often presented as new or different, which it clearly is not. Many TQ ideas are based on management theories that are familiar to readers. The organization of this book enables readers to appreciate the ways in which TQ really is different.

The book has four parts. Part I, Introduction to Total Quality, presents the core principles of TQ and begins to explain how they relate to familiar management concepts. This section also explains many of the most common TQ techniques readers are likely to encounter. Part II, Total Quality and Organization Theory, introduces the idea of customer-supplier relations and shows how TQ relates to topics such as organization-environment relations, organizational design, and change.

Part III, Total Quality and Organizational Behavior, discusses the themes of teamwork and empowerment and relates TQ to the topics of groups, motivation, and leadership. Part IV, Total Quality and Strategic

Management, deals with the impact of TQ on both the content and process of competitive strategy. The bibliography at the end of the book provides a number of references for readers who wish to expand their understanding of various aspects of TQ.

Because the topics in this book are presented in different orders in different courses, we have tried to make each chapter as freestanding as possible. In most cases, users should read Part I first as an introduction to TQ. After that, the chapters can be covered in virtually any order, thus giving instructors in classroom settings a great deal of flexibility.

ACKNOWLEDGMENTS

We are extremely grateful to the following reviewers who provided excellent feedback and suggestions for improvement on drafts of the first edition of this book and in preparation for the second edition:

Charles Schrader, Iowa State University
Stephen Beckstead, Utah State University
Arthur L. Darrow, Bowling Green State University
Allen Bluedorn, University of Missouri-Columbia
John Alderson, East Arkansas Community College
Uttarayan Bagchi, University of Texas at Austin
David A. Waldman, Concordia University
Cynthia Lengnick-Hall, Wichita State University
Janet Barnard, Rochester Institute of Technology
Karen Hawley, University of Minnesota
Benjamin Abramowitz, University of Central Florida
Barbara Price, Georgia Southern University

In addition, we would like to thank Carole Barnett, Richard Buck, Richard Garula, Gerry Kaminski, Dick McKeever, Todd Molfenter, Barbara Reckers, Ann Schooley, and Charles Seeley, all of whom also contributed to this project in various ways. Finally, we greatly appreciate the help of our editors at South-Western Publishing Company, Charles McCormick and Alice Denny, as well as our former editors from West Publishing Company, Richard Fenton and Esther Craig.

We have come to believe, like many business and academic leaders, that quality is an absolute essential not only for competitive success in business, but also for meaningful work and integrity in many aspects of life. If this book helps readers to contribute to the quality of their organizations' products and services and to understand the importance of quality in all their endeavors, then our efforts will have been worthwhile.

James R. Evans
James W. Dean, Jr.

PART

I

Introduction to Total Quality

1

Introduction

CHAPTER OUTLINE

A Brief History
The Concept of Quality
Quality in Manufacturing
Quality in Services
Principles of Total Quality
Customer Focus
Strategic Planning and Leadership
Continuous Improvement and Learning
Empowerment and Teamwork
TQ and Traditional Management Practices
TQ and Organizational Models
Summary
Review and Discussion Questions
Cases

In this chapter we will introduce you to the basic principles of total quality. Specifically, we will

- provide reasons why attention to quality should be a part of every organization's culture and management systems,
- provide a brief history of the "quality revolution,"
- provide an overview of the key principles of total quality,
- compare and contrast quality-focused management with traditional management practices, and
- discuss relationships of total quality with organizational models in management theory.

To appreciate the impact that quality has had on business, especially in the United States, one need only look at Xerox Corporation. Xerox experienced rapid growth through the 1960s after introducing its 914 copier, called "the most successful business product ever introduced." They reached $1 billion in revenue faster than any other company. They could sell all they produced. They had little competition. And they thought they knew what the customer needed.

In the 1970s Japanese competitors entered the market with cost-competitive machines. Customers now had a choice. As Xerox began to lose market share, the company realized that a tremendous amount of change would be required to compete successfully. Xerox began a process of benchmarking—comparing their products and processes with those of others—to gauge how much improvement was needed. The results shocked top management. Xerox had ten times as many assembly line rejects as their Japanese competitors, twice the product lead time, nine times as many suppliers, and seven times as many defects per hundred machines. Most startling was that their unit manufacturing cost equaled the selling price of their overseas competition.

In 1983 President David Kearns convened the company's top 25 managers. As a result of this meeting, they agreed to focus on quality as the main strategy for running their business. Their agenda for the future was summarized in the Xerox Quality Policy:

- Xerox is a quality company.
- Quality is the basic business principle for Xerox.
- Quality means providing our external and internal customers with innovative products and services that fully satisfy their requirements.
- Quality improvement is the job of every Xerox employee.

Xerox established an initiative called Leadership Through Quality, a 34-step strategy designed to instill quality as the basic business principle throughout the company, ensure that all employees focus on their customers, and pursue quality improvement.

Profitability increased annually as the quality process took root. Between 1986 and 1990 return on assets increased from 7.8 percent to 14.6 percent, and revenues increased from $9.42 billion to $12.69 billion. In 1989 Xerox Business Products and Systems won the Malcolm Baldrige National Quality Award in recognition of its achievements in implementing quality throughout the organization. (The Baldrige Award will be discussed in the next chapter.)

Xerox represents one of the most celebrated turnarounds in American business, and David Kearns became a mentor to many other corporate CEOs. For example, Scott McNealy, CEO of Sun Microsystems, invited Kearns as well as CEOs of FedEx and Motorola to learn about their quality processes. From those meetings came the core principles and strategies that Sun uses today. Although many believe that quality has been simply one of the endless business fads to capture managers' attention, the focus on quality has not diminished at Xerox. In 1997 another division, Xerox Business Services, also won the Baldrige Award, using a much tougher and more comprehensive set of criteria than in 1989.

Total quality—a comprehensive, organization-wide effort to improve the quality of products and services—applies not only to such large manufacturers as Xerox, but also to small companies like Trident Precision Manufacturing (see box). All organizations—large and small, manufacturing and service, profit and not-for-profit—can benefit from applying the principles of total quality. Empirical evidence shows that firms implementing effective total quality approaches improve their performance on measures of income, sales growth, cost control, and growth in employment and total assets.[1]

Quality Starts with a Vision[2]

Unless you live in Webster, New York, you probably have never heard of Trident Precision Manufacturing, Inc. The privately held company, formed in 1979 with three people, today manufactures precision sheet metal components, electromechanical assemblies, and custom products, mostly in the office equipment, medical supply, computer, and defense industries with a workforce of about 170. In 1995 revenues totaled $14.5 million. Trident has established quality as its basic business plan to accomplish short- and long-term goals for five key business drivers: customer satisfaction, employee satisfaction, shareholder value, operational performance, and supplier partnerships. Trident's human resource strategies emphasize training, involvement through teams, empowerment, and reward and recognition. Since 1989, Trident has invested 4.4 percent of its payroll on training and education, two to three times the average for all U.S. industry and especially large for a small firm.

Employee turnover has declined dramatically, from 41 percent in 1988 to 5 percent in 1994 and 1995. Defect rates have fallen so much that Trident offers a full guarantee against defects in its custom products. On-time delivery has increased from 87 percent in 1990 to 99.94 percent in 1995. Rates of return on assets consistently exceed industry averages, customers have rated the quality of their products at 99.8 percent or better, and the company has never lost a customer to a competitor. In 1996, Trident received the Malcolm Baldrige National Quality Award.

How did Trident achieve such success? Trident's total quality quest began in 1988, when CEO Nicholas Juskiw attended a symposium offered by Xerox Corporation about their Leadership Through Quality strategy. When Juskiw wrote his vision statement he said:

"My Vision for Trident is one in which each of us shares in the responsibility, growth, and benefits of becoming a world-class organization. How will we, as a team, achieve this? Through quality! Not just the quality of each individual part but through Total Quality—in everything we say and do. . . . As a strong team, with each headed in the same direction, we can become the unquestionable leader that our Customers, Industry, and Community look up to."

A Brief History

To understand the importance of quality in business today, we need to review some history. Before the Industrial Revolution, skilled craftspeople served both as manufacturers and inspectors, building quality into their products through their considerable pride in their workmanship. Customers expected quality, and craftspeople understood it.

The Industrial Revolution changed everything. Thomas Jefferson brought Honoré Le Blanc's concept of interchangeable parts to America. Eli Whitney mistakenly believed that this idea would be easy to carry out. The government awarded him a contract in 1798 to supply 10,000 muskets in two years. He designed special machine tools and trained unskilled workmen to make parts according to a standard design, measure them, and compare them to a model. Unfortunately, Whitney grossly underestimated the effect of variation in the production process and its impact on quality. It took more than 10 years to complete the project, perhaps the first example of cost-overrun in government contracts! This same obstacle—variation—continues to plague American managers to this day.

Frederick W. Taylor's concept of "scientific management" greatly influenced the nature of quality in manufacturing organizations. By focusing on production efficiency and decomposing jobs into small work tasks, the modern assembly line destroyed the holistic nature of manufacturing. To ensure that products were manufactured correctly, independent "quality control" departments assumed the tasks of inspection. Thus, the separation of good from bad product became the chief means of ensuring quality.

Statistical approaches to quality control had their origins at Western Electric when the inspection department was transferred to Bell Telephone Laboratories in the 1920s. The pioneers of quality control—Walter Shewhart, Harold Dodge, George Edwards, and others—developed new theories and methods of inspection to improve and maintain quality. Control charts, sampling techniques, and economic analysis tools laid the foundation for modern quality assurance activity and influenced the thinking of two of their colleagues, W. Edwards Deming and Joseph M. Juran.

Deming and Juran introduced statistical quality control to Japanese workers after World War II as part of General MacArthur's rebuilding program. Although this was not much different from what was being done in America, there was one vital difference. They convinced top Japanese managers that quality improvement would open new world markets and was necessary for the survival of their nation. The managers believed in, and fully supported, the concept of quality improvement. The Japanese were in an ideal position to embrace this philosophy. The country was devastated from the war, and they had few natural resources with which to compete, except their people. During the next 20 years, while the Japanese were improving quality at an unprecedented rate, quality levels in the West remained stagnant. Western manufacturers had little need to focus on quality. America had a virtual monopoly in manufacturing, and the postwar economy was hungry for nearly any kind of consumer good. Top managers focused their efforts on marketing, production quantity, and financial performance.

During the late 1970s and early 1980s, many businesses in the United States lost significant market share to other global competitors, Japan in particular. For example, U.S.-made computers purchased in the United States dropped from 94 percent in 1979 to 66 percent in 1989. In 1980 domestic automobile manufacturers commanded a 71.3 percent share of the U.S. market; by 1991 this had declined to 62.5 percent. Although the U.S. auto industry has made remarkable progress in slowing and even reversing this trend in recent years, other industries such as machine tool, electronics, and steel have been devastated. Fueling the competitive crisis were the facts that consumers became increasingly quality-conscious and that the technological complexity of modern electronics made sophisticated consumer products more difficult to make.

By 1987 *Business Week* posed a stern warning to American management:

> Quality. Remember it? American manufacturing has slumped a long way from the glory days of the 1950s and '60s when "Made in U.S.A." proudly stood for the best that industry could turn out. . . . While the Japanese were developing remarkably higher standards for a whole host of products, from consumer electronics to cars and machine tools, many U.S. managers were smugly dozing at the switch. Now, aside from aerospace and agriculture, there are few markets left where the U.S. carries its own weight in international trade. For American industry, the message is simple. Get better or get beat.[3]

The "quality revolution" in America can be traced to 1980, when NBC aired a white paper entitled "If Japan Can . . . Why Can't We?" This program introduced the 80-year-old Deming, who was virtually unknown in the United States, to corporate executives across America. Ford Motor Company was among the first to invite Deming to help transform its operations. Within a few years, Ford's earnings were the highest for any company in automotive history, despite a 7 percent drop in U.S. car and truck industry sales, higher capital spending, and increased marketing costs. In 1992 the media celebrated the fact that the Ford Taurus outsold the Honda Accord to become the leader in domestic sales. Former CEO Donald Petersen stated:

> The work of Dr. Deming has definitely helped change Ford's corporate leadership. . . . Dr. Deming has influenced my thinking in a variety of ways. What stands out is that he helped me crystallize my ideas concerning the value of teamwork, process improvement, and the pervasive power of the concept of continuous improvement.

America woke up to quality during the 1980s as most major companies embarked on extensive quality improvement campaigns. In 1984 the U.S. government designated October as National Quality Month. In 1987—some 34 years after Japan established the Deming Prize—Congress established the Malcolm Baldrige National Quality Award, spawning a remarkable interest in quality among American business. By the end of the decade, Florida Power and Light became the first non-Japanese company to win Japan's coveted Deming Prize for quality. After the publicity that quality received from the manufacturing sector, the quality movement shifted to services. Companies like FedEx, the Ritz-Carlton Hotel Company, and AT&T Universal Card Services (now a part of CitiBank) demonstrated clearly that quality principles can be applied effectively in the service sector.

By 1991 *Business Week* was calling quality "a global revolution affecting every facet of business. . . . For the 1990s and far beyond, quality must remain the priority for business." Dr. Joseph Juran, one of the premier leaders in the quality movement, observed:

> I have become optimistic for the first time since the quality crisis descended on the United States. I now believe that, during the 1990s, the number of U.S. companies that have achieved stunning results will increase by orders of magnitude. I also believe that, during the l990s, the United States will make great strides toward making "Made in the U.S.A." a symbol of world class quality.[4]

During the 1990s, health care, government, and education began to pay increased attention to quality. As more public and government attention focuses on the nation's health care system, its providers turn toward quality as a means of achieving better performance and lower costs.[5] One hospital, for example, lowered its rate of postsurgical infections to less than one-fifth of the acceptable national norms by using quality tools. In 1993, Vice President Al Gore spearheaded the National Performance Review, an initiative driven by the need to improve quality. The review made 384 recommendations and indicated 1,214 specific actions that the federal government should take to improve operations and reduce costs. In 1991, a consortium of professional associations, business associations, and individual businesses and universities incorporated a nonprofit group called the National Education Quality Initiative to improve educational processes through quality principles. Many local school systems, colleges, and universities have made considerable progress.

As quality principles have matured in organizations, attention to quality as "something new" has faded. The term "total quality management (TQM)," popular throughout the 1980s and early 1990s, has all but fallen out of the business vernacular. Critics such as *Business Week*'s John Byrne have suggested that "TQM is as dead as a pet rock" (23 June 1997, p. 47). Perhaps it is unfortunate that a three-letter acronym was chosen to represent such a powerful management concept. It is equally unfortunate that people point to the demise of faddish terminology as the death of the concepts themselves. Reasons for failure of quality initiatives are rooted in organizational approaches and systems, many of which this book addresses. Nevertheless, successful organizations have found that the fundamental principles of total quality are essential to effective management practice and represent a sound approach for achieving business success.

The world has become more quality conscious, and companies that resist implementing total quality principles may not survive. In actuality, the quality management discipline is quite young. Companies that have invested millions of dollars in improving quality are not about to let their investment go to waste; however, they need to be both persistent and patient to achieve desired results. A Conference Board (a non-profit business membership organization with over 2,900 worldwide members) study, based on more than five years of research on hundreds of U.S. companies, found that companies need at least 4 years to persuade employees to buy into the quality philosophy and 8 to 10 years to fully establish a quality culture.[6] As Edwin L. Artzt, former CEO of Procter & Gamble and chairman of the 1992 National Quality Month campaign, stated, "Quality has been, and will remain, the key management imperative. Leaders of the best companies profoundly believe in, and promote, the core values of customer-focused quality."

THE CONCEPT OF QUALITY

People define quality in many ways. Some think of quality as superiority or excellence, others view it as a lack of manufacturing or service defects, still others think of quality as related to product features or price (see box). Today most managers agree that the main reason to pursue quality is to satisfy customers. The American National Standards Institute (ANSI) and the American Society for Quality (ASQ) define quality as "the totality of features and characteristics of a product or service that bears on its ability to satisfy given needs." The view of quality as the satisfaction of customer needs is often called *fitness for use*. In highly competitive markets, merely satisfying customer needs will not achieve success. To beat the competition, organizations often must *exceed* customer expectations. Thus, one of the most popular definitions of quality is *meeting or exceeding customer expectations*. Deer Valley Resort is one example of an organization dedicated to exceeding customer expectations (see box on page 10).

You Don't Always Get What You Pay For[7]

The Associated Press reported that a Florida man, who purchased a $262,000 Lamborghini Diablo Roadster, has filed a lawsuit alleging that Lamborghini knew about the car's defects and ignored them. Among his woes: a roof that leaks so badly he can't drive when it rains, a battery that quits without notice, a sunroof that detaches when he drives over a bump, and doors that jam—causing him to have to bang on the windows until a stranger can help get him out.

Quality Is Not a Snow Job[8]

Deer Valley Resort in Park City, Utah, is viewed by many as the Ritz-Carlton of ski resorts, providing exceptional services and a superior ski vacation experience. The resort offers curbside ski valet service to take equipment from vehicles, parking lot attendants to ensure efficient parking, and a shuttle to transport guests from the lot to Snow Park Lodge. Guests walk to the slopes on heated pavers that prevent freezing and assist in snow removal. The central gathering area by the base lifts is wide and level, allowing plenty of room to put on equipment and easy access to the lifts. At the end of the day, guests can store their skis without charge at each lodge. The resort limits the number of skiers on the mountain to reduce lines and congestion and offers complimentary mountain tours for both expert and intermediate skiers. Everyone is committed to ensuring that each guest has a wonderful experience, from "mountain hosts" stationed at the top of the lifts to answer questions and provide directions, to the friendly workers at the cafeterias and restaurants, whose food is consistently rated number one by ski enthusiast magazines. "Our goal is to make each guest feel like a winner," says Bob Wheaton, vice president and general manager. "We go the extra mile on the mountain, in our ski school, and throughout our food-service operation because we want our guests to know they come first."

Managers of manufacturing and service functions deal with different types of quality issues. The following sections provide a brief overview of these issues. Although the details of quality management differ between manufacturing and service industries, the customer-driven definition eliminates these artificial distinctions and provides a unifying perspective.

Quality in Manufacturing

Manufactured products have several quality dimensions[9] including the following:

1. *Performance:* a product's primary operating characteristics.
2. *Features:* the "bells and whistles" of a product.
3. *Reliability:* the probability of a product's surviving over a specified period of time under stated conditions of use.
4. *Conformance:* the degree to which physical and performance characteristics of a product match preestablished standards.
5. *Durability:* the amount of use one gets from a product before it physically deteriorates or until replacement is preferable.
6. *Serviceability:* the ability to repair a product quickly and easily.
7. *Aesthetics:* how a product looks, feels, sounds, tastes, or smells.
8. *Perceived quality:* subjective assessment resulting from image, advertising, or brand names.

Most of these dimensions revolve around the design of the product. In designing the initial Lexus automobile for instance, Toyota bought several competitors' cars, including Mercedes, Jaguar, and BMW, and put them through grueling test track runs before taking them apart.[10] The chief engineer decided that he could match Mercedes on performance and reliability, as well as on luxury and status features. He developed 11 performance goals. The final design had a drag coefficient smaller than any other luxury car (resulting in higher aerodynamic performance), a lighter weight, a more fuel-efficient engine, and a lower noise level. Sturdier materials were used for seat edges to maintain their appearance longer. The engine was designed with more torque than German models to give the car the quick start that Americans prefer. Ford's director of North American interior design called the instrument cluster "a work of art."

Quality control in manufacturing is usually based on conformance, specifically conformance to specifications. Specifications are targets and tolerances determined by designers of products and services. Targets are the ideal values for which production strives; tolerances are acceptable deviations from these ideal values. For example, a computer chip manufacturer might specify that the distance between pins on a computer chip should be .095 ± .005 inches. The value .095 is the target, and ± 0.005 is the tolerance. Thus, any pin distance between .090 and .100 would be acceptable.

A lack of defects has constituted quality in manufacturing for many years. Many studies comparing domestic and foreign products focus on statistical measures of defects. However, the lack of defects alone will not satisfy or exceed customer expectations. Many top managers have stated that good quality of conformance is simply the "entry into the game." A better way to achieve distinction and delight customers is through improved product design. Thus, manufacturers are turning their attention toward improved design for achieving their quality and business goals.

Quality in Services

Today services account for more than 75 percent of the U.S. workforce. The importance of quality in services cannot be underestimated, as statistics from a variety of studies reveal:[11]

- The average company never hears from more than 90 percent of its unhappy customers. For every complaint it receives, the company has at least 25 customers with problems, about one-fourth of which are serious.
- Of the customers who make a complaint, more than half will do business again with that organization if the complaint is resolved. If the customer feels that the complaint was resolved quickly, this figure jumps to about 95 percent.
- The average customer who has had a problem will tell 9 or 10 others about it. Customers who have had complaints resolved satisfactorily will only tell about 5 others.
- It costs six times more to get a new customer than to keep a current customer.

So why do many companies treat customers as commodities? In Japan the notion of customer is equated with "honored guest." Service clearly should be at the forefront of a firm's priorities.

Many of the key dimensions of product quality apply to services. For instance, "on time arrival" for an airline is a measure of service performance; frequent flyer awards and "business class" sections represent features. Banks and hotels have specifications that employees should greet customers using their names or that receptionists should answer telephones within three rings.

Many service organizations have well-developed quality assurance systems. Most of them, however, are based on manufacturing analogies and tend to be more product-oriented than service-oriented. For example, a typical hotel's quality assurance system focuses on technical specifications such as properly made-up rooms. However, service organizations have special requirements that manufacturing systems cannot fulfill. The most important dimensions of service quality include the following:[12]

- *Time:* How much time must a customer wait?
- *Timeliness:* Will a service be performed when promised?
- *Completeness:* Are all items in the order included?
- *Courtesy:* Do frontline employees greet each customer cheerfully?
- *Consistency:* Are services delivered in the same fashion for every customer, and every time for the same customer?
- *Accessibility and convenience:* Is the service easy to obtain?
- *Accuracy:* Is the service performed right the first time?
- *Responsiveness:* Can service personnel react quickly and resolve unexpected problems?

Service organizations must look beyond product orientation and pay significant attention to customer transactions and employee behavior. Several points that service organizations should consider are as follows:[13]

- The quality characteristics that a firm should control may not be the obvious ones. Customer perceptions are critical, although it may be difficult to define what the customer wants. For example, speed of service is an important quality characteristic, yet perceptions of speed may differ significantly among different service organizations and customers. Marketing and consumer research can play a significant role.
- Behavior is a quality characteristic. The quality of human interaction is vital in every transaction that involves human contact. For example, banks have found that the friendliness of tellers is a principal factor in retaining depositors.
- Image is a major factor in shaping customer expectations of a service and in setting standards by which customers evaluate that service. A breakdown in image can be as harmful as a breakdown in delivery of the service itself. Top management is responsible for shaping and guiding the image that the firm projects.

- Establishing and measuring service levels may be difficult. Service standards, particularly those relating to human behavior, are often set judgmentally and are hard to measure. In manufacturing, it is easy to quantify output, scrap, and rework. Customer attitudes and employee competence are not as easily measured.
- Quality control activity may be required at times or in places where supervision and control personnel are not present. Often work must be performed at the convenience of the customer. This calls for more training of employees and self-management.

These issues suggest that the approach to managing quality in services differs from that used in manufacturing. However, manufacturing can be seen as a set of interrelated services, not only between the company and the ultimate consumer, but within the organization. Manufacturing is a customer of product design; assembly is a customer of manufacturing; sales is a customer of packaging and distribution. If quality is meeting and exceeding customer expectations, then manufacturing takes on a new meaning, far beyond product orientation. Total quality provides the umbrella under which everyone in the organization can strive to create customer satisfaction. The Baldrige Award criteria, discussed in chapter 2, do not distinguish between manufacturing and service, even though awards are given in both categories.

PRINCIPLES OF TOTAL QUALITY

A definition of total quality was endorsed in 1992 by the chairs and CEOs of nine major U.S. corporations in cooperation with deans of business and engineering departments of major universities and recognized consultants:

> Total Quality (TQ) is a people-focused management system that aims at continual increase in customer satisfaction at continually lower real cost. TQ is a total system approach (not a separate area or program) and an integral part of high-level strategy; it works horizontally across functions and departments, involves all employees, top to bottom, and extends backward and forward to include the supply chain and the customer chain. TQ stresses learning and adaptation to continual change as keys to organizational success.
>
> The foundation of total quality is philosophical: the scientific method. TQ includes systems, methods, and tools. The systems permit change; the philosophy stays the same. TQ is anchored in values that stress the dignity of the individual and the power of community action.[14]

There probably are as many different approaches to TQ as there are businesses. However, most share some basic elements: (1) customer focus, (2) strategic planning and leadership, (3) continuous improvement and learning, and (4) empowerment and teamwork.

Customer Focus

The customer is the judge of quality. A business can achieve success only by understanding and fulfilling the needs of customers. From a total quality perspective, all strategic decisions a company makes are "customer-driven." In other words, the company shows constant sensitivity to emerging customer and market requirements. This requires an awareness of developments in technology and rapid and flexible response to customer and market needs.

Perceptions of value and satisfaction are influenced by many factors throughout the customer's overall purchase, ownership, and service experiences. Companies must focus on all product and service attributes that contribute to perceived value to the customer and lead to customer satisfaction. To accomplish this task, a company's efforts need to extend well beyond merely meeting specifications, reducing defects and errors, or eliminating complaints. They must include designing new products that truly delight the customer and responding rapidly to changing consumer and market demands. Nevertheless, reducing defects and errors and eliminating causes of dissatisfaction contribute significantly to customers' views of quality and so are important parts of TQ. In addition, the company's approach to recovering from defects and errors that do occur is crucial to its improving both quality and relationships with customers.

Customer-driven firms measure the factors that drive customer satisfaction. A company close to its customer knows what the customer wants, knows how the customer uses its products, and anticipates needs that the customer may not even be able to express. It also continually develops new techniques to obtain customer feedback. Customer opinion surveys and focus groups can help companies understand customer requirements and values. Some companies require their sales and marketing executives to meet with random groups of key customers on a regular basis. Other companies bring customers and suppliers into internal product design and development meetings. The Coca-Cola Company is one example of good customer relationship management (see box).

A firm also must recognize that internal customers—the recipients of any work output, such as the next department in a manufacturing process or the order picker who receives instructions from an order entry clerk—are as important in ensuring quality as are external customers who purchase the product. Failure to meet the needs of internal customers will likely affect external customers. Employees must view themselves as customers of some employees and suppliers to others. Employees who view themselves as both customers of and suppliers to other employees understand how their work links to the final product. After all, the responsibility of any supplier is to understand and meet customer requirements in the most efficient and effective manner possible.

Coke Stays Close to the Customer[15]

While companies concerned about quality try to minimize problems that cause customer dissatisfaction, all companies occasionally receive complaints from customers. Often the response to such a complaint can make the difference between keeping and losing a loyal customer. The Coca-Cola Company's Industry & Consumer Affairs department is responsible for all consumer contacts with the company's headquarters in Atlanta. The mission of the department is "to protect and enhance Coca-Cola's trademarks and image by providing a communications link between consumers and company management." The department's 60 employees handle over 500,000 contacts each year, both by mail and via the company's toll-free hotline (800 GET COKE). Most of the contacts are inquiries about the product.

If a customer does call with a complaint, Coca-Cola sends the customer a letter apologizing for the problem, as well as coupons that allow the customer to replace the unacceptable product. As Roger Nunley, director of Industry & Consumer Affairs, puts it, "We strive to exceed customer expectations every time. We want our customers to be excited and pleased with our response." In certain circumstances, the local Coca-Cola bottler may also follow up with the customer.

A Service Quality Survey is mailed to the customer two weeks after the initial contact. The survey asks the customer to rate the quality of the response, as well as the quality of the phone agent or letter writer (for example, how courteous or professional the company representative was). The survey also asks whether the customer will continue to purchase products of the Coca-Cola Company. According to the company's most recent data, 90 percent of customers were satisfied with how their complaint was handled, but in the spirit of continuous improvement, the company aspires to 100 percent satisfaction.

Customer focus extends beyond the consumer and internal relationships, however. Society represents an important customer of business. A world-class company, by definition, is an exemplary corporate citizen. Business ethics, public health and safety, environment, and sharing of quality-related information in the company's business and geographic communities are necessary activities. In addition, company support—within reasonable limits of its resources—of national, industry, trade, and community activities and the sharing of nonproprietary quality-related information demonstrate far-reaching benefits.

Strategic Planning and Leadership

Achieving quality and market leadership requires a strong future orientation and a willingness to make long-term commitments to key stakeholders—customers, employees, suppliers, stockholders, the public, and the community. Strategic planning needs to anticipate many changes, such as customers' expectations, new business opportunities, technological developments, new customer and market segments, evolving regulatory requirements, community and societal expectations, and competitors' actions. Plans, strategies, and resource allocations need to reflect these commitments and changes. Improvements do not happen overnight. The success of market penetration by Japanese manufacturers evolved over several decades.

Leadership for quality is the responsibility of top management. Senior leadership must set directions; create a customer orientation, clear quality values, and high expectations that address the needs of all stakeholders; and build them into the way the company operates. Senior leaders need to commit to the development of the entire workforce and should encourage participation, learning, innovation, and creativity throughout the organization. Reinforcement of the values and expectations requires the substantial personal commitment and involvement of senior management. Through their personal roles in planning, reviewing company quality performance, and recognizing employees for quality achievement, the senior leaders serve as role models, reinforcing the values and encouraging leadership throughout the organization.

If commitment to quality is not a priority, any initiative is doomed to failure. Lip service to quality improvement is the kiss of death. The CEO of Motorola, one of the first Baldrige winners, had quality as the first agenda item at every top management meeting. He frequently left after quality was discussed, sending the message that once quality was taken care of, financial and other matters would take care of themselves. When the Ritz-Carlton Hotel Company opens a new facility, the CEO works alongside the housekeeping and kitchen staffs, making beds and washing dishes. Imagine the message these actions send to the workers! Many companies have a corporate quality council made up of top executives and managers, which sets quality policy and reviews performance goals within the company. Quality should be a major factor in strategic planning and competitive analysis processes.

Many of the management principles and practices required in a TQ environment may be contrary to long-standing practice, as discussed later in this chapter. Top managers, ideally starting with the CEO, must be the organization's TQ leaders. The CEO should be the focal point, providing broad perspectives and vision, encouragement, and recognition. The leader must be determined to establish TQ initiatives and committed to sustaining TQ activities through daily actions in order to overcome employees' inevitable resistance to change.

Unfortunately, many organizations do not have the commitment and leadership of their top managers. This does not mean that these organizations cannot develop a quality focus. Improved quality can be fostered through the strong leadership of middle managers and the involvement of the workforce. In many cases, this is where quality begins. In the long run, however, an organization cannot sustain quality initiatives without strong top management leadership.

Continuous Improvement and Learning

Continuous improvement is part of the management of all systems and processes. Achieving the highest levels of performance requires a well-defined and well-executed approach to continuous improvement and learning. "Continuous improvement" refers to both incremental and "breakthrough" improvement. Improvements may be of several types:

- enhancing value to the customer through new and improved products and services;
- developing new business opportunities;
- reducing errors, defects, and waste;
- improving responsiveness and cycle time performance; and
- improving productivity and effectiveness in the use of all resources.

"Learning" refers to adaptation to change, leading to new goals or approaches. Improvement and learning need to be embedded in the way an organization operates. This means they should be a regular part of daily work, seek to eliminate problems at their source, and be driven by opportunities to do better as well as by problems that need to be corrected.

Improving Products and Services

Careful research is required to determine the needs of customers, and those needs must be reflected in the design of products and services. A Japanese professor, Noriaki Kano, suggests that three classes of customer needs exist:

- *Dissatisfiers*—needs that are expected in a product or service, such as a radio, heater, and required safety features in an automobile. Such items generally are not stated by customers but are assumed as given. If they are not present, the customer is dissatisfied.
- *Satisfiers*—needs that customers say they want, such as air conditioning or a compact disc player in a car. Fulfilling these needs creates satisfaction.
- *Delighters/exciters*—new or innovative features that customers do not expect. When first introduced, antilock brakes and air bags were examples of exciters. Newer concepts still under development, such as collision-avoidance systems, offer other examples. The presence of such unexpected features, if valued, leads to high perceptions of quality.

The importance of this classification is realizing that although satisfiers are relatively easy to determine through routine marketing research, special effort is required to elicit customer perceptions about dissatisfiers and delighters/exciters. Over time, delighters/exciters become satisfiers as customers become used to them (as is the case today with antilock brakes and air bags), and eventually satisfiers become dissatisfiers (customers are dissatisfied if they are not provided). Therefore, companies must innovate continually and study customer perceptions to ensure that their needs are being met. Scandinavian Airlines is one organization that set about to delight its customers (see box).

Scandinavian Airlines Improves Its Products and Services[16]

Improving the design of its service system transformed Scandinavian Airlines System (SAS) in Sweden. When president and CEO Jan Carlzon took over SAS in 1980, the company was suffering from the effects of an oil shock, two years of financial losses, and high labor costs. These factors prevented the company from competing on price alone with U.S. and Asian airlines. Carlzon set about creating a quality image by instituting low standby fares for passengers under age 27; reconfiguring airplanes to give more comfort and amenities to business-class passengers; training and empowering employees to handle problems swiftly, competently, and without excessive "red tape"; and improving ground service. In the latter category, changes included providing better express check-in service, new business facilities such as computers and fax machines, and automatic delivery of luggage to hotels owned by or linked to SAS's full-service travel agency.

To attain their quality objectives, Carlzon stressed the need to have behavioral change take place at the "moment of truth" where the employee comes in contact with the customer during the process of delivering the company's service.

Designing and Improving Work Processes

Quality excellence derives from well-designed and well-executed work processes and administrative systems that stress prevention. Improvements in the work processes may lead to major reductions in scrap and defects and, hence, to lower costs, as the example about Dell Computer Corporation shows (see box).

Fast response to customers is a major quality attribute. Success in competitive markets increasingly demands shorter product and service introduction cycles and faster response to customers. Reductions in cycle and response time can occur when work processes are designed to meet both quality and response goals. Major improvement in response time often requires simplification of work processes. To accomplish this, the time performance of

---

Michael Dell's Touch for Quality[17]

Although Dell Computer Corporation's PCs have had some of the highest quality ratings in the industry, CEO Michael Dell became obsessed with finding a way to reduce their failure rates. The key, he believed, was to reduce the number of times that each hard drive—the most sensitive part of a PC—was handled during assembly. Production lines were revamped, and the number of "touches" were reduced from more than 30 to less than 15. Soon after, the rate of rejected hard drives fell by 40 percent, and the overall failure rate for the company's PCs dropped by 20 percent.

work processes should be among the most important process measures. Response time improvements often drive simultaneous improvements in organization, quality, and productivity. Hence, it is beneficial to consider response time, quality, and productivity objectives together.

Measuring and Assessing Improvement

The process of continuous improvement must contain regular cycles of planning, execution, and evaluation. This requires a basis—preferably a quantitative basis—for assessing progress and for deriving information for future cycles of improvement. Measurements provide critical data and information about key processes, outputs, and results. When supported by sound analytical approaches that project trends and infer cause-and-effect relationships, measurements provide an objective foundation for learning, leading to better customer, operational, and financial performance.

A company should select performance measures and indicators that best represent the factors that lead to improved customer, operational, and financial performance. These typically include

- customer satisfaction,
- product and service performance,
- market assessments,
- competitive comparisons,
- supplier performance,
- employee performance, and
- cost and financial performance.

A comprehensive set of measures and indicators tied to customer and company performance requirements provides a clear basis for aligning all activities of the company with its goals.

Analyzing the costs of poor quality is one approach that many firms use to identify improvement opportunities. The cost of poor quality includes such items as inspection costs, costs of scrap and rework, customer returns and warranty claims, and other related expenses. The boxed example about Travenol Laboratories (see page 20) illustrates the effective use of such information. The cost of poor quality also goes beyond that of direct costs to the firm. When goods and services fail to meet customers' needs, substantial losses—in the form of lost customers and tarnished reputations—lead to lost income. The cost of poor quality extends to society and the environment in the form of products that cannot be recycled easily, wasted energy needed to run them, or environmental damage from manufacturing wastes and pesticides.

Empowerment and Teamwork

A company's success depends increasingly on the knowledge, skills, and motivation of its work force. Employee success depends increasingly on having opportunities to learn and to practice new skills. This can be fostered through teamwork. Teamwork can be viewed in three ways:

> ### Travenol Laboratories Studies Quality Costs[18]
>
> Travenol Laboratores, Inc. instituted a program to incorporate quality costs and decision support systems to assist managers in discovering significant improvement opportunities in one of its northern Illinois manufacturing facilities. A committee consisting of the plant manager, the engineering manager, and the controller meets each month to identify areas of opportunity for improving quality and reducing costs. They use a computerized system to track trends in quality-related costs.
>
> The system has a high degree of flexibility that allows managers to view monthly or year-to-date data, total costs, costs divided by the value of production or machine hours, and other statistics. Once the committee has found an area of opportunity, it assigns a diagnostic team of technical and operations staff to investigate the problem. The diagnostic team seeks to discover causes and remedies, evaluates the quality and economic impact of various alternatives, and recommends courses of action to the committee.

1. *Vertical*—teamwork between top management and lower-level employees. Vertical teamwork is usually evidenced by *empowerment*—giving people authority to make decisions and have control over their work; for example, employees can make decisions that satisfy customers without a lot of bureaucratic hassles, and barriers between levels are removed.
2. *Horizontal*—teamwork within work groups and across functional lines (often called cross-functional teams). A product development team might consist of designers, manufacturing personnel, suppliers, salespeople, and customers.
3. *Interorganizational*—partnerships with suppliers and customers. Rather than dictating specifications for purchased parts, a company might develop specifications jointly with suppliers to take advantage of the suppliers' manufacturing capabilities.

Vertical Teamwork

Everyone must participate in quality improvement efforts. The person in any organization who best understands his or her job and how it can be improved is the one performing it. Employees must be empowered to make decisions that affect quality and to develop and implement new and better systems. This often represents a profound shift in the philosophy of senior management, as the traditional philosophy is that the workforce should be "managed" to conform to existing business systems. As an example, Dana Commercial Credit Corporation has a "just do it" policy to empower its people to act on ideas for improvement without prior approval.

Companies can encourage participation by recognizing team and individual accomplishments, sharing success stories throughout the organization, encouraging risk taking by removing the fear of failure, encouraging the formation of employee involvement teams, implementing suggestion systems that act rapidly, provide feedback, and reward implemented suggestions, and providing financial and technical support to employees to develop their ideas. Marriott and American Express[19] are two examples of companies that exemplify the empowering and rewarding of employees for service quality. At Marriott, customer service representatives are called "associates" and have wide discretion to call on any part of the company to help customers. Indeed, they earn lush bonuses for extraordinary work. At American Express cash awards of up to $1,000 have been given to "Great Performers" such as Barbara Weber, who in 1986 cut through miles of State Department and Treasury Department red tape to refund $980 of stolen traveler's checks to a customer stranded in Cuba.

Employees need training in skills related to performing their work and to understanding and solving quality-related problems. Frontline workers need the skills to listen to customers; manufacturing workers need specific skills in developing technologies; and all employees need to understand how to use measurements to drive continuous improvement. Training brings all employees to a common understanding of goals and objectives and the means to attain them. Training usually begins with awareness of quality management principles and is followed by specific skills in quality improvement. Training should be reinforced through on-the-job applications of learning, involvement, and empowerment.

Increasingly, training and participation need to be tailored to a more diverse workforce. All employees, from the CEO on down, must be suitably trained and involved in quality activities. Managers must view training as a continuous effort, not a one-time project. This requires a commitment of significant resources that many firms are reluctant to make.

Horizontal Teamwork

Problem solving and process improvement are best performed by cross-functional work teams. For example, Texas Instruments Defense Systems & Electronics Group (now Raytheon Systems Company) uses corporation teams to work on corporate-level goals, employee effectiveness teams to prevent potential problems in specific work areas, and department action teams to solve departmental problems. Granite Rock Company, with fewer than 400 employees, has about 100 functioning teams, ranging from 10 corporate quality teams, to project teams, purchasing teams, task forces, and function teams composed of people who do the same job at different locations.

Interorganizational Partnerships

Partnerships must be created both internally and externally. Companies should seek to build partnerships that serve mutual and larger community interests. Partnerships might include those that promote labor-management cooperation, such as agreements with unions that entail employee development, cross-training, or new work organizations. Internal partnerships might also involve creating network relationships among company units to improve flexibility, responsiveness, and knowledge sharing. External partnerships might be with suppliers, customers, or educational organizations. Partnerships permit the blending of a company's core competencies with complementary strengths and capabilities of partners.

One example of supplier partnerships involves local telephone companies who provide AT&T access to their customers. Following divestiture, AT&T established a Financial Assurance Organization to check the accuracy of access charges and to correct errors. By 1989, AT&T employed 1,100 people working to duplicate the supplier's access-billing system, anticipate charges, and resolve problems. In 1990, AT&T began a joint effort with Pacific Bell to design a single access billing verification process that involved both supplier and customer. The new process shifted focus from correction to prevention, moved account-ability for accuracy to the supplier, and replaced postbill resolution with prebill certification. As a result, validation time declined from three months to 24 hours, accuracy went up, and costs came down.

These principles will continue to develop in organizations. Armand Feigenbaum, one of the international leaders in the quality movement, talked about the future of quality management in the new millenium.[20] Feigenbaum stated that competitive organizations in the future will

- make quality the epicenter of increasing revenue growth and competitive leadership;
- achieve complete customer satisfaction by offering essentially perfect goods and services whose quality the customer determines;
- accelerate sales and earnings growth through quality failure reduction;
- innovate in product and service leadership and cycle-time management;
- restore the "fizz" in jobs by using tools and resources to encourage employee participation in quality improvement;
- develop effective supplier partnerships;
- create a seamless quality value network among customers, producer, and supplier relationships;
- provide environmental and safety leadership; and
- ensure that quality remains the company's international business language.

TQ AND TRADITIONAL MANAGEMENT PRACTICES

TQ is quite different from traditional management practices, requiring changes in organizational processes, beliefs and attitudes, and behaviors. "Traditional management" means the way things are usually done in most organizations in the absence of a TQ focus. Many "traditional" organizations have been ap-plying TQ principles all along, so not all of these comments pertain to every organization. The nature of TQ differs from common management practices in many respects. Among the key differences that will be explored in greater depth throughout this book are the following:[21]

1. Strategic Planning and Management
    In traditional management, financial and marketing issues such as prof-itability, return on investments, and market share drive strategic plan-ning. Quality planning activities are delegated to the "quality control"

department. Long-term quality initiatives are viewed as being costly and not contributing to the ultimate performance measure—profit. Quality planning and strategic business planning are indistinguishable in TQ. Quality goals are the cornerstone of the business plan. Measures such as customer satisfaction, defect rates, and process cycle times receive as much attention in the strategic plan as financial and marketing objectives.

2. Changing Relationships with Customers and Suppliers
    In traditional management, quality is defined as adherence to internal specifications and standards. Quality is measured only by the absence of defects. Inspection of people's work by others is necessary to control defects. In TQ, quality is defined as products and services beyond present needs and expectations of customers. Innovation is required to meet and exceed customers' needs.

    Traditional management places customers outside of the enterprise and within the domain of marketing and sales. TQ views everyone inside the enterprise as a customer of an internal or external supplier, and a supplier of an external or internal customer. Marketing concepts and tools can be used to assess internal customer needs and to communicate internal supplier capabilities.

    In traditional management, suppliers are pitted against each other to get the lowest price. The more competing suppliers there are, the better it is for the customer company. In TQ, suppliers are partners with their customers. The aim of the partnership is innovation, reduction in variation of critical characteristics of supplied materials, lower costs, and better quality. The aim may be enhanced by reducing the number of suppliers and establishing long-term relationships.

3. Organizational Structure
    Traditional management views an enterprise as a collection of separate, highly specialized individual performers and units, loosely linked by a functional hierarchy. Lateral connections are made by intermediaries close to the top of the organization. TQ views the enterprise as a system of interdependent processes, linked laterally over time through a network of collaborating (internal and external) suppliers and customers. Each process is connected to the enterprise's mission and purpose through a hierarchy of micro- and macroprocesses. Every process contains subprocesses and is also contained within a higher process. This structure of processes is repeated throughout the hierarchy.

    In traditional management, hierarchical "chimney" organization structures promote identification with functions and tend to create competition, conflict, and adversarial relations between functions. In TQ, formal and informal mechanisms encourage and facilitate teamwork and team development across the entire enterprise.

    Traditional managers oversee departments or functions that do not know they are interdependent, and each department acts as if it were the whole. Problems are seen as the result of individual people or departments not doing their best. TQ managers run interdependent systems and processes and exercise managerial leadership through participative management in carrying out their roles as mentors, facilitators, innovators, and so on. Quality results from the enterprise's systems. People working in the system cannot do better than the system allows. The vast majority of problems will be prevented and improvement will be promoted when people understand where they fit in and have the knowledge to maximize their contribution to the whole. Only management can foster an environment that nurtures a team-oriented culture that can prevent problems and continually improve.

4. Organizational Change
    Once a traditional organization has found a formula for success, it keeps following it. Management's job is to prevent change, to maintain the status quo. In TQ, the environment in which the enterprise interacts is changing constantly. If the enterprise continues to do what it has done in the past, its future performance relative to the competition will deteriorate. Management's job, therefore, is to provide the leadership for continual improvement and innovation in processes and systems, products, and services. External change is inevitable, but a favorable future can be shaped.

5. Teamwork
    In traditional management, individuals and departments work for themselves. Individuals are driven by short-term performance measures, have narrowly defined jobs, and rarely see how they fit into the whole process or system. Little communication and cooperation exists between design and manufacturing, manufacturing and marketing, and sales/service and design. In TQ, individuals cooperate in team structures such as quality circles, steering committees, and self-directed work teams. Departments work together toward system optimization through cross-functional teamwork.

    The adversarial relationship between union and management is inevitable in traditional management. The only room for negotiation is in areas such as wages, health, and safety. In TQ, the union is a partner and a stakeholder in the success of the enterprise. The areas for partnership and collaboration are broad, particularly in education, training, and meaningful employee involvement in improving processes that they affect and that affect their work.

6. Motivation and Job Design
    Traditional management motivates employees through fear of punishment. People are motivated to perform in order to avoid failure and punishment, rather than to contribute something of value to the enterprise. Employees are afraid to do anything that would displease the boss or not be in compliance with company regulations. The system makes people feel like losers. TQ managers provide leadership rather than overt intervention

Procter & Gamble Embraces TQ[22]

Quality is not new at Procter & Gamble. In 1987 William Cooper Procter, grandson of the company's founder, told his employees, "The first job we have is to turn out quality merchandise that consumers will buy and keep on buying. If we produce it efficiently and economically, we will earn a profit, in which you will share. Today, P&G focuses on delivering superior consumer satisfaction using four basic principles:

- Really know our customers and consumers. Know those who resell our products and those who finally use them—and then meet and exceed their expectations.
- Do right things right. This requires hard data and sound statistical analysis to select the "right things" and to direct continual improvement in how well we do those things.
- Concentrate on improving systems. In order to achieve superior customer and consumer satisfaction and leadership financial goals, we must continually analyze and improve the capability of our basic business systems and subsystems.
- Empower people. This means removing barriers and providing a climate in which everyone in the enterprise is encouraged and trained to make his or her maximum contribution to business objectives.

The P&G Statement of Purpose captures the "what," "how," and expected "results" of their quality efforts:

We will provide products of superior quality and value that best fill the needs of the world's consumers.

We will achieve that purpose through an organization and a working environment that attracts the finest people; fully develops and challenges our individual talents; encourages our free and spirited collaboration to drive the business ahead; and maintains the company's historic principles of integrity and doing the right thing.

Through the successful pursuit of our commitment, we expect our brands to achieve leadership share and profit positions that, as a result, our business, our people, our shareholders, and the communities in which we live and work, will prosper.

in the processes of their subordinates, who are viewed as process managers rather than functional specialists. People are motivated to make meaningful contributions to what they believe is an important and noble cause, of value to the enterprise and society. The system enables people to feel like winners.

In traditional management, competition is inevitable and inherent in human nature. Performance appraisal, recognition and reward systems place people in an internally competitive environment. Individualism is reinforced to the detriment of teamwork. Competitive behavior—one person against another or one group against another—is not a natural state in TQ. TQ reward systems recognize individual as well as team contributions and reinforce cooperation.

7.   Management and Leadership
Traditional management views people as interchangeable commodities, developed to meet the perceived needs of the enterprise. People are passive contributors with little autonomy—doing what they are told and nothing more. TQ views people as the enterprise's true competitive edge. Leadership provides people with opportunities for personal growth and development. People are able to take pride and joy in learning and accomplishment, and the ability of the enterprise to succeed is enhanced. People are active contributors, valued for their creativity and intelligence. Every person is a process manager presiding over the transformation of inputs to outputs of greater value to the enterprise and to the ultimate customer.

In traditional management, control is achieved by preestablished, inflexible response patterns given in the book of rules and procedures. People are customers of a "book" that prescribes appropriate behaviors. In TQ, control is achieved by shared values and beliefs and by knowledge of mission, purpose, and customer requirements.

The principles of total quality management are embodied in the business philosophy of many leading companies, such as Procter & Gamble (see box on page 25). Our purpose in this book is to provide a solid link between concepts of total quality and the traditional management areas of organization theory, organizational behavior, and strategy. When any company begins to think about how to improve, it will be led to the various approaches that are united under the TQ concept. Today, total quality is a matter of survival.

TQ AND ORGANIZATIONAL MODELS[23]

TQ is a new way of thinking about the management of organizations. However, it is not a totally new paradigm. When we compare TQ with well-known organizational models, we can see that it captures many aspects of these established models and amplifies them by providing a useful methodology. Three major organizational models that management theorists have studied are the mechanistic, organismic, and cultural models of organizations. Contrasts between TQ and these models are summarized in Table 1.1.

The mechanistic model, described by classical management theorists, views an organization as a tool or a machine designed solely to create profits for its owners. Work is reduced to elementary tasks, with a focus on efficiency, conformity, and compliance. While both the mechanistic model and TQ assume that the organization exists to achieve a specific performance goal, TQ has a broader definition of quality. TQ takes more of an open-systems perspective, which views managers as leaders and visionaries rather than as individuals who plan, organize, direct, and control. It broadens employees' roles; em-

TABLE 1.1 SUMMARY OF TQ AND ORGANIZATIONAL MODELS

Dimension	TQ Paradigm	Mechanistic Model	Organismic Model	Cultural Model
Goal	Long-term survival	Organizational efficiency and performance	Organizational survival	Meet individual needs; human development
Definition of quality	Satisfying or delighting the customer	Conformance to standards	Customer satisfaction	Constituent satisfaction
Role/ nature of environment	Blurred organization and environmental boundaries	Objective, outside boundary	Objective; inside boundary	Enacted/boundaries defined through relationships
Role of management	Focus on improvement and creating a system that can produce quality outcomes	Coordinate and provide visible control	Coordinate and provide invisible control by creating vision and system	Coordinate and mediate negotiations regarding vision, system, rewards
Role of employees	Employees are empowered; training and education provide needed skills	Passive, follow orders	Reactive/self-control within system parameters	Active/self-control; participate in creation of vision, system
Structural rationality	Horizontal processes beginning with suppliers and ending with customers and supported by teams	Chain of command (vertical) Technical rationality	Process flow (horizontal and vertical) Organizational rationality	Mutual adjustment in any direction Political rationality
Philosophy toward change	Change, continuous improvement, and learning are encouraged	Stability is valued; learning arises from specialization	Change and learning assist adaptation	Change and learning are valued in themselves

Republished with permission of the Academy of Management, P.O. Box 3020, Briarcliff Manor, New York 10510-8020. *Models of Organization and Total Quality Management: A Comparison and Critical Evaluation* (Table), Barbara A. Spencer, *Academy of Management Review*, 1994, Vol. 19, No. 3. Reproduced by permission of the publisher via Copyright Clearance Center, Inc.

phasizes a horizontal, rather than vertical, work organization; and focuses on continuous improvement rather than stability. Narrow-minded managers and those who criticize TQ often view it in a mechanistic sense and do not see the broader implications.

The organismic model views organizational systems as living organisms that depend on their environments for resources and adjust the behavior of their parts to maintain the properties of the whole within acceptable limits. This model assumes that systems goals, such as the need to survive, displace performance goals, such as profit. TQ is similar in that survival in competitive environments is often the primary motivation for adopting it. Customer satisfaction as a definition of quality is compatible with this notion. In the organismic model, organizations are not autonomous entities. This is consistent with the notion of partnership development espoused by TQ: Vision replaces fear as a motivator and driver of management actions; employees work for shared beliefs and values; horizontal communication becomes as important as vertical communication and direction in stressing coordination and organizational rationality; and the organization must adapt to a broad array of external forces. It is evident that TQ shares many similarities with this organizational model. This helps explain why many practitioners have viewed TQ as something new, while many academics recognize its roots in systems theory that was popular decades ago.

The cultural model views an organization as a collection of cooperative agreements entered into by individuals with free will. The organization's culture and social environment are enacted or socially constructed by organization members. From the perspective of this model, the goal of an organization is to serve the diverse needs of all whom it affects—its stakeholders—a view often expressed by TQ philosophers. Because of the multiplicity of stakeholders, quality has many meanings, although some degree of consensus is needed regarding the organization's values and purposes. Although TQ generally assumes that organizations must adapt to the expectations of customers, more recent views of building partnerships and sharing of best practices (even with competitors) are consistent with the cultural model. In the cultural model, managers take on a more distinctive leadership role, relinquishing control and sharing power in order to meet the needs of the many individuals in the organization; employees have greater voice in establishing organizational goals; all structural decisions are value based and have clear implications for individual autonomy (political rationality); and learning needs are driven not by adaptation to environmental forces but in response to individual needs. Many of these attributes are characteristic of recent trends in the evolution of TQ themes in high-performing organizations.

In summary, TQ appears to have evolved from reactionary influences against the mechanistic model of management and embraced many of the characteristics of the organismic model. Recent trends, however, suggest that ideas from the cultural model are influencing the maturity of TQ in modern organizations. This will become more evident as we discuss the Malcolm Baldrige Criteria for Performance Excellence in the next chapter.

SUMMARY

Quality—meeting and exceeding customer expectations—is a major concern to all manufacturing and service organizations. Foreign competition has made companies focus on quality as a key business strategy. *Total quality* denotes a comprehensive effort involving everyone in an organization to meet customer needs and continuously improve products and services.

The key elements of TQ are customer focus, strategic planning and leadership, continuous improvement, and empowerment and teamwork. Total quality represents a radical change from traditional management practices. In this sense, an organization that pursues total quality must address issues of organizational and behavioral change. The remainder of this book develops these concepts further and ties them together with theories of management, organization, and strategy. However, from the perspective of management theory, TQ is not entirely new, but an adaptation of principles that have been known for many years.

REVIEW AND DISCUSSION QUESTIONS

1. Explain why quality became the most important issue facing American business in the 1980s. In addition to the economic competition from Japan, what other factors may have contributed to the importance that quality has assumed?
2. Cite several examples in your own experience in which your expectations were met, exceeded, or not met in purchasing goods or services. How did you regard the company after your experience?
3. How might the definition of quality apply to your college or university? Provide examples of who some customers are and how their expectations can be met or exceeded.
4. Think of a product with which you are familiar. Describe the eight "multiple quality dimensions" for this product that are listed in this chapter.
5. What might the eight "multiple quality dimensions" mean for a college or university? For a classroom?
6. Explain the differences between manufacturing and service organizations and their implications for quality.
7. Describe the key elements of total quality.
8. How might you apply the concepts of total quality to your personal life? Consider your relations with others and your daily activities, such as being a student, belonging to a fraternity or professional organization, and so on.
9. Why is a customer focus a critical element of TQ?
10. Make a list of your personal "customers." What steps might you take to understand their needs and remain "close" to them?
11. Cite an example in which you did not purchase a product or service because it lacked "dissatisfiers" as defined in the chapter. Cite another example in which you received some "exciters/delighters" that you did not expect.
12. In what ways might the lack of top management leadership in a quality effort hinder or destroy it?

13. Explain the various areas within an organization in which continuous improvement may take place.
14. Why is measurement important in a TQ effort?
15. Examine some process with which you are familiar. Make a list of ways that the process can be measured and improved. What difficulties might you face in implementing these ideas?
16. Describe the three ways of viewing teamwork.
17. Describe some possible ways in which vertical, horizontal, and interorganizational teamwork can be applied at a college or university.
18. What does empowerment mean? How might an employee really know that he or she is truly empowered?
19. Have you ever felt restricted in your work because of a lack of empowerment? Can you cite any experiences in which you noticed a lack of empowerment in a person who was serving you? Why is this such a difficult concept to implement in organizations?
20. Explain the key differences between "traditional" management practices and those in a TQ environment.
21. Prepare a self-assessment questionnaire designed to determine if an organization follows traditional management practices or a TQ approach. You might consider applying it to some organization.

CASES

Hillshire Farm/Kahn's[24]

In 1971, Consolidated Foods Incorporated (later to be renamed Sara Lee) acquired Quality Packing Company, the forerunner of Hillshire Farm, to complete the meat product lines for their Kahn's division and compete in the smoked sausage market. In 1988, Hillshire Farm merged with Kahn's to gain economies of scale and buying power.

Milton Schloss, president of Kahn's at the time of the acquisition, wanted to produce smoked sausage products that were equal to or superior to the market leader, Eckrich. Hillshire Farm later surpassed Eckrich as the leader in the smoked sausage market.

As president of Hillshire Farm and Kahn's, Schloss was a firm believer in "managing by walking around." He made a habit of making a daily tour of the plant and asking employees "what's new?" One day an employee asked him if he really meant it. This surprised Schloss, and he arranged to meet privately with the employee early the next morning. The employee arrived with a balsa wood model of a new plant layout he had been working on at home. Recognizing the superiority of his ideas, Schloss asked him why he had not come forward sooner. The employee said that nobody had ever asked him. The design was implemented and portions are still in place at Hillshire Farm in Cincinnati. This event was a catalyst for further quality efforts.

Drawing from a similar program at Procter & Gamble, Hillshire Farm developed a system called Deliberate Methods Change (DMC) to seek ways for continually improving their processes. Using DMC, semivoluntary groups of salaried employees met to improve current processes. By emphasizing the positive aspects of improvement and refusing to place blame on workers for process design flaws, these groups built trust among the workforce.

Schloss was a firm believer in quality within the meat industry, and especially at Hillshire Farm. He used customer complaints—or more accurately, what customers found unacceptable—as the basis for defining quality. Schloss personally answered all customer complaints promptly, something that was unheard of at the time. Frequently customers were so surprised to hear from the company president that they apologized for their complaints. However, Schloss listened carefully to understand the nature of the complaint so he could improve product quality. Also, he believed that a phone call from the company president would allow Hillshire Farm to keep the customer for life.

Schloss took a variety of steps to show his commitment and improve quality. He kept the plant grounds free of litter, freshly painted all the walls, and kept the grass and the shrubbery neatly trimmed. In this way he communicated to employees the attitude they should adopt when they entered the building. Schloss also required that all telephone calls be answered after two rings and that the caller not be kept on hold for long.

The company defined four dimensions of quality—taste, particle definition, color, and packaging—and kept all employees continually informed of the company's quality standards. The accounting and finance departments judged quality according to how promptly and accurately they could make invoices and payments. Marketing and sales were responsible for identifying the features of the product that the customer perceived as most valuable and differentiable and for convincing the customer of Hillshire Farm's leadership in these features.

Schloss personally saw to it that these activities were performed throughout the company. He believed that management must act immediately on new ideas and suggestions. Getting commitment from supervisors was the most difficult task. Management had to explain the "hows and whys" behind the changes, motivate the workers, and recognize the top performers.

When Bill Geoppinger became the CEO at Hillshire Farm and Kahn's, he realized that a great challenge lay ahead. He had inherited an organization that, although focused on quality, was essentially an autocracy. Employees were used to management making the decisions, and Geoppinger realized that it would be difficult to make significant changes because of the cultural tradition.

To implement a total quality effort successfully, Geoppinger realized that the corporate culture would have to change, to become more open, flexible, and responsive. He brought in a new management team that emphasized total quality and team approaches and discontinued many of the personal initiatives devised by Milton Schloss. The 1988 merger of Hillshire Farm and Kahn's further served to change the corporate culture. Empowerment of employees became a priority. Management held regular meetings with line employees to give them the opportunity to share their concerns. Geoppinger encouraged line employees to participate as members of DMC teams. This open culture and focus on empowerment was adapted to all aspects of the business, including accounting, finance, and marketing. However, the total quality effort is most visible in production operations.

In 1991 the Deli Select Line implemented statistical process control (SPC). The company was the market leader in this product category and wished to keep its competitive advantage in this low-margin business. The division was relatively new and had new employees who could be empowered with little resistance. Before implementing SPC, the only data they collected was yield, the "efficient use of inputs." The team decided that yield improvement would be a good objective for improving costs. However, they could not sacrifice quality for yield, so they also monitored defect rates. They tracked defect rates by monitoring product specifications of the output and tracking customer complaints.

Calculating product defects was challenging. They had to quantify customers' perceptions of quality from complaint records. Through team efforts, they defined specifications for the product and its packaging. The product was inspected from the customer's point of view, as seen through the package window. Because they continually monitored incoming meat quality in identifying yields, they felt that this amount of inspection was sufficient.

To track defect rates, they pulled a box of finished products at random every hour and inspected it for product and packaging characteristics. Points were assigned based on severity and graphed on a control chart. Improvements in defects and yields were both realized using SPC. By statistically tracking customer complaints, they could determine which factors were the greatest cause of concern. For example, fat is a major concern because it is highly visible in darker meat products.

Discussion Questions

1. Based on the facts presented in this case, assess the company in the areas of
   - customer focus
   - strategic planning and leadership
   - continuous improvement
   - empowerment and teamwork
2. List strengths and opportunities for improvement that you would suggest in each of these categories. Would you state that Hillshire Farm/Kahn's has fully adopted TQ? Why or why not? What steps would you recommend that the company take next?

Mercantile Stores[25]

Mercantile Stores Co., Inc., acquired by Dillard's Inc. in 1998, was one of the most successful retailers in the nation, operating under 13 different names in 17 states. Mercantile's mission statement stated that "Mercantile Stores is dedicated to creating excitement in merchandising by providing the highest level of service to our customers and a broad assortment of fashionable products that offer superior quality and value." In 1983, Mercantile initiated a program for processing incoming merchandise at regional distribution centers. This was seen as more efficient than receiving merchandise in the individual stores. In 1986, they remodeled and expanded existing stores to accommodate a greater selection of fashion merchandise. Designer apparel offerings were increased in 1987.

In 1989 a major technological initiative called Quick Response was instituted. It integrated all facets of operations, from inventory planning to purchasing and inventory control, to provide customers with better service. Some of the technologies introduced were price lookup and point-of-sale laser scanning systems, electronic purchase ordering and replenishment, and electronic invoicing and funds transfer. Stronger partnerships were developed with suppliers to help ensure that suppliers had sufficient merchandise for stocking the stores. The company was in constant contact with its suppliers for mutual benefit. For example, Hanes hosiery used selling information furnished electronically and shipped 97 percent of Quick Response orders. Sales increased 17 percent, and the inventory level decreased by 15 percent.

The Quick Response program eliminated bottlenecks within the merchandise processing functions. Previously, shipments had required a high amount of labor-intensive efforts: opening cartons, physical counts, sorting, and manual ticketing. Under the new program, advance shipping notice capability provided the means of knowing exactly what was coming and when. Shipments arrived preticketed by suppliers with external shipping container marking. Entire containers were scanned for contents and matched to purchase orders.

Mercantile Stores established Mercantile Stores University, modeled after Disney, GM, and McDonald's, for training its management associates to implement quality practices within the company. The school's motto, "Investing in excellence through education," reflected the company's commitment to the development of its people. New hires participated in a four-day learning course that included world-class customer service training as well as routine job skills. Sales associates, department managers, and store managers were empowered and challenged to embrace ownership and responsibility in their jobs. They planned and monitored their own forecasts from start to finish, for example.

A focus on the customer included special services such as Personal Shopper Service, which was devoted to helping customers select merchandise for their own needs or for gifts—with wrapping and delivery provided at no additional charge. Complete customer satisfaction was seen as the responsibility of all associates. Customer contact skills were reflected in the company's three As—Attitude, Appearance, and Attention—and C.A.R.E. (Customers are Really Everything). Associates were empowered to recognize problems and respond to complaints. Decisions were made as close to the customer as possible, and promotions were made from within the company.

Discussion Questions

1. How did Mercantile view quality? Explain the roles of people and information technology in achieving quality in the Mercantile organization.
2. Compare the importance of "internal quality" (what the company sees) and "external quality" (what the customer sees). Do they conflict? What is needed to ensure that they are consistent?

Surf and Turf Quality[26]

Kelley's Seafood Restaurant was founded about 15 years ago by Tim Kelley, who has run it from the start. The restaurant is very profitable because of its excellent quality of food, but lately it has been having problems with consistency because of numerous suppliers. The restaurant operations are divided into front-end (servers) and back-end (kitchen). The kitchen has Post-it notes to boost employee morale, employees are cross-trained in all areas, and the kitchen staff continually seek improvements in cooking. Servers, however, have few perks and minimal wages, and turnover is a bit of a problem. Tim's primary criterion for selecting servers is their ability to show up on time. There is little communication between the front-end and back-end operations, other than fulfilling orders. Tim makes sure that any complaints are referred to him immediately by the servers.

The restaurant has no automation, as Tim believes that it would get in the way of customers' special requests. "This is the way we've done it for the past 15 years and how we will continue to do it," was his response to a suggestion of using a computerized system to speed up orders and eliminate delays. Tim used to hold staff meetings regularly, but recently they have dropped from once each week to one every five or six months. Most of the time is spent focusing on negative behavior, and Tim has often said "You can't find good people anymore."

Jim's SteakHouse is a family-owned restaurant in the same state. Jim uses only the freshest meats and ingredients from the best suppliers and gives extra-large portions of food so customers feel they are getting their money's worth. Jim pays his cooks high wages to attract quality employees. Servers get 70 percent of tips, bussers 20 percent, and the kitchen staff 10 percent to foster teamwork. Many new hires come from referrals from current employees. Jim interviews all potential employees and asks them many pointed questions relating to courtesy, responsibility, and creativity. The restaurant sponsors bowling nights, golf outings, picnics, and holiday parties for its employees. At Jim's, birthday customers receive a free dinner, children are welcomed with balloons, candy, and crayons, and big-screen TVs cater to sports fans. Jim walks around and constantly solicits customer feedback. Jim visits many other restaurants to study their operations and learn new techniques. As a result of these visits, Jim installed computers to schedule reservations and enter orders to the kitchen.

Discussion Questions

1. Contrast these two restaurants from the perspective of TQ. What conclusions can you make and what advice would you recommend to the owners?
2. What type of management model (mechanistic, organismic, or cultural) do you think each organization represents?

Saturn Corporation[27]

General Motors' Saturn project has become a test of whether U.S. industry can adapt and beat the Japanese automakers at what they do best. Saturn was born in June 1982, when GM began a top-secret project aimed at revolutionizing car making in the United States. They named it Saturn after the rocket that propelled the United States past the Soviets' lead in space exploration. The Saturn Corporation was formed as a wholly owned subsidiary of General Motors in January 1985. GM's chairman Roger Smith called Saturn "the key to GM's long term competitiveness, survival, and success."

In the small car market in which Saturn vehicles compete, quality is a "must." Meeting and exceeding customers' requirements and expectations on a consistent basis is a key strategy in Saturn's success. To accomplish its objective, the Saturn project began with a clean slate. Nothing in GM's manufacturing past was required for building the Saturn; all design and engineering approaches were new. The Saturn manufacturing complex was built to be self-sufficient, with its own stamping plants, power train assembly, and foundries. Saturn was originally intended to be a high-tech factory full of automated equipment and robots. But GM's joint venture with Toyota proved that labor-management relations could do more for quality and productivity than automation. Workers are chosen more for their interpersonal skills than for technical skills.

Saturn machines and assembles both manual and automatic transmissions on the same line in any sequence, a first for a U.S. manufacturer. Cars move along the line on wooden pallets and workers travel with them, which is easier on workers' legs than standing on concrete floors and eliminates the need to walk down the line to install parts. GM even overhauled the administrative systems that operate within Saturn. As each finished car exits the plant, Saturn's computers automatically authorize payment to suppliers. Saturn uses only one database for all its financial operations, including purchasing, payroll, and dealer billing.

Saturn does not have a formal quality department. There is no one director of quality. Saturn uses a series of quality councils to set quality goals and provide general direction. These councils are composed of both UAW union members and management team members who meet on a periodic basis. The highest quality council is chaired by the president of the local UAW union and the president of Saturn Corporation. In addition to quality councils, Saturn also has specific quality resource areas to aid and support the team members assembling the vehicles on the factory floor. These quality resource areas are also responsible for developing and auditing quality procedures, quality methods, and quality systems.

Saturn's corporate philosophy reads as follows:

We, the Saturn Team, in concert with the UAW and General Motors, believe that meeting the needs of customers, Saturn members, suppliers, dealers, and neighbors is fundamental to fulfilling our mission.

To meet our customers' needs:
• Our products and services must be world leaders in value and satisfaction.

To meet our members' needs:

• We will create a sense of belonging in an environment of mutual trust, respect, and dignity.
• We believe that all people want to be involved in decisions that affect them, care about their jobs, take pride in themselves and their contributions, and want to share in the success of their efforts.
• We will develop the tools, training, and education for each member, recognizing individual skills and knowledge.
• We believe that creative, motivated, and responsible team members who understand that change is critical to success are Saturn's most important asset.

To meet our suppliers' and dealers' needs:

• We will create real partnerships with them.
• We will be open and fair in our dealings, reflecting trust, respect, and their importance to Saturn.
• We want dealers and suppliers to feel ownership in Saturn's mission and philosophy as their own.

To meet the needs of our neighbors and the communities in which we live and operate:

• We will be good citizens, protect the environment, and conserve natural resources.
• We will seek to cooperate with government at all levels and strive to be sensitive, open, and candid in our public statements.

This statement represents a fundamental commitment not to be compromised or undermined by decisions that could be attractive in the short term but would lead the organization in an undesired direction in the long run. Every decision must fit Saturn's philosophy.

Starting from ground level, Saturn defined the values necessary to compete effectively and to attract the best GM managers and UAW workers willing to assume the challenges and risks associated with those values. Saturn's culture, created with these values, can be summed up in one word: partnership. A close partnership between GM and the UAW influences every strategic, tactical, and operational decision. Such sharing of decision making and building mutual trust is unique in the U.S. auto industry. Educational initiatives directed at improving union leaders' business knowledge and managers' people knowledge strengthen communication and contribute an important element to this partnership.

One of Saturn's major innovations is GM's agreement with the UAW. Teams of workers have broad decision-making powers and responsibilities. They undergo hundreds of hours of training and learn the economics behind each car. This UAW contract differs significantly from previous contracts. It includes the following features:

- The contract has no specific expiration date. Exactly one year from the date that the first car comes off the line, management and labor may begin modifying the contract, if necessary, on a day-to-day basis.
- Saturn workers have a hand in the design of the vehicle and the factory.
- Job classifications, which number in the dozens in traditional automobile factories, have been cut to only a few. As a result, a production worker can do a simple repair without waiting for an electrician while production grinds to a halt.
- Saturn employees work on salary and receive 80 percent of the wages other UAW members receive, but they are eligible for bonuses depending on the car's success.

Worker involvement is unprecedented. Intensive training and elimination of barriers between management and labor characterize Saturn. Teams of line workers do more than just assemble parts; they "hire" workers, approve parts from suppliers, choose their own equipment, and handle administrative matters, such as their budgets. Workers and union representatives have a great deal of input on business issues. In 1991, when managers increased production that wound up raising the number of defects, line workers staged a slowdown during the visit of GM's chairman. The president of the UAW stated, "We are not going to sacrifice quality to get productivity." Managers eventually eased their production goals.

The heart of the organizational structure of Saturn is a work unit, a team of about 15 people who make decisions by consensus. Work units evolve, starting as conventional teams with an external union and management advisor. They then begin to assume the responsibilities traditionally assigned to a supervisor or foreman. As the team hires other members, it teaches them Saturn's mission, philosophy, and values and ensures that they develop the necessary skills to perform the team's tasks. With increased group interaction, the team moves toward a completely self-directed team. Team members, most of whom have worked from 5 to 25 years in the auto industry, receive from 250 to 750 hours of intensive education and training just to prepare for their jobs. The education covers behavioral subjects, leadership, and team development and even includes learning to read a balance sheet. Saturn opens its books internally and expects employees to know how much their operations add to the cost of the car.

Partnerships necessarily extend to suppliers and dealers. Saturn's goal is to establish a long-term partnership with only one supplier for each input. These partnerships are based on mutual trust, high quality standards, just-in-time delivery, and continuous improvement. Saturn believes that each dealer must not be threatened by competition from other Saturn dealers, a practice that has proven to be counterproductive in the automobile industry. Instead, Saturn dealers have designated market areas and help other regions as needed. The no-dicker sticker price also reduces internal competition.

Day-to-day monitoring of product quality is accomplished through statistical methods, adherence to Saturn quality systems and procedures, appropriate use of various problem-solving tools, quality-related education in a team environment, and inherent team motivation and enthusiasm. Work unit members receive customer feedback from the field within 24 hours to facilitate rapid analysis and appropriate corrective action.

By 1993, Saturn had captured 2.39 percent of the U.S. car market. Seventy-three percent of the buyers were classified as "plus business" to General Motors, meaning that had Saturn not been available, these buyers would not have purchased a GM product. Ongoing surveys show that 97 percent of Saturn owners say they would "enthusiastically recommend the purchase of a Saturn car" to a friend, relative, or neighbor.

Discussion Questions

1. Explain how the infrastructure at Saturn was designed to support the principles of total quality management.
2. Discuss why a "clean sheet" approach to designing the Saturn organization can more successfully implement TQ than attempting to change a traditional organization.
3. Summarize the performance of Saturn over the last five years. You might wish to search business and consumer periodicals, GM annual reports, JD Power and Associates ratings, and so on.

ENDNOTES

1. Kevin B. Hendricks and Vinod R. Singhal, "Does Implementing an Effective TQM Program Actually Improve Operating Performance? Empirical Evidence from Firms that Have Won Quality Awards," *Management Science*, Vol. 43, No. 9, September 1997.
2. Malcolm Baldrige National Quality Award Profiles of Winners, U.S. Department of Commerce, National Institute of Standards and Technology, and Trident Precision Manufacturing Award Application Summary.
3. "The Push for Quality," *Business Week*, June 8, 1987, p. 131.
4. J.M. Juran, "Strategies for World-Class Quality," *Quality Progress*, March 1991, pp. 81–85.
5. "Reinventing Health Care," *Fortune*, July 12, 1993, advertisement section.
6. Ronald E. Yates, "TQM is Alive and Well—and Not Just a Fad, Study Finds," *Chicago Tribune*, February 9, 1994, 1, business section.
7. "Lamborghini owner says he got $262,000 lemon," *Cincinnati Enquirer*, June 23, 1998, p. B5.
8. Courtesy of Deer Valley Resort.

9. David A. Garvin, "What Does 'Product Quality' Really Mean?" *Sloan Management Review*, Vol. 26, No. 1, 1984, pp. 25–43.

10. "A New Era for Auto Quality," *Business Week*, October 2, 1990, pp. 84–96.

11. Karl Albrecht and Ronald E. Zemke, *Service America*, Homewood, Ill.: Dow Jones-Irwin, 1985.

12. A. Parasuraman, V.A. Zeithaml, and L.L. Berry, "SERVQUAL: A Multiple-Item Scale for Measuring Consumer Perceptions of Service Quality," *Journal of Retailing*, Vol. 64, No. 1, Spring 1988, pp. 12–40.

13. Carol A. King, "Service Quality Assurance is Different," *Quality Progress*, Vol. 18, No. 6, June 1985, pp. 14–18.

14. Procter & Gamble, "Report to the Total Quality Leadership Steering Committee and Working Councils," Cincinnati, Ohio, 1992.

15. Based on personal communication from Roger Nunley, Director, Industry & Consumer Affairs, Coca-Cola, the Service Quality Survey, and the Industry & Consumer Affairs Department Overview.

16. Kenneth Labich. "An Airline that Soars on Service," *Fortune*, December 31, 1990, pp. 94–96.

17. Andrew E. Serwer, "Michael Dell Turns the PC World Inside Out," *Fortune*, September 8, 1997, pp. 76–86.

18. Adapted from Joseph J. Tsiakals, "Management Team Seeks Quality Improvement from Quality Costs," *Quality Progress*, Vol. 16, No. 4, April l983, pp. 26–27.

19. Bro Uttal, "Companies that Serve You Best," *Fortune*, December 7, 1987, p. 101.

20. Armand V. Feigenbaum, "The Future of Quality Management," *Quality Digest*, May 1998, pp. 33–38.

21. Adapted in part from Ed Baker, "The Chief Executive Officer's Role in Total Quality: Preparing the Enterprise for Leadership in the New Economic Age," Proceedings of the William G. Hunter Conference on Quality, Madison, Wis., 1989.

22. "Total Quality at Procter & Gamble," The Total Quality Forum, Cincinnati, Ohio, August 6–8, 1991.

23. Based on Barbara A. Spencer, "Models of Organization and Total Quality Management: A Comparison and Critical Evaluation," *Academy of Management Review*, Vol. 19, No. 3, 1994, pp. 446–471.

24. Appreciation is given to our former colleague, Dr. Reginald Bruce, and his students at the University of Cincinnati for this case.

25. Based on student projects prepared by Burton Phillips, Stefanie Steward, Travis Beuerlein, Branndi Beverly, and Megan Gallagher. Their contribution is gratefully acknowledged. Information was obtained through interviews of various store managers, training videos, and Web sites.

26. Based on a student project prepared by Stacey Bizzell, Suzanne Lee, and Kenneth Shircliff. Their contribution is gratefully acknowledged.

27. Based on a variety of materials provided by the Saturn Assistance Center, Saturn Corporation, Spring Hill, Tenn.; Frederick Standish, "As Saturn's Debut Nears, Skepticism Still Abounds," *Cincinnati Enquirer*, July 7, 1990, F-2; "Here Comes GM's Saturn," *Business Week*, April 9, 1990, pp. 56–62; "Saturn Workers Say 'No' to Speed Up," *APICS—The Performance Advantage*, February 1992, p. 11; "Saturn," *Business Week*, August 17, 1992, pp. 86–91; Richard G. LeFauve and Arnold C. Hax, "Managerial and Technological Innovations at Saturn Corporation," *MIT Management*, Spring 1992, pp. 8–19.

CHAPTER

2

Approaches to Total Quality

CHAPTER OUTLINE

Many individuals have made substantial contributions to the theory and practice of quality management. These include the well-known "gurus": W. Edwards Deming, Joseph M. Juran, and Philip B. Crosby, as well as many other consultants, business executives, and academic researchers. Their philosophical writings and lectures have helped shape management thought as well as provide the foundation for practical management frameworks designed around quality.

This chapter introduces you to several key philosophies and frameworks used to guide total quality initiatives. The objectives of this chapter are

- to understand that total quality is simply a means of achieving performance excellence in any organization,
- to describe the Deming philosophy and compare it to traditional management approaches,
- to discuss the quality management philosophies of Juran and Crosby, and
- to provide an overview of ISO 9000, QS-9000, the Malcolm Baldrige National Quality Award, and other international quality awards as frameworks for total quality.

TOTAL QUALITY AS PERFORMANCE EXCELLENCE

A major study conducted in the late 1980s by the MIT Commission on Industrial Productivity cited five basic reasons why many American companies had lost their ability to compete during the 1970s and 1980s:[1]

1. *Outdated strategies*—Firms neglected manufacturing, because business strategies were driven by marketing and finance. Many firms did not invest in the human and physical capital necessary to sustain a competitive manufacturing capability.

2. *Short time horizons*—American business was (and in many cases, still is) preoccupied with short-term financial results. Companies have not made sufficient investment in research and development, facilities, and the training and education of the workforce. Short-term focus has overshadowed long-term issues, such as a firm's ability to satisfy the true needs of customers and stay in business.

3. *Technological weaknesses in development and production*—Although many companies had made significant technological advances, they did not develop them into affordable and reliable manufactured goods or design effective manufacturing systems to produce them. Foreign competitors took ideas invented here and developed cost-effective processes to produce them quickly with high quality to meet consumer demands.

4. *Neglect of human resources*—U.S. firms had tended to view labor as a cost rather than a productive and critical resource. The importance of well-trained, well-motivated, and flexible workers was frequently underestimated.

Toyota Management Overhauls Failing GM Plant

In working with General Motors on a joint venture, the New United Motor Manufacturing, Inc. (NUMMI), Toyota transformed a failing California assembly plant into GM's most efficient factory, producing the Toyota Corolla and the Geo Prizm. Before GM closed the plant in 1982, it was a battleground between inflexible managers and a workforce whose rate of absenteeism was 20 percent. Toyota quickly turned it around by hiring the best of the former workforce and replacing GM's 100 job classifications with teams of multiskilled workers. Absenteeism dropped to less than 2 percent. Productivity grew to twice the average level in GM plants. This occurred without any special technology or automation; the difference is in the way Toyota managers organize and operate the plant.

---

5. *Failures of cooperation*—Many organizational barriers existed within firms that separated research and development, design, manufacturing, and marketing. These barriers were often bolstered by short-term, protective interests and excessive specialization.

The MIT commission's findings pointed to *poor management practices* as the key factor in our lack of competitiveness. Japanese start-ups in the U.S. support this assertion (see box). Sony claims that the production lines in its San Diego plant have the same rate of productivity as those in its Japanese factories. Workers are different, but management standards are the same. A Honda executive has stated that "the quality and productivity of workers depend on management. When Detroit changes its management system, we'll see more powerful American companies."

Each of the shortcomings identified by the commission is effectively addressed by total quality principles. Total quality philosophies have redefined management systems, evolving from relatively narrow "programs" delegated to quality professionals to a philosophy of *performance excellence* that permeates all aspects of how an organization should be managed. In world-class organizations, TQ principles are synonymous with "how we run our business."

Approaches to Total Quality

Despite a lot of rhetoric, most firms in the United States and Europe have not come anywhere near fully adopting total quality. Adoption requires significant changes in organization design, work processes, and culture. Organizations use a variety of approaches. Some emphasize the use of quality tools, such as statistical process control or quality function deployment, but have not made the necessary fundamental changes in their processes and culture. Although these firms will realize limited improvements, the full potential of total quality is lost due to a lack of complete understanding by the entire organization.

Others have adopted a problem-solving focus in which they identify defects in both production and customer service and work to correct them through quality circles or other team approaches. Although improvements are achieved, they are sporadic and limited. The lack of involvement by management prevents the development of a culture focused on the customer.

A third approach emphasizes error prevention and "building in" quality. Although this approach is customer focused, firms that follow it may overlook many opportunities for continuous improvement. Still other companies focus on continuous improvement coupled with innovations in work processes and organization strategy.

Single approaches, such as statistical process control or quality circles, can have some short-term success, but they do not seem to work well over time. Total quality requires a comprehensive effort that encompasses all of these approaches. A total change in thinking, not a new collection of tools, is needed. Unfortunately, it is easy to focus on tools and techniques but very hard to understand and achieve the necessary changes in human attitudes and behavior.

The biggest dangers lie in the lack of complete understanding and the tendency to imitate—the easy way out. The "one best model" of TQ for one organization may not mesh with another organization's culture. Most successful companies have developed unique approaches to fit their own requirements. Research shows that imitating the TQ efforts of one successful organization may not lead to good results in another. To use one of Deming's often-quoted phrases, "There is no instant pudding."

Companies adopt TQ for two basic reasons:

1. to react to competitive threats, and
2. as an opportunity to improve.

Most firms have moved toward TQ for the first reason. Xerox, for example, saw its market share fall from 90 percent to less than 15 percent in a decade; Milliken faced increased competition from Asian textile manufacturers; Zytec Corporation found itself in financial difficulties because of reliance on a single customer. Although not facing dire crises, future threats were also the impetus for the TQ efforts of FedEx, Solectron, and IBM Rochester.

When faced with a threat to survival, companies have less difficulty embracing TQ. Since a cultural change is necessary, it is more difficult to gain support for TQ when a crisis is not imminent. Some firms—such as IBM Rochester, which embarked on TQ even when it was not facing a crisis—suggest that a crisis mentality, whether real or perceived, is necessary to effect change. To rally the troops, management might have to "manufacture" a crisis.

Total quality requires a set of guiding principles. Of the three "quality gurus," Deming has generated the most interest—and controversy. A discussion of his philosophy, which is actually more about management than quality, follows.[2]

THE DEMING MANAGEMENT PHILOSOPHY

Deming was trained as a statistician and worked for Western Electric during its pioneering era of statistical quality control development in the 1920s and 1930s. During World War II he taught quality control courses as part of the national defense effort. Although Deming taught many engineers in the United States, he was not able to reach upper management. After the war, Deming was invited to Japan to teach statistical quality control concepts. Top managers there were eager to learn, and he addressed 21 top executives who collectively represented 80 percent of the country's capital. They embraced Deming's message and transformed their industries. By the mid-1970s, the quality of Japanese products exceeded that of Western manufacturers, and Japanese companies had made significant penetration into Western markets.

Deming's contributions were recognized early by the Japanese. The Deming Application Prize was instituted in 1951 by the Union of Japanese Scientists and Engineers in recognition and appreciation for his achievements in statistical quality control. Deming also received the nation's highest honor, the Royal Order of the Sacred Treasure, from the emperor of Japan.

Deming was virtually unknown in the United States until 1980 when NBC aired a white paper entitled "If Japan Can . . . Why Can't We?" This program made Deming a household name among corporate executives, and companies such as Ford invited him to assist them in revolutionizing their quality approaches. Deming worked with passion until his death in December 1993 at the age of 93, knowing he had little time left to make a difference in his home country. When asked how he would like to be remembered, Deming replied, "I probably won't even be remembered." Then after a long pause, he added, "Well, maybe . . . as someone who spent his life trying to keep America from committing suicide."[3]

Deming's philosophy is based on improving products and services by reducing uncertainty and variability in the design and manufacturing processes. In Deming's view, variation is the chief culprit of poor quality. In mechanical assemblies, for example, variations from specifications for part dimensions lead to inconsistent performance and premature wear and failure. Likewise, inconsistencies in service frustrate customers and damage a firm's image. To achieve reduced variation, he advocates a never-ending cycle of product design, manufacture, test, and sales, followed by market surveys, then redesign, and so forth.

Deming stresses that higher quality leads to higher productivity, which in turn leads to long-term competitive strength. The Deming "chain reaction," shown in Figure 2.1, summarizes this view. This theory states that improvements in quality lead to lower costs because of less rework, fewer mistakes, fewer delays and snags, and better use of time and materials. Lower costs, in turn, lead to productivity improvements. With better quality and lower prices, the firm can achieve a higher market share and thus stay in business, providing more and more jobs. Deming states emphatically that top management has the overriding responsibility for quality improvement.

FIGURE 2.1 THE DEMING CHAIN REACTION

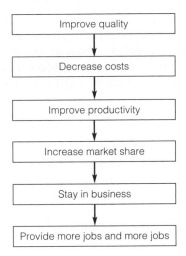

The Deming philosophy of quality and management is complex; indeed, several books have been written in an effort to explain and interpret it. Many of the principles are very basic yet difficult to put into practice. Deming has summarized his philosophy in what he calls "A System of Profound Knowledge."

Profound Knowledge

Profound knowledge consists of four parts: (1) appreciation for a system, (2) some knowledge of the theory of variation, (3) theory of knowledge, and (4) psychology.

Systems

A system is a set of functions or activities within an organization that work together to achieve organizational goals. For example, a McDonald's restaurant can be viewed as a system. It consists of the order-taker/cashier subsystem, grill and food preparation subsystem, drive-through subsystem, and so on.

The components of any system must work together for the system to be effective. When parts of a system interact, the system as a whole cannot be understood or managed solely in terms of its parts. To run any system, managers must understand the interrelationships among all subsystems and the people that work in them. One example is performance appraisal. Some of the factors within a system that affect the individual performance of an employee are

- training received,
- information and resources provided,
- leadership of supervisors and managers,
- disruptions on the job, and
- management policies and practices.

However, most performance appraisals do not recognize these factors.

Management must have an aim, a purpose to which the system continually strives. Deming believes that the aim of any system is for everybody—stockholders, employees, customers, community, the environment—to gain over the long term. Stockholders can realize financial benefits, employees can have opportunities for training and education, customers can receive products and services that meet their needs and create satisfaction, the community can benefit from business leadership, and the environment can benefit from socially responsible management.

Deming emphasizes that management's job is to optimize the system. By making decisions that are best for only a small part of the system (often encouraged by competition), we suboptimize. Suboptimization results in a loss to everybody in the system. For example, a common practice is to purchase materials or services at the lowest bid. Inexpensive materials may be of such inferior quality that they will cause excessive costs in adjustment and repair during manufacture and assembly. Although purchasing's track record will look good, the system will suffer.

This theory applies to managing people also. Pitting individuals or departments against each other for resources is self-destructive. The individuals or departments will perform to maximize their expected gain, not that of the firm as a whole. Employees must cooperate with each other. Likewise, sales quotas or arbitrary cost reduction goals do not motivate people to improve the system and, ultimately, customer satisfaction; workers will only perform to meet the quotas and goals.

Variation

The second part of Profound Knowledge is some understanding of statistical theory, particularly as it applies to variation. Just as no two snowflakes are exactly alike, no two outputs from any production process are exactly alike. A production process contains many sources of variation. Different lots of material will vary in strength, thickness, or moisture content, for example. Cutting tools will have inherent variation in strength and composition. During manufacturing, tools will experience wear, machine vibrations will cause changes in settings, and electrical fluctuations will cause variations in power. Operators may not position parts on fixtures consistently.

The complex interaction of all these variations in materials, tools, machines, operators, and the environment cannot be understood. Variation due to any individual source appears random; however, their combined effect is stable and can usually be predicted statistically. Factors that are present as a natural part of a process are called *common causes of variation*.

Common causes generally account for about 80 to 90 percent of the observed variation in a production process. The remaining 10 to 20 percent result from *special causes of variation*, often called *assignable causes*. Special causes arise from external sources that are not inherent in the process. A bad batch of material purchased from a supplier, a poorly trained operator, excessive tool wear, and miscalibration of measuring instruments are examples of special causes. Special causes result in unnatural variations that disrupt the random pattern of common causes. Hence, they are generally easy to detect using statistical methods, and it is usually economical to remove them.

A system governed only by common causes is said to be stable. Understanding a stable system and the differences between special and common causes of variation is essential for managing any system. Management can make two fundamental mistakes in attempting to improve a process:

1. To treat as a special cause any fault, complaint, mistake, breakdown, accident, or shortage when it actually came from common causes.
2. To attribute to common causes any fault, complaint, mistake, breakdown, accident, or shortage when it actually came from a special cause.

In the first case, tampering with a stable system will actually increase the variation in the system. In the second case, we can miss the opportunity to eliminate unwanted variation by assuming that it is not controllable. Changing a system on the basis of a special cause can damage the system and add cost. Variation should be minimized. The producer and consumer both benefit from reduced variation. The producer benefits by having less need for inspection, less scrap and rework, and higher productivity. The consumer is assured that all products have similar quality characteristics; this is especially important when the consumer is another firm using large quantities of the product in its own manufacturing or service operations.

Variation increases the cost of doing business. An example was published in the Japanese newspaper *Asahi* comparing the cost and quality of Sony televisions at plants in Japan and San Diego.[4] The color density of all the units produced at the San Diego plant was within specifications, although the density of some of those shipped from the Japanese plant was not (Figure 2.2). However, the average loss per unit at the San Diego plant was $0.89 greater than that of the Japanese plant. This was because units out of specification at the San Diego plant were adjusted within the plant, adding cost to the process. Furthermore, a unit adjusted to just within specifications was more likely to generate customer complaints than a unit that was closer to the original target value, therefore incurring higher field service costs. Figure 2.2 shows that fewer U.S.-produced sets met the target value for color density. The distribution of quality in the Japanese plant was more uniform around the target value, and even though some units were out of specification, the total cost was less.

The only way to reduce variation due to common causes is to change the technology of the process—the machines, people, materials, methods, or measurement system. The process is under the control of management, not the production operators. Pressuring operators to perform at higher quality levels may not be possible and may be counterproductive.

Variation due to special causes can be identified through the use of control charts, which are introduced in chapter 3. The responsibility for using control charts to identify special causes of variation and to make the necessary cor-

FIGURE 2.2   VARIATION IN U.S.-VERSUS JAPANESE-MADE TELEVISION COMPONENTS

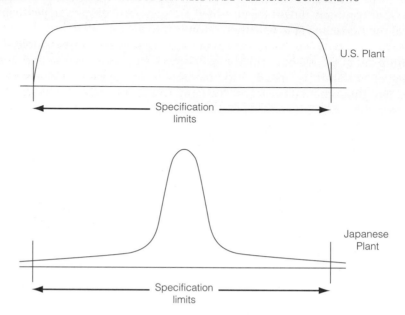

rections should lie with the production operators and their immediate supervisors.

Theory of Knowledge

The third part of Profound Knowledge is the theory of knowledge—a branch of philosophy concerned with the nature and scope of knowledge, its presuppositions and bases, and the general reliability of claims to knowledge. Deming was influenced greatly by Clarence Irving Lewis, author of *Mind and the World*.[5] Lewis stated, "There is no knowledge without interpretation. If interpretation, which represents an activity of the mind, is always subject to the check of further experience, how is knowledge possible at all? . . . An argument from past to future at best is probable only, and even this probability must rest upon principles which are themselves more than probable."

Deming emphasizes that there is no knowledge without theory and that experience alone does not establish a theory. To copy an example of success without understanding it with the aid of theory may lead to disaster. Experience only describes; it cannot be tested or validated. Theory establishes a cause-and-effect relationship that can be used for prediction. Theory leads to questioning and can be tested and validated; it explains why. Many companies have jumped on the latest fads advocated by popular business consultants. Methods that have sustained success are grounded in theory. Managers have a responsibility to learn and apply theory.

Psychology

Psychology helps us to understand people, interactions between people and circumstances, interactions between leaders and employees, and any system of management. People differ from one another. A leader must be aware of these differences and use them to optimize everybody's abilities and inclinations.

Many managers operate under the supposition that all people are alike and treat them as interchangeable components of a process. However, people learn in different ways and at different speeds and perform at different levels. Leaders have an obligation to make changes in the system of management that will bring improvement. People have an innate need for relationships with other people and for self-esteem and respect. Circumstances provide some people with dignity and self-esteem and deny them to other people. People inherit the right to enjoy work. Psychology helps us to nurture and preserve people's positive innate attributes.

Little in Deming's system of Profound Knowledge is original: The concept of common and special causes of variation was developed by Walter Shewhart in the 1920s; behavioral theories to which Deming subscribes were developed in the 1960s; systems theory was refined by management scientists from the 1950s through the 1970s; and scientists in all fields have long understood the relationships among prediction, observation, and theory. Deming's contribution was in tying together some basic concepts. He recognized the synergy among these diverse subjects and developed them into a theory of management.

Peter Scholtes, a noted consultant, makes some salient observations about the failure to understand the components of Profound Knowledge: [6]

1. When people don't understand systems,
   - they see events as individual incidents rather than the net result of many interactions and interdependent forces;
   - they see the symptoms but not the deep causes of problems;
   - they don't understand how an intervention in one part of an organization can cause havoc in another place or at another time;
   - they blame individuals for problems even when those individuals have little or no ability to control the events around them; and
   - they don't understand the ancient African saying, "It takes a whole village to raise a child."

2. When people don't understand variation,
   - they don't see trends that are occurring;
   - they see trends where there are none;
   - they don't know when expectations are realistic;
   - they don't understand past performance so they can't predict future performance;
   - they don't know the difference between prediction, forecasting, and guesswork;
   - they are less likely to distinguish between fact and opinion; and
   - they give others credit or blame when those people are simply either lucky or unlucky. This usually occurs because people tend to attribute everything to human effort, heroics, frailty, error, or deliberate sabotage, no matter what the systemic cause.

3.   When people don't understand psychology,
   • they don't understand motivation or why people do what they do;
   • they resort to carrots and sticks and other forms of induced motivation that have no positive effect and impair the relationship between the motivator and the one being motivated;
   • they don't understand the process of change and the resistance to it;
   • they revert to coercive and paternalistic approaches when dealing with people; and
   • they create cynicism, demoralization, demotivation, guilt, resentment, burnout, craziness, and turnover.

4.   When people don't understand the theory of knowledge,
   • they don't know how to plan and accomplish learning and improvement;
   • they don't understand the difference between improvement and change; and
   • problems will remain unsolved, despite their best efforts.

Deming's 14 Points for Management

The 14 Points for Management, listed in Table 2.1, have been the subject of considerable controversy and debate. They have their basis in Profound Knowledge. Many companies have studied and applied them to their organizations.

1.   *Statement of Purpose*—Businesses should not exist simply for profit; their true purpose should be to serve their customers and employees. To do this, they must take a long-term view and invest in innovation, training, and research. Japanese companies spend considerably more on research and development than those in the United States. Japanese firms are willing to give up short-term profits knowing that they will achieve a high market share several years in the future. Thus, an organization needs a clear mission and statement of purpose.

2.   *Learn the New Philosophy*—American management has been built on the Taylor system, which has led to numbers-driven production, quotas, and adversarial work relationships. Old methods of management create mistrust, fear, and anxiety with a focus on "satisficing" (a term derived from "satisfy" and "suffice") rather than on "optimizing." Eliminating defects is not good enough. Defect-free production is taken for granted in Japan. Achieving competitive success in today's global economy requires a customer-driven approach based on mutual cooperation between labor and management and a never-ending cycle of improvement. Everyone, from the boardroom to the stockroom, must learn the new philosophy.

3.   *Understand Inspection*—Routine inspection acknowledges defects but does not add value to the product. Instead, it encourages defects because "someone else" catches and fixes the problems. This procedure increases costs and decreases productivity. Workers must take responsibility for

TABLE 2.1 DEMING'S 14 POINTS FOR MANAGEMENT[7]

1. Create and publish to all employees a statement of the aims and purposes of the company or other organization. The management must demonstrate constantly their commitment to this statement.

2. Learn the new philosophy, top management and everybody.

3. Understand the purpose of inspection, for improvement of processes and reduction of cost.

4. End the practice of awarding business on the basis of price tag alone.

5. Improve constantly and forever the system of production and service.

6. Institute training.

7. Teach and institute leadership.

8. Drive out fear. Create trust. Create a climate for innovation.

9. Optimize toward the aims and purposes of the company the efforts of teams, groups, staff areas.

10. Eliminate exhortations for the workforce.

11. (a) Eliminate numerical quotas for production. Instead, learn and institute methods for improvement.
    (b) Eliminate MBO (management by objective). Instead, learn the capabilities of processes and how to improve them.

12. Remove barriers that rob people of pride of workmanship.

13. Encourage education and self-improvement for everyone.

14. Take action to accomplish the transformation.

their own work and be able to take appropriate action to ensure good quality. Managers need to understand how variation affects their processes and to take steps to reduce the causes of variation. Inspection should be used as an information-gathering tool for improvement, not as an end in itself.

4. *End Price Tag Decisions*—Purchasing decisions traditionally have been driven by cost through competitive bidding, not by quality. Costs due to inferior materials and components increase costs in later stages of production and can far exceed the "savings" realized through competitive bidding. The purchasing department is a supplier to the production department and must understand its new role. Suppliers themselves are part of the whole system.

Deming urged businesses to establish long-term relationships with a few suppliers, leading to loyalty and enhanced opportunities for improvement. Management has always justified multiple vendors for reasons such as protection against strikes or natural disasters but has ignored hidden costs such as increased travel to visit suppliers, loss of volume discounts, added setup charges resulting in higher unit costs, and higher inventory and administrative expense. More importantly, using multiple suppliers increases the variation in purchased items and, hence, in the final product.

In contrast, a reduced supply base decreases variation and reduces scrap, rework, and the need to adjust to this variation. Long-term relationships between suppliers and customers allow the supplier to produce in greater quantities and reduce unit costs, foster improved communication, and enhance opportunities for process improvements.

5. *Improve Constantly*—Western management has typically thought of improvement in the context of large, expensive innovations such as robotics and computer-integrated manufacturing. The success of Japanese manufacturers, however, is due primarily to continuous, small, incremental improvements in design and production. Improved design results from understanding customer needs and from continual market surveys and other sources of feedback. Improved production is achieved by reducing the causes of variation in order to establish a stable, predictable production process. Statistical methods provide one means for doing this. Improvement should go beyond production, encompassing transportation, engineering, maintenance, sales, service, and administration— all areas of the organization.

6. *Institute Training*—Employees need the proper tools and knowledge to do a good job, and it is management's responsibility to provide these. In addition to specific job skills, all employees should be trained in statistical tools for quality problem solving and continuous improvement. Training not only improves quality and productivity, but also enhances workers' morale by showing them that the company is dedicated to helping them and is investing in their future. Deming notes that in Japan, entry-level managers spend 4 to 12 years on the factory floor, and in other activities to learn the problems of production. At Honda of America in Marysville, Ohio, all employees start out on the production floor, regardless of their job classification.

7. *Institute Leadership*—The job of management is leadership and guidance, not supervision and work direction. Supervisors should be coaches, not policemen, and supervision should provide the link between management and the workforce. Leadership can help to eliminate fear and encourage teamwork.

8. *Drive Out Fear and Innovate*—Fear in work manifests in many ways: fear of reprisal, fear of failure, fear of the unknown, fear of change. Many

workers fear punishment or reprisals for not meeting quotas and for problems of the system that are beyond their control. Managers compete against each other to protect their own jobs or to receive higher performance ratings. Fear encourages short-term, selfish thinking, not long-term improvement for the benefit of all.

9. *Optimize Team Efforts*—Barriers between individuals and departments lead to poor quality, because "customers" do not receive what they need from their "suppliers." This is often the result of internal competition for raises or performance ratings. Teamwork helps to break down barriers between internal customers and suppliers. The focus should be on meeting customer needs and improving processes. Teamwork is an important means of achieving a company's goals.

    Perhaps the biggest barrier to team efforts in the United States is between unions and management. With some notable exceptions, the history of management-labor relations in the United States has been largely adversarial. Lack of sensitivity to worker needs, exploitation of workers, and poor management practices and policies have frequently resulted in strained relations. Labor also bears its share of the blame. It has tended to resist any management effort to reduce rigid, rule-based tasks, preferring to adhere to structured approaches that stem from the Taylor principles. Unions, as Deming has said, are a part of the system and must work within the system.

10. *Eliminate Exhortations*—Motivation can be better achieved through trust and leadership than slogans. Slogans calling for improved quality usually assume that poor quality results from a lack of motivation. Workers cannot improve solely through motivational methods when the system in which they work constrains their performance. On the contrary, they will become frustrated, and their performance will decrease further.

11. *Eliminate Quotas and MBO; Institute Improvement; and Understand Processes*—Numerical quotas reflect short-term perspectives and do not encourage long-term improvement, particularly if rewards or performance appraisals are tied to meeting quotas. Workers may shortcut quality to reach the goal. If the quota is met, they have no incentive to continue production or to improve quality. Arbitrary management goals without a method for achieving them have no meaning. Further, variation in the system makes year-to-year or quarter-to-quarter comparisons meaningless. The typical American MBO system focuses on results, not processes, and encourages short-term behavior. Management must understandthe system and the variation within it and seek to improve it in the long term.

12. *Remove Barriers*—The Taylor system has promulgated the view of workers as a "commodity." Factory workers are given monotonous tasks, provided with inferior machines, tools, or materials, told to run defective items to meet sales pressures, and report to supervisors who know

Ford Becomes a Deming Company

Dr. Deming came to Ford in 1981 to meet with the president, Donald Petersen, and other company officials who were stimulated by the program "If Japan Can . . . Why Can't We?" Deming began by giving seminars for top executives and meeting with various employees, suggesting changes corresponding to his 14 points. Ford managers visited Nashua Corporation, the first American company to incorporate Deming's philosophy, to learn how statistical methods were used there. Chief executives from many of Ford's major suppliers visited Japan. Petersen himself took a course on statistical methods. The 14 points became the basis for a transformation in Ford's management.

Ford's quality commitment is evident from its "Guiding Principles:"
Quality comes first. To achieve customer satisfaction, the quality of our products and services must be our number one priority.

- Customers are the focus of everything we do. Our work must be done with customers in mind, providing better products and services than our competition.
- Continuous improvement is essential to our success. We must strive for excellence in everything we do: in our products, in their safety and value—and in our services, our human relations, our competitiveness, and our profitability.
- Employee involvement is our way of life. We are a team. We must treat each other with trust and respect.
- Dealers and suppliers are our partners. The company must maintain mutually beneficial relationships with dealers, suppliers, and our other business associates.
- Integrity is never compromised. The conduct of our company worldwide must be pursued in a manner that is socially responsible and commands respect for its integrity and for its positive contributions to society. Our doors are open to men and women alike without discrimination and without regard to ethnic origin or personal beliefs.

Petersen has stated that "The work of Dr. Deming has definitely helped change Ford's corporate leadership. It is management's responsibility to create the environment in which everyone can contribute to continuous improvement in processes and systems. . . . Dr. Deming has influenced my thinking in a variety of ways. What stands out is that he helped me crystallize my ideas concerning the value of teamwork, process improvement, and the pervasive power of the concept of continuous improvement."

nothing about the job. Salaried employees are expected to work evenings and weekends to make up for cost-cutting measures that resulted in layoffs of their colleagues. Many are given the title of "management" so that overtime need not be paid. Management assumes it is smarter than workers and does not use the workers' knowledge and experience to the fullest extent. The key to the loss of pride in workmanship is the loss of control.

Deming believes that one of the biggest barriers to pride in workmanship is performance appraisal. Performance appraisals

- destroy teamwork by promoting competition among employees for limited resources;
- foster mediocrity since objectives typically are driven by numbers and what the boss wants;
- focus on short-term results and discourage risk taking; and are not focused on serving the customer.

Deming suggests that there are three categories of performance: the majority who work within the system, those outside the system on the superior side, and those outside the system on the inferior side. Statistical methods provide the means of making this classification. Superior performers should be compensated specially; inferior performers need extra training or a different job.

13. *Encourage Education*—"Training" in number 6 refers to job skills; education refers to self-development. Firms have a responsibility to develop the value and self-worth of the individual. Investing in people is a powerful motivation method.

14. *Take Action*—The TQ philosophy is a major cultural change, and many firms find it difficult. Top management must institute the process and include everyone in it.

One of the first American companies that has embraced the Deming philosophy is Ford Motor Company (see box on page 54).

The Juran Philosophy

Joseph M. Juran joined Western Electric in the 1920s during its pioneering days in the development of statistical methods for quality. He spent much of his time as a corporate industrial engineer. In 1951 Juran wrote, edited, and published the *Quality Control Handbook*, now in its fourth edition.

Juran taught quality principles to the Japanese in the 1950s just after Deming and was a principal force in their quality reorganization. Like Deming, he concluded that we faced a major crisis due to the loss of sales to foreign competition and the huge costs of poor quality. Solving this crisis required new thinking about quality, thinking that included all levels of the managerial hierarchy. Upper management in particular required training and experience in managing for quality.

Juran's programs are designed to fit into a company's current strategic business planning with minimal risk of rejection. This is in contrast to Deming, who proposes sweeping cultural change. Juran contends that employees at different levels of an organization speak in different "languages." (Deming believes statistics should be the common language.) Top management speaks in the language of dollars, workers speak in the language of things, and middle management must be able to speak both languages and translate between dollars and things. Thus, to get top management's attention, quality issues must be cast in the language they understand—dollars. Juran advocates the accounting and analysis of quality costs to focus attention on quality problems. At the operational level, Juran's focus is on increasing conformance to specifications through elimination of defects, supported extensively by statistical tools for analysis. Thus, his philosophy fits well into existing management systems.

Juran defines quality as "fitness for use." (Deming advocates no specific definition.) This is broken down into four categories: quality of design, quality of conformance, availability, and field service. Quality of design focuses on market research, the product concept, and design specifications. Quality of conformance includes technology, manpower, and management. Availability focuses on reliability, maintainability, and logistical support. Field service quality comprises promptness, competence, and integrity.

Juran views the pursuit of quality on two levels: (1) the mission of the firm as a whole is to achieve high product quality, and (2) the mission of each individual department in the firm is to achieve high production quality. Like Deming, Juran advocates a never-ending spiral of activities that includes market research, product development, design, planning for manufacture, purchasing, production process control, and inspection and testing, followed by customer feedback. Because of the interdependence of these functions, the need for competent company-wide quality management is great. Senior management must play an active and enthusiastic leadership role in the quality management process.

Juran's prescriptions focus on three major aspects of quality called the Quality Trilogy (a registered trademark of the Juran Institute): quality planning—the process for preparing to meet quality goals; quality control—the process for meeting quality goals during operations; and quality improvement—the process for breaking through to unprecedented levels of performance.

Quality planning begins with identifying customers, both external and internal, determining their needs, and developing product features that respond to customer needs. Like Deming, Juran asks people to know who uses their products, whether in the next department or in another organization. Quality goals are then established that meet the needs of customers and suppliers alike at a minimum combined cost. The process must be designed to produce the product that meets customers' needs and can meet the quality goals under operating conditions. Strategic planning for quality should be similar to the firm's financial planning process. The process should determine short-term and long-term goals, set priorities, compare results with previous plans, and mesh the plans with other corporate strategic objectives.

Quality control involves determining what to control, establishing units of measurement so data may be objectively evaluated, establishing standards of performance, measuring actual performance, interpreting the difference between actual performance and the standard, and taking action on the difference. In many ways this parallels Deming's emphasis on identifying sources of variation and improving the work system.

Unlike Deming, Juran specifies a detailed program for quality improvement. The quality improvement process involves proving the need for improvement, identifying specific projects for improvement, organizing to guide the projects, diagnosing the causes, providing remedies for the causes, proving that the remedies are effective under operating conditions, and providing control to hold improvements. At all times, hundreds or even thousands of quality improvement projects should be under way in every area of the firm.

Juran's assessment of most companies is that quality control is far and away the top priority among the trilogy, and most companies feel they are strong in this category. Quality planning and quality improvement, however, are not important priorities and are significantly weaker in most organizations. He feels that more effort must be placed on quality planning and even more on quality improvement.

Juran supports these conclusions with several case examples in which Japanese firms using the same technology, materials, and processes as American firms had much higher levels of quality and productivity. He explains that since the 1950s the Japanese have implemented quality improvement projects at a far greater pace than their Western counterparts. The result is that sometime in the 1970s Japanese product quality exceeded Western quality and continues to improve at a greater pace.

Japanese efforts at quality improvement were supported by massive training programs and top management leadership. Training in managerial quality-oriented concepts as well as training in the tools for quality improvement, cost reduction, data collection, and analysis is one of the most important components of Juran's philosophy. Juran maintains that the Japanese experience leaves little doubt as to the significance of the return on quality training in competitive advantage, reduced failure costs, higher productivity, smaller inventories, and better delivery performance.

The Crosby Philosophy

Philip B. Crosby was corporate vice president for quality at International Telephone and Telegraph (ITT) for 14 years after working his way up from line inspector. After leaving ITT, he established Philip Crosby Associates in 1979 to develop and offer training programs. He is also the author of several popular books. His first book, *Quality Is Free*, sold about one million copies.

The essence of Crosby's quality philosophy is embodied in what he calls the Absolutes of Quality Management and the Basic Elements of Improvement. Crosby's Absolutes of Quality Management are as follows:

- *Quality means conformance to requirements, not elegance.* Crosby dispels the myth that quality is simply a feeling of "excellence." Requirements must be clearly stated so they cannot be misunderstood. Requirements are communication devices and are ironclad. Once a task is done, one can take measurements to determine conformance to requirements. The nonconformance detected is the absence of quality. Quality problems become nonconformance problems—that is, variation in output. Setting requirements is the responsibility of management.

- *There is no such thing as a quality problem.* Problems must be identified by the individuals or departments that cause them. There are accounting problems, manufacturing problems, design problems, front-desk problems, and so on. Quality originates in functional departments, not in the quality department, and the burden of responsibility for such problems lies with the functional departments. The quality department should measure conformance, report results, and lead the drive to develop a positive attitude toward quality improvement. This is similar to number 3 of Deming's points.

- *There is no such thing as the economics of quality. It is always cheaper to do the job right the first time.* Crosby supports the premise that "economics of quality" has no meaning. Quality is free. What costs money are all the actions that involve not doing jobs right the first time. The Deming chain reaction provides a similar message.

- *The only performance measurement is the cost of quality.* The cost of quality is the expense of nonconformance. Crosby notes that most companies spend 15 to 20 percent of their sales dollars on quality costs. A company with a well-run quality management program can achieve a cost of quality that is less than 2.5 percent of sales, primarily in the prevention and appraisal categories. Crosby's program calls for measuring and publicizing the cost of poor quality. Quality cost data are useful in calling problems to management's attention, selecting opportunities for corrective action, and tracking quality improvement over time. Such data provide visible proof of improvement and recognition of achievement. Juran also supports this theme.

- *The only performance standard is Zero Defects.* Crosby feels that the Zero Defects (ZD) concept is widely misunderstood and resisted. Zero Defects is not a motivational program. It is as follows:

> Zero Defects is a performance standard. It is the standard of the craftsperson regardless of his or her assignment. . . . The theme of ZD is do it right the first time. That means concentrating on preventing defects rather than just finding and fixing them.
>
> People are conditioned to believe that error is inevitable; thus they not only accept error, they anticipate it. It does not bother us to make a few errors in our work. . . . To err is human. We all have our own standards in business or academic life—our own points at which errors begin to bother us. It is good to get an A in school, but it may be OK to pass with a C.
>
> We do not maintain these standards, however, when it comes to our personal life. If we did, we should expect to be shortchanged every now and then when we cash our paycheck; we should expect hospital nurses to drop a constant percentage of newborn babies. . . . We as individuals do not tolerate these things. We have a dual standard: one for ourselves and one for our work.

Most human error is caused by lack of attention rather than lack of knowledge. Lack of attention is created when we assume that error is inevitable. If we consider this condition carefully and pledge ourselves to make a constant conscious effort to do our jobs right the first time, we will take a giant step toward eliminating the waste of rework, scrap, and repair that increases cost and reduces individual opportunity.[8]

Juran and Deming, on the other hand, would argue that it is pointless, if not hypocritical, to exhort a line worker to produce perfection, since the overwhelming majority of imperfections are due to poorly designed manufacturing systems beyond the workers' control.

Crosby's Basic Elements of Improvement include *determination, education,* and *implementation.* By determination, Crosby means that top management must be serious about quality improvement. The Absolutes should be understood by everyone; this can be accomplished only through education. Finally, every member of the management team must understand the implementation process.

Unlike Juran's and Deming's, Crosby's program is primarily behavioral. He places more emphasis on management and organizational processes for changing corporate culture and attitudes than on the use of statistical techniques. Like Juran's and unlike Deming's, his approach fits well within existing organizational structures.

Crosby's approach, however, provides relatively few details about how firms should address the finer points of quality management. The focus is on managerial thinking rather than on organizational systems. By allowing managers to determine the best methods to apply in their own firm's situations, his approach tends to avoid some of the implementation problems experienced by firms that have adopted the Deming philosophy.

Crosby's philosophy has not earned the respect of his rivals. Although they agree that he is an entertaining speaker and a great motivator, they say he lacks substance in the methods of achieving quality improvement. Nevertheless, hundreds of thousands have taken his courses in-house or at his Quality College in Winter Park, Florida.

FRAMEWORKS FOR QUALITY AND PERFORMANCE EXCELLENCE

The philosophies of Deming, Juran, and Crosby provide fundamental principles on which total quality is based. Business firms tend to be highly individualized. As a result, it is difficult to apply one specific philosophy. Company leaders must understand the differences and commonalities in the three philosophies and tailor an approach that fits their unique culture. The most successful firms, such as Xerox and Motorola, have done this. Aspects of implementation are addressed further in chapter 11.

None of these philosophies, however, provide a framework for how to implement total quality within an organization or a means of assessing total quality efforts relative to one's peers or world-class companies. Award criteria and certification procedures fill this important role. The most prominent frameworks for quality that have had worldwide influence are ISO 9000, and its derivative QS-9000, and the Malcolm Baldrige National Quality Award Criteria for Performance Excellence.

ISO 9000

As quality became a major focus of businesses throughout the world, various organizations developed standards and guidelines. Terms such as *quality management*, *quality control*, *quality system*, and *quality assurance* acquired different, and sometimes conflicting, meanings from country to country, within a country, and even within an industry.[9] As the European Community moved toward the European free trade agreement, which went into effect at the end of 1992, quality management became a key strategic objective. To standardize quality requirements for European countries within the Common Market and those wishing to do business with those countries, a specialized agency for standardization, the International Organization for Standardization, was founded in 1946. Composed of representatives from the national standards bodies of 91 nations, the agency adopted a series of written quality standards in 1987, which were revised in 1994. The standards have been adopted in the United States by the American National Standards Institute (ANSI) with the endorsement and cooperation of the American Society for Quality Control (ASQC). The U.S. standards are called the ANSI/ASQC Q9000–1994 series. The standards are recognized by about 100 countries, including Japan. In some foreign markets, companies will not buy from noncertified suppliers. Thus, meeting these standards is becoming a requirement for international competitiveness. The standards are intended to apply to all types of businesses, including electronics and chemicals, and to services such as health care, banking, and transportation.

The ISO 9000 family of standards defines *quality system standards* that guide a company's performance of specified requirements in the areas of design/ development, production, installation, and service. They are based on the premise that certain generic characteristics of management practices can be standardized and that a well-designed, well-implemented, and carefully managed quality system provides confidence that the outputs will meet customer expectations and requirements. The standards prescribe documentation for all processes affecting quality and suggest that compliance through auditing leads to continuous improvement. Thus, the standards have five objectives:

1. achieve, maintain, and seek to continuously improve product quality (including services) in relationship to requirements,
2. improve the quality of operations to continually meet customers' and stakeholders' stated and implied needs,

3. provide confidence to internal management and other employees that quality requirements are being fulfilled and that improvement is taking place,
4. provide confidence to customers and other stakeholders that quality requirements are being achieved in the delivered product, and
5. provide confidence that quality system requirements are fulfilled.

Structure of the ISO 9000 Standards

The standards define three levels of quality assurance:

- *Level 1* (ISO 9001) provides a model for quality assurance in firms that design, develop, produce, install, and service products.
- *Level 2* (ISO 9002) provides a quality assurance model for firms engaged only in production and installation.
- *Level 3* (ISO 9003) applies to firms engaged only in final inspection and test.

Two other standards, ISO 9000 and ISO 9004, define the basic elements of a comprehensive quality assurance system and provide guidance in applying the appropriate level. ISO 9000 describes the principal concepts of quality assurance, such as the objectives and responsibilities for quality, stakeholder expectations, the concept of a process, the role of processes in a quality system, the roles of documentation and training in support of quality improvement, and how to apply the different standards. ISO 9004 guides the development and implementation of a quality system. It examines each of the elements of the quality system in detail and can be used for internal auditing purposes. Together, these five standards are referred to as the ISO 9000 series.

ISO 9001 focuses on 20 key requirements; some of these requirements are not applicable to the ISO 9002 and ISO 9003 standards. To illustrate the scope of the requirements, consider the first one, Management Responsibility. To meet this standard a company must

- establish, document, and publicize its policy, objectives, and commitment to quality;
- designate a representative with authority and responsibility for implementing and maintaining the requirements of the standard;
- provide adequate resources for managing, performing work, and verifying activities including internal quality audits;
- conduct in-house verification and review of the quality system. These reviews should consider the results of internal quality audits, management effectiveness, defects and irregularities, solutions to quality problems, implementation of past solutions, handling of nonconforming product, results of statistical score-keeping tools, and the impact of quality methods on actual results.

A brief summary of the basic requirements for the remaining 19 elements of ISO 9001 are summarized below.

- *Quality system*—The company must write and maintain a quality manual that meets the criteria of the applicable standard (9001, 9002, or 9003) and defines conformance to requirements. The company must effectively implement the quality system and its documented procedures and prepare quality plans for determining how requirements will be met.
- *Contract review*—The company must review contracts to assess whether requirements are adequately defined and whether the capability exists to meet requirements.
- *Design control*—The company must verify product design to ensure that requirements are being met and that procedures are in place for design planning and design changes. This includes documenting plans for each design and development activity, defining organizational and technical interfaces, validating outputs against design input requirements, and describing design verification and validation procedures.
- *Document and data control*—The company must establish and maintain procedures for controlling documentation and data through approval, distribution, change, and modification.
- *Purchasing*—The company must have procedures to ensure that purchased products conform to requirements. This includes evaluating subcontractors, preparing clearly written purchasing documents, and verifying purchased products.
- *Control of customer-supplied products*—Procedures to verify, store, and maintain items supplied by customers must be established.
- *Product identification and traceability*—The company must identify and trace products during all stages of production, delivery, and installation.
- *Process control*—The company must carry out production processes under controlled conditions. The processes must be documented and monitored, and workers must use approved equipment and have specified criteria for workmanship.
- *Inspection and testing*—The company must maintain records of inspection and testing at all stages to verify that requirements are met. This includes receiving, in-process, and final inspection and testing.
- *Control of inspection, measuring, and test equipment*—The company must establish procedures to control, calibrate, and maintain equipment used to demonstrate conformance to requirements.
- *Control of nonconforming product*—Procedures should ensure that the company avoids inadvertent use of nonconforming product. This includes how nonconforming product is reviewed and how repaired or reworked product is reinspected.
- *Corrective and preventive action*—The company should investigate causes of nonconformance and take action both to correct the problems and to prevent them in the future. Corrective action includes handling customer complaints, investigating causes of nonconformities, and applying appropriate controls. Preventive action includes detecting, analyzing, and eliminating potential causes of nonconformities and initiating preventive actions.

- *Handling, storage, packaging, preservation, and delivery*—The company should develop procedures for properly handling, storing, packaging, preserving, and delivering products.
- *Control of quality records*—The company should identify, collect, index, file, and store all records relating to the quality system.
- *Internal quality audits*—The company must establish a system of internal audits to verify whether its activities comply with requirements and to evaluate the effectiveness of the quality system.
- *Training*—The company must establish procedures for identifying training needs and provide for training of all employees who perform activities that affect quality.
- *Servicing*—The company must develop procedures to ensure that service is performed as required by its contracts with customers.
- *Statistical techniques.* Procedures should identify statistical techniques used to control processes, products, and services and how they are implemented.

ISO 9000 requires that all published standards be reviewed on a periodic basis. Many of the changes in the 1994 revision were improvements in language, such as clarifying a "product" to be "hardware, software, processed materials, or services," reducing the manufacturing focus of the standards. (A college in England achieved ISO registration in 1994, and Surgical Focused Care, a New York City orthopedic practice, received registration in 1996.) The current set of complete standards can be purchased through the American Society for Quality (http://www.asq.org).

ISO 9000 Registration

The ISO 9000 standards originally were intended to be advisory in nature and to be used for two-party contractual situations (between a customer and supplier) and for internal auditing. However, they quickly evolved into criteria for companies who wished to "certify" their quality management or achieve "registration" through a third-party auditor, usually a laboratory or some other accreditation agency (called a *registrar*). This process began in the United Kingdom. Rather than a supplier being audited by each customer for compliance to the standards the registrar certifies the company, and this certification is accepted by all of the supplier's customers.

The registration process includes the registrar's review of the quality system documents or quality manual; preassessment, which identifies potential noncompliance in the quality system or in the documentation; assessment by a team of two or three auditors of the quality system and its documentation; and surveillance, or periodic re-audits, to verify conformity with the practices and systems registered. During the assessment, typical questions auditors might ask (about Management Responsibility, for example) are: Does a documented policy on quality exist? Have management objectives for quality been defined? Have the policy and objectives been transmitted and explained to all levels of the organization? Have job descriptions been documented for people who manage or perform work that affects quality? Are descriptions of functions that affect quality available? Has management designated a person or group with the authority to prevent nonconformities in products, identify and record quality problems, and recommend solutions? What means are used to verify the solutions?[10]

Recertification is required every three years. Individual sites—not entire companies—must achieve registration. All costs are borne by the applicant, so the process can be quite expensive. A registration audit may cost anywhere from $10,000 to over $40,000, and the internal cost for documentation and training may exceed $100,000.

Perspectives on ISO 9000

Many misconceptions exist about what ISO 9000 actually is. The standards do not specify any measure of quality performance; specific product quality levels are set by the company. The standards only require that the supplier have a verifiable process in place to ensure that it consistently produces what it says it will produce, thus providing confidence to customers and company management that certain principles of good management are followed. The standards emphasize documenting conformance of quality systems to the company's quality manual and established quality system requirements. As one consultant explained it, "Document it, and do it like you document it. If it moves, train it. If not, calibrate it." A supplier can comply with the standards and still produce a poor quality product—as long as it does so consistently! In addition, ISO 9000 does not consider activities such as leadership, strategic planning, or customer relationship management.

Having just read the preceding sentences, do not think that the standards are not useful. They provide a set of good common practices for quality assurance systems and are an excellent starting point for companies with no formal quality assurance program. Many companies find that their current quality systems already comply with most of the standards. For companies in the early stages of formal quality programs, the standards enforce the discipline of control that is necessary before they can seriously pursue continuous improvement. The requirements of periodic audits reinforce the stated quality system until it becomes ingrained in the company (see box).

The rigorous documentation standards help companies uncover problems and improve their processes. At DuPont, for example, ISO 9000 has been credited with increasing on-time delivery from 70 to 90 percent, decreasing cycle time from 15 days to 1.5 days, increasing first-pass yields from 72 to 92 percent, and reducing the number of test procedures by one-third. Sun Microsystems' Milpitas plant was certified in 1992, and managers believe that it has helped deliver improved quality and service.[11] In Canada, Toronto Plastics, Ltd., reduced defects from 150,000 per million to 15,000 after one year of ISO implementation.[12] Thus, using ISO 9000 as a basis for a quality system can improve productivity, decrease costs, and increase customer satisfaction.

In addition to improving internal operations, the most important reasons why companies seek ISO 9000 certification include:

• *Meeting contractual obligations*—Some customers now require certification of all their suppliers. Suppliers that do not pursue registration will eventually lose customers.

Some Unusual ISO 9000 Approaches[13]

The Rosemount Measurement Division of the Fisher-Rosemount Group of the Emerson Electric Company was named one of the "Best Plants in America" by *Industry Week* in 1993. Since achieving ISO certification that year, every department is audited internally at least once each year for conformance to the standards. Discrepancies found during an audit are fed back to the area on a corrective action form. Every corrective action is verified within about a month of a stated completion date. In most ISO 9000 systems, the quality department tends not to hold specific people responsible for system deficiencies. But if a Rosemount department head is tardy resolving a discrepancy, his or her name is found blinking in red letters on the computer monitor. In other words, the person is held responsible for the lateness of the solution, not the actual problem. All discrepancies are therefore resolved in a timely manner.

As the audit teams visit all areas in the organization, they get very good at understanding which departments are best in class for certain process control features. Although most auditors tend to be neutral, the Rosemount system gives complete feedback of information. At postaudit meetings, the positive discoveries are shared first, and the department may be judged best in class in some process categories. In categories where some improvement is needed, the auditors may suggest that the audited department visit other departments that are best in class in those categories.

The auditors try to let the departments learn from one another rather than reinvent the wheel. The external auditors told the quality group that Rosemount has made great improvements in the two years that the best-in-class feedback method has been used.

- *Meeting trade regulations*—Many products sold in Europe, such as telecommunications terminal equipment, medical devices, gas appliances, toys, and construction products require product certifications to assure safety. Often, ISO certification is necessary to obtain product certification.
- *Marketing goods in Europe*—ISO 9000 is widely accepted within the European Union. It is fast becoming a de facto requirement for doing business within the trading region.
- *Gaining a competitive advantage*—Many customers use ISO registration as a basis for supplier selection. Companies without it may be at a market disadvantage.

As of early 1993, only about 550 company sites in the United States were certified. In contrast, some 20,000 companies were certified in the United Kingdom. During the first nine months of 1993, registrations grew by 70 percent to about 45,000 worldwide, evidence of the growing global interest in the standards, driven primarily by marketplace demands. By 1997, the United States had more than 12,000 registrations, and Europe had more than 200,000. Diverse organizations such as schools, physician's offices, and even a ski resort in France have achieved ISO 9000 registration.

Nevertheless, ISO 9000 has been quite controversial. Many now question its usefulness.[14] The European Union has called for de-emphasizing ISO 9000 registration, citing that companies are focused more on "passing a test" than on developing quality processes. New quality policies are being debated at this time. The Australian government has stopped requiring it for government contracts. The Australian *Business Review Weekly* noted that "its reputation among small and medium businesses continues to deteriorate. Some small businesses have almost been destroyed by the endeavor to implement costly and officious quality assurance ISO 9000 systems that hold little relevance to their businesses." It will certainly be interesting to observe what happens in the near future.

QS-9000

Late in 1994, the big three automobile manufacturers—Ford, Chrylser, and General Motors—released QS-9000, an interpretation and extension of ISO 9000 for automotive suppliers. QS-9000 is a collaborative effort of these firms to standardize their individual quality requirements while drawing upon the global ISO standards. Truck manufacturers—Mack Trucks, Freightliner, Navistar International, PACCAR Inc, and Volvo GM—also participated in the process. Their goal was to develop fundamental quality systems that provide for continuous improvement, emphasizing defect prevention and the reduction of variation and waste in the supply chain. This standardized quality system is aimed at reducing the cost of doing business with suppliers and enhancing the competitive position of the automakers and suppliers alike. QS-9000 applies to all internal and external suppliers of production and service parts and materials. Chrysler, Ford, GM, and truck manufacturers require all suppliers to establish, document, and implement quality systems based on these standards according to individual customers' timing.

QS-9000 is based on ISO 9000 and includes all ISO requirements. However, QS-9000 goes well beyond ISO 9000 standards by including additional requirements such as continuous improvement, manufacturing capability, and production part approval processes. QS-9000 not only states *what* must be done, but often *how* to do it. For example, under Management Responsibility (the first element in the ISO standards), the QS-9000 standard requires companies to use a formal, documented, comprehensive business plan; to develop both short- and longer-term goals and plans based on the analysis of competitive products and benchmarking information; and to revise and review the plan appropriately. The standard also requires methods to determine current and future customer expectations, an objective and valid process to collect the information, and a process for determining customer satisfaction. The company must document trends in quality and in operational performance (productivity, efficiency, and effectiveness, and current quality levels for key product and service features). The company must then compare their trends with those of competitors and/or appropriate benchmarks to measure progress toward overall business objectives. Trends in customer satisfaction and key indicators of customer dissatisfaction must be documented and supported by objective information; compared to competitors or to benchmarks; and reviewed by senior management.

In addition, registration to QS-9000 requires demonstration of effectiveness in meeting the intent of the standards, rather than simply the "do it as you document it" philosophy. For instance, under process control, ISO 9000 requires "suitable maintenance of equipment to ensure continuing process capability;" QS-9000 requires suppliers to identify key process equipment, to provide appropriate resources for maintenance, and to develop an effective, planned total preventive maintenance system. The system should include a procedure that describes the planned maintenance activities, scheduled maintenance, and predictive maintenance methods. Also, extensive requirements for documenting process monitoring and operator instructions and process capability and performance requirements are built into the standards. Finally, additional requirements pertain specifically to Ford, Chrysler, and GM suppliers. Thus, registration under QS-9000 standards will also achieve ISO 9000 registration, but ISO-certified companies must meet the additional QS-9000 requirements to achieve QS certification.

The latest release of QS-9000, in January 1999, adds other new requirements. These include informing management responsible for corrective action as soon as possible when a product or process becomes noncompliant with specific requirements, using the cost of poor quality to document operational performance, incorporating product safety into design and process control procedures, maintaining production environments to prevent nonconformities due to working conditions, and mistake-proofing methods in corrective and preventive action processes.

The Malcolm Baldrige National Quality Award

The Malcolm Baldrige National Quality Award (MBNQA) has been one of the most powerful catalysts of total quality in the United States and, indeed, throughout the world. More importantly, the award's Criteria for Performance Excellence establish a framework for integrating total quality principles and practices in any organization. In this section we present an overview of the award, the criteria, and the award process.

Recognizing that U.S. productivity was declining, President Reagan signed legislation mandating a national study/conference on productivity in October 1982. The American Productivity and Quality Center (formerly the American Productivity Center) sponsored seven computer networking conferences in 1983 to prepare for an upcoming White House Conference on Productivity. The final report on these conferences recommended that "a National Quality Award, similar to the Deming Prize in Japan, be awarded annually to those firms that successfully challenge and meet the award requirements. These requirements and the accompanying examination process should be very similar to the Deming Prize system to be effective." The Baldrige Award was signed into law (Public Law 100-107) on August 20, 1987. The award is named after President Reagan's secretary of commerce, who was killed in an accident shortly before the Senate acted on the legislation. Malcolm Baldrige was highly regarded by world leaders, having played a major role in carrying out the administration's trade policy, resolving technology transfer differences with China and India, and holding the first Cabinet-level talks with the Soviet Union in seven years, which paved the way for increased access for U.S. firms in the Soviet market. The award is a public-private partnership, funded primarily through a private foundation.

The purposes of the award are to

- help stimulate American companies to improve quality and productivity for the pride of recognition while obtaining a competitive edge through increased profits;
- recognize the achievements of those companies that improve the quality of their goods and services and provide an example to others;
- establish guidelines and criteria that can be used by business, industrial, governmental, and other enterprises in evaluating their own quality improvement efforts;
- provide specific guidance for other American enterprises that wish to learn how to manage for high quality by making available detailed information on how winning enterprises were able to change their cultures and achieve eminence.

The Baldrige Award recognizes U.S. companies that excel in quality management practice and performance. The Baldrige Award does not exist simply to recognize product excellence, nor does it exist for the purpose of "winning." Its principal focus is on promoting high-performance management practices that lead to customer satisfaction and business results. Up to two companies can receive an award in each of the categories of manufacturing, small business, and service. Table 2.2 shows the recipients through 1998. In 1995, pilot programs in education and health care were instituted, and late in 1998, Congress approved awards in these sectors for 1999.

The Criteria for Performance Excellence

The Baldrige Award's Criteria for Performance Excellence were designed to encourage companies to enhance their competitiveness through efforts toward two results-oriented goals:

- delivery of ever-improving value to customers, resulting in improved marketplace success; and
- improvement of overall company performance and capabilities.

The criteria consist of a hierarchical set of *categories*, *items*, and *areas to address*. The seven categories are:

1. *Leadership*—This category examines how an organization's senior leaders address values and performance expectations and a focus on customers

TABLE 2.2   MALCOLM BALDRIGE AWARD RECIPIENTS

Year	Manufacturing	Small Business	Service
1988	Motorola, Inc. Westinghouse Commercial Nuclear Fuel Division	Globe Metallurgical, Inc.	
1989	Xerox Corp. Business Products and Systems Milliken & Co.		
1990	Cadillac Motor Car Division IBM Rochester	Wallace Co. Inc.	Federal Express (FedEx)
1991	Solectron Corp. Zytec Corp.	Marlow Industries	
1992	AT&T Network Systems Texas Instruments Defense Systems & Electronics Group	Granite Rock Co.	AT&T Universal Card Services The Ritz-Carlton Hotel Co.
1993	Eastman Chemical Co.	Ames Rubber Corp.	
1994		Wainwright Industries, Inc.	AT&T Consumer Communication Services GTE Directories
1995	Armstrong World Industries Building Products Operations Corning Telecommunications Products Division		
1996	ADAC Laboratories	Custom Research Inc. Trident Precision Manufacturing, Inc.	Dana Commercial Credit Corp.
1997	3M Dental Products Division Solectron Corp.		Merrill Lynch Credit Corp. Xerox Business Services
1998	Boeing Airlift and Tanker Programs Solar Turbines, Inc.	Texas Nameplate Company, Inc.	

and other stakeholders, as well as empowerment, innovation, learning, and organizational directions. Also examined are how the organization addresses its responsibilities to the public and supports its key communities.

2. *Strategic Planning*—This category examines an organization's strategy development process, including how it develops strategic objectives, action plans, and related human resource plans. Also examined are how plans are deployed and how performance is tracked.

3. *Customer and Market Focus*—This category examines how an organization determines requirements, expectations, and preferences of customers and markets. Also examined is how the organization builds relationships with customers and determines their satisfaction.

4. *Information and Analysis*—This category examines an organization's performance measurement system and how it analyzes performance data and information.

5. *Human Resource Focus*—This category examines how an organization enables employees to develop and use their full potential, aligned with the organization's objectives. Also examined are efforts to build and maintain a work environment and an employee support climate conducive to performance excellence, full participation, and personal and organizational growth.

6. *Process Management*—This category examines the key aspects of an organization's process management, including customer-focused design, product and service delivery processes, support processes, and supplier and partnering processes involving all work units.

7. *Business Results*—This category examines an organization's performance and improvement in key business areas—customer satisfaction, product and service performance, financial and marketplace performance, human resource results, supplier and partner results, and operational performance. Also examined are performance levels relative to competitors.

You should consult the actual criteria document (which is updated annually) for clarifying notes and explanations. A single free copy of the criteria can be obtained from the National Institute of Standards and Technology. Contact the Malcolm Baldrige National Quality Award, National Institute of Standards and Technology (NIST), Route 270 & Quince Orchard Road, Administration Building, Room A537, Gaithersburg, MD 20899, phone 301-975-2036; fax 301-948-3716; or visit the Web site (http://www.quality.nist.gov/).

The seven criteria categories form an *integrated management system*, as illustrated in Figure 2.3. Leadership, Strategic Planning, and Customer and Market Focus represent the "leadership triad," and suggest the importance of integrating these three functions. Senior leaders must set organizational direction and seek future opportunities—this is the role of strategic planning. They must also

FIGURE 2.3 MALCOLM BALDRIGE NATIONAL QUALITY AWARD CRITERIA FRAMEWORK

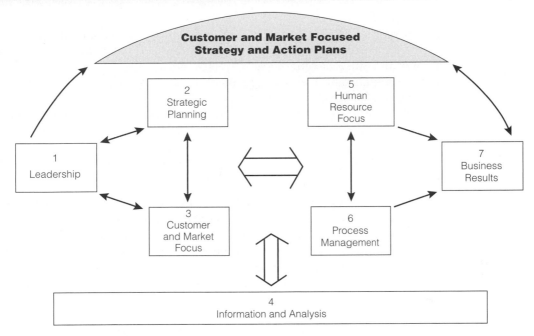

focus on customers; if they don't, the organization as a whole will lack that focus. Human Resource Focus, Process Management, and Business Results represent the "results triad." An organization's employees and its key processes accomplish the work of the organization that yields its business results, toward which all actions point. Finally, Information and Analysis supports the entire framework by providing the foundation for performance measurement and a fact-based approach for improving performance and competitiveness.

Each category consists of several *items* or major requirements on which businesses should focus. Each item, in turn, consists of a small number of *areas to address*, which seek specific information on *approaches* used to ensure and improve competitive performance, *deployment* of these approaches, or *results* obtained from such deployment.

For example, the Leadership category in the 1999 criteria consists of two items and four areas to address:

1.1 Organizational Leadership
   a. Senior Leadership Direction
   b. Organizational Performance Review

1.2 Public Responsibility and Citizenship
   a. Responsibilities to the Public
   b. Support of Key Communities

The Senior Leadership Direction area to address seeks the following information:

- how senior leaders set, communicate, and deploy organizational values, performance expectations, and a focus on creating and balancing value for customers and other stakeholders;
- how communication and deployment to all employees is accomplished through the leadership structure;
- how senior leaders establish and reinforce an environment for empowerment and innovation, and encourage and support organizational and employee learning; and
- how senior leaders set directions and seek future opportunities for the organization.

Areas to address that request information on approach or deployment begin with the word "how"; that is, they define a set of key actionable management practices (see Table 2.3). Thus, the MBNQA Criteria define both an integrated infrastructure and a set of fundamental practices for a high-performance management system. These practices represent the collective wisdom of the nation's leading business experts and reflect what a truly world-class high-performance organization must do to succeed.

One thing the criteria do not do is prescribe specific quality tools, techniques, technologies, systems, or starting points. Companies are encouraged to develop and demonstrate creative, adaptive, and flexible approaches to meeting basic requirements. Many innovative approaches have been developed by Baldrige winners and are now commonly used by many other companies.

The Baldrige Award Evaluation Process

The Baldrige evaluation process is rigorous. In the first stage, each application is thoroughly reviewed by at least 10 examiners (all volunteers) chosen from among leading quality professionals in business, academia, health care, and government. Examiners evaluate the applicant's response to each examination item, listing major strengths and areas for improvement relative to the criteria. Strengths demonstrate an effective and positive response to the criteria. Areas for improvement do not prescribe specific practices or examiners' opinions on what the company should be doing, but rather deficiencies in responding to the criteria. Based on these comments, a percentage score from 0 to 100 in increments of 10 is given to each item. Each examination item is evaluated on approach/deployment or results.

Approach refers to the methods the company uses to achieve the requirements addressed in each category. The factors used to evaluate approaches include:

- the appropriateness of the methods to the requirements,
- the effectiveness of methods,
- the degree to which the approach is systematic, integrated, and consistently applied,

TABLE 2.3 KEY MANAGEMENT PRACTICES REFLECTED IN THE 1999 MBNQA CRITERIA
(Note that not all specific areas to address are reflected here, because some deal explicitly with key information or results.)

Leadership

1. How senior leaders set, communicate, deploy organizational values, performance expectations, and a focus on creating and balancing value for customers and other stakeholders.
2. How senior leaders establish and reinforce an environment for empowerment and innovation, and encourage and support organizational and employee learning.
3. How senior leaders set directions and seek future opportunities.
4. How senior leaders review organizational performance and capabilities to assess organizational health, competitive performance, and progress relative to performance goals and changing organizational needs.
5. How organizational performance review findings are translated into priorities for improvement and opportunities for innovation.
6. How key recent performance review findings, priorities for improvement, and opportunities for innovation are deployed throughout the organization and to suppliers/partners and key customers to ensure organizational alignment.
7. How senior leaders use organizational performance review findings and employee feedback to improve their leadership effectiveness and the effectiveness of management throughout the organization.
8. How the organization addresses the impacts on society of products, services, and operations, anticipates public concerns with current and future products, services, and operations, and prepares for these concerns in a proactive manner.
9. How the organization ensures ethical business practices in all stakeholder transactions and interactions.
10. How the organization, senior leaders, and employees actively support and strengthen their key communities.

Strategic Planning

1. How the organization considers the following key factors in its strategic planning process:
   - customer and market needs/expectations, including new product/service opportunities
   - competitive environment and capabilities, including use of new technology
   - financial, societal, and other potential risks
   - human resource capabilities and needs
   - operational capabilities and needs, including resource availability
   - supplier and/or partner capabilities and needs
2. How the organization evaluates options to assess how well they respond to the factors most important to performance in setting objectives.
3. How the organization develops action plans and key human resource requirements that address key strategic objectives.

TABLE 2.3   KEY MANAGEMENT PRACTICES REFLECTED IN THE 1999 MBNQA CRITERIA *CONTINUED*

4. How the organization allocates resources to ensure accomplishment of its overall action plan and uses key performance measures and/or indicators for tracking progress relative to action plans.

5. How the organization communicates and deploys strategic objectives, action plans, and performance measures/indicators to achieve overall organizational alignment.

Customer and Market Focus

1. How the organization determines target customers, customer groups, and/or market segments.

2. How the organization listens and learns to determine key requirements and drivers of purchase decisions for current, former, and potential customers.

3. How the organization determines and/or projects key product/service features and their relative importance/value to customers for purposes of current and future marketing, product planning, and other business developments, and uses relevant information from current and former customers, including marketing/sales information, customer retention, won/lost analysis, and complaints, in this determination.

4. How the organization keeps its listening and learning methods current with business needs and directions.

5. How the organization determines key access mechanisms to facilitate the ability of customers to conduct business, seek assistance and information, and make complaints.

6. How the organization determines key customer contact requirements and deploys these requirements to all employees involved in the response chain.

7. How the organization ensures that complaints are resolved effectively and promptly, and that all complaints received are aggregated and analyzed for use in overall organizational improvement.

8. How the organization builds relationships with customers for repeat business and/or positive referral.

9. How the organization keeps its approaches to customer access and relationships current with business needs and directions.

10. How customer satisfaction and dissatisfaction measurements capture actionable information that reflects customers' future business and/or potential for positive referral.

11. How the organization follows up with customers on products/services and recent transactions to receive prompt and actionable feedback.

12. How the organization obtains and uses information on customer satisfaction relative to competitors and/or benchmarks.

13. How the organization keeps its approaches to satisfaction determination current with business needs and directions.

TABLE 2.3   Key Management Practices Reflected in the 1999 MBNQA Criteria *continued*

Information and Analysis

1. How the organization addresses the major components of an effective performance measurement system, including the following key factors:
   - selection of measures/indicators, and extent and effectiveness of their use in
     daily operations
   - selection and integration of measures/indicators and completeness of data to
     track overall organizational performance
   - selection, and extent and effectiveness of use, of key comparative data and infor-
     mation
   - data and information reliability
   - a cost/financial understanding of improvement options
   - correlations/projections of data to support planning
2. How the organization keeps its performance measurement system current with
   business needs and directions.
3. How the organization performs analyses to support senior executives' organizational performance review and organizational planning, and ensures that the analyses address the overall health of the organization, including key business results
   and strategic objectives.
4. How the organization ensures that the results of organizational-level analysis are
   linked to work group and/or functional-level operations to enable effective support
   for decision making.
5. How analysis supports daily operations throughout the organization, and ensures
   that analysis measures align with action plans.

Human Resource Focus

1. How the organization designs, organizes, and manages work and jobs to promote
   cooperation and collaboration, individual initiative, innovation, and flexibility, and to
   keep current with business needs.
2. How managers and supervisors encourage and motivate employees to develop and
   utilize their full potential.
3. How the employee performance management system, including feedback to
   employees, supports high performance.
4. How compensation, recognition, and related reward/incentive practices reinforce
   high performance.
5. How the organization ensures effective communication, cooperation, and
   knowledge/skill sharing across work units, functions, and locations.
6. How the organization identifies characteristics and skills needed by potential
   employees, and recruits and hires new employees, taking into account key performance requirements, diversity of the community, and fair workforce practices.
7. How education and training approaches balance short- and longer-term organizational and employee needs, including development, learning, and career progres-
   sion.

TABLE 2.3   KEY MANAGEMENT PRACTICES REFLECTED IN THE 1999 MBNQA CRITERIA *CONTINUED*

8. How education and training are designed to keep current with business and individual needs.
9. How the organization seeks and uses input from employees and their supervisors/managers on education and training needs, expectations, and design.
10. How the organization delivers and evaluates education and training.
11. How the organization addresses key developmental and training needs, including diversity training, management/leadership development, new employee orientation, and safety.
12. How the organization addresses performance excellence in its education and training, and how employees learn to use performance measurements, performance standards, skill standards, performance improvement, quality control methods, and benchmarking.
13. How the organization reinforces knowledge and skills on the job.
14. How the organization addresses and improves workplace health, safety, and ergonomic factors and how employees take part in identifying these factors and in improving workplace safety, including performance measures and/or targets for each key environmental factor and significant differences, if any, based on different work environments for employee groups and/or work units.
15. How the organization enhances employees' work climate via services, benefits, and policies, and how these enhancements are selected and tailored to the needs of different categories and types of employees, and to individuals.
16. How the work climate considers and supports the needs of a diverse workforce.
17. How the organization determines the key factors that affect employee well-being, satisfaction, and motivation.
18. How the organization conducts assessments to understand employee well-being, satisfaction, and motivation, and tailors the methods and measures to a diverse workforce and to different categories and types of employees.
19. How the organization relates assessment findings to key business results to identify work environment and employee support climate improvement priorities.

Process Management
1. How the organization identifies its design processes for products/services and their related production/delivery processes, and incorporates changing customer/market requirements into product/service designs and production/delivery systems and processes.
2. How the organization incorporates new technology into products/services and into production/delivery systems and processes.
3. How design processes address design quality and cycle time, transfer of learning from past projects and other parts of the organization, cost control, new design technology, productivity, and other efficiency/effectiveness factors.
4. How the organization ensures that its production/delivery process design accommodates all key operational performance requirements.

TABLE 2.3 KEY MANAGEMENT PRACTICES REFLECTED IN THE 1999 MBNQA CRITERIA *CONTINUED*

5. How the organization coordinates and tests design and production/delivery processes to ensure capability for trouble-free and timely introduction of products/services.
6. How the organization identifies its key production/delivery processes and their key performance requirements, and ensures they meet key performance requirements.
7. How key performance measures and/or indicators are used for the control and improvement of production/delivery processes, and how real-time customer input is sought.
8. How the organization improves its production/delivery processes to achieve better process performance and improvements to products/services, and shares improvements with other organizational units and processes.
9. How the organization determines key support process requirements, incorporates input from internal and/or external customers, and designs and manages these processes to meet all the key requirements.
10. How the organization improves its support processes to achieve better performance and to keep them current with business needs and directions, and shares improvements with other organizational units and processes.
11. How the organization incorporates performance requirements into supplier and/or partner process management, ensures that performance requirements are met, and provides timely and actionable feedback to suppliers and/or partners.
12. How the organization seeks to minimize overall costs associated with inspections, tests, and process and/or performance audits.
13. How the organization provides business assistance and/or incentives to suppliers and/or partners to help them improve their overall performance and to improve their abilities to contribute to current and longer-term performance.
14. How the organization improves supplier and/or partner processes, including the organization's role as supportive customer/partner, to keep current with business needs and directions, and shares improvements throughout the organization.

- the degree to which the approach embodies effective evaluation/improvement cycles,
- the degree to which the approach is based upon reliable information and data,
- alignment with organizational needs, and
- evidence of innovation.

Deployment refers to the extent to which the approaches are applied to all requirements of the item. The factors used to evaluate deployment include:

- use of the approach in addressing item requirements relevant to the organization, and
- use of the approach by all appropriate work units.

Results refers to the outcomes and effects in achieving the purposes given in the item. The factors used to evaluate results include:

- current performance,
- performance relative to appropriate comparisons and/or benchmarks,
- rate, breadth, and importance of performance improvements, and
- linkage of results measures to key customer, market, process, and action plan performance requirements identified by the applicant.

Table 2.4 summarizes the scoring guidelines.

Scores for each examination item are computed by multiplying the examiner's score by the maximum point value that can be earned (see Table 2.5 on page 81). The scores are reviewed by a panel of nine judges without knowledge of the specific companies. The higher scoring applications enter a consensus stage in which a selected group of examiners discusses variations in individual scores and arrives at consensus scores for each item. The panel of judges then reviews the scores and selects the highest scoring applicants for site visits. At this point, six or seven examiners visit the company for up to a week to verify information contained in the written application and resolve issues that are unclear. The judges use the site visit reports to recommend award recipients. Final contenders each receive more than 1,000 hours of evaluation.

Like quality itself, the specific award criteria are continually improved each year. The initial set of criteria in 1988 had 62 items with 278 areas to address. By 1991, the criteria had only 32 items and 99 areas to address. The 1995 criteria were streamlined significantly to 24 items and 54 areas to address. In 1997, further refinements to develop the shortest list of key requirements necessary to compete in today's marketplace, improve the linkage between process and results, and make the criteria more generic and user-friendly resulted in 20 items and 30 areas to address. These were further streamlined to 19 items and 27 areas to address in 1999.

More significantly, the word *quality* has been judiciously dropped throughout the document. For example, until 1994, the Strategic Planning category had been titled Strategic Quality Planning. The change to Strategic Planning signifies that quality should be a part of business planning, not a separate issue.

TABLE 2.4 BALDRIGE AWARD SCORING GUIDELINES

Score	Approach/Deployment
0%	• no systematic approach evident; anecdotal information
10% to 20%	• beginning of a systematic approach to the basic purposes of the item • major gaps exist in deployment that would inhibit progress in achieving the basic purposes of the item • early stages of a transition from reacting to problems to a general improvement orientation
30% to 40%	• a sound, systematic approach, responsive to the basic purposes of the item • approach is deployed, although some areas or work units are in early stages of deployment • beginning of a systematic approach to evaluation and improvement of basic item processes
50% to 60%	• a sound, systematic approach, responsive to the overall purposes of the item • approach is well deployed, although deployment may vary in some areas or work units • a fact-based, systematic evaluation and improvement process is in place for basic item processes • approach is aligned with basic organizational needs identified in the other criteria categories
70% to 80%	• a sound, systematic approach, responsive to the multiple requirements of the item • approach is well deployed, with no significant gaps • a fact-based, systematic evaluation and improvement process and organizational learning/sharing are key management tools; clear evidence of refinement and improved integration as a result of organizational-level analysis and sharing • approach is well integrated with organizational needs identified in the other criteria categories
90% to 100%	• a sound, systematic approach, fully responsive to all the requirements of the item • approach is fully deployed without significant weaknesses or gaps in any areas or work units • a very strong, fact-based, systematic evaluation and improvement process and extensive organizational learning/sharing are key management tools; strong refinement and integration, backed by excellent organizational-level analysis and sharing • approach is fully integrated with organizational needs identified in the other criteria categories

TABLE 2.4   BALDRIGE AWARD SCORING GUIDELINES *CONTINUED*

Score	Results
0%	• no results or poor results in areas reported
10% to 20%	• some improvements *and/or* early good performance levels in a few areas • results not reported for many to most areas of importance to the organization's key business requirements
30% to 40%	• improvements *and/or* good performance levels in many areas of importance to the organization's key business requirements • early stages of developing trends and obtaining comparative information • results reported for many to most areas of importance to the organization's key business requirements
50% 60%	• improvement trends *and/or* good performance levels reported for most areas of importance to the organization's key business requirements • no pattern of adverse trends and no poor performance levels in areas of importance to the organization's key business requirements • some trends *and/or* current performance levels—evaluated against relevant comparisons *and/or* benchmarks—show areas of strength *and/or* good to very good relative performance levels • business results address most key customer, market, and process requirements
70% to 80%	• current performance is good to excellent in areas of importance to the organization's key business requirements • most improvement trends *and/or* current performance levels are sustained • many to most trends *and/or* current performance levels—evaluated against relevant comparisons *and/or* benchmarks—show areas of leadership and very good relative performance levels • business results address most key customer, market, process, and action plan requirements
90% to 100%	• current performance is excellent in most areas of importance to the organization's key business requirements • excellent improvement trends *and/or* sustained excellent performance levels in most areas • evidence of industry and benchmark leadership demonstrated in many areas • business results fully address key customer, market, process, and action plan requirements

TABLE 2.5 1999 BALDRIGE AWARD ITEM POINT VALUES

1999 Categories/Items	Point Values
1 Leadership	**125**
1.1 Organizational Leadership	85
1.2 Public Responsibility and Citizenship	40
2 Strategic Planning	**85**
2.1 Strategy Development	40
2.2 Strategy Deployment	45
3 Customer and Market Focus	**85**
3.1 Customer and Market Knowledge	40
3.2 Customer Satisfaction and Relationships	45
4 Information and Analysis	**85**
4.1 Measurement of Organizational Performance	40
4.2 Analysis of Organizational Performance	45
5 Human Resource Focus	**85**
5.1 Work Systems	35
5.2 Employee Education, Training, and Development	25
5.3 Employee Well-Being and Satisfaction	25
6 Process Management	**85**
6.1 Product and Service Processes	55
6.2 Support Processes	15
6.3 Supplier and Partnering Processes	15
7 Business Results	**450**
7.1 Customer Focused Results	115
7.2 Financial and Market Results	115
7.3 Human Resource Results	80
7.4 Supplier and Partner Results	25
7.5 Organizational Effectiveness Results	115
Total Points	**1,000**

Throughout the document, the term *performance* has been substituted for *quality* as a conscious attempt to recognize that the principles of total quality are the foundation for a company's entire management system, not just the quality system. As Curt Reimann, former director and architect of the Baldrige Award Program noted, "The things you do to win a Baldrige Award are exactly the things you'd do to win in the marketplace. Our strategy is to have the Baldrige Award criteria be a useful daily tool that simulates real competition."

All applicants receive a feedback report that critically evaluates the company's strengths and opportunities for improvement relative to the award criteria. The feedback report, frequently 30 or more pages in length, contains the evaluation team's response to the written application. It includes a distribution of numerical scores of all applicants and a scoring summary of the individual applicant. This feedback is one of the most valuable aspects of the Baldrige Award program.

Using the Baldrige Criteria

The Baldrige Award criteria form a model for business excellence in any organization—manufacturing or service, large or small (see box). Many small businesses (defined as those with 500 or fewer employees) believe that the Baldrige criteria are too difficult to apply to their organizations because they cannot afford to implement the same types of practices as large companies. However, approaches to address the issues in Table 2.3 need not be formal or complex. For example, the ability to obtain customer and market knowledge through independent third-party surveys, extensive interviews, and focus groups, which are common practices among large companies, may be limited by the resources of a small business. What is important, however, is whether the company is using appropriate mechanisms to gather information and use it to improve customer focus and satisfaction. Similarly, large corporations frequently have sophisticated computer/information systems for data management, while small businesses may perform data and information management with a combination of manual methods and personal computers. Also, systems for employee involvement and process management may rely heavily on informal verbal communication and less on formal written documentation. Thus, the size or nature of a business does not affect the appropriateness of the criteria, but rather the context in which the criteria are applied.

Many companies use the award criteria to evaluate their own quality programs, set up and implement quality initiatives, communicate better with suppliers and partners, and for education and training, even if they do not intend to apply for the award. Even the U.S. Postal Service has decided to use the Baldrige criteria as a basis for reestablishing a quality system by identifying the areas that need the most improvement and providing a baseline to track progress. Using the award criteria as a self-assessment tool provides an objective framework, sets a high standard, and compares units that have different systems or organizations.

Most states have developed award programs similar to the Baldrige Award. State award programs generally are designed to promote an awareness of productivity and quality, foster an information exchange, encourage firms to

Baldrige Pays Off for Texas Instruments[15]

Texas Instruments (TI) Defense Systems & Electronics Group (acquired by Raytheon Corporation in 1997 and now called Raytheon Systems Company) faced a critical issue that many businesses struggle with: Is the payoff of greater competitive advantage worth the effort of achieving total quality, specifically competing for the Baldrige Award? Their answer is a definite yes. TI understands firsthand that the real benefit of applying for the Baldrige Award lies in adopting its quality criteria. The application itself is the single most powerful catalyst for the kinds of organizational and cultural changes that companies must make to compete.

TI's commitment to quality and productivity improvement dates back to the 1950s. But, like most corporations, most of its efforts were aimed at improving manufacturing and product quality. In the early 1980s, a total quality initiative was formalized across the entire corporation. Some business units made tremendous progress; the semiconductor operation in Japan won the Deming Prize in 1985.

When the Baldrige Award criteria appeared, TI used them to provide focus and coherence to the activities across the corporation. Using the criteria, they were able to tackle a part of total quality that previously had been unreachable: implementing quality efforts in staff, support, and nonmanufacturing areas. In 1989, TI asked every business unit to prepare a mock award application as a way of measuring its progress. This task represented a radical change for some operations because, until that time, most staff functions were not required to measure their processes or their results.

The Defense Systems & Electronics Group's self-assessment revealed that they were a long way from applying for and winning the Baldrige Award. But the group aggressively adopted the criteria as a blueprint for improving its business. Many executives did not believe that the criteria could be applied to defense contractors. Similarly, many executives today question whether small businesses can realistically meet the Baldrige Award criteria. TI discovered that all companies have one thing in common: customers. Focusing on customers to make the company more competitive provides meaning to the award.

The Baldrige Award application process changed almost everything within the Defense Systems & Electronics Group. Before applying, the group had no way of systematically measuring how well it understood its customers' concerns, captured customers' feedback, or made improvements in interacting with customers. Mountains of data were being collected, but most of the data measured internal criteria, not customer satisfaction. The structured, hierarchical management environment made it difficult to adopt ideas from outside sources.

The Baldrige Award process provided a way to make the customer the centerpiece of daily activities. It led to much better communication with customers and employees and accelerated progress toward less hierarchical, more functional work teams. It changed the management process from an individual activity to a team effort, leading to better decisions. Finally, it introduced two radical new ideas: benchmarking and stretch goals. Changing the culture was not easy and did not happen quickly. It took teamwork, consensus building, and buy in. At TI, it took about five years of dedicated pulling in the same direction to begin seeing measurable results.

adopt quality and productivity improvement strategies, recognize firms that have instituted successful strategies, provide role models for other businesses in the state, encourage new industry to locate in the state, and establish a quality-of-life culture that will benefit all residents of the state.[16] Each state is unique, however, so the specific objectives vary. For instance, the primary objectives of Minnesota's quality award are to encourage all Minnesota organizations to examine their current state of quality and to become more involved in the movement toward continuous quality improvement, as well as to recognize outstanding quality achievements in the state. Missouri, on the other hand, has as its objectives to educate all Missourians in quality improvement, to foster the pursuit of quality in all aspects of Missouri life, and to recognize quality leadership. Information about state award programs can be found at the NIST Web site cited earlier in this section.

The Baldrige Criteria and the Deming Philosophy

It is no secret that W. Edwards Deming was not an advocate of the Baldrige Award.[17] (Joseph Juran, however, was highly influential in its development.) The competitive nature of the award is fundamentally at odds with Deming's teachings. However, many of Deming's principles are reflected directly or in spirit within the Baldrige criteria. In fact, Zytec Corp. implemented its total quality system around Deming's 14 points and received a Baldrige Award. Specific portions of the Baldrige criteria that support each of Deming's 14 points are summarized next.

1. *Statement of Purpose*—Strategy development requires a mission and vision. Commitment to aims and purposes by senior leaders is specifically addressed in the Leadership category and in enhancing customer satisfaction and relationships.
2. *Learn the New Philosophy*—Communication of values, expectations, customer focus, and learning is a key area of the Organizational Leadership item.
3. *Understand Inspection*—The Process Management category addresses the development of appropriate measurement plans. In the Management of Supplier and Partnering Processes item, the Baldrige criteria seek evidence of how a company aims to minimize the costs associated with inspection.
4. *End Price Tag Decisions*—This is implicitly addressed throughout the Process Management category and in the criteria's emphasis on overall performance and linkages among processes and results.
5. *Improve Constantly*—Continuous improvement and learning is a core value of Baldrige. The criteria specifically seek "how the company evaluates and improves [its processes for . . .]" throughout.
6. *Institute Training*—The Human Resource Focus category recognizes the importance of training and employee development in meeting performance objectives.

7. *Institute Leadership*—Category 1 is devoted exclusively to leadership, and it is recognized as the principal driver of the management system in Figure 2.3.

8. *Drive Out Fear and Innovate*—The Human Resource Focus, Customer and Market Focus, and Strategic Planning categories focus on work design, empowerment, and implementation issues that support this point.

9. *Optimize Team Efforts*—The Baldrige criteria have a significant focus on teamwork and customer knowledge in product/process design and process management, as well as in the Human Resource Focus category.

10. *Eliminate Exhortations*—While not directly addressed, the focus on work and job design as the driver of high performance makes this a moot point.

11. *Eliminate Quotas and MBO; Institute Improvement; and Understand Processes*—The Organizational Leadership and Strategy Deployment items, as well as the Information and Analysis and Process Management categories deal with fact-based management and understanding processes.

12. *Remove Barriers*—The Leadership and Human Resource Focus categories, as well as Customer Satisfaction and Relationship Enhancement item support this goal.

13. *Encourage Education*—This is addressed directly in the Employee Education, Training, and Development and Employee Well-Being and Satisfaction items.

14. *Take Action*—This is the role of leadership, addressed directly in the Organizational Leadership item.

The consistencies among Deming's 14 points and the Baldrige criteria attest to the universal nature of quality management principles.

Baldrige versus ISO 9000[18]

With all the publicity surrounding the Baldrige Award and ISO 9000, many misconceptions about them have arisen. Two common misconceptions are that the Baldrige Award and ISO 9000 registration cover similar requirements and that both address improvement and results. In reality, the Baldrige Award and ISO 9000 are distinctly different instruments that can reinforce one another when properly used. ISO 9000 is a minor subset of Baldrige, and most of it falls in Category 6, Process Management. The Baldrige criteria go far beyond ISO 9000 and address such issues as leadership, continuous improvement, use of information, and customer satisfaction. Many companies are using the Baldrige Award criteria and ISO 9000 compatibly, sometimes sequentially and sometimes simultaneously.

INTERNATIONAL QUALITY AWARD PROGRAMS

A focus on total quality has permeated organizations throughout the world. Numerous countries and regions of the world have established awards and award criteria. Many other award programs are similar in nature to the Baldrige criteria.

The Deming Prize

The Deming Application Prize was instituted in 1951 by the Union of Japanese Scientists and Engineers (JUSE) in recognition and appreciation of W. Edwards Deming's achievements in statistical quality control and his friendship with the Japanese people. The Deming Prize has several categories, including prizes for individuals, factories, and small companies, as well as the Deming application prize, which is an annual award presented to a company or a division of a company that has achieved distinctive performance improvements through the application of companywide quality control (CWQC). As defined by JUSE, CWQC

> is a system of activities to assure that quality products and services required by customers are economically designed, produced, and supplied while respecting the principle of customer orientation and the overall public well-being. These quality assurance activities involve market research, research and development, design, purchasing, production, inspection, and sales, as well as all other related activities inside and outside the company. Through everyone in the company understanding both statistical concepts and methods, through their application to all the aspects of quality assurance, and through repeating the cycle of rational planning, implementation, evaluation, and action, CWQC aims to accomplish business objectives.[19]

The judging criteria consist of a checklist of 10 major categories: policies; the organization and its operations; education and dissemination; information gathering, communication and its utilization; analysis; standardization; control/management; quality assurance; effects; and future plans. Each major category is divided into subcategories, or "checking points." For example, the policies category includes policies pursued for management, quality, and quality control; methods for establishing policies; appropriateness and consistency of policies; utilization of statistical methods; communication and dissemination of policies; checks of policies and the status of their achievement; and the relationship between policies and long- and short-term plans. Each category is weighted equally.

Hundreds of companies apply for the award each year. After its initial application is accepted as eligible for the process, a company must submit a detailed description of its quality practices. Sorting through and evaluating a large number of applications is an extraordinary effort in itself. Based on review of the written descriptions, only a few companies believed to be successful in CWQC are selected for a site visit. The site visit consists of a company presentation, in-depth questioning by examiners, and an executive session with top managers. Examiners visit plants and are free to ask any worker any question. For example, at Florida Power and Light, the first non-Japanese company to win the Deming Prize, examiners asked questions of specific individuals such as "What are your main accountabilities?" "What are the important priority issues for the corporation?" "What indicators do you have for your performance? For your target?" "How are you doing today compared to your target?" They request examples of inadequate performance. Documentation must be made available immediately. The preparation is extensive and sometimes frustrating.

The Deming Prize is awarded to all companies that meet the prescribed standard. However, the small number of awards given each year is an indication of the difficulty achieving the standard. The objectives are to ensure that a company has so thoroughly deployed a quality process that it will continue to improve long after a prize is awarded. The application process has no "losers." For companies that do not qualify, the examination process is automatically extended up to two times over three years.

The European Quality Award

In October 1991, the European Foundation for Quality Management (EFQM) in partnership with the European Commission and the European Organization for Quality announced the creation of the European Quality Award. The award was designed to increase awareness throughout the European Community, and businesses in particular, of the growing importance of quality to their competitiveness in the increasingly global market and to their standards of life. The European Quality Award consists of two parts: the European Quality Prize, given to companies that demonstrate excellence in quality management practice by meeting the award criteria, and the European Quality Award, awarded to the most successful applicant. In 1992, four prizes and one award were granted for the first time.

Applicants must demonstrate that their quality approach has contributed significantly to satisfying the expectations of customers, employees, and other constituencies. The award process is similar to those for the Deming Prize and the Baldrige Award. The assessment is based on customer satisfaction, business results, processes, leadership, people satisfaction, resources, people management, policy and strategy, and impact on society. As for the Baldrige Award, results—including customer satisfaction, people (employee) satisfaction, and impact on society—constitute a high percentage of the total score. These are driven by "enablers"—the means by which an organization approaches its business responsibilities. The categories are roughly equivalent to those in the Baldrige criteria. However, the results criteria of people satisfaction, customer satisfaction, impact on society, and business results are somewhat different.[20] The impact on society results category focuses on the perceptions of the company by the community at large and the company's approach to the quality of life, the environment, and the preservation of global resources. The European Quality Award criteria place greater emphasis on this category than is placed on the public responsibility item in the Baldrige Award criteria.

Canadian Awards for Business Excellence

Canada's National Quality Institute (NQI) recognizes Canada's foremost achievers of excellence through the prestigious Canada Awards for Business Excellence. NQI is a nonprofit organization designed to stimulate and support quality-driven innovation within all Canadian enterprises and institutions, including business, government, education, and health care. The quality criteria for the Canadian Awards for Business Excellence are similar in structure to the Baldrige Award criteria. The major categories and items within each category are as follows.

1. *Leadership*—strategic direction, leadership, involvement outcomes
2. *Customer Focus*—voice of the customer, management of customer relationships, measurement outcomes
3. *Planning for Improvement*—development and content of improvement plan, assessment outcomes
4. *People Focus*—human resource planning, participatory environment, continuous learning environment, employee satisfaction outcomes
5. *Process Optimization*—process definition, process control, process improvement outcomes
6. *Supplier Focus*—partnering, outcomes

These categories seek similar information as the Baldrige Award criteria. For example, the people focus category examines the development of human resource planning and implementation and operation of a strategy for achieving excellence through people. It also examines the organization's efforts to foster and support an environment that encourages and enables people to reach their full potential.

Australian Quality Awards

The Australian Quality Awards were developed independently from the MBNQA in 1988. The awards are administered by the Australian Quality Awards Foundation, a subsidiary of the Australian Quality Council. The assessment criteria address leadership, strategy, policy and planning, information and analysis, people, customer focus, processes, products and services, and organizational performance. In this model, leadership and customer focus are the drivers of the management system and enablers of performance. Strategy, policy and planning, information and analysis, and people are the key internal components of the management system. The quality of process, product, and service category focuses on how work is done to achieve the required results and obtain improvement. Organizational performance is the outcome of the management system—a results category. As with Baldrige, the framework emphasizes the holistic and interconnected nature of the management process. The criteria are benchmarked with the Baldrige and the European award criteria. One of the distinctive aspects of Australia's program is solid union support.

SUMMARY

Total quality can be viewed as a philosophy of management that provides a foundation for sound procedures and approaches for managing an enterprise. The philosophical underpinnings of total quality stem from the writings and teachings of W. Edwards Deming, Joseph Juran, and Philip Crosby, who focused on basic ideas of customers, continuous improvement, and organizational transformation. Their work captured the attention of quality practitioners and managers during the 1980s. Many of their management principles are no longer viewed as part of a "quality program" but are now embedded in "how we run our business."

These philosophies have led to frameworks for implementing total quality within an organization. The most prominent frameworks are ISO 9000 and the Malcolm Baldrige National Quality Award Criteria for Performance Excellence. ISO 9000 is a set of fundamental procedures for ensuring a level of consistency in products and services, with assurances that certified companies adhere to these procedures. ISO 9000 is a good way to begin to develop a quality framework, particularly if a firm has never developed any formalized procedures for assuring quality of its products. The Baldrige criteria represent a more comprehensive management framework that focuses on approaches that lead to improving customer value and organizational effectiveness. The Baldrige criteria form the basis not only for a national and many state awards, but also for organizational assessment. Many industrial nations in the world have quality awards that are based on similar requirements, attesting to the universal nature of quality management principles.

REVIEW AND DISCUSSION QUESTIONS

1. Explain the relationship of quality to the five reasons for the lack of competitiveness cited by the MIT Commission. How does TQ address these issues?
2. Prepare a report investigating Japanese "transplants" in the United States. Focus on the differences in management styles between these firms and their traditional American counterparts. What conclusions do you draw?
3. Do you believe that organizations are more successful in adopting TQ when they are reacting to a competitive threat or simply looking to improve?
4. Summarize the Deming management philosophy. Why has it been very controversial?
5. Explain Deming's 14 points in the context of the four categories of Profound Knowledge.
6. How might Deming's concepts of variation be applied to the classroom?
7. Why doesn't the Deming Chain Reaction terminate with "Increased Profits"? Would this contradict the basis of Deming's philosophy?

8. Provide an example of a system with which you are familiar and define its purpose. Examine the interactions within the system and whether the system is managed for optimization.

9. Describe a process with which you are familiar. List some factors that contribute to common cause variation. Cite some examples of special causes of variation in this process.

10. How does the theory of knowledge apply to education? What might this mean for improving the quality of education?

11. Extract three or four key themes in Deming's 14 points. How might the 14 points be grouped in a logical fashion?

12. What implications might Deming's 14 points have for college education? What specific proposals might you suggest as a means of implementing the 14 points at your school?

13. Summarize Juran's philosophy. How is it similar to and different from Deming's?

14. What is Juran's Quality Trilogy? Is it any different from management approaches in other functional areas of business, such as finance?

15. What implications might Juran's Quality Trilogy have for colleges and universities? Would most faculty and administrators agree that the emphasis has been on quality control rather than planning and improvement?

16. How could you apply Juran's Quality Trilogy to improve your personal approach to study and learning?

17. Summarize the Crosby philosophy. How does it differ from Deming's and Juran's?

18. Which quality philosophy—Deming's, Juran's, or Crosby's—do you personally feel most comfortable with? Why?

19. Explain the benefits of and controversy surrounding ISO 9000. Can ISO 9000 lead an organization to world-class quality?

20. Summarize the framework of the Baldrige Award. What are its key philosophical underpinnings?

21. Prepare a list of specific actions that a high-scoring company in the Baldrige Award process might take in each of the seven categories. How difficult do you think it is for a company to score well in all the categories?

CASES

The Rise and Fall of WonderTech[21]

In the mid-1960s a new electronics company, WonderTech, was founded with a unique high-tech product—a new type of computer. Because of its engineering expertise, WonderTech had a virtual lock on its market. The demand for its products was enormous, and the investors were plentiful. Sales in the first three years were so good that backlogs of orders began to pile up midway through their second year. Even with steadily increasing manufacturing capacity (more factories, more shifts, more advanced technology), the demand grew so fast that delivery times began to slip. Originally, WonderTech promised to deliver machines within eight weeks. They intended to return to that standard, but management told investors, "Our computers are so good that some customers are willing to wait 14 weeks for them. We know it's a problem, and we're working to fix it, but nonetheless they're still glad to get the machines, and they love 'em when they get 'em."

The top management knew they had to add production capacity. After six months of study, they decided to borrow the money to build a new factory. To make sure the growth continued, they pumped much of the incoming revenue directly back into sales and marketing. The company sold its products only through a direct sales force, so they had to hire and train more salespeople. During the company's third year, the sales force doubled.

Despite these efforts, sales started to slump at the end of the third year. At this point, the new factory came on-line. Top management began to panic. The marketing VP was under fire to turn sales around. He held high-powered sales meetings with a single message: "Sell! Sell! Sell!" He fired the low performers and increased sales incentives, added special discounts, and ran new advertising promotions.

Sales rose again, as did order backlogs. After delivery times began to rise again—first to 10 weeks, then to 12, and eventually to 16—the debate over adding capacity started anew. This time, management was more cautious. Eventually the approval of a new facility was granted, but no sooner had the papers been signed than a new sales crisis began. The same situation recurred over the next several years. High sales growth occurred in spurts, followed by periods of low or no growth. The company prospered modestly but never came close to fulfilling its original potential. Gradually, top managers began to fear competition and frantically introduced ill-conceived improvements in the product. They continued to push hard on marketing, but sales never returned to its original rate of growth. Eventually the company collapsed.

Discussion Questions

1. What factors led to the demise of WonderTech?
2. Could these factors have been overcome through a better understanding of a system as advocated in Deming's Profound Knowledge?

The Pursuit of ISO 9000 Registration[22]

A major national manufacturer of chemical products has a well-established TQ program. Its most recent effort involved preparing for ISO 9000 registration. The director of quality, who had spent some time in the European division, saw the emphasis on ISO in Europe and felt that the firm would be at a significant competitive disadvantage if it did not pursue registration. In the spring of 1992, additional staff was hired in an attempt to register a Midwest plant by the end of the first quarter of 1993.

In the purchasing department, the additional work required to document the purchase of raw materials required three additional employees, bringing the number up to 10. All have been intimately involved in the preparation for registration. Many thousands of raw materials are used, and ISO requires that each of their specifications be reviewed, updated, and documented. One of the new employees focuses primarily on training the department's employees in the new procedures. Purchasing agents see many potential benefits. Documentation of specifications will ensure more consistent materials purchases. Training documentation allows the department to tell what training requirements will be needed by new employees.

In manufacturing, ISO appears to be just another quality program. In the past, management would be gung-ho over the newest program, but then enthusiasm would die. Employees were never told that the program had ended and never saw any benefits. One technician saw no real incentives to participate and felt that management was simply forcing the program on the employees. He felt that employees on different shifts had their own way of performing their work, and that standard operating procedures would never be followed. The technician compared the ISO effort to a previous program on safety. With the safety program, improvements were made at the insistence of the employees. The benefit that the workers derived was quite evident. The benefits to be gained through ISO are not as clear.

Discussion Questions

1. Contrast the attitudes in the purchasing department and manufacturing about the ISO registration process. How might these be explained in terms of organizational behavior theories?
2. How might the company's pursuit of ISO registration be viewed using expectancy theory?
3. What must this company do to be successful in its efforts?

Modern Steel Technology, Inc.[23]

Modern Steel Technology, Inc. (MST) is a supplier of custom-designed, hardened steel components and replacement parts to heavy industry worldwide. Steel mills and mining companies account for 75 percent of sales. Aluminum, paper, chemical, and cement industries account for the remaining 25 percent. The main product groups are gears, couplings, wheels, and rolls. MST operates three plants—two in Pennsylvania and one in Canada—and employs 374 people.

The MST mission is to "serve our customers by producing and delivering products of superior quality and value, maintain a commitment to continuous improvement, and provide long-term value to our shareholders." Each year the president and his staff meet off-site to develop and refine a plan for the next year. Here they discuss goals, strategies, and objectives, and make capacity, personnel, and quality decisions. The plan is passed down to middle management for review and suggestions. Middle management takes the yearly plan and determines monthly goals for sales, production, inventory, backlog, expenses, and revenues. All employees have access to these plans. Every three months, managers review their department's progress against the plan and present the results to the president. If the plan is not being met, suggestions for improvement are discussed.

MST is conscious of its community responsibilities at its Pennsylvania headquarters. The CEO is a board member of the United Way, the Fine Arts Council, and other local community efforts. Annually, MST employees are encouraged to contribute to these causes. MST complies with all EPA and OSHA regulations and offers flu shots and health-related seminars to its employees.

MST understands its customer requirements. In a highly competitive industry, failure to meet a customer need usually results in a lost customer. For example, European Union customers required ISO 9000 certification, which MST was able to obtain in June 1995. Customer satisfaction is determined by on-time delivery and quality results. Each year, the roll product manager visits all customers and conducts a survey on product performance. Often, a latent customer need is determined, and MST seeks ways to fulfill this need.

MST uses a mainframe computer–based information system to track quotes, orders, inventory, schedules, and purchasing activities. Networked PCs within the company allow different departments to access the same information. Departments have access only to those databases they use. For example, the Quality Department monitors on-time delivery, cycle time, and cost. Several improvements have been made. For example, roll heat treat recipes were kept in duplicate books by both the Metallurgy and Heat Treat departments, resulting in errors if only one book was updated. These are now maintained in a common database, accessible to both departments.

MST compares its performance to that of competitors by examining product performance of rolls at steel mills. In addition, the company uses annual surveys of the gear industry published by a manufacturing association to compare its gears against others, based on performance and production cost. The company also uses cost-of-quality indicators to measure performance. An external measure is defined as the cost to repair or replace a product after if fails, and an internal measure is the cost of rework and scrap. Each internal incident is traced back and charged to the budget of the responsible department. These are analyzed in total to determine possible corrective actions.

Employee excellence is recognized through the use of annual employee appraisals. The employee and his or her immediate supervisor sit down and discuss the appraisal and the employee's score. Merit raises are based on the appraisal. The discussion also identifies any weaknesses the employee may have, and additional training may be suggested to strengthen weak areas. Vacancies are usually filled by promotion from within MST. Consequently, turnover of salaried employees is relatively high. MST has an employee stock ownership plan. In 1997, the last of the company stock was distributed. New employees contribute to a base retirement plan and are unable to participate in company ownership.

Customer requirements are transmitted through blueprints. Blueprints are generated by the Engineering Department and contain product dimensions, specified hardness requirements, and other information necessary to manufacture the product.

Quality control measurement techniques are defined and vary by product. Key product characteristics, such as gear tooth thickness, are measured against tolerances. Inspection personnel are trained and certified in applicable testing techniques. If a dimension is out of tolerance, the inspector must call a technician who will decide if immediate corrective action should be taken. A department manager makes the decision to take preventive action to stop an undesirable condition from recurring.

MST maintains an informal partnership with a supplier of forgings. MST meets periodically to convey its requirements.

Currently, on-time delivery is above 90 percent for all product groups except gears, which is at a 60 percent level. Delivery dates for gears are difficult to determine because the product mix is constantly changing, cycle times vary, and machines used for production are common to several products, creating a challenge for capacity planners.

Discussion Questions

1. Refer to Table 2.3, which lists the key management practices reflected in the MBNQA Criteria. What are MST's key strengths relating to its approach and deployment of these practices? Where are its major weaknesses or gaps?

2. How well does MST address the three core principles of total quality?

ENDNOTES

1. Michael L. Dertouzos, Richard K. Lester, and Robert M. Solow, and the MIT Commission on Industrial Productivity, *Made in America: Regaining the Productive Edge*, Cambridge, Mass.: The MIT Press, 1989.

2. W. Edwards Deming, *Out of the Crisis*, Cambridge, Mass.: MIT Center for Advanced Engineering Study, 1986.

3. John Hillkirk, "World-famous Quality Expert Dead at 93," *USA Today*, December 21, 1993.

4. April 17, 1979; cited in L.P. Sullivan, "Reducing Variability: A New Approach to Quality," *Quality Progress*, Vol. 17, No. 7, July 1984, pp. 15–21.

5. Mineola, N.Y.: Dover, 1929.

6. Peter R. Scholtes, "Communities as Systems," *Quality Progress*, July 1997, pp. 49–53.

7. Reprinted from *Out of the Crisis* by W. Edwards Deming by permission of MIT and The W. Edwards Deming Institute. Published by MIT, Center for Advanced Educational Services, Cambridge, MA 02139. Copyright © 1986 by The W. Edwards Deming Institute.

8. Philip B. Crosby, *Quality Is Free*, New York: McGraw-Hill, 1979, pp. 200–201.

9. Michael J. Timbers, "ISO 9000 and Europe's Attempts to Mandate Quality," *Journal of European Business*, March/April 1992, pp. 14–25.

10. AT&T Corporate Quality Office, "Using ISO 9000 to Improve Business Processes," July 1994.

11. ISO 9000 Update, *Fortune*, September 30, 1996, p. 134[J].

12. Astrid L.H. Eckstein and Jaydeep Balakrishnan, "The ISO 9000 Series: Quality Management Systems for the Global Economy," *Production and Inventory Management Journal*, Vol. 34, No. 4, Fourth Quarter 1993, pp. 66–71.

13. Hank Rogers, "Benchmarking Your Plant against TQM Best-Practices Plants, Part 2," *Quality Progress*, April 1998, pp. 60–64.

14. Amy Zuckerman, "ISO/QS-9000 Registration Issues Heating Up Worldwide," *The Quality Observer*, June 1997, pp. 21–23.

15. Adapted from Jerry R. Junkins, "Insights of a Baldrige Award Winner," *Quality Progress*, Vol. 27, No. 3, March 1994, pp. 57–58.

16. Paul M. Bobrowski and John H. Bantham, "State Quality Initiatives: Mini-Baldrige to Baldrige Plus," *National Productivity Review*, Vol. 13, No. 3, Summer 1994, pp. 423–438.

17. Letter from W. Edwards Deming, *Harvard Business Review*, January–February 1992, p. 134.

18. Curt W. Reimann and Harry S. Hertz, "The Malcolm Baldrige National Quality Award and ISO 9000 Registration," *ASTM Standardization News*, November 1993, pp. 42–53. This paper is a contribution of the U.S. Government not subject to copyright.

19. JUSE, The Deming Prize Guide for Oversea Companies (TOKYO, 1992), p. 5.

20. B. Nakkai and J. Neves, "The Deming, Baldrige, and European Quality Awards," *Quality Progress*, April 1994, pp. 24–29.

21. Adapted from Peter Senge, *The Fifth Discipline*, New York: Doubleday, 1990.

22. We thank our former colleague, Dr. Reginald Bruce, and his students, Susan Bennet, Jane Glazer, and Jeff Hempfling, for providing the facts in this case.

23. Developed from a term paper by Ms. Debra Bergerhouse. Her contribution is gratefully acknowledged.

3

Total Quality Tools
and Statistical Thinking

CHAPTER OUTLINE

Joseph Juran describes quality management as the "Quality Trilogy": *planning*, *control*, and *improvement*. He says that most managers devote too much attention to control and too little to planning and improvement—which may be the most important activities for meeting and exceeding customer expectations and gaining competitive advantage. Quality practitioners have adapted a variety of tools from other disciplines, such as statistics, operations research, and creative problem solving, to aid the planning and improvement processes. These tools provide a means by which problems can be viewed objectively, data can be used as a basis for fact-driven decisions, and managers can deal with variation in a logical fashion. This chapter describes and illustrates some of the most useful and popular tools and describes how they support process-driven statistical thinking. Since the focus of this book is management, organization, and strategy, this chapter is intended to be only an elementary introduction. The list presented here is by no means exhaustive. The bibliography at the end of the book provides supplementary reading on these and other tools for quality improvement.

The objectives of this chapter are

- to describe how quality function deployment and concurrent engineering can improve the process of designing products and services to achieve better customer satisfaction;
- to show how simple graphical tools can improve management planning;
- to describe and illustrate the Deming Cycle—a simple methodology for continuous improvement;
- to illustrate the application of basic statistical tools, mistake-proofing approaches, and benchmarking for quality improvement;
- to discuss the importance of creativity and innovation for quality improvement and the management environment that fosters these characteristics; and
- to describe principles of statistical thinking as a basis for effective management.

The tools we describe in this chapter can be broadly categorized into two groups: *tools for planning* and *tools for continuous improvement*. Planning tools—which include quality function deployment, concurrent engineering, and the "new seven" management and planning tools—are designed to assist managers in planning the quality effort and making efficient use of information. They are often used by cross-functional teams in their quality planning efforts. Tools for continuous improvement—which include the Deming cycle, tools for data analysis, poka-yoke (mistake-proofing), and benchmarking—are means of improving the manufacturing and service systems. The Deming cycle and basic statistical tools are usually found in basic quality training for all employees of an organization and are used by problem-solving teams to attack specific quality problems. Benchmarking is used at all levels of the firm to better understand its processes relative to its competitors' and to make significant improvements in operations.

TOOLS FOR QUALITY PLANNING

Customers' needs and expectations drive the planning process for products and the systems by which they are produced. Marketing plays a key role in identifying customer expectations. Once these expectations are identified, managers must translate them into specific product and service specifications that manufacturing and service delivery processes must meet. In some cases the product or service that customers receive is quite different from what they expect. It is management's responsibility to minimize such gaps. Firms use several tools and approaches to help them focus on their external and internal customers. This section introduces three of these tools: quality function deployment, concurrent engineering, and the "new seven" management and planning tools.

Quality Function Deployment

Quality function deployment (QFD) is a methodology used to ensure that customers' requirements are met throughout the product design process and in the design and operation of production systems. QFD is both a philosophy and a set of planning and communication tools that focuses on customer requirements in coordinating the design, manufacturing, and marketing of goods.

QFD originated in 1972 at Mitsubishi's Kobe shipyard site. Toyota began to develop the concept shortly thereafter, and it has been used since 1977. The results have been impressive: Between January 1977 and October 1979, for example, Toyota realized a 20 percent reduction in start-up costs on the launch of a new van. By 1982 start-up costs had fallen 38 percent from the 1977 baseline, and by 1984 they were reduced by 61 percent. In addition, development time fell by one-third, and quality had improved.

Today QFD is successfully used by manufacturers of electronics, appliances, clothing, and construction equipment, and by firms such as General Motors, Ford, Mazda, Motorola, Xerox, Kodak, IBM, Procter & Gamble, Hewlett-Packard, and AT&T. The 1992 Cadillac was planned and designed entirely with QFD. The concept has been publicized and developed in the United States by the American Supplier Institute, Inc., a nonprofit organization, and by GOAL/QPC, a consulting firm in Massachusetts.

A major benefit of QFD is improved communications and teamwork among all constituencies in the production process—marketing, design, manufacturing, purchasing, and suppliers. With QFD, product objectives are more likely to be understood and interpreted correctly during the production process. QFD helps to determine the causes of customer dissatisfaction and is a useful tool for competitive analysis of product quality by top management. Productivity as well as quality improvements result, and, most significantly, the time needed for new product development is reduced. QFD allows companies to simulate the effects of new design ideas and concepts. This allows them to bring new products into the market sooner and to gain competitive advantage.

The term *quality function deployment* represents the overall concept that provides a means of translating customer requirements into the appropriate technical requirements for each stage of product development and production. The customers' requirements—expressed in their own terms—are appropriately called *the voice of the customer*. These requirements are the collection of customer needs, including all satisfiers, delighters/exciters, and dissatisfiers—the "whats" that customers want from a product.

For example, a consumer might ask that a dishwashing liquid be "long lasting" and "clean effectively" or that a portable stereo have "good sound quality." Sometimes these requirements are referred to as *customer attributes*. Under QFD, all operations of a company are driven by the voice of the customer, rather than by top management edicts or design engineers' opinions.

Technical features are the translation of the voice of the customer into technical language. They are the "hows" that determine the means by which customer attributes are met. For example, a dishwashing detergent loosens grease and soil from dishes. The soil becomes trapped in the suds so dishes can be removed from the water without picking up grease. Eventually the suds become saturated with soil and break down. Thus, a technical feature of a dishwashing liquid would be the weight of greasy soil that the suds generated by a fixed amount of dishwashing liquid can absorb before breaking down. Another might be the size of the soap bubble (which, incidently, has been found to be a key attribute of customers' perception of cleaning effectiveness!). Technical features of a stereo system that affect sound quality include the frequency response, flutter (the wavering in pitch) and the speed accuracy (a cassette tape player should have a speed of 1⅞ inch/second—inconsistency affects the pitch and tempo of the sound).

A set of matrices is used to relate the voice of the customer to technical features and production planning and control requirements. The basic planning document is called the customer requirement planning matrix. Because of its structure (Figure 3.1), it is often referred to as the **House of Quality**. The House of Quality relates customer attributes to technical features to ensure that any engineering decision has a basis in meeting a customer need. Building the House of Quality requires six basic steps:

1. Identify customer attributes.
2. Identify technical features.
3. Relate the customer attributes to the technical features of a design.
4. Evaluate competing products based on customer attributes.
5. Evaluate technical features of a design and develop targets.
6. Determine which technical features to deploy in the production process.

The first step is identifying customer attributes. In applying QFD, it is important to use the customer's own words so as not to have customer needs misinterpreted by designers and engineers. Recall that not all customers are end users. For a manufacturer, customers might include government regulators, wholesalers, and retailers. Thus, many classes of customer needs may exist.

The second step is listing the technical features that are necessary to meet customer requirements. These technical features are design attributes expressed in the language of the designer and engineer. They form the basis for subsequent design, manufacturing, and service process activities. They must be

FIGURE 3.1 THE HOUSE OF QUALITY

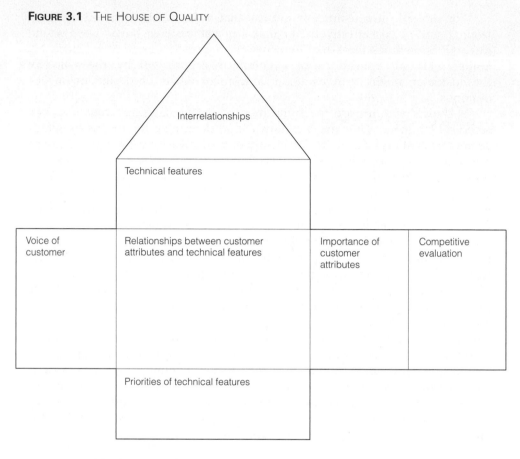

measurable, because the output will be controlled and compared to objective targets.

The roof of the House of Quality shows the interrelationships between any pair of technical features. Various symbols are used to denote these relationships. A typical scheme is to use the symbol ⊙ to denote a very strong relationship, ○ for a strong relationship, and △ to denote a weak relationship. These notations help determine the effects of changing one product characteristic and enable planners to assess the tradeoffs between characteristics. This process enables designers to focus on features collectively rather than individually.

Next, a relationship matrix between the customer attributes and the technical features is developed. Customer attributes are listed down the left column, and technical features are written across the top. In the matrix itself, a symbol is used to indicate the degree of relationship in a manner similar to that used in the roof of the house. The purpose of the relationship matrix is to show whether the final technical features adequately address the customer attributes. This assessment may be based on expert experience, customer responses, or controlled experiments.

Technical features can affect several customer attributes. The lack of a strong relationship between a customer attribute and any of the technical features suggests that the attributes are not being addressed and that the final product will have difficulty meeting customer needs. Similarly, if a technical feature does not affect any customer attribute, it may be redundant or the designers may have missed an important customer attribute.

The next step is adding market evaluation and key selling points. This step includes rating the importance of each customer attribute and evaluating existing products on each of the attributes. Customer importance ratings represent the areas of greatest interest and highest expectations to the customer. Competitive evaluation helps highlight the absolute strengths and weaknesses of competing products. This step enables designers to seek opportunities for improvement. It also links QFD to a company's strategic vision and allows priorities to be set in the design process. For example, focusing on an attribute that receives a low evaluation on all competitors' products can help to gain a competitive advantage. Such attributes become key selling points and help establish promotion strategies.

Next comes the evaluation of the technical features of competitive products and the development of targets. This is usually accomplished through in-house testing and translated into measurable terms. These evaluations are compared with the competitive evaluation of customer attributes to find inconsistencies. If a competing product best satisfies a customer attribute, but the evaluation of the related technical feature indicates otherwise, then either the measures used are faulty or the product has an image difference (either positive toward the competitor or negative toward the product) that affects customer perceptions. Targets for each technical feature are set on the basis of customer importance ratings and existing product strengths and weaknesses.

The final step in building the House of Quality is selecting technical features to be deployed in the remainder of the process. This means identifying the characteristics that have a strong relationship to customer needs, have poor competitive performance, or are strong selling points. These characteristics need to be deployed—or translated into the language of each function—in the design and production process, so that proper actions and controls are taken to maintain the voice of the customer. Characteristics that are not identified as critical do not need such rigorous attention.

A simple example of a House of Quality is shown in Figure 3.2 for the hypothetical case of a quick-service franchise that wishes to improve its hamburger. The voice of the customer consists of four attributes. The hamburger should

- be tasty,
- be healthy,
- be visually appealing, and
- provide good value.

The technical features that can be designed into the product are price, size, calories, sodium content, and fat content. The symbols in the matrix show the

FIGURE 3.2   HOUSE OF QUALITY EXAMPLE

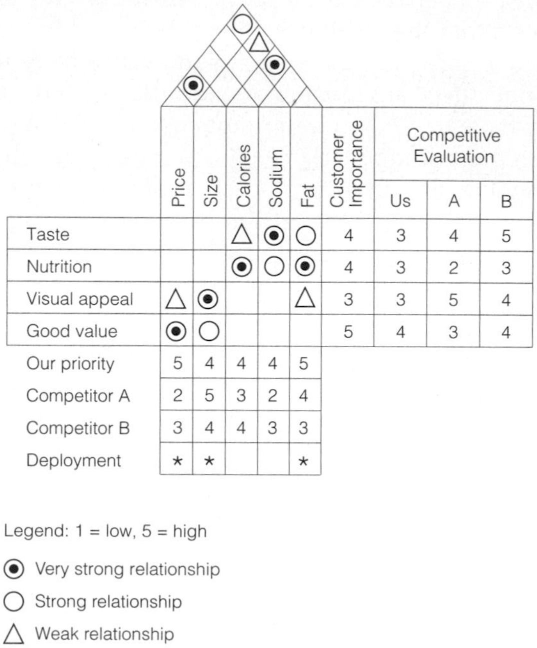

	Price	Size	Calories	Sodium	Fat	Customer Importance	Competitive Evaluation		
							Us	A	B
Taste			△	◉	◯	4	3	4	5
Nutrition			◉	◯	◉	4	3	2	3
Visual appeal	△	◉			△	3	3	5	4
Good value	◉	◯				5	4	3	4
Our priority	5	4	4	4	5				
Competitor A	2	5	3	2	4				
Competitor B	3	4	4	3	3				
Deployment	★	★			★				

Legend: 1 = low, 5 = high

◉ Very strong relationship

◯ Strong relationship

△ Weak relationship

relationships between each customer attribute and technical feature. For example, taste bears a strong relationship to sodium content, a moderate relationship to fat content, and a weak relationship to caloric content. In the roof of the house, price and size are seen to be strongly related (as size increases, the price must increase). The competitive evaluation shows that competitors are currently weak on nutrition and value; these can become key selling points in a marketing plan if the franchise can capitalize on them. Finally, at the bottom of the house, are targets for the technical features based on an analysis of customer importance ratings and competitive ratings. The features assigned asterisks will be deployed in subsequent design and production activities.

The House of Quality provides marketing with an important tool to understand customer needs and gives top management strategic direction. However, it is only the first stage in the QFD process. The voice of the customer must be carried throughout the production process. Three other Houses of Quality are used to deploy the voice of the customer to component parts characteristics, process planning, and production planning. These are

- *technical features deployment matrix*, which translates technical features of the final product into design requirements for critical components;
- *process plan and quality control charts*, which translates component features into critical process and product parameters and control points for each; and
- *operating instructions*, which identifies operations to be performed by plant

personnel to ensure that important process and product parameters are achieved.

Most of the QFD activities represented by the first two Houses of Quality (customer attributes matrix and technical features deployment matrix) are performed by people in the product development and engineering functions. At the next stage, the planning activities begin to involve supervisors and production-line operators. This represents the transition from planning to execution. If a product component parameter is critical and is created or affected during the process, it becomes a control point. This tells the company what to monitor and inspect and forms the basis for a quality control plan for achieving those critical characteristics that are crucial to achieving customer satisfaction. The last house relates the control points to specific requirements for quality assurance activity. This includes specifying control methods, sample sizes, and so on, to achieve the necessary level of quality.

The majority of QFD applications in the United States concentrate on the first, and to some extent the second, House of Quality. Lawrence Sullivan, who brought QFD to the West, suggests that the third and fourth houses offer far more significant benefits, especially in the United States.[1] Japanese managers, engineers, and workers are more naturally cross-functional and tend to promote group effort and consensus thinking. U.S. workers are more vertically oriented and tend to suboptimize for individual and/or departmental achievements. Beginning to emphasize effective cross-functional interactions as supported by QFD will enable U.S. firms to be more competitive with foreign rivals. The third and fourth houses of quality utilize the knowledge of about 80 percent of a company's employees—if they are not used, this potential is wasted.

Concurrent Engineering

A topic closely related to QFD is concurrent engineering. This is the concept that all major functions that contribute to getting a product to market have continuing product-development involvement and responsibility from original concept through sales.

The designer's objective is to create a product that meets the desired functional requirements. The manufacturing engineer's objective is to produce the designed product efficiently. The salesperson's goal is to sell the product, and that of finance personnel is to make a profit. Purchasing must ensure that purchased parts meet quality requirements. Packaging and distribution personnel must ensure that the product reaches the customer in good operating condition. Since all these functions have a stake in the product, they must all work together.

Unfortunately, the product development process in many large firms is carried out in a serial fashion with little cooperation among departments. In the early stages of development, design engineers dominate the process. Later the prototype is transferred to manufacturing for production. Finally, marketing and sales personnel are brought in.

This approach has several disadvantages. First, product development time is long. Second, up to 90 percent of manufacturing costs may be committed before manufacturing engineers have any input to the design. Third, the final product may not be the best one for market conditions when it is introduced.

Ford Motor Company was the first U.S. automotive firm to move away from this traditional approach when developing the Taurus/Sable.[2] "Team Taurus" took an approach in which representatives from all the various units—planning, design, engineering, and manufacturing—worked together as a group. Communication was dramatically improved, and many problems were resolved much earlier in the process. For instance, manufacturing suggested changes in design that resulted in higher productivity and better quality.

Comprehensive market surveys were conducted to determine customers' wants and preferences. Ford even asked assembly-line workers for their advice before the car was designed. Workers complained that they had trouble installing doors because the body panels were made up of too many pieces. Designers reduced the number of panels from eight to two. One worker suggested that all bolts should have the same head size so that they would not have to change wrenches constantly. The Taurus/Sable has been one of Ford's biggest success stories and has established new levels of quality for American automakers. Chrysler and General Motors have moved toward similar styles of product development. In fact, Chrysler's expertise in product development has been noted as one of the key reasons it was acquired by Daimler-Benz.

Multifunctional teams of 4 to 20 members typically comprise concurrent engineering teams. The functions of such teams include the following:

1. Distinguishing the character of the product in order to determine appropriate design and production methods, and ensuring that the product can be repaired easily.
2. Analyzing product functions so all design decisions can be made with full knowledge of how the item is supposed to work and so all team members understand it well enough to contribute.
3. Relating product function to production methods. Computer-aided design tools allow a designer to simulate product performance by varying assumptions within a computer model.
4. Performing a design-for-manufacturability study to determine if the design can be made easier to produce without affecting performance.
5. Designing an assembly sequence that integrates quality control and ensures that each part is designed so that its quality is compatible with the assembly method.
6. Designing a factory system that fully involves workers in the production strategy, operates on minimal inventory, and is integrated with suppliers' methods and capabilities.

One example of an aggressive product-development effort based on concurrent engineering is Milacron Inc. (formerly Cincinnati Milacron). Milacron code-named its effort "Wolfpack" because wolves work in packs, are known for their speed and cunning, and can bring down prey much larger and powerful than themselves. Cross-functional teams of managers drawn from different areas of the company are responsible for developing globally competitive products of the future at significantly lower costs. The Wolfpack concept has cut lead time for new products from 3 years to 18 months and allowed Milacron to regain lost market leadership in several areas. Wolfpack design goals include 40 to 60 percent fewer parts, 25 to 50 percent less floor space, 50 percent less installation time, and 50 percent less product development time.[3]

The New Seven Management and Planning Tools

Many of the problems in implementing Quality Function Deployment are due to the way that American managers have become accustomed to planning and organizing businesses based on Frederick W. Taylor's philosophy.[4] The barriers to effective planning and quality improvement efforts have been

- strict departmentalization that has separated the planners (staff specialists, such as QA and industrial engineers) from the doers (line and functional managers), thus limiting the abilities of both to make significant improvements;
- relegating planning to a seat-of-the-pants approach, due to the perception that it is either too theoretical to be of practical use or too detailed to be interesting or action oriented; and
- a lack of available tools to make planning available and timely for managers to use.

The "new seven management and planning tools" had their roots in post–World War II operations research developments in the United States, but they were combined and refined by several Japanese companies over the past several decades as part of their planning processes. The tools were popularized in the United States by the consulting firm GOAL/QPC and have been used by a number of firms since 1984 to improve their quality planning and improvement efforts. They are only new to managers who have not previously seen what powerful aids they can be in improvement processes.

These tools can be used to address problems typically faced by managers who are called upon to structure unstructured ideas, make strategic plans, and organize and control large, complex projects. They have helped to overcome the barriers listed previously and have given managers tools appropriate to their specific needs for planning and implementing quality improvement efforts. Due to space limitations, only a brief discussion of each tool follows. (See books by Brossart, Brassard, and Mizuno[5] for further details and examples.)

Affinity Diagram/KJ Method
This is a technique for gathering and organizing a large number of ideas, opinions, and facts relating to a broad problem or subject area. It enables problem solvers to sift through large volumes of information efficiently and to identify natural patterns or groupings in the information. This method was

FIGURE 3.3 EXAMPLE OF AN AFFINITY DIAGRAM

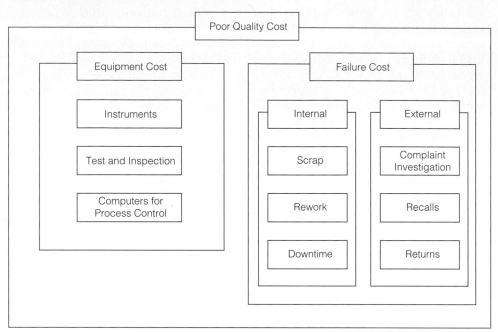

developed in the 1960s by Kawakita Jiro, a Japanese anthropologist. "KJ" is a trademark registered by the Kawayoshida Research Center.

The technique requires that a group of six to eight people meet to consider a broad issue, such as identifying the elements of poor quality cost for their organization. Responses can be recorded on a flip chart or on small cards that can be posted and moved around on a board. For example, in determining the elements of quality cost, the group will probably list various elements in a random fashion. Once many ideas have been generated, they can be grouped according to their "affinity," or relationship, to each other. An example is shown in Figure 3.3. This technique helps managers focus on the key issues and their elements rather than an unorganized collection of information.

The Affinity Diagram/KJ Method is intended to be a creative, rather than a logical process. It resembles brainstorming and storyboarding, a technique developed by Walt Disney to create cartoons and movies.

Interrelationship Digraphs

The purpose of an interrelationship digraph is to take a central idea and map out logical or sequential links among related categories. It shows that every idea can be logically linked with more than one idea at a time, and it allows for "lateral" rather than "linear" thinking. This technique often is used after the affinity diagram has brought issues and problems into clearer focus. Figure 3.4 shows an example of how failure costs are influenced by other factors.

Like affinity diagrams, this technique also depends on getting together a team of people who own the problem. Some of the same cards or flip-chart lists

FIGURE 3.4 EXAMPLE OF AN INTERRELATIONSHIP DIGRAPH

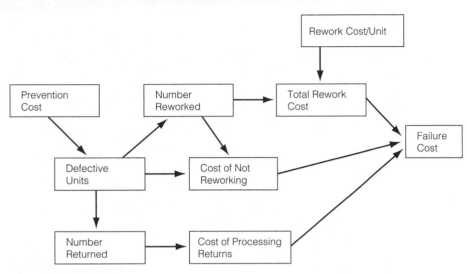

developed in the affinity diagram can be duplicated and used in this technique. New cards or lists of specific items must be added frequently as the issue becomes more focused.

Tree Diagram

A tree diagram maps out the paths and tasks that need to be accomplished to complete a specific project or to reach a specified goal. A planner uses this technique to seek answers to such questions as "What sequence of tasks needs to be completed to address the issue?" or "What are all of the factors that contribute to the existence of the key problem?"

This technique brings the issues and problems disclosed by the affinity diagram and the interrelationship digraph down to the operational planning stage. A clear statement of the problem or process must be specified. From this general statement, a team can be established to recommend steps required to solve the problem or implement the plan. The "product" produced by this group would be a tree diagram with activities and recommendations for timing the activities. Figure 3.5 shows an example of some of the key elements in establishing a quality cost system.

Matrix Diagrams

These are spreadsheets that graphically display relationships between characteristics, functions, and tasks in such a way as to provide logical connecting points between items. The House of Quality is an example of one of the many matrix diagrams now used for planning and quality improvement.

Matrix Data Analysis

This process takes data from matrix diagrams and seeks to arrange it quantitatively to display the strength of relationships among variables so they can be

FIGURE 3.5   EXAMPLE OF A TREE DIAGRAM

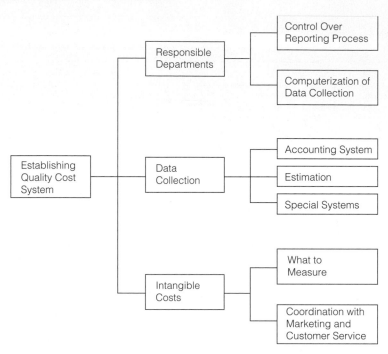

easily viewed and understood. Matrix data analysis is a rigorous, statistically based "factor analysis" technique. GOAL/QPC feels that this method, although worthwhile for many applications, is too quantitative to be used on a daily basis, so they have developed an alternative tool called a prioritization matrix, which is easier to understand and implement. This approach bears a lot of similarity to decision matrices that you may have studied in a quantitative methods course. Interested readers should consult Brassard's book for further details.

Process Decision Program Chart (PDPC)

This is a method for mapping out every conceivable event and contingency that can occur when moving from a problem statement to possible solutions. It is used to plan for each possible chain of events that could occur when a problem or goal is unfamiliar. A PDPC takes each branch of a tree diagram, anticipates possible problems, and provides countermeasures that will prevent the deviation from occurring or be in place if the deviation does occur. Figure 3.6 shows one example.

Arrow Diagrams

These have been used by construction planners for years in the form of CPM and PERT project planning techniques. Arrow diagramming has also been taught extensively in quantitative methods, operations management, and other business and engineering courses in the United States for a number of years.

FIGURE 3.6 EXAMPLE OF A PROCESS DECISION PROGRAM CHART

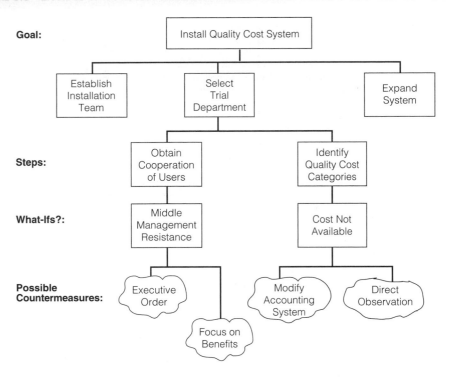

Unfortunately, its use has been confined to technical experts. By adding it to the "quality toolbox," it has become more widely available to general managers and other nontechnical personnel.

Implementation of process improvements is an essential, but frequently ignored, step. Process improvements often are not implemented because they are too complex to work in practice or are not accepted by those who have the responsibility to carry them out. These seven quality improvement tools assist managers in implementing improvements through active involvement.

TOOLS FOR CONTINUOUS IMPROVEMENT

Many tools have been created or adapted from other disciplines (such as operations research and industrial engineering) to facilitate the process of continuous improvement. In this section we describe the most common ones used in quality improvement applications.

Tools for Data Collection and Analysis

Seven simple statistically based tools are used extensively to gather and analyze data. Like the seven management and planning tools, these tools—flowcharts, check sheets, histograms, pareto diagrams, cause-and-effect diagrams, scatter diagrams, and control charts—are visual in nature and simple

FIGURE 3.7 EXAMPLE OF A FLOWCHART FOR TRAINING NEW PRINTING PRESS OPEARATORS

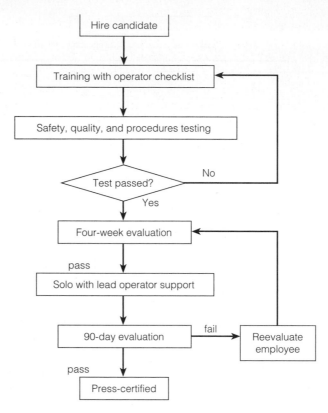

enough for anyone to understand. Historically, these tools preceded the seven management and planning tools and often are called the "seven QC (quality control) tools." The seven management and planning tools have been referred to as the "new seven."

Flowcharts

A flowchart is a picture of a process that shows the sequence of steps performed. Figure 3.7 is an example. Flowcharts are best developed by the people involved in the process—employees, supervisors, managers, and customers. A facilitator often is used to provide objectivity, to ask the right questions, and to resolve conflicts. The facilitator can guide the discussion through questions such as "What happens next?" "Who makes the decision at this point?" and "What operation is performed here?" Often the group does not agree on the answers to these questions, due to misconceptions about the process or a lack of awareness of the "big picture."

Flowcharts help the people involved in the process to understand it better. For example, employees realize how they fit into a process—that is, who their suppliers and customers are. By helping to develop a flowchart, workers begin to feel a sense of ownership in the process and become more willing to work on improving it. Using flowcharts to train employees on standard procedures leads to more consistent performance.

Once a flowchart is constructed, it can be used to identify quality problems as well as areas for improvement. Questions such as "How does this operation affect the customer?" "Can we improve or eliminate this operation?" or "Should we control a critical quality characteristic at this point?" help to identify such opportunities. Flowcharts help people to visualize simple but important changes that could be made in a process.

Check Sheets

These tools aid in data collection. When designing a process to collect data, one must first ask basic questions such as:

- What question are we trying to answer?
- What type of data will we need to answer the question?
- Where can we find the data?
- Who can provide the data?
- How can we collect the data with minimum effort and minimum chance of error?

Check sheets are data collection forms that facilitate the interpretation of data. Quality-related data are of two general types—attribute and variable. Attribute data are obtained by counting or from some type of visual inspection: the number of invoices that contain errors, the number of parts that conform to specifications, and the number of surface defects on an automobile panel, for example. Variable data are collected by numerical measurement on a continuous scale. Dimensional characteristics such as distance, weight, volume, and time are common examples. Figure 3.8 is an example of an attribute data check sheet, and Figure 3.9 shows a variable data check sheet.

Histograms

Variation in a process always exists and generally displays a pattern that can be captured in a histogram. A histogram is a graphical representation of the variation in a set of data. It shows the frequency or number of observations of a particular value or within a specified group. Histograms provide clues about the characteristics of the population from which a sample is taken. Using a his-

FIGURE 3.8   EXAMPLE OF A CHECK SHEET FOR ATTRIBUTE DATA: AIRLINE COMPLAINTS

Type	Week 1	Week 2	Week 3	Week 4
Lost baggage			||		
Baggage delay	||||		||||	|||| |||	||||
Missed connection	||			|||		
Poor cabin service	|||	||||	|||	|||
Ticketing error						

FIGURE 3.9 EXAMPLE OF A CHECK SHEET FOR VARIABLE DATA

Frequency

	1	2	3	4	5	6	7	8	9	10	11	12	13	14	15	16	17	18	19	20
20																				
19																				
18																				
17																				
16																				
15																				
14																				
13										X										
12										X										
11									X	X										
10									X	X	X									
9									X	X	X									
8								X	X	X	X									
7								X	X	X	X									
6								X	X	X	X									
5								X	X	X	X	X								
4						X	X	X	X	X	X									
3							X	X	X	X	X	X	X							
2							X	X	X	X	X	X	X							
1						X	X	X	X	X	X	X	X		X			X		

Time to process loan request (days)

togram, the shape of the distribution can be seen clearly, and inferences can be made about the population. Patterns can be seen that would be difficult to see in an ordinary table of numbers.

The check sheet in Figure 3.9 was designed to provide the visual appeal of a histogram as the data are tallied. It is easy to see how the output of the process varies and what proportion of output falls outside of any specification limits.

Pareto Diagrams

Pareto analysis is a technique for prioritizing types or sources of problems. Pareto analysis separates the "vital few" from the "trivial many" and provides help in selecting directions for improvement. It is often used to analyze the attribute data collected in check sheets. In a Pareto distribution the characteristics are ordered from largest frequency to smallest. For example, if the data in Figure 3.8 are placed in order of decreasing frequency, the result is

> Baggage delay
> Poor cabin service
> Missed connection
> Lost baggage
> Ticketing error

A Pareto diagram is a histogram of these data, as shown in Figure 3.10. A cumulative frequency curve is usually drawn on the histogram, as shown. Such pictures clearly show the relative magnitude of defects and can be used to

FIGURE 3.10 EXAMPLE OF A PARETO DIAGRAM

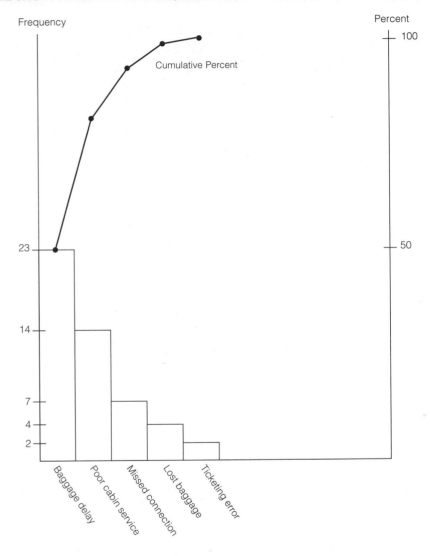

identify the most promising opportunities for improvement. They can also show the results of improvement projects over time.

Cause-and-Effect Diagrams

The most useful tool for identifying the causes of problems is a cause-and-effect diagram, also known as a fishbone or Ishikawa diagram, named after the Japanese quality expert who popularized the concept. A cause-and-effect diagram is simply a graphical representation of an outline that presents a chain of causes and effects.

An example is shown in Figure 3.11. At the end of the horizontal line is the problem to be addressed. Each branch pointing into the main stem represents a possible cause. Branches pointing to the causes are contributors to these

FIGURE 3.11   EXAMPLE OF A CAUSE-AND-EFFECT DIAGRAM

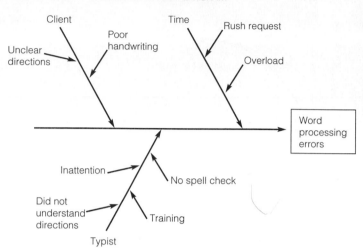

causes. The diagram is used to identify the most likely causes of a problem so that further data collection and analysis can be carried out.

Cause-and-effect diagrams are usually constructed in a brainstorming setting so that everyone can contribute their ideas. Usually small groups drawn from operations or management work with an experienced facilitator. The facilitator guides the discussion to focus attention on the problem and its causes, on facts, not opinions. This method requires significant interaction among group members. The facilitator must listen carefully to the participants and capture the important ideas.

Scatter Diagrams

Scatter diagrams illustrate relationships between variables, such as the percentage of an ingredient in an alloy and the hardness of the alloy, or the number of employee errors and overtime worked (Figure 3.12). Typically the variables represent possible causes and effects obtained from cause-and-effect diagrams.

A general trend of the points going up and to the right indicates that an increase in one variable corresponds to an increase in the other. If the trend is down and to the right, an increase in one variable corresponds to a decrease in the other. If no trend can be seen, then it would appear that the variables are not related. Of course, any correspondence does not necessarily imply that a change in one variable *causes* a change in the other. Both may be the result of something else. However, if there is reason to believe causation, the scatter diagram may provide clues on how to improve the process.

Control Charts

These tools, the backbone of statistical process control (SPC), were first proposed by Walter Shewhart in 1924. Shewhart was the first to distinguish between common causes and special causes in process variation. He developed the control chart to identify the effects of special causes. Much of the Deming philosophy is based on the use of control charts to understand variation.

FIGURE 3.12   EXAMPLE OF A SCATTER DIAGRAM

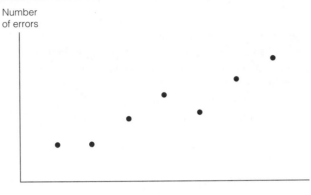

Number
of errors

Volume of work

A control chart displays the state of control of a process (Figure 3.13). Time is measured on the horizontal axis, and the value of a variable on the vertical axis. A central horizontal line usually corresponds to the average value of the quality characteristic being measured.

Two other horizontal lines represent the upper and lower control limits, chosen so there is a high probability that sample values will fall within these limits if the process is under control—that is, affected only by common causes of variation. If points fall outside the control limits or if there are unusual patterns such as shifts up or down, trends up or down, cycles, and so forth, special causes may be present.

FIGURE 3.13   EXAMPLE OF A CONTROL CHART

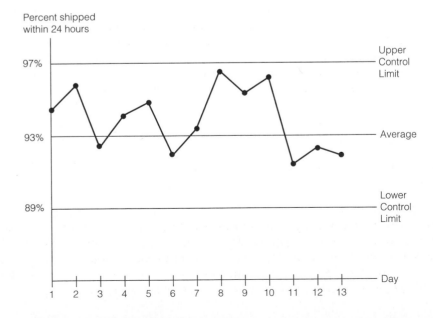

Shooting for Quality[6]

Timothy Clark observed that in basketball games his son Andrew's free-throw percentage averaged between 45 and 50 percent. Andrew's process was simple: Go to the free throw line, bounce the ball four times, aim, and shoot. To confirm these observations, Andrew shot five sets of 10 free throws with an average of 42 percent, showing little variation among the five sets. Timothy developed a cause-and-effect diagram (Figure 3.14) to identify the principal causes. After analyzing the diagram and observing his son's process, he believed that the main causes were not standing in the same place on the free-throw line every time and having an inconsistent focal point. They developed a new process in which Andrew stood at the center of the line and focused on the middle of the front part of the rim. The new process resulted in a 36 percent improvement in practice (Figure 3.15). Toward the end of the 1994 season, he improved his average to 69 percent in the last three games.

During the 1995 season, Andrew averaged 60 percent. A control chart (Figure 3.16) showed that the process was quite stable. In the summer of 1995, Andrew attended a basketball camp where he was advised to change his shooting technique. This process reduced his shooting percentage during the 1996 season to 50 percent. However, his father helped him to reinstall his old process, and his percentage returned to its former level, also improving his confidence.

As we noted in chapter 2, two fundamental mistakes that can be made concerning variation are

1. treating special causes as common causes, and
2. treating common causes as special causes.

Control charts minimize the risk of making these two types of mistakes. As a problem-solving tool, they allow workers to identify quality problems as they occur and base their conclusions on hard facts.

The seven QC tools provide excellent communication vehicles both vertically and horizontally across organizational boundaries (see box).

The Deming Cycle

Managers need systematic approaches to drive continuous improvement programs. One approach that can be learned and applied by everyone in an organization is the Deming cycle. The **Deming cycle** is a methodology for improvement, based on the premise that improvement comes from the application of knowledge.[7] Knowledge of engineering, management, or operations may make a process easier, more accurate, faster, less costly, safer, or better-suited to customer needs. Three fundamental questions to consider are

1. What are we trying to accomplish?
2. What changes can we make that will result in improvement?
3. How will we know that a change is an improvement?

This methodology was originally called the Shewhart cycle after Walter Shewhart, its founder, but it was renamed for Deming by the Japanese in 1950. The Deming cycle is composed of four stages: Plan, Do, Study, Act (Figure 3.17). Sometimes it is called the PDSA cycle.

The Plan stage consists of studying the current situation, gathering data, and planning for improvement. In the Do stage, the plan is implemented on a trial basis in a laboratory, pilot production process, or with a small group of customers. The Study stage is designed to determine if the trial plan is working correctly and to see if any further problems or opportunities can be found. The last stage, Act, is the implementation of the final plan to ensure that the improvements will be standardized and practiced continuously. This leads back to the Plan stage for further diagnosis and improvement (see box on page 119).

As Figure 3.17 suggests, this cycle is never ending. That is, it is focused on continuous improvement, so the improved standards serve as a springboard for further improvements. This distinguishes it from more traditional problem-solving approaches and is one of the essential elements of the Deming philosophy.

FIGURE 3.14   FREE-THROWING CAUSE-AND-EFFECT DIAGRAM

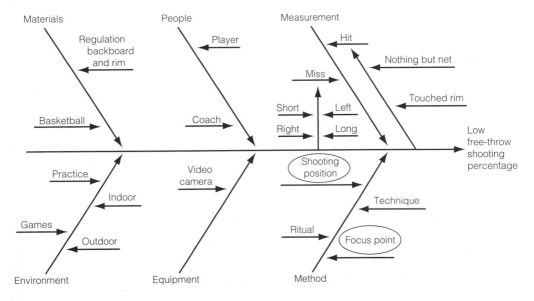

FIGURE 3.15   FREE-THROWING SHOTS MADE BEFORE AND AFTER IMPLEMENTING THE IMPROVEMENT (3/17/94–11/23/94)

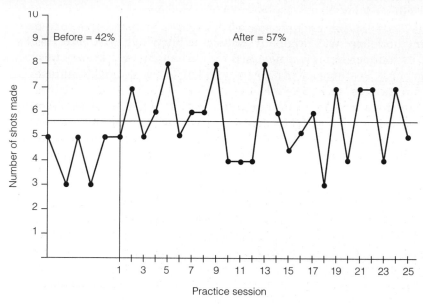

FIGURE 3.16   DETERMINING WHETHER THE FREE-THROW PROCESS IS STABLE (3/17/94–1/18/96)

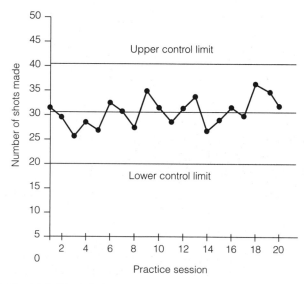

Crying Out for the Deming Cycle[8]

Kevin Dooley and his wife applied the Deming Cycle and various quality tools to help stop their infant daughter from crying whenever her diaper was changed, which as any new parent or older sibling knows, can break your heart or drive you crazy. Their first cycle involved creating an experiment to determine the percentage of time crying while on the diaper changing table (Plan); collecting data on 15 diaper changes and plotting them on a run chart (Do); observing that the data appeared to be random (Study); and focusing on the steps involved in the changing process. The second cycle involved developing a flowchart to document the steps in changing a diaper (Plan); constructing the chart (Do); studying the process (which did not appear complex or incorrect—Study); and deciding to seek other causes (Act). Cycles 3, 4, and 5 involved developing a cause-and-effect diagram, collecting data to test the hypothesis that the type of outfit worn caused her to cry more (studied with a Pareto diagram), and looking for correlations between the time crying and the time since last changing. In cycle 6, the Dooleys collected data to determine if she cried less when being changed by her mother. Histograms confirmed a difference between the parents! Cycle 7 was to observe what Kevin's wife did differently (Plan); make a list of key differences (Do); Study the differences (his wife had captured the baby's attention better); and develop some attention-getting strategies (Act). The last cycle implemented these, and data indeed confirmed an improvement! We're sure the Dooleys can't wait to apply the Deming Cycle to their daughter's driving. . . .

FIGURE 3.17   THE DEMING CYCLE

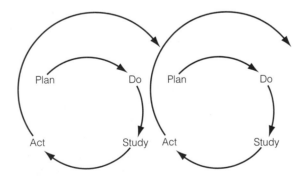

Poka-Yoke (Mistake-Proofing)

Poka-yoke is an approach for mistake-proofing processes using automatic devices or methods to avoid simple human error. The poka-yoke concept was developed and refined by the late Shigeo Shingo, a Japanese manufacturing engineer who developed the Toyota production system. The idea is to avoid repetitive tasks or actions that depend on vigilance or memory in order to free workers' time and minds to pursue more creative and value-adding activities.

Poka-yoke is focused on two aspects: prediction, or recognizing that a defect is about to occur and providing a warning; and detection, or recognizing that a defect has occurred and stopping the process. Many applications of poka-yoke are deceptively simple, yet creative. Usually, they are inexpensive to implement. Many machines have limit switches connected to warning lights that tell the operator when parts are positioned improperly on the machine. Another example, a device on a drill counts the number of holes drilled in a workpiece; a buzzer sounds if the workpiece is removed before the correct number of holes has been drilled. As a final example, one production step at Motorola involves putting alphabetic characters on a keyboard, then checking to ensure each key is placed correctly. A group of workers designed a clear template with the letters positioned slightly off center. By holding the template over the keyboard, assemblers can quickly spot mistakes.

Poka-yoke techniques are also applied to the design of consumer products to prevent inadvertent user errors or safety hazards. For example, a 3.5-inch diskette is designed so that it cannot be inserted unless the disk is oriented correctly (try it!). These disks are not perfectly square, and the bevelled right corner of the disk allows a stop in the disk drive to be pushed away if it is inserted correctly. Power lawn mowers now have a safety bar on the handle that must be engaged in order to start the engine. Computer software such as Microsoft Word will automatically check for any unsaved files before closing down. A proxy ballot for an investment fund will not fit into the return envelope unless a small strip is detached. The strip asks the respondent to check if the ballot is signed and dated.

Richard B. Chase and Douglas M. Stewart suggest that the same concepts can be applied to services.[9] The major differences are that service mistake-proofing must account for the customers' activities as well as those of the producer, and mistake-proofing methods must be set up for interactions conducted directly or by phone, mail, or other technologies, such as ATM. Chase and Stewart classify service poka-yokes by the type of error they are designed to prevent: server errors and customer errors.

Examples of server errors include doing work incorrectly, in the wrong order, or too slowly; lack of courteous behavior; and physical anomalies, such as unclean facilities, dirty uniforms, or inappropriate temperature. Examples of poka-yoke devices for dealing with some of these are computer prompts, color-coded cash register keys, and measuring tools such as McDonald's french fry scoop. Poka-yoke devices may be very simple: One bank encourages eye contact by requiring tellers to record the customer's eye color on a checklist as they start the transaction. Hotels wrap paper strips around towels to help the housekeeping staff distinguish clean linen from towels that should be replaced.

Some poka-yoke devices help prevent customer errors, such as not bringing necessary materials to a service encounter, not understanding their role in the service transaction, or failing to remember steps in a process or to follow instructions. Digital Equipment provides a flowchart that specifies how to place a service call. By guiding customers through three yes-or-no questions, the flowchart prompts them to have the necessary information before calling. Other poka-yoke examples include beepers that signal customers to remove cards from ATM machines, airplane lavatory doors that must be locked to turn on the lights, and spell-checkers in word processing software (provided they are used!).

Benchmarking

Benchmarking is the search for best practices that will lead to superior performance. Benchmarking helps a company learn its strengths and weaknesses— and those of other industrial leaders—and incorporate the best practices into its own operations. Benchmarking was initiated by Xerox, an eventual winner of the Malcolm Baldrige National Quality Award.

Xerox initially studied their direct competitors and discovered that

- their unit manufacturing cost equalled the Japanese selling price in the United States,
- the number of production suppliers was nine times that of the best companies,
- assembly line rejects were 10 times higher,
- product lead times were twice as long, and
- defects per hundred machines were seven times higher.

These results helped them to understand the amount of change that would be required and to set realistic targets to guide their planning efforts.

Two major types of benchmarking are competitive and generic. Competitive benchmarking usually focuses on the products and manufacturing of a company's competitors, as Xerox initially did. Generic benchmarking evaluates processes or business functions against the best companies, regardless of their industry. Xerox recognized the potential for improving all business processes and realized that better practices in service companies and other types of manufacturing firms could be adapted to their operations. For example, the warehousing and distribution practices of L.L. Bean were adopted by Xerox. Thus, benchmarking should not be aimed solely at direct competitors (see box on page 122).

In order to be effective, benchmarking must be applied to all facets of a business. For example, Motorola encourages everyone in the organization to ask "Who is the best person in my own field and how might I use some of their techniques and characteristics to improve my own performance in order to be the best (executive, machine operator, chef, purchasing agent, and so on) in my 'class'"?

The benchmarking process can be described as follows:

1. *Determine which functions to benchmark.* These should have a significant impact on business performance and key dimensions of competitiveness.

Smart Bombs and Pink Cadillacs

Although Xerox is credited with developing modern approaches to benchmarking, the concept of benchmarking is not new.[10] In the early 1800s, Francis Lowell, a New England industrialist, traveled to England to study manufacturing techniques of the best British mill factories. Henry Ford created the assembly line after taking a tour of a Chicago slaughterhouse and watching carcasses, hung on hooks mounted on a monorail, move from one work station to another. Toyota's just-in-time production system was influenced by replenishment practices of U.S. supermarkets. Convex Computer Corporation sent its facilities manager to Disney World to see what they could learn about facilities management. And Texas Instrument's former Defense Systems and Electronics Group, makers of "smart bombs" and other advanced weapon systems, studied the kitting (order preparation) practices of six companies, including Mary Kay Cosmetics (the pink Cadillac being a reward to their top sales-people), and designed a process that captured the best practices of each of them, cutting kitting cycle time in half.

If fast response is an important dimension of competitive advantage, then processes that might be benchmarked would include order processing, purchasing, production planning, and product distribution. There should also be an indication that the potential for improvement exists.

2. *Identify key performance indicators to measure.* These should have a direct link to customer needs and expectations. Typical performance indicators are quality, performance, and delivery.

3. *Identify the best-in-class companies.* For specific business functions, benchmarking might be limited to the same industry: A bank in one state might benchmark the check-processing operations of a bank in another state. For generic business functions, it is best to look outside one's own industry: A university financial aid office might benchmark a bank's loan operation, for example. Selecting companies requires knowledge of which firms are superior performers in the key areas. Such information can be obtained from published reports and articles, industry experts, trade magazines, professional associations, former employees, or customers and suppliers.

4. *Measure the performance of the best-in-class companies, and compare the results to your own performance.* Such information might be found in published sources or might require site visits and in-depth interviews.

5. *Define and take actions to meet or exceed the best performance.* This usually requires changing organizational systems. Simply to emulate the best is like shooting at moving target—their processes will continually improve. Therefore, attempts should be made to exceed the performance of the best.

CREATIVITY AND INNOVATION

Creativity is the ability to discover useful new relationships or ideas; *innovation* refers to the practical implementation of such ideas. Paul E. Plsek states five reasons why organizations should be concerned with creativity and innovation:

1. Superior long-term financial performance is associated with innovation.
2. Customers are increasingly demanding innovation.
3. Competitors are getting increasingly better at copying past innovations.
4. New technologies enable innovation.
5. What used to work, doesn't anymore.[11]

From the perspective of total quality, creativity and innovation are needed to better respond to customer needs, particularly to recognize the "exciters/delighters" that customers cannot articulate, and to develop the products and services that will position an organization strategically ahead of its competitors. They also are needed to support continuous improvement efforts, for example the poka-yoke devices and methods discussed in this chapter. Finally, an environment that fosters creativity and innovation can motivate employees more than any extrinsic reward—"joy in work" as Deming used to say (see box on page 124). Thus, creativity and innovation are instrumental in achieving the principles of total quality discussed in the first chapter.

In Japanese, the word *creativity* has a literal translation as *dangerous opportunity*. In the Toyota production system, which has become the benchmark for world-class efficiency, a key concept is *soikufu*—creative thinking or inventive ideas, which means capitalizing on worker suggestions. The chairman of Toyota once observed: "One of the features of Japanese workers is that they use their brains as well as their hands. Our workers provide 1.5 million suggestions a year, and 95 percent of them are put to practical use. There is an almost tangible concern for improvement in the air at Toyota."[12]

Creativity is often motivated by an individual's or group's need to invent solutions from limited resources. The Japanese have shown remarkable creativity in developing solutions to manufacturing quality problems. This is no wonder, given the limited natural resources in Japan and the Japanese cultural focus on eliminating waste and conserving every precious resource available. The largest source of creativity in any organization are the frontline employees. They gather a wealth of data and information about their work every day. To tap into their knowledge, companies must make creativity a key part of their culture and think of improvement as everybody's job. This requires companies to empower their employees to allow them to put their ideas to work. We will address this further in chapter 8.

Creativity is the foundation of successful problem solving teams in the workplace. Quality circles and other forms of teams that address quality and productivity problems often use a "scientific" approach to solving problems.

Often, the approach overshadows the need for creativity. Creative approaches to problem solving rely on four key steps:

1. redefining and analyzing the perceived problem,
2. generating ideas,

Creativity in the Heartland

In 1994, three companies received the Malcolm Baldrige National Quality Award: AT&T Consumer Communications Services (CCS), GTE Directories Corporation, and Wainwright Industries. AT&T CCS (the long-distance provider) and GTE Directories (which publishes and sells advertising for telephone directories) are large, innovative firms, with sophisticated technologies and human resource development activities that support empowered teams and foster an atmosphere of creativity throughout their organizations. Both companies also offer a wide variety of training and education courses, including courses devoted specifically to creativity and innovation. It is not surprising that they have achieved remarkable results in product and service quality, in customer satisfaction, and in various operational and financial measures.

Wainwright Industries, headquartered in rural St. Peters, Missouri, is considerably different from CCS and GTE. Wainwright is a small, family-owned business that manufactures stamped and machined parts for the automotive and other industries. Since initiating continuous improvement processes in 1991, Wainwright has seen continual, and sometimes dramatic, improvements in customer satisfaction, defect and scrap rates, work-related accidents, manufacturing cycle times, and quality costs. At the same time, market share, productivity gains, and profit margins have all increased.

Innovation is a way of life at Wainwright. Each associate averages more than one *implemented improvement* per week! That's over 50 each year, in an industry that averages at most one *suggestion* per employee per year in the U.S. Wainwright does not have the comparable resources available to large corporations like AT&T and GTE. The company spends a relatively high proportion of its budget on training, some of which is outsourced, yet no formal creativity training is offered. What the company does have is a *culture* that exudes a spirit of creativity and innovation—far different from the culture at most large corporations. The plant has a folksy, Midwestern atmosphere. Everyone—up to the chairman of the board—wears a company uniform with his or her first name stitched on it. The human resources function is called "The People Zone." The training director is known simply as "The Training Guy." And a stuffed duck is the company's mascot and symbol of quality leadership.

Wainwright is an excellent example of how creativity, integrated within a traditional American company, can lead to exceptional improvements in quality and business performance. More importantly, when visitors tour the plant, they see clearly the spirit and enthusiasm exuded by Wainwright associates. The associates are having *fun*! Improving quality—and work itself—*should* be fun, and people have fun when they are creative.

3. evaluating ideas and selecting a workable solution, and

4. implementing the solution.

In redefining and analyzing a problem, information is collected and organized, the data and underlying assumptions are analyzed, and the problem is re-examined from new perspectives. At this stage, the goal of the problem solver is to collect facts and achieve a useful problem definition. The purpose of generating ideas is to develop novel solutions. After ideas have been generated, they are evaluated, and the best one is identified and selected. Finally, the solution must be put to work. The Deming Cycle is just one specific example of a creative problem-solving approach.

Innovation and creativity are important aspects of the Malcolm Baldrige National Quality Award Criteria for Performance Excellence. Mechanisms used to encourage innovation and creativity include:

1. The nonprescriptive nature of the criteria, which encourages innovative approaches and breakthrough thinking toward meeting the purpose of the specific items in the criteria. This channels activities toward purpose, not toward following procedures.

2. Customer-driven quality, which places major emphasis on the positive side of quality and stresses enhancement, new services, and customer relationship management. Enhancing the positive side of quality relies heavily on creativity, usually more so than steps to reduce errors and defects, which tend to rely more on well-defined techniques.

3. Continuous improvement and cycles of learning, which are stressed as integral parts of the activities of all work units. This encourages analysis and problem solving everywhere within the company.

4. Strong emphasis on cycle time reduction in all company operations, which encourages companies to analyze work processes, work organizations, and the value-added contributions of all process steps. This fosters change, innovation, and creative thinking in how work is organized and conducted.

5. Focus on future requirements of customers, which encourages companies to seek innovative and creative ways to serve needs.

Many examples of creativity and innovation are seen in firms that have received the Baldrige Award. Among the many examples are:

- Motorola's original "six sigma" stretch goal.

- The benchmarking process, pioneered by Xerox.

- GraniteXpress, an automatic loading system for rock, sand, aggregates, and other construction materials, developed by Granite Rock. The system is similar to an automatic teller machine and allows customers to rapidly, accurately, and automatically order, load, and invoice materials 24 hours a day, seven days a week.

- Wainwright Industries' practice of reenacting and videotaping workplace accidents for study and prevention.
- The Ritz-Carlton Hotel Company's guest-profiling system that records the individual preferences of hundreds of thousands of guests who have stayed at least three times at any of its hotels. The system gives front-desk employees immediate access to such information as whether the guest smokes and what kind of pillow he or she prefers.

While the tools discussed in this chapter all help to promote creative thinking, they cannot be applied effectively in a noncreative environment. Because management designs the organizational systems, management is responsible for developing a climate conducive to creativity and innovation. The organizational literature contains many different recommendations for fostering creativity. Some of these are listed below:[13]

- *Remove or reduce obstacles to creativity within an organization.* These obstacles include various environmental blocks such as autocratic bosses, distractions (constant meetings or phone calls), and lack of management support. In addition, creative people should be relieved of routine duties and administrative chores.
- *Match jobs to individuals' creative abilities.* Some people are best working alone; others are better in groups. Some work well in 9-to-5 time frames; others require flex time. Managers need to be tolerant of individual idiosyncrasies, nonconformity of dress codes, frequent coffee breaks, and so on.
- *Tolerate failures and establish direction.* Creative people need an atmosphere that allows radical ideas without being harshly judged. Seemingly silly ideas often turn into the best products. However, appropriate direction must be given, and realistic goals and objectives must be set to maintain a sense of urgency.
- *Improve motivation to increase productivity and solve problems creatively.* Creative accomplishments should be recognized publicly, to peers, superiors, and upper management. Such recognition increases both self-esteem and motivation.
- *Enhance the self-esteem and build the confidence of organization members.* Creative individuals are at their best when their minds are challenged—not their security or ego. Job security, adequate wages, and job satisfaction enhance an individual's self-confidence and security.
- *Improve communication so ideas can be better shared.* This is certainly true within an organization. Creative individuals also have the need to communicate with peers outside the organization; such activities should be encouraged. Creative people need a sounding board for their ideas and continuous feedback from their efforts.
- *Place highly creative people in special jobs and provide training to take advantage of their creativity.* Establish career paths and financial rewards so as not to disadvantage creative people who are not part of the line organization.

If you examine carefully the underlying principles of Deming's 14 points, you see many similarities with attitudes and organizational structures that support creativity. This is particularly true in the elimination of fear, the removal of barriers that inhibit joy in work, elimination of numbers-driven and short-term goal-driven management, a focus on continuous improvement, leadership, and continual training and education. Fear, in particular, is a creativity killer. The head of a corporate legal office commented that "when someone tries to use fear to motivate me, I get all tied up. I get less creative and less willing to take chances, and you've got to take risks to do good work." A midlevel manager observed, "Where there is a lot of fear of screwing up, people don't change behaviors or work systems. Creativity is inhibited. People work one day at a time, rather than looking to the future."[14] Generally, the cultures of most organizations do not support the conditions that lead to creative behavior. Cultural change, education, and training are necessary to develop a creative climate.

STATISTICAL THINKING

Statistical thinking is at the heart of the Deming philosophy and is the basis for good management. **Statistical thinking** is a philosophy of learning and action based on the principles that

1. all work occurs in a system of interconnected processes,
2. variation exists in all processes, and
3. understanding and reducing variation are keys to success.[15]

Statistical thinking is more than simply applying statistical methods. Statistical thinking focuses on understanding and reducing variation, not merely quantifying it. Nevertheless, statistical methods are important to be a good statistical thinker.

A sign in the office of the president of the former Texas Instruments Defense Systems and Electronics Group (now Raytheon Systems Company) office said: "Unless you change the process, why would you expect the results to change?" By viewing work as a process, we can apply management-by-fact and various quality tools to establish consistent, predictable processes, study them, and improve them. By viewing processes as interconnected components of a system, we avoid suboptimization—one of the key principles of Deming's Profound Knowledge. When managers make decisions in isolation, they often fail to see chains of events that might occur throughout the company because of their decisions. A typical example is designing a product without consideration of the capability of processes to manufacture it or the support systems required to service it in the field.

Recognizing and understanding variation is the essence of statistical thinking. We discussed principles of variation within the context of Deming's Profound Knowledge in chapter 2, particularly the differences between common and special causes of variation. While variation exists everywhere, many business decisions do not often account for it. How often do managers make decisions based on a single data point or two, seeing trends when they don't exist or manipulating financial figures they cannot truly control (see the box below)?

The lack of broad and sustained use of statistical thinking in many organizations is due to two reasons.[16] First, statisticians historically have functioned as problem solvers in manufacturing, research, and development, and thereby focused on individual clients rather than on organizations. Second, statisticians have focused primarily on technical aspects of statistics rather than emphasizing the focus on process variation that will lead to bottom-line results. Process management—category 6 in the Baldrige criteria—includes process definition, measurement, control, and improvement. Each of these is fundamental to statistical thinking. Understanding processes provides the context for determining the effects of variation and the proper type of managerial action to

---

The VP's Dilemma[17]

Brian Joiner, a noted quality management consultant, relates the following case:

> Ed was a regional VP for a service company that had facilities around the world. He was determined that the facilities in his region would get the highest customer satisfaction ratings in the company. If he noticed that a facility had a major drop in satisfaction ratings in one month or had "below average" ratings for three months in a row, he would call the manager and ask what had happened—and make it clear that next month's rating had better improve. And most of the time, it did!

As the average satisfaction score dropped from 65 to 60 between February and March, Ed's memo to his managers read:

> Bad news! We dropped five points! We should all focus on improving these scores right away! I realize that our usage rates have increased faster than anticipated, so you've really got to hustle to give our customers great service. I know you can do it!

As Joiner observed,

> Do you look at data this way? This month versus last month? This month versus the same month last year? Do you sometimes look at the latest data point? The last two data points?
>
> "I couldn't understand why people would only want to look at two data points. Finally, it became clear to me. With any two data points, it's easy to compute a trend: "Things are down 2 percent this month from last month. This month is 30 percent above the same month last year." Unfortunately, **we learn nothing of importance by comparing two results when they both come from a stable process . . . and most data of importance to management are from stable processes.**

Black Belts and Statistical Thinking at General Electric[18]

A "Black Belt" means one thing to karate students; at General Electric, Black Belts (along with Green Belts and Master Black Belts), are employees who are highly trained in quality improvement principles and techniques. They roam manufacturing plants to improve quality as a part of a major initiative introduced by CEO Jack Welch in 1996. This "Six Sigma" initiative, which was benchmarked from Motorola, includes many TQ principles, such as a better focus on customers, data-driven decisions, improved design and manufacturing capabilities, and individual rewards for process improvements. The effort aims to reduce defect levels to only a few parts per million for strategic products and processes. Accomplishing such a daunting task requires effective implementation of many of the process management tools that we described in this chapter, as well as the principles of TQ and management infrastructure discussed in chapter 1. As one manager stated, "Because it's data driven, Six Sigma helps you to make better decisions faster and ensures better results than the trial and error method."

General Electric embarked on this initiative to achieve Six Sigma quality levels by the year 2000, down from a starting level of about 35,000 defects per million. All of GE's businesses are engaged in Six Sigma process improvements, ranging from making jet engine blades to executing credit transactions and minimizing "dead air" between segments in broadcasting. The Black Belts and their associates work in teams to reduce variation and defects by using a four-phase approach:

1. *Measure:* Select critical quality characteristics, determine the frequency of defects, define performance standards, validate the measurement system, and establish product capability. Measurements include output, process, and input (supplier) measures to evaluate current performance.

2. *Analyze:* Understand when, where, and why defects occur by defining performance objectives and sources of variation. This step includes process mapping, identifying potential root causes, discovering cause-effect relationships, and establishing operating tolerances.

3. *Improve:* Generate ideas. Narrow the list of potential solutions, select a solution, validate it, and develop an implementation strategy.

4. *Control:* Maintain improvements by validating the measurement system, determining process capability, and implementing process control systems to monitor performance.

To address customer issues, a program known as Work-Out, in which an individual or team devotes all their time and energy to solving one problem and designing solutions with customers' assistance, helps to minimize bureaucracy in supporting the Six Sigma initiative.

From 1996 to 1998, GE has increased the number of Six Sigma projects from 200 to 6,000. This effort has required massive training and new incentives. A typical

continued on next page

Black Belt training curriculum includes four weeks of training on statistical thinking (tools such as quality function deployment), measurement systems analysis, correlation, design of experiments, statistical process control, and mistake-proofing. Forty percent of managerial bonuses are tied to progress in Six Sigma results. Most importantly, the effort is driven by top management leadership. CEO Welch has made it clear that if an employee is not enthusiastic about Six Sigma, then GE is not the right company for them. From all these efforts, GE hopes to save $7 to $10 billion over a decade.

be taken. This variation is quantified through statistical analysis of process data and requires understanding the sources, magnitude, and nature of the variation.

Senior management needs to champion the use of statistical thinking by defining the strategy and goals of the approach, communicating the benefits and results clearly and consistently, providing the necessary resources, coaching others, and recognizing and rewarding the desired behavior. To help managers work in this fashion, many organizations create core groups of highly trained professionals who are skilled in statistical thinking tools and can help others to use them effectively (see the box on GE's Six Sigma program). This requires an environment conducive to learning new behaviors and concepts.

Statistical thinking can be applied at all levels of an organization.[19] At the strategic level, statistical thinking helps to generate long-term activities that will guide organizational functions. For example, strategic statistical thinking can motivate executives to

- flowchart a system and its core processes,
- create a strategy and communicate it throughout the organization,
- use data from various sources to assess the organization,
- develop and implement measurement systems to assess progress, and
- encourage employees to experiment to find better ways to do their work.

At the managerial level, statistical thinking helps to align operational activities with strategic directions. For example, managers can

- develop and institute good meeting management practices,
- develop, implement, and assess standardized project management systems,
- set goals, keeping in mind that measurement systems are processes and all processes exhibit variation,
- use various methods of communication to keep employees informed and involved, and
- focus on the process and never blame employees for process variation.

At the operational level, statistical thinking helps to improve daily work processes by helping employees to

- be knowledgeable of variation,

- plot data to analyze processes, and
- identify key measures and improvement opportunities.

Thus, every manager and employee can benefit from statistical thinking and using total quality tools. Technology, including today's powerful PCs and user-friendly software for data analysis and visualization such as Microsoft Excel and other spreadsheet packages, has facilitated greatly the ability to use statistics and quality tools in daily work.

SUMMARY

Quality practitioners have compiled many different tools and techniques to assist quality planning, implementation, and improvement processes. Among these are:

- *quality function deployment*—a planning technique to ensure that customer requirements are incorporated into the design of products and the systems that produce them;
- *concurrent engineering*—an approach to streamline product development to improve quality and reduce development time, thereby meeting customer needs faster;
- The *"new seven" management and planning tools*—a set of graphical aids to assist in planning and implementing new projects and ideas and reduce "surprises" later on;
- The *"seven QC tools"*—a set of graphically based tools for collecting, analyzing, and interpreting data to facilitate the solution of quality problems for continuous improvement;
- the *Deming cycle*—a simple methodology for continuous improvement that is based on the scientific approach to problem solving; and
- *benchmarking*—the search for best practices to improve operations in any business function.

None of these tools or approaches requires rocket science; they are simple, effective, and easy to learn. Moreover, they provide common means of communication among managers, supervisors, and hourly workers so that all can focus their efforts on quality improvement. In addition, they promote statistical thinking—a process-driven approach to managing by facts and data rather than by opinions. To gain the most from these tools, however, management must develop an organizational climate that fosters and rewards creativity and innovation.

REVIEW AND DISCUSSION QUESTIONS

1. Why is good planning important to quality improvement? Why should managers invest in the time to learn many of the tools presented in this chapter?

2. Explain the benefits of the quality function deployment approach. How does it help organizations to design better products and services?

3. Using whatever "market research" techniques you feel are appropriate, define a set of customer attributes for (a) an "excellent" cup of coffee and (b) a college registration process. How might QFD be used to improve these processes? Define a set of "hows" and try to construct the relationship matrix for the House of Quality for each of these examples.

4. Most organizations have well-defined mission statements that include a set of goals for the firm and actions the firm can take. How might QFD be used to ensure that the actions are consistent with the goals? Find some company's mission statement to illustrate this.

5. What is concurrent engineering? What quality-related advantages does it have?

6. What type of organizational culture would be required to make concurrent engineering successful?

7. Explain the purpose of the seven management and planning tools.

8. How might you use the seven management and planning tools in your daily activities (schoolwork, fraternity or honor society operations, and so on)? Provide specific examples.

9. Explain the purpose and uses of each of the "seven QC tools."

10. Select a process that you do routinely and draw a flowchart of it. Explain how the flowchart helps you to understand and improve the process.

11. A flowchart for a fast-food drive-through window is shown in Figure 3.18. Discuss the important quality characteristics inherent in this process and suggest possible improvements.

12. Design a check sheet to help a high school student who is getting poor grades on a math quiz determine the source of his or her difficulty.

13. Develop cause-and-effect diagrams for
    a. a poor exam grade
    b. no job offers
    c. too many speeding tickets
    d. late for work or school

14. What is the Deming cycle? How is it used to improve quality?

15. Many books in business describe some sort of problem-solving process. Find two or three descriptions of systematic problem-solving processes. How are they similar to or different from the Deming cycle?

16. Choose some process in which you are involved. Devise a plan to use the Deming cycle to improve it.

17. How might a professor use the Deming cycle to improve his or her teaching performance?

18. Describe the purpose and role of benchmarking in business organizations. How much effort do you believe companies should spend in benchmarking efforts?

19. Discuss how a college or university might apply benchmarking to improving its operations. You might solicit views from academic adminis-

FIGURE 3.18 FLOWCHART OF A FAST-FOOD DRIVE-THROUGH PROCESS

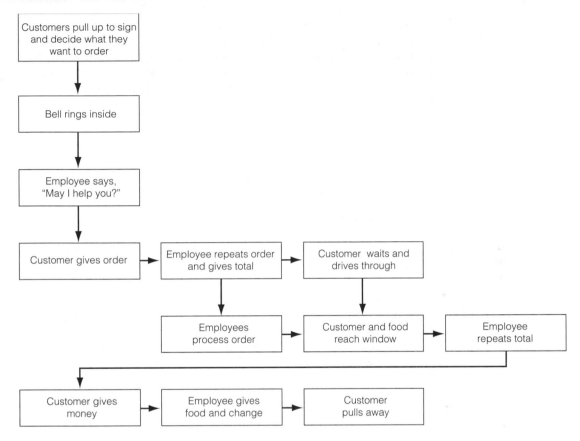

trators and from businesspeople. (You might find some differences of opinion!)

20. Explain how creativity is embodied in the various tools and approaches described in this chapter.

21. What is statistical thinking? How might the traditional teaching of statistics be improved by incorporating this notion? Draw your response from your own experiences in learning statistics.

CASES

Welz Business Machines[20]

Welz Business Machines sells and services a variety of copiers, computers, and other office equipment. The company receives many calls daily for service, sales, accounting, and other departments. All calls are handled centrally by customer service representatives and routed to other individuals as appropriate. A number of customers had complained about long waits when calling for service. A market research study found that customers became irritated if the call was not answered within five rings. Scott Welz, the company president, authorized the customer service department manager, Tim, to study this problem and find a method to shorten the call-waiting time. Tim met with the service representatives who answered the calls to attempt to determine the reasons for long waiting times. The following conversation ensued:

Tim: This is a serious problem. How a customer phone inquiry is answered is the first impression the customer receives from us. As you know, this company was founded on efficient and friendly service to all our customers. It's obvious why customers have to wait: You're on the phone with another customer. Can you think of any reasons that might keep you on the phone for an unnecessarily long time?

Robin: I've noticed quite often that the person to whom I need to route the call is not present. It takes time to transfer the call and to see if it is answered. If the person is not there, I end up apologizing and transferring the call to another extension.

Tim: You're right, Robin. Sales personnel often are out of the office on sales calls, away on trips to preview new products, or away from their desks for a variety of reasons. What else might cause this problem?

Ravi: I get irritated at customers who spend a great deal of time complaining about a problem that I cannot do anything about except refer to someone else. Of course, I listen and sympathize with them, but this eats up a lot of time.

Lamarr: Some customers call so often, they think we're long-lost friends and strike up a personal conversation.

Tim: That's not always a bad thing, you realize.

Lamarr: Sure, but it delays my answering other calls.

Nancy: It's not always the customer's fault. During lunch, we're not all available to answer the phone.

Ravi: Right after we open at 9 A.M., we get a rush of calls. I think that many of the delays are caused by these peak periods.

Robin: I've noticed the same thing between 4 and 5 P.M.

Tim: I've had a few comments from department managers who received calls that didn't fall in their areas of responsibility and had to be transferred again.

Mark: But that doesn't cause delays at our end.

Nancy: That's right, Mark, but I just realized that sometimes I simply don't understand what the customer's problem really is. I spend a lot of time trying to get him or her to explain it better. Often, I have to route it to someone because other calls are waiting.

Ravi: Perhaps we need to have more knowledge of our products.

Tim: Well, I think we've covered most of the major reasons why many customers have to wait. It seems to me that we have four major reasons: the phones are short-staffed, the receiving party is not present, the customer dominates the conversation, and you may not understand the customer's problem. Next we need to collect some information about these possible causes. I will set up a data collection sheet that you can use to track some of these things. Mark, would you help me on this?

Over the next two weeks the staff collected data on the frequency of reasons why some callers had to wait. The results are summarized as follows:

Reason	Total number
A. Operators short-staffed	172
B. Receiving party not present	73
C. Customer dominates conversation	19
D. Lack of operator understanding	61
E. Other reasons	10

Discussion Questions

1. From the conversation between Tim and his staff, draw a cause-and-effect diagram.
2. Perform a Pareto analysis of the data collected.
3. What actions might the company take to improve the situation?

The Quarterly Sales Report[21]

Suppose that Ron Hagler, the vice president of sales for Selit Corp., had just gotten a report on the past five years of quarterly sales data for the regions under his authority (see Figure 3.19). Not happy with the results, he got on the phone to his secretary. "Marsha, tell the regional managers I need to speak with them this afternoon. Everyone must attend."

Marsha had been Hagler's secretary for almost a decade. She knew by the tone in his voice that he meant business, so she contacted the regional managers about the 2 P.M. impromptu meeting. At 1:55 P.M., the regional managers filed into the room. The only time they were called into a meeting together was when Hagler was unhappy.

Hagler wasted no time. "I just received the quarterly sales report. Northeast sales were fantastic. Steve, you not only improved 17.6 percent in the fourth quarter, you also increased sales a whopping 20.6 percent over the previous year. I don't know how you do it!" Steve smiled. His philosophy to end the year with a bang by getting customers to stockpile units paid off again. Hagler had failed to notice that Steve's first quarter sales were always sluggish.

Hagler continued: "Terry, Southwest sales were also superb. You showed an 11.7 percent increase in the fourth quarter and an 11.8 percent increase over the previous year." Terry also smiled. She wasn't sure how she did so well, but she sure wasn't going to change anything.

"Jan, Northwest sales were up 17.2 percent in the fourth quarter, but down 8.2 percent from the previous year," said Hagler. "You need to find out what you did previously to make your sales go through the roof. Even so, your performance in the fourth quarter was good." Jan tried to hide his puzzlement.

FIGURE 3.19   SALES BY REGION FOR SELIT CORP., 1994–1998

1994 Sales (in thousands)

Region	First Quarter	Second Quarter	Third Quarter	Fourth Quarter
Northeast	$ 924	$ 928	$ 956	$1,222
Southwest	1,056	1,048	1,129	1,073
Northwest	1,412	1,280	1,129	1,181
North Central	431	470	439	431
Mid-Atlantic	539	558	591	556
South Central	397	391	414	407

1995 Sales (in thousands)

Region	First Quarter	Second Quarter	Third Quarter	Fourth Quarter
Northeast	$ 748	$ 962	$ 983	$1,024
Southwest	1,157	1,146	1,064	1,213
Northwest	1,149	1,248	1,103	1,021
North Central	471	496	506	573
Mid-Atlantic	540	590	606	643
South Central	415	442	384	448

1996 Sales (in thousands)

Region	First Quarter	Second Quarter	Third Quarter	Fourth Quarter
Northeast	$ 991	978	1,040	$1,295
Southwest	1,088	4,322	1,256	1,132
Northwest	1,085	1,125	910	999
North Central	403	440	371	405
Mid-Atlantic	657	602	596	640
South Central	441	366	470	426

1997 Sales (in thousands)

Region	First Quarter	Second Quarter	Third Quarter	Fourth Quarter
Northeast	$ 756	$1,008	$1,038	$ 952
Southwest	4,352	1,353	1,466	1,196
Northwest	883	851	997	878
North Central	466	536	551	670
Mid-Atlantic	691	723	701	802
South Central	445	455	363	462

1998 Sales (in thousands)

Region	First Quarter	Second Quarter	Third Quarter	Fourth Quarter
Northeast	$1,041	$1,020	$ 976	$1,148
Southwest	1,330	1,003	1,197	1,337
Northwest	939	834	688	806
North Central	588	699	743	702
Mid-Atlantic	749	762	807	781
South Central	420	454	447	359

Although he had received a big order in November, it was the first big order he had received in a long time. Overall, sales for the Northwest were declining.

Hagler was now ready to deal with the "problem" regions. "Leslie, North Central sales were down 5.5 percent in the fourth quarter, but up 4.7 percent from the previous year. I don't understand how your sales vary so much. Do you need more incentive?" Leslie looked down. She had been working very hard the past five years and had acquired numerous new accounts. In fact, she received a bonus for acquiring the most new business in 1994.

"Kim, Mid-Atlantic sales were down 3.2 percent in the fourth quarter and down 2.6 percent from the previous year. I'm very disappointed in your performance. You were once my best sales representative. I had high expectations for you. Now, I can only hope that your first quarter results show some sign of life." Kim felt her face get red. She knew she sold more units in 1996 than in 1995. "What does Hagler know anyway," she thought to herself. "He's just an empty suit."

Hagler turned to Dave, who felt a surge of adrenaline. "Dave, South Central sales were the worst of all! Sales were down 19.7 percent in the fourth quarter and down 22.3 percent from the previous year. How can you explain this? Do you value your job? I want to see a dramatic improvement in this quarter's results or else!" Dave felt numb. This was a tough region, with a lot of competition. Sure, accounts were lost over the years, but those lost were always replaced with new ones. How could he be doing so badly?

Discussion Question

1. How can Ron improve his approach by applying principles of statistical thinking? Use any analyses of the data that you feel are appropriate to fully explain your thinking and help him.

The HMO Pharmacy Crisis[22]

John Dover just completed an intensive course, "Statistical Thinking for Continuous Improvement," that was offered to all employees of a large health maintenance organization (HMO). There was no time to celebrate, however, because he was already under a lot of pressure. Dover worked as a pharmacy assistance in the HMO's pharmacy, and his manager, Juan de Pacotilla, was about to be fired. Pacotilla's dismissal appeared imminent because of numerous complaints—and even a few lawsuits—over inaccurate prescriptions. Pacotilla now was asking Dover for his assistance in trying to resolve the problem.

"John, I really need your help," said Pacotilla. "If I can't show some major improvement or at least a solid plan by next month, I'm history."

"I'll be glad to help," replied Dover, "But what can I do? I'm just a pharmacy assistant."

"Your job title isn't important. I think you're just the person who can get this done," said Pacotilla. "I realize that I've been too far removed from day-to-day operations in the pharmacy, but you work there every day. You're in a much better position to find out how to fix the problem. Just tell me what to do, and I'll do it."

"But what about the statistical consultant you hired to analyze the data on inaccurate prescriptions?" asked Dover.

"To be honest, I'm really disappointed with that guy. He has spent two weeks trying to come up with a new modeling approach to predict weekly inaccurate prescriptions. I tried to explain to him that I don't want to predict the mistakes, I want to eliminate them. I don't think I got through, however, because he said we need a month of additional data to verify the model before he can apply a new method he just read about in a journal to identify 'change points in the time series,' whatever that means. But get this, he will only identify the change points and send me a list. He says it's my job to figure out what they mean and how to respond. I don't know much about statistics. The only thing I remember from my course in college is that it was the worst course I ever took. I'm becoming convinced that statistics really doesn't have much to offer in solving real problems. Since you've just gone through the statistical thinking course, maybe you can see something I can't. I realize it's a long shot, but I was hoping you could use this as the project you need to officially complete the course."

"I used to feel the same way about statistics," replied Dover. "But the statistical thinking course was interesting because it didn't focus on crunching numbers. I have some ideas about how we can approach making improvements in prescription accuracy. I think it would be a great project. But we might not be able to solve this problem ourselves. As you know, there is a lot of finger pointing going on. Pharmacists blame the doctors' sloppy handwriting and incomplete instructions for the problem. Doctors blame the pharmacy assistants, who do most of the computer entry of the prescriptions, claiming that they are incompetent. Pharmacy assistants blame the pharmacists for assuming too much about their knowledge of medical terminology, brand names, known drug interactions, and so on."

"It sounds like there's no hope," said Pacotilla.

"I wouldn't say that at all," replied Dover. "It's just that there might be no quick fix we can do by ourselves in the pharmacy. Let me explain what I'm thinking about doing and how I would propose attacking the problem using what I just learned in the statistical thinking course."

Discussion Question

1. How do you think John should approach this problem, using what he has just learned? Assume that he really did pick up a solid understanding of the concepts and tools of statistical thinking in the course.

ENDNOTES

1. L.P. Sullivan, "Quality Function Deployment: The Latent Potential of Phases III and IV," in A. Richard Shores, *A TQM Approach to Achieving Manufacturing Excellence*, Milwaukee: ASQC Quality Press, 1990.

2. "How Ford Hit the Bull's Eye With Taurus," *Business Week*, June 30, 1986, pp. 69–70.

3. Mike Boyer, "Milacron Seeks Killer Instinct," *Cincinnati Enquirer*, August 31, 1990, B6, and www.milacron.com/wolfhome.htm.

4. James L. Brossert, *Quality Function Deployment: A Practitioner's Approach*, Milwaukee: ASQC Quality Press/Marcel Dekker, Inc., 1991, Part 2.

5. Michael Brassard, *The Memory Jogger Plus +*, Meuthen, Mass.: GOAL/QPC, 1989; Brossert, *Quality Function Deployment*; Shigeru, Mizuno, *Management for Quality Improvement: The 7 New QC Tools*, Cambridge, Mass.: Productivity Press, 1988.

6. Timothy Clark and Andrew Clark, "Continuous Improvement on the Free Throw Line," *Quality Progress*, October 1997, pp. 78–80. © 1997 American Society for Quality, reprinted with permission.

7. Gerald Langley, Kevin Nolan, and Thomas Nolan, "The Foundation of Improvement," Sixth Annual International Deming User's Group Conference, Cincinnati, Ohio, August, 1992.

8. Adapted from Kevin Dooley, "Use PDSA for Crying Out Loud," *Quality Progress*, October 1997, pp. 60–63.

9. Excerpts reprinted from Richard B. Chase and Douglas M. Stewart, "Make Your Service Fail-Safe," *Sloan Management Review*, Vol. 35, No. 3, Spring 1994. Copyright © 1994 by the Sloan Management Review Association. All rights reserved.

10. Christopher E. Bogan and Michael J. English, "Benchmarking for Best Practices: Winning Through Innovative Adaptation," *Quality Digest*, August 1994, pp. 52–62.

11. Paul E. Plsek, *Creativity, Innovation, and Quality*, Milwaukee: WI: ASQ Quality Press, 1997, p. 11.

12. Masaaki Imai, *Kaizen: The Key to Japan's Competitive Success*, New York: McGraw-Hill, 1986, p. 15.

13. Mark R. Edwards and J. Ruth Sproull, "Creativity: Productivity Gold Mine?" *Journal of Creative Behavior*, Vol. 18, No. 3, 1984, pp. 175–184; and Michael K. Badawy, "How to Prevent Creativity Mismanagement," *Research Management*, Vol. 29, No. 4, 1986, p. 28.

14. Kathleen D. Ryan and Daniel K. Oestreich, *Driving Fear Out of the Workplace*, San Francisco: Jossey-Bass, Inc., 1991, pp. 63, 64.

15. Adapted from Galen Britz, Don Emerling, Lynne Hare, Roger Hoerl, and Janice Shade, "How to Teach Others to Apply Statistical Thinking," *Quality Progress*, June 1997, pp. 67–79. © 1997 American Society for Quality, reprinted with permission.

16. Ronald D. Snee, "Getting Better Business Results: Using Statistical Thinking and Methods to Shape the Bottom Line," *Quality Progress*, June 1998, pp. 102–106.

17. Adapted from Brian L. Joiner, *Fourth Generation Management*, New York: McGraw-Hill, 1994, p. 129.

18. William M. Carley, "To Keep GE's Profits Rising, Welch Pushes Quality-Control Plan," *Wall Street Journal*, January 13, 1997, A1, A8; "Changing the Way Aircraft Engines Works," *GE Aircraft Engines News*, January 1998; Roger W. Hoerl, "Six Sigma and the Future of the Quality Profession," *Quality Progress*, June 1998, pp. 35–42; and presentation notes provided by Stefanie A. Darlington, Leader–Total Product Quality, GE Aircraft Engines, Cincinnati, Ohio.

19. Britz, et al. See Note 15.

20. This problem was developed from a classic example published in "The Quest for Higher Quality: The Deming Prize and Quality Control" by RICOH of America, Inc.

21. Adapted from Britz, et al. See Note 15.

22. Adapted from Britz, et al. See Note 15.

II

Total Quality and Organization Theory

Quality in Customer-Supplier Relationships

CHAPTER OUTLINE

The needs of customers too often are overshadowed by short-term business objectives. Peter Senge of MIT tells a story about a company that embraced total quality management but found its stock price steadily declining. One of the main objectives of their quality initiative was to reduce new product introduction time. In the effort to meet this objective (on which the managers were measured and rewarded), the new products became increasingly simple and mundane.

In Japanese the same word—*okyakusama*—means both "customer" and "honorable guest." World-class organizations are obsessed with meeting and exceeding customer expectations. Many companies such as Disney and Nissan Motor Co.'s Infiniti division were built on the notion of satisfying the customer. The service philosophy of Home Depot, cited by Wal-Mart's CEO as *the* best retail organization in the United States, is "Every customer has to be treated like your mother, your father, your sister, or your brother."

Many businesses traditionally have kept suppliers at arm's length, but the quality of output can be no better than the quality of the input. In 1982 IBM purchased some parts from a Japanese manufacturer. According to the specifications, IBM would accept 300 defective parts per million of the product. The response from Japan raised a lot of questions and gave IBM the opportunity to change its perspective on quality and relationships with suppliers. The Japanese commented, "We have a hard time understanding North American business practices. But the 3 defective parts per 10,000 have been included and are wrapped separately. Hope this pleases."[1]

Developing strong and positive relationships with customers and suppliers is a basic principle of total quality. This chapter will

- demonstrate the importance of customer-supplier relationships to achieving total quality;
- identify the principles and practices of quality customer-supplier relationships;
- give examples of effective partnerships between customers and suppliers; and
- compare the TQ approach to customers and suppliers to conventional organizational theories.

CUSTOMER-SUPPLIER RELATIONSHIPS AND TOTAL QUALITY

From the TQ perspective, every company is part of a long chain (actually many long chains) of customers and suppliers.[2] Each company is a customer to its suppliers and a supplier to its customers, so it does not make sense to think of a company as only one or the other (Figure 4.1). One implication of this concept is that your customer's customers are, in a sense, your customers as well. Sometimes a company must focus on both their immediate customers and those next in the chain. Procter & Gamble, for example, works hard to satisfy the needs of both the people who use their products and the retail establishments that sell them, labeling the former "consumers" and the latter "customers."

Companies should try to establish the same kinds of productive relationships with their suppliers that they have with their customers. By developing partnerships, customers and suppliers can build relationships that will help them satisfy their shared customers further along the customer-supplier chain.

FIGURE 4.1   THE CUSTOMER-SUPPLIER CHAIN

Customer/
Supplier ⟶ Customer/
Supplier ⟶ Customer/
Supplier ⟶ Customer/
Supplier ⟶

(Coal mine)   (Steel mill)   (Auto plant)   (Car rental agency)

This is why we have written one chapter on customer-supplier relationships, rather than separate chapters on customers and suppliers.

The idea of creating mutually beneficial relationships with both customers and suppliers is a major departure from the traditional approach to customer and supplier relationships (CSRs). As one book on quality recently put it, "The historical picture of customer-supplier relationships has been one of self-interested adversaries negotiating against each other to maximize their slice of the pie at the expense of the other."[3] The authors go on to say that the focus of CSRs under TQ is on expanding the pie rather than on arguing over its division.

The Importance of Customers

The importance of customers has evolved over the years, from viewing the customer as a buyer to increase profitability, to viewing the customer as an active partner and the focus of all quality activities. Customer satisfaction translates directly into increased profits. Loyal customers spend more, refer new clients, and are less costly to do business with. Studies have shown that it costs about five times more to attract new customers than to keep old ones and that satisfied customers purchase more and are willing to pay higher prices. At IBM, for instance, each percentage point in improved customer satisfaction translates into $500 million more revenue over five years.[4] Although Home Depot customers spend only about $38 each visit, they shop 30 times annually and spend more than $25,000 throughout a lifetime.[5] Poor quality products and services, on the other hand, lead to customer dissatisfaction in the form of complaints, returns, and unfavorable word-of-mouth publicity. Dissatisfied customers purchase from competitors. One study found that customers are five times more likely to switch because of perceived service problems than for price concerns or product quality issues.[6] Studies have also shown that dissatisfied customers tell at least twice as many friends about bad experiences than they tell about good ones.

For many companies, "The Customer Comes First" is a guiding principle (see the box about Southwest Airlines). It is impossible to overstate the importance of customers to TQ. Customers are at the very center of every TQ activity, and devotion to satisfying them is the first principle of TQ. Customers are recognized as the guarantee of the organization's continued existence. Therefore, a focus on customers, rather than internal issues, is the foundation of the TQ approach to management. Customer-driven quality is recognized as a core value of the Malcolm Baldrige National Quality Award. The award guidelines state:[7]

> Quality is judged by customers. Thus, quality must take into account all product and service features and characteristics that contribute value to customers and lead to customer satisfaction, preference, and retention. Value and satisfaction may be influenced by many factors throughout the customer's overall purchase, ownership, and service

---

Flying the Customer-Friendly Skies[8]

Southwest Airlines began on June 18, 1971, with flights to Houston, Dallas, and San Antonio. It has grown to become the fifth largest U.S. airline in terms of domestic customers carried. The airline operates more than 2,150 flights daily with more than 23,000 employees. Known for its legendary service, the Southwest culture ensures that it serves the needs of its Customers (with a capital C) in a friendly, caring, and enthusiastic manner. Kevin and Jackie Freiberg, authors of *NUTS! Southwest Airlines' Crazy Recipe for Business and Personal Success*, note that legendary service is a key component of Southwest's culture.

> Southwest wants its customers to experience service that makes a lasting impression, service that is kind and loving, service that is fun and makes them laugh. . . . Thus, Southwest will go a long way to defend and support an employee who may violate a company policy to bend toward the customer. The company instills in every employee the idea that happy, satisfied customers who return again and again create job security.

Every one of the approximately 1,000 customers who write to the airline gets a personal response (not a form letter) within four weeks, and frequent fliers even get birthday cards. The airline even moved a flight up a quarter hour when five medical students who commuted weekly to an out-of-state medical school complained that the flight got them to class 15 minutes late.

Customer focus applies to internal customers also; each operating division identifies an internal customer. Mechanics who service planes target the pilots who fly them, and marketers treat reservation agents as customers. It is not unusual to find pilots helping ground crews unload baggage. As Executive VP Colleen Barrett stated: "We are not an airline with great customer service. We are a great customer service organization that happens to be in the airline business."

Southwest has been one of the most profitable airlines in the United States. In many years, the airline has been recognized for best baggage handling, fewest customer complaints, and best on-time performance. It has been recognized with numerous honors, including one of America's Most Admired Corporations by *Fortune* magazine in 1995.

experiences. These factors include the company's relationship with customers that helps build trust, confidence, and loyalty.

The Importance of Suppliers

Suppliers—those companies that provide the organization with goods and services that help them to satisfy the needs of their own customers—are also crucial to successful TQ. A manufacturing company assembling parts made by suppliers illustrates this point: The final product cannot be any better than the parts that go into it. If a supplier's performance is of consistently high quality, its customer can decrease or eliminate costly incoming inspections that add no value to the product. For these reasons, organizations such as Ford Motor Company and Motorola have increasingly demanded tangible progress in quality from all their suppliers. Companies that do not accept this requirement are dropped from supplier lists. The importance of suppliers is at least as great when they provide training, software, or other goods or services that do not physically become part of the final product; they will influence its quality, nevertheless, by shaping the quality of the processes used to produce it.

However, as Terry A. Carlson, corporate vice president of purchasing for Maytag stated, "Superior quality, consistent service, and competitive pricing are just the price of entry to get into the game." What sets world-class suppliers apart from the rest are a formal company-wide effort to continually improve their products and services, the ability and willingness to align products, processes, and business strategies with customers for mutual success, and a proven ability to be an industry leader in developing new technologies and products.[9]

In business today, operations are often highly decentralized and dispersed around the world. Consequently, managing a complex network of suppliers becomes a critical interorganizational issue. Suppliers play a vital role throughout the product development process, from design through distribution. Suppliers can provide technology or production processes not internally available, early design advice, and increased capacity, which can result in lower costs, faster time-to-market, and improved quality for their customers. In turn, they are assured of stable and long-term business. At Chrysler, for example, suppliers are involved early in the design process.[10] As a result, Chrysler often finds out about new materials, parts, and technologies before other automakers.

Increasingly, suppliers are viewed as *partners* with customers, because there usually is a co-dependent relationship. A powerful example of supplier partnerships is the response that occurred when a fire destroyed the main source of a crucial $5 brake valve for Toyota.[11] Without it, Toyota had to shut down its 20 plants in Japan. Within hours of the disaster, other suppliers began taking blueprints, improvising tooling systems, and setting up makeshift production lines. Within days, the 36 suppliers, aided by more than 150 other subcontractors, had almost 50 production lines making small batches of the valve. Even a sewing-machine company that had never made car parts spent 500 person-hours refitting a milling machine to make just 40 valves a day. Toyota promised the suppliers a bonus of about $100 million "as a token of our appreciation."

PRINCIPLES FOR CUSTOMER-SUPPLIER RELATIONSHIPS

Three governing principles describe CSRs under total quality:

- recognition of the strategic importance of customers and suppliers,
- development of win-win relationships between customers and suppliers, and
- establishing relationships based on trust.

First, an organization must recognize that its customers and suppliers are absolutely crucial to its success. Although this may sound obvious, many organizations seem to be driven by the need to observe standard operating procedures. Those companies maintain rigid boundaries between jobs, rather than trying to meet customer expectations. Consider the following letter from a hotel desk clerk to the popular newspaper columnist Abigail Van Buren:

> Dear Abby:
>
> I am a desk clerk at a resort hotel. I would like the public to know that we are not maintenance men. We cannot repair television sets or break into their automobiles when they have locked their keys inside the car. We do not unplug toilets or change lightbulbs, and we can't repair the telephone.
>
> Also, we are not in "housekeeping," so we can't bring them extra wash cloths, towels, pillows, blankets, or toilet paper. We are not bellmen either, so please don't ask us to carry luggage or run errands.
>
> Now I will tell you what front desk clerks *are* paid to do: greet and register incoming guests, and make sure that outgoing guests see the cashier about paying their bill and turning in their key before departing. Thank you.
>
> Desk Clerks[12]

Although some division of labor is to be expected in any organization, the writer seems ignorant of his or her responsibility for guaranteeing customer satisfaction, preferring to focus on what he or she can't do. As the first and last contact a guest makes with the hotel, front desk personnel probably have the largest impact on guest satisfaction of anyone. It is frightening to imagine how much damage this individual's attitude has done to his or her organization. Of course, the responsibility for this attitude may ultimately rest with the hotel organization that apparently has created a system in which people are more interested in maintaining boundaries than in serving customers.[13]

Fortunately, Abby seems to have grasped the central principle of TQ much better than her correspondent:

I doubt that you can speak for all hotel and motel desk clerks through-out the world. In the name of good customer relations, you should be prepared to handle all questions and complaints to the satisfaction of the guests so they will want to return to your establishment.[14]

Customers must be at the center of the organizational universe. Satisfying their needs leads to repeat business and positive referrals, as opposed to one-shot business and negative referrals. Suppliers must also be considered crucial to organizational success, because they make it possible to create customer sat-isfaction. Neither the quality nor the cost of the organization's product can be brought to competitive levels and continuously improved without the contri-butions of suppliers.

The second principle of customer-supplier relationships is the need to develop mutually beneficial (often called win-win) relationships between cus-tomers and suppliers. This was discussed previously as working together to increase the size of the pie, rather than competing over how to divide it. The goal of building partnerships with customers and suppliers can be seen as an extension of the teamwork principle that applies to all TQ activities and as a recognition that the needs of both partners must be satisfied if productive long-term relationships are to be created. W. Edwards Deming has advocated these principles for decades, as is evident in his 14 points (chapter 2). Joseph Juran suggests some key differences between adversarial and teamwork rela-tionships with suppliers.[15] Traditionally, customers have used many different suppliers for the same purchased item, and they typically have been awarded short-term (annual) contracts. This practice fosters a competitive situation in which suppliers strive to outbid each other, and may sacrifice quality for cost. A teamwork relationship results in the need for fewer suppliers, with many items being single-sourced. With few suppliers, companies do not have to rely on annual bidding, and can award longer-term contracts. This enhances the motivation to work together for mutual benefits. For instance, quality planning is performed jointly, rather than independently. This helps both the customer and supplier focus on "fitness for use" to meet customer needs rather than simply trying to conform to specifications. It also fosters a spirit of continuous improvement, in which larger customers often help smaller suppliers develop their quality management systems and process capabilities. Similar ideas were also advocated by Deming in his 14 points.

The third principle of effective CSRs is that they must be based on trust rather than suspicion. The point noted by Juran observes that a critical dis-tinction between adversarial and teamwork relationshps is a "pattern of col-laboration." Adversarial relationships are characterized by secrecy and a tendency to look over suppliers' shoulders. Teamwork relationships, on the other hand, are characterized by openness and full disclosure of both capa-bilities and problems.

The costs of mistrust are staggering: Witness the tremendous number, detail, and rigidity of rules that characterize the U.S. Department of Defense's contracts with suppliers. The suppliers often incur substantial costs in terms of

Partnering with Internal Customers[16]

GTE Supply negotiates contracts, purchases products, and distributes a vast array of goods needed for telephone operations, from office supplies to telecommunications equipment. Its major customers are internal network, business, and telephone operations customer groups at each GTE local telephone company. The company created a systematic, highly effective process of obtaining and using information from internal customers, making partners of previously adversarial groups, reducing costs, and improving customer satisfaction. This was based on systematically surveying internal customers and using the results as a basis for quality improvement. Respondents rate GTE Supply on how well it

- Provides complete information,
- Understands customers' needs,
- Does the job right the first time,
- Provides timely responses to questions and requests,
- Makes it easy to do business with,
- Follows up on services, and
- Provides clear communication.

Other questions seek information about overall satisfaction, quality, and value, and open-ended questions ask about improvement opportunities. Detailed reports and analyses are provided to managers, who use the information to set objectives and to develop and implement action plans.

The survey and quality improvement process has transformed the organization from one of the worst-regarded to one of the best-regarded organizations in the company. They learned that extensive, focused communication with internal customers can produce spectacular increases in satisfaction levels and decrease costs and cycle times.

both money and time due to multiple levels of review and inspection. Although a certain level of rigidity is to be expected in the acquisition of weapons, it is harder to understand when applied to more ordinary items.

Aside from the obvious teamwork implications for relationships based on trust versus suspicion, monitoring supplier or customer behavior does not add any value to the product. If a trusting relationship between customers and suppliers can be developed so that neither must check up on the behavior of the other, the costs of monitoring, such as inspection and auditing, can be avoided. Many Japanese firms do not inspect items purchased from other companies in Japan; they do, however, often inspect those purchased from America. Trust is not a blind leap into the unknown; it is developed over time "through a pattern of success by all parties to fully and faithfully deliver that which was promised."[17] In other words, trust depends upon trustworthy behavior by both parties in a CSR.

Practices for Dealing with Customers

How can these principles be translated into specific practices? The most basic practices for dealing with customers are (1) to collect information constantly on customer expectations, (2) to disseminate this information widely within the organization, (3) to use this information to design, produce, and deliver the organization's products and services, and (4) to effectively manage relationships with customers.

Collect Customer Information

As seen in the GTE Supply example, acquiring customer information is critical to understanding customer needs and identifying opportunities for improvement. The Japanese auto industry is known for trying to understand customer needs so thoroughly that they can incorporate design features that customers would never have asked for but love once they experience them. Teams of automobile designers visit people at home and observe how they live in order to anticipate their automotive needs. Hideo Sugiura, executive vice president of Honda, comments on his company's efforts to anticipate customer needs: "We should not try to sell things just because the market is there, but rather we should seek to create a new market by accurately understanding the potential needs of customers and society."[18] Lexus, Toyota's luxury car line, has succeeded dramatically in this manner and is consistently at the top of owner satisfaction surveys.

Perhaps one of the best examples of understanding customer needs and using this information to improve competitiveness is Frank Perdue's chicken business.[19] Perdue learned what customers' key purchase criteria were. These included a yellow bird, high meat-to-bone ratio, no pinfeathers, freshness, availability, and brand image. He also determined the relative importance of each criterion and how well the company and its competitors were meeting each one. By systematically improving his ability to exceed customers' expectations relative to the competition, Perdue gained market share even though his chickens were premium priced. Among Perdue's innovations was a used jet engine that dried the chickens, allowing the pinfeathers to be singed off. As discussed in chapter 1, Perdue not only addressed his customer's satisfiers, but also their exciters/delighters as well.

Some of the most popular ways to collect information about customers are surveys, service evaluation cards, focus groups, and listening to what customers say during business transactions, especially when they complain. Some companies, such as Marriott Hotels, have developed elaborate methods for keeping abreast of customer needs. This is not a low-profile activity at Marriott: Chairman Bill Marriott, Jr., himself reads approximately 800 letters from customers and 15,000 guest questionnaires every month![20] The rewards of taking customer information seriously are also apparent at Marriott, where occupancy rates are consistently 10 percent above the industry average. (For an example from manufacturing, see box, "Promoting Customer Delight at U.S. Precision Lens," on page 153.)

Sending employees into customer facilities, another popular practice, provides not only feedback from customers, but also valuable information to employees about the importance of what they do. A manager in a foundry that follows this practice commented:

> We take shop floor people and take them out to the customer's plant. We want them to see the final product in place. It gets our employees out in the world to meet the customers. They get to know the customers better and really by doing that, the employees get to have a better, more caring attitude. Because they know more about what's going on.

Having top managers of the company act as customers of their own organizations—renting a room in their own hotel or buying a suit from a retail outlet—is another way to better understand customer needs. This not only gives them a sense of the quality of service, but also makes them more sensitive to how the organizational policies they have created actually affect customers.[21]

A newer approach to collecting customer information is to monitor the Internet.[22] In recent years, the growth of the Internet is offering companies a fertile arena for finding out what consumers think of their products. Internet users frequently seek advice from other users on strengths and weaknesses of products, share experiences on service quality, or pose specific problems they need to resolve. By monitoring the conversations on Usenet discussion groups, managers can obtain valuable insights on customer perceptions and product or service quality problems. In open forums, customer comments can often be translated into creative product improvements. In addition, the Internet can be a good source of information about competitors' products. The cost of monitoring Internet conversations is minimal compared to the costs of other types of survey approaches, and customers are not biased by any questions that may be asked. However, the conversations may be considerably less structured and unfocused and thus may contain less usable information. Also, unlike a focus group or telephone interview, inaccurate perceptions or factual errors cannot be corrected.

Beyond getting a thorough understanding of customer needs, companies also need to assess how well their products and services are meeting customer needs. Some companies have developed unconventional and innovative ways of understanding customers. British Airways has installed video kiosks at Heathrow Airport outside London and at Kennedy Airport in New York. Upset customers can enter the booth and create a video message for BA's management. The videos have proven so informative that, although they were initially viewed only by executives, frontline employees demanded and were given access to them. One important aspect of this method is that it gives people a sense of the emotion associated with customer response to the quality of service ("You lost my *&%$# baggage!"), which cannot easily be conveyed by checking a number from one through five on a customer satisfaction survey, especially when done weeks later. Texas Instruments created a simulated

Promoting Customer Delight at U.S. Precision Lens[23]

U.S. Precision Lens (USPL) is the world's largest manufacturer of lens systems for projection televisions. Since 1986 USPL has been a wholly-owned subsidiary of Corning, Inc. The major requirements for success in selling to projection television manufacturers such as Philips and Sony are product quality, delivery, product innovation, and customer service. USPL's goal in each area is "customer delight" through exceeding customer expectations.

USPL understands customer needs through a system it describes as "simple, reliable, and effective"—they ask them what their needs are. Company executives travel frequently to Europe and the Far East to meet with senior members of customer organizations, and customers visit USPL with similar frequency. During these visits, competitors' products are also discussed, so USPL can set a direction for continuous (they say "relentless") improvement. Planning sessions prior to visits allow input to the data-gathering process from across the organization. Trips are not the exclusive preserve of senior managers; hourly "associates" (employees) also visit customers and share their impressions on their return.

Interestingly, the primary medium of day-to-day communication between USPL and its customers is the fax. This is partly due to the time zone differences between USPL and its customers. The CEO sees every fax message from customers, and USPL's policy is to respond to all faxes within 24 hours. Also, the home telephone numbers of USPL's senior executives are provided to customers, and they use them.

USPL uses a survey to procure ratings of its own service quality, as well as that of its competitors, on the dimensions of assurance, responsiveness, reliability, empathy, and "tangibles." In response to feedback through this and other means, USPL has bar-coded container labels, vacuum sealed parts, and placed a native speaker in Japan to represent the company.

These and other TQ-oriented practices at USPL have paid tremendous dividends to the company. USPL received the SONY President Award in 1991 as the highest-rated supplier for quality and delivery. Philips presented USPL the Supplier Total Quality Award that same year. Electrohome made USPL its supplier of the year for 1990. The ultimate reward for quality, however, is in attracting and maintaining demand for the organization's products. In this category as well USPL is outstanding: The company's market share is approaching 70 percent.

classroom to understand how mathematics teachers use calculators, and a manager at Levi Strauss used to talk with teens who were lined up to buy rock concert tickets.

Disseminate Customer Information

After people in the organization have gathered information about customer needs, the next step is to broadcast this information within the organization. After all, if the people in the firm are going to work as a team to meet customer expectations, they must all be "singing from the same hymnbook," as the saying goes. Information does little good if it stays with the person or department that brought it into the organization. Wainwright Industries has a unique approach. A room at the headquarters building, named Mission Control by one of the managers who is a Star Trek fan, serves as the company's key information center. Not only are customer report cards displayed on a wall (along with other key quality and business information), but green and red flags are used to designate customers for whom everything is going well or a problem has arisen. Red flags signal the convening of a customer team to address the problem.

Richard Whiteley, vice chairman of The Forum Corporation, a customer satisfaction–oriented consulting firm, has a vivid way to describe this need: "Saturate your company with the voice of the customer."[24] Saturation is an attractive way of describing what organizations need to do: If the organization is awash in information about customer needs, it is much harder to downplay customer expectations in favor of administrative convenience or the need to follow procedures.

AT&T, which won two Baldrige Awards in 1992 and another in 1994, is one organization trying to maintain a constant customer focus. Jerre Stead, president of Global Business Communications Systems, tells people in his unit: "I say if you're in a meeting, any meeting, for 15 minutes and we're not talking about customers or competitors, raise your hand and ask why. If it goes on for half an hour, leave! Leave the meeting!"[25]

Customer information must be translated into the features of the organization's products and services. This is the bottom line of quality customer-supplier relations from the supplier's point of view: giving the customers what they want. Translating customer needs into product features can be done in a structured manner using Quality Function Deployment (QFD), a technique discussed in chapter 3. QFD allows people to see how aspects of their products and services relate to customer satisfaction and to make informed decisions about how their products should be improved. The overall process of using information from customers to provide quality products is summarized in Figure 4.2.

Use Customer Information

Customer information is worthless unless it is used. Customer feedback should be integrated into continuous improvement activities. For example, by listening to customers, Bank One opened nearly 60 percent of its 1,377 branches in Ohio and Texas on Saturdays and 20 percent on Sundays. A 24-hour customer hotline is also available. Since the early 1980s, Xerox has surveyed tens of thousands of customers annually and tracked the results through its Customer Satisfaction Measurement System (CSMS).[26] The data guide continuous improvements within the corporation. For instance, the CSMS uncovered the fact that customers wanted one-call, one-person problem resolution. As a result, Xerox created six Customer Care Centers, staffed by specially trained customer care representatives who handle some 1.2 million telephone calls and about one

FIGURE 4.2   THE CUSTOMER-DRIVEN QUALITY CYCLE

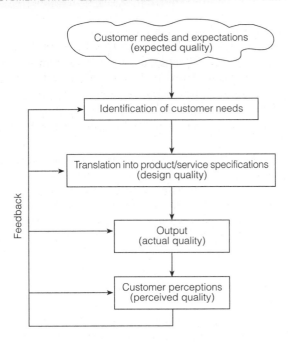

million written inquiries each year. Employees are cross-trained and empowered to adjust bills, correct forms, or take other steps to solve problems single-handedly. Any problems that cannot be resolved instantly are given a 10-day resolution deadline. The files remain open until customers confirm that they are totally satisfied with Xerox actions. CSMS data also showed that customer satisfaction is linked to cycle time—the elapsed time between the reporting phone call and the solution of the problem. The data also showed that simply knowing when a technician will arrive has a positive effect on customer satisfaction. Xerox modified the system to call customers shortly after problems are reported and give them an estimated time of arrival.

Binney & Smith, the company that produces Crayola crayons and markers, makes it a point to improve its products by taking advantage of customer feedback. Many of the letters the company receives from parents laud the role that crayons play in the artistic development of their children. Some letters complained that the markers created permanent stains in children's clothes. After two years of research, Binney & Smith responded by developing a new line of washable markers. Marker sales doubled, demonstrating the company's ability to learn and provide what customers are looking for.[27] More recently Binney & Smith sponsored a contest in which customers could name one of 16 new crayon colors the company created for its Big Box. "Part of our reason for introducing new colors came from consumer suggestions. More than 50 percent said they wanted us to expand and add new colors," according to Brad Dexler, a company spokesman.

Manage Customer Relationships

A company builds customer loyalty by developing trust and effectively managing the interactions and relationships with customers through customer-contact employees. Truly excellent companies foster close and total relationships with customers. These companies also provide easy access to their employees. AT&T Universal Card Services, for instance, has an 800 number, fax, and access for the hearing impaired 24 hours every day throughout the year, translation services for 140 languages, and bilingual Spanish/English operators. Customers are also informed if they will have to wait more than a minute. Customers of Ames Rubber Corporation have immediate access to top division management, manufacturing personnel, quality engineers, sales and service representatives, and technical support staff.

In services, customer satisfaction or dissatisfaction takes place during *moments of truth*—every instance in which a customer comes in contact with an employee of the company. Moments of truth may be direct contacts with customer representatives or service personnel, or when customers read letters, invoices, or other company correspondence. One study concluded that 70 percent of customers leave a supplier because of poor quality service, not problems with products per se, and many companies are struggling to bring their service up to the level of their products.[28] One of the main areas on which companies have focused is telephone service, especially how long it takes to get someone on the phone and to get one's question answered or order taken. Many companies have worked to make sure that phone calls are answered on the third ring, but to AMP, Inc., the world's largest manufacturer of electronic interconnection systems, three rings is an eternity. Customer calls to AMP are answered within six seconds—that is, on the first ring. Why such an ambitious goal? AMP found that 8 percent of their customers were hanging up before their calls were answered under the three-ring standard. They don't lose many calls now.[29]

Customer-contact employees are particularly important. They are the people whose main responsibilities bring them into regular contact with customers—in person, by telephone, or through other means. Companies must carefully select these employees, then extensively train and empower them to meet and exceed customer expectations. Job applicants often go through rigorous screening processes. At Universal Card Services, for instance, every applicant completes a two-part general aptitude test. The company then invites successful candidates to participate in additional testing, which includes a customer service role-playing exercise. Each applicant is asked to handle simulated incoming and outgoing calls. After completing the initial screening test, each candidate must pass a background check, credit check, and a medical evaluation, including drug testing, before being hired.

Service standards are measurable performance levels or expectations that define the quality of customer contact. Service standards might include technical standards, such as response time (answering the telephone within two rings), or behavioral standards (using a customer's name whenever possible). Companies need to communicate and continually reinforce their service standards. Finally, a company should implement a process for tracking adherence to the standards and providing feedback to the employees to improve their performance. Information technology supplies the data for effectively tracking conformance to customer service standards.

Despite all efforts to satisfy customers, every business experiences unhappy customers. Complaints can adversely affect business if not dealt with effectively. Many customers do not complain because they feel it wouldn't do any good or they are uncomfortable with the process. World-class organizations make it easy for customers to complain. Besides providing easy access to the company using toll-free telephone numbers (which should be adequately staffed and supported), many firms actively solicit complaints. Nissan, for instance, telephones each person who buys a new car or brings one in for significant warranty work. Its objective is to resolve all dissatisfaction within 24 hours.[30] Effective resolution of complaints increases customer loyalty and retention. At the Ritz-Carlton Hotel Company, for example, employees can spend up to $2,000 to resolve complaints with no questions asked.

Customers in the Fine Arts[31]

Car dealers have customers, bookstores have customers, but how about symphony orchestras and art museums? Traditionally, such organizations have acted as if they were your customer. But fine arts organizations in Cincinnati, spurred both by economic necessity and the proximity and influence of several quality-conscious corporations, have begun to think hard about satisfying customers. Some of the results:

- The Cincinnati Symphony Orchestra has initiated a series of concerts on Thursday nights. Dress is more casual for these concerts, and tickets can be easily exchanged.
- The Taft Museum has doubled the number of events it holds—from 20 to 40 per season.
- The Cincinnati Opera has begun scheduling series of operas linked by a popular theme. For example, "Pretty Women" included *Carmen* and *The Barber of Seville*.

The increased focus on satisfying customers, which has begun to pay off economically, is reflected by statements from leaders in these organizations. Paul A. Stuhireyer III, managing director of the opera, believes that "the goal should not be an international reputation while losing sight of what [local customers] want. . . . I want to make sure we're still putting 3,000 people into Music Hall for each performance. Then I know we're taking care of the citizens of Cincinnati." Gretchen Mehring, Cincinnati Art Museum director of public service, puts it: "Our primary focus is the family, especially the children. We're not operating a museum or creating exhibitions to appeal to art experts."

Practices for Dealing with Suppliers[32]

Although the principles of CSRs are the same in dealing with suppliers as they are with customers, the practices are somewhat different. In many companies, suppliers are treated as if they were actually a part of the organization. For example, functions such as cafeteria service, mailroom operations, and information processing are being performed by suppliers at their customers' facilities. As more and more of this type of outsourcing is done, the lines between customer and supplier become increasingly blurred.

To ensure that suppliers can provide high quality and reduce costs associated with incoming inspection or testing, many companies provide many types of assistance to their suppliers in developing quality assurance programs or solving quality problems. Joint conferences, training, incentives, recognition, and long-term agreements help to improve suppliers' abilities to meet key quality requirements. The Delco Moraine Division, a manufacturer of automotive brake controls, uses an awareness program that includes a videotape presentation emphasizing quality shown at supplier plants. After viewing the tape, supplier employees were better able to relate their work to Delco. Similarly, Chrysler instituted a program with its suppliers to identify cost reduction ideas; both parties benefit from the lower costs.

Many companies segment suppliers into categories based on their importance to the business and manage them accordingly. For example, at Corning, Level 1 suppliers, who provide raw materials, cases, and hardware, are deemed critical to business success and are managed by teams that include representatives from engineering, materials control, purchasing, and the supplier company. Level 2 suppliers provide specialty materials, equipment, and services and are managed by internal customers. Level 3 suppliers provide commodity items and are centrally managed by purchasing.[33]

In general, the fundamental practices for dealing with suppliers are (1) to base purchasing decisions on quality as well as cost, (2) to reduce the number of suppliers, (3) to establish long-term contracts, (4) to measure and certify suppliers' performance, and (5) to develop cooperative relationships and strategic alliances."

Base Purchasing Decisions on Quality and Cost

The first and most obvious practice is that purchasing decisions should be based on the quality of the product and not just its cost.[34] This, however, goes against the grain in most organizations. Generally speaking, the technical people will determine the specifications for a product to be purchased, and then the purchasing department will solicit bids or check prices with several suppliers and negotiate the contract with the one that fills the order. Purchasing personnel have traditionally been rewarded primarily for negotiating low prices, and thus this has been their focus. Supplier firms have often responded to this situation in the obvious way: by doing whatever they need to do (including sacrificing quality) to maintain low prices.

Beyond the compromises this creates for the quality of the final product, there are two other problems with this approach. First, low purchase cost often does not equal low overall cost. If a cheap (in both senses of the word) part causes a large amount of scrap or leads to high warranty costs, it may end up with a higher overall cost, often referred to as life-cycle cost. Second, pressing suppliers for ever-lower prices will minimize their profits. Although this benefits the customer in the short run, in the long run it keeps suppliers operating so close to the bone that they forgo capital investments, maintenance, and other expenses necessary to improve or even maintain their quality.[35]

Reduce the Number of Suppliers

Firms pursuing TQ also reduce the number of suppliers they work with to the point of having only one supplier for some components. Xerox has reduced its suppliers by about 90 percent—from more than 4,000 to about 450 in 1990.[36] In the automotive industry, General Motors had cut domestic suppliers by 45 percent, from 10,000 down to 5,500, by 1991. Ford Motor Company had likewise reduced their number of suppliers from 1,800 down to 1,000.[37] This also goes against the grain of conventional purchasing practices, as it increases the dependence of the organization on the supplier, thus weakening its bargaining position and exposing it to the possibility of an interruption in supply in the case of a labor stoppage or similar problem with the supplier.

Several advantages offset these disadvantages. For one thing, administrative costs are greatly reduced.[38] (Imagine the time to be saved by eliminating the paperwork associated with 90 percent of suppliers!) Also, cutting the number of suppliers reduces the variability in the incoming products, making it much easier to control the quality of outgoing products. This is because there are fewer "special causes" of variation, to use Deming's term.

The type of intensive CSRs that characterize TQ simply cannot be maintained with a large number of suppliers. The significance of partners (like friends or vice presidents) is lost if you have too many of them. For these reasons, many organizations continue to reduce the number of suppliers with which they do business.

Establish Long-Term Contracts

Related to the idea of fewer suppliers is the practice of establishing long-term contracts with suppliers (see box, "Changing Ford's Supplier Relationships: Easier Said Than Done," on page 161). Establishing long-term contracts allows suppliers to make greater commitments to improving the quality of products and provides greater opportunity for joint improvement efforts and the development of teamwork across organizational boundaries.

Measure and Certify Supplier Performance

Texas Instruments measures suppliers' quality performance by parts per million defective, percentage of on-time deliveries, and cost of ownership.[39] An electronic requisitioning system allows a paperless procurement process. More than 800 suppliers are linked to Texas Instruments through an information exchange system. Integrated data systems track the incoming quality and timeliness of deliveries as materials are received. Analytical reports and on-line data are used to identify material defect trends. Performance reports are sent each month to key suppliers. Joint customer-supplier teams are formed to communicate and improve performance. A supplier management task force of top managers directs current and strategic approaches to improving supplier management practices.

Supplier certification is used by many companies as the focal point of their supplier management system. Formal programs typically are established to rate and certify suppliers who provide quality materials in a cost-effective and timely manner. At the Gillette Company, the supplier certification program begins with Gillette identifying those suppliers with a proven ability to meet its specifications.[40] Once a supplier is selected to participate, Gillette expects them to establish a preproduction planning system to assess the capability of their process to meet Gillette's specifications. Feedback is offered in the form of recommended changes that will improve quality, reduce cost, or facilitate ease of manufacture.

Some companies, such as Motorola, have suppliers rate them as customers. Motorola uses a 15-member council of suppliers that rates Motorola's practices and offers suggestions for improving, for example, the accuracy of production schedules or design layouts that Motorola provides.[41]

Develop Cooperative Relationships and Strategic Alliances

The cornerstone of TQ-style customer-supplier relationships is cooperation. In a sense, practices such as long-term contracts and fewer suppliers create an environment in which cooperation can flourish. Similar to the operation of teamwork within an organization (see chapter 7), quality customer-supplier relations help both parties to achieve their goals.

One common form that cooperation takes is the early involvement of suppliers in the design of new products.[42] Early involvement allows suppliers to make cost-cutting and quality-improving suggestions about the design while changes are relatively easy and inexpensive to make. When the product design is not revealed to suppliers until late in the process, often out of concern that it will be leaked to competitors, such opportunities are lost. Security concerns can be dealt with through nondisclosure agreements.[43]

Another indication of cooperation is the effort of customers to help suppliers improve quality, which can take many forms. Many TQ-oriented corporations present quality-improvement seminars for their suppliers.[44] Juran recommends joint quality planning between customers and suppliers, featuring the exchange of quality-related information.[45] Although customers traditionally have hammered suppliers to lower their prices, in a cooperative relationship the focus is on helping suppliers to lower their costs, which will ultimately benefit both parties.[46]

Today, suppliers are being asked to take on greater responsibilities to help their customers. As companies focus more on their core competencies—the things they do best—they are looking outside their organizations for assistance with noncritical support processes. Customer-supplier partnerships represent an important strategic alliance in achieving excellence and business success. Benefits of such partnerships include access to technology or distribution channels not available internally, shared risks in new investments and product development, improved products through early design recommendations

---

Changing Ford's Supplier Relationships: Easier Said Than Done[47]

Ford Motor Company was among the first companies to try to change its relationships with suppliers to be consistent with total quality. In 1983 Ford's purchasing vice president, L.M. Chicoine, sent a statement throughout Ford's purchasing organization to the effect that he would like to see more supplier contracts written for periods of more than one year. After six months he learned that there was virtually no increase in the number of long-term contracts.

Mr. Chicoine found that the reason for this lack of change was a procedure requiring buyers to get authorization from two levels of supervision for any contract greater than one year. Most buyers, not seeing any great rewards to them from negotiating long-term contracts, and seeing very clearly the extra hassle involved in getting two additional levels of approval, simply did not attempt to negotiate long-term contracts. A one-word change was all that was needed. The new policy stated that any contract for less than one year would require two additional levels of authorization, leading to historic changes in the nature of Ford's supplier relationships.

---

based on supplier capabilities, and reduced operations costs through better communications. For example, FedEx and Jostens formed a strategic partnership that enabled both to benefit from new sales of scholastic jewelry and yearbooks.[48] They took advantage of each others' strengths: Josten provided a high-quality product with superior service, and FedEx provided reliable high-volume, short-interval delivery for these time-critical products.

QUALITY CUSTOMER–SUPPLIER RELATIONSHIPS IN ACTION

Many of the aspects of quality CSRs we have been discussing are illustrated by the relationship between GE Appliance and DJ Inc., both of Louisville, Kentucky.[49] In nine years, DJ went from being one of 100 GE suppliers of plastic parts to being its sole source. DJ improved its quality by taking advantage of GE's supplier seminars in statistical process control (SPC). The company must have studied hard, as it has not had a single lot of parts rejected by GE since 1978. Early involvement in product design is commonplace for these two companies. In one typical case, DJ recommended a minor change in product design that reduced the cost of a part by more than 5 percent and increased its expected life by 16 percent. This example typifies the advantages enjoyed by companies with quality customer-supplier relationships.

Granite Rock Company of Watsonville, California, a 1992 Malcolm Baldrige Award winner, has also devoted itself to absorbing and making use of information from customers.[50] Bruce Woolpert, who shares with his brother Steve the CEO title at Granite Rock, believes that the role of manager is "to make sure there's a flood of information coming into the company." Where does the flood come from? Granite Rock has its customers rate its performance against its competitors in "report cards," longer surveys, quick-response cards, and focus groups. Information on what customers need and what is being done to satisfy them is distributed throughout the company via team meetings, an annual recognition day, and the appropriately titled company newsletter, *Rock Talk.*

Granite Rock learned that quarry customers wanted to pick up rock very quickly at any time of the day or night. To satisfy this need, the company invested a great deal of money in Granite Xpress, a system that allows customers to pull up to the quarry, check the computer for their order, and insert a magnetic card to load their own orders. Not only does this system operate 24 hours a day, but it has reduced the time at the quarry for truckers from 30 minutes to 10.

Granite Rock personnel also frequently make trips to benchmark other companies, both in their industry (aggregate and concrete producers) and out of their industry (a gold mine). Perhaps the furthest afield they have roamed is to Domino's Pizza, another company that is concerned about on-time delivery. Domino's told Granite Rock where to get better maps and suggested that they adopt Domino's practice of writing house numbers on maps.

CUSTOMER–SUPPLIER RELATIONS IN ORGANIZATION THEORY

Much of the organization literature has argued that firms should consider customers as partners for success.[51] As far back as 1973, Gersuny and Rosengren argued that diverse customer roles require new bonds of interdependence and an increasingly complex social network that crosses traditional organizational boundaries.[52] They identified four distinct roles for customers:

1.   resource,
2.   worker (or co-worker),
3.   buyer, and
4.   beneficiary (or user).

A fifth role has emerged from work in the human service area: Customers can be a key outcome, or product, of value-creating transformation activities, such as education and health delivery. In the first two roles, customers act as inputs to the transformation process, while in the last three, they act as outputs. Each of these roles is instrumental in creating competitive quality within a firm.

In reviewing the organizational literature for these roles, Lengnick-Hall[53] suggests that the following organizational practices are positively related to the competitive quality of production processes and outcomes:

• practices that deliberately select and carefully manage customer resources, foster an effective alliance between the firm and its customer resources, and improve the quality of its customer resources;

- practices that provide clear opportunities for coproduction, enhance customer abilities as coproducers, and increase customer motivation toward coproduction;
- activities that foster trust, develop interdependence, share information, and initiate friendly, mutually beneficial customer-organization bonds;
- activities that foster unambiguous communication with users, focus on meeting customer needs, offer realistic previews, achieve dimensions of quality that customers truly care about, and ensure that actual use is consistent with intended use; and
- activities that create opportunities for direct communication and interaction between users and production/core service personnel.

Thus, firms should design systems that involve and empower customers throughout the input-transformation-output system, rather than merely rely on customers to define their preferences and evaluate the products and services provided to them. This conclusion is certainly the foundation of modern TQ approaches and is reflected in the Baldrige Award criteria.

One example of this in practice is ADAC Laboratories, a manufacturer of high-technology health care equipment and a 1996 Baldrige winner. Not only does ADAC survey customers and potential customers and measure satisfaction, they invite customers to participate in strategic planning meetings, have lunch with customers attending new equipment training sessions, and host formal user group meetings to help prioritize product enhancements, share tips on new uses, and provide other information.

Total quality can also be related to a number of traditional organizational theories. The following sections discuss TQ's relationship with the resource dependence perspective and the theory of integrative bargaining.

The Resource Dependence Perspective

The organizational theory most directly comparable to the TQ view of customer-supplier relations is the resource dependence perspective (RDP) developed by Jeffrey Pfeffer and Gerald Salancik.[54] This perspective—which deals with how organizations manage to get the resources they need from their environment—resembles TQ in some ways, yet differs in others.

The most important similarity between the two perspectives is their mutual emphasis on the idea that the sources of an organization's success lie outside its boundaries. Although the idea that customers ultimately grant the organization its continued existence has become familiar as a fundamental principle of TQ, Pfeffer and Salancik point out that much organization theory focuses on the internal operations of organizations, giving less emphasis to the organization's environment:

> Most current writers give only token consideration to the environmental context of organizations. The environment is there, somewhere outside the organization, and the idea is mentioned that environments

constrain or affect organizations. . . . After this, the task of management is considered. Somehow, the things to be managed are usually within the organization, assumed to be under its control, and often have to do with the direction of low-level hired personnel. When authors get down to the task of describing the running of the organization, the relevance of the environment fades.[55]

According to the RDP, the effectiveness of an organization should be understood in terms of how well it meets the demands of external groups and organizations that are concerned with its actions and products. This is similar to the TQ conception of quality as meeting or exceeding customer expectations. There is an interesting difference, however, between the RDP concept of effectiveness and the TQ concept of quality.

TQ has traditionally focused almost exclusively on the organization's customers—that is, those who purchase the organization's products and provide the wherewithal for the organization's continued survival. The RDP perspective, however, recognizes that organizations must satisfy the demands of not only customers, but also other entities in the environment, including various government agencies, interest groups, shareholders, and—to some extent—society as a whole.

A government regulatory agency can make life miserable for an organization it does not believe is following government regulations—for example, a coal mine with inadequate safety procedures or a restaurant with unsanitary practices. In the extreme case, the government can even shut down an operation. Interest groups can influence customers to boycott a product for reasons unrelated to the quality of the product itself. Certain brands of California wine were boycotted for years because of alleged mistreatment of the migrant farmworkers who picked their grapes.

In recent years, shareholders of public corporations have become a constituency to be reckoned with. They are making increasing demands on how corporations operate, including not only economic but also social and environmental aspects of performance, such as minority hiring and use of recyclable materials.

From this perspective it is clear that although customers are important, groups and organizations other than customers can play a major role in determining an organization's success. TQ advocates can take two avenues in dealing with this issue. The first is to enlarge the concept of customers to include all those who have a stake in the organization. Following this logic, an organization would not be seen as practicing TQ unless it met the expectations of all of its constituencies, not just its customers in the traditional sense. However, different groups are apt to have very different expectations for the behavior of an organization, thus making it quite difficult to satisfy all parties.

The other avenue is for TQ advocates to recognize that although providing quality to customers is the overriding focus of an organization's activities, satisfying customers alone will not necessarily guarantee continued success, due to the potential influence of other constituencies. Interestingly, this perspective has recently been incorporated into the Baldrige Award criteria:

A company's leadership needs to stress its responsibilities to the public and needs to practice good citizenship. This responsibility refers to basic expectations of the company—business ethics and protection of public health, safety, and the environment. . . . Company planning should seek to prevent problems, to provide forthright company response if problems occur, and to make available information needed to maintain public awareness, safety, and confidence. Companies should not only meet all local, state, and federal laws and regulatory requirements. They should treat these and related requirements as areas for continuous improvement "beyond mere compliance."

Another similarity between TQ and RDP is in their recognition of interdependence between organizations as a fact of organizational life that must be managed effectively.

In the current dense environment . . . interdependencies are the problem. The dominant problems of the organization have become managing its exchanges and its relationships with the diverse interests affected by its actions. . . . The increasing density of relationships among diverse interests has led to less willingness to rely on unconstrained market forces. Negotiation, political strategies, the management of the organization's institutional relationships—these have all become more important.[56]

Thus the RDP shares with TQ the idea that managing interdependencies with other organizations is a key to success. The two perspectives diverge again, however, when it comes to how such interdependencies should be managed. Quality customer-supplier relationships are seen from the TQ perspective as consisting of mutually beneficial partnerships. Such an option, however, is not anticipated in the RDP. From this perspective, interdependence should be managed by some combination of gaining as much control as possible over the other organization, minimizing the other party's control over one's own organization, making it difficult for the other organization to monitor and influence one's behavior, and so on.

When compared to the protection of self-interest inherent in the recommendations of the RDP, the TQ win-win doctrine sounds somewhat naive. Yet most organizations practicing TQ and building partnerships with their customers and suppliers have traditionally managed customer-supplier relationships in the manner suggested by the RDP and have been dissatisfied with the results. The partnership efforts are mostly in their early stages, and there is no guarantee that they will ultimately succeed. As of now, however, they are the preferred method of many firms for managing interdependence.

Integrative Bargaining

The idea of building cooperative relationships that benefit both parties to a negotiation is not something that was created by writers or practitioners of TQ.

The idea of mutually beneficial relationships and win-win bargaining comes from a long tradition of research and writing on conflict management and negotiation.[57]

The idea behind this research tradition is that both parties will benefit more in the long run if they work together to help each other, rather than each one striving to win each round of negotiation. This tradition has been appropriated by writers on TQ, perhaps because it is consistent with the idea of customer orientation and teamwork. This is another area where TQ doctrine derives in a straightforward manner from existing organizational theory.

SUMMARY

Customers are the focus of companies practicing TQ, and those companies recognize that they cannot satisfy their customers without strong partnerships with their suppliers. The principles for developing quality customer-supplier relationships are

- recognizing the centrality of customers and the importance of suppliers,
- developing win-win relationships, and
- building up and acting on trust.

The practices for implementing these principles in dealing with customers are

- collecting information relentlessly about what customers want,
- distributing this information broadly within the organization,
- designing one's products and services in accord with customer demands, and
- managing customer relationships.

Practices for creating effective relationships with suppliers include developing long-term relationships with a limited number of suppliers chosen on the basis of quality, developing cooperative relations characterized by early supplier involvement in product design, and working together to improve quality and reduce costs. TQ principles and practices for customer-supplier relations are related to organizational theories of resource dependence and negotiation.

REVIEW AND DISCUSSION QUESTIONS

1. What can be learned about customer-supplier relationships from the story about IBM and its Japanese supplier?
2. Draw a diagram of a customer-supplier chain that includes at least four organizations. What attributes of quality are required at each link in the chain? How does quality at the beginning of the chain influence quality at the end?
3. Why are suppliers important to a company's quality efforts?
4. Identify three practices through which companies can better understand their customers' needs.

5.   Think of a type of customer that you know reasonably well. Try to identify some unmet needs of this type of customer and to think of some new features of the products and/or services they purchase that would excite them. Why do you think these features are not being offered?

6.   Identify a customer-supplier relationship in which you are involved. How does it compare to the principles and practices of TQ relationships? In what specific ways could adopting some of the principles and practices discussed in this chapter improve this relationship?

7.   How do the terms used for customers in different industries and occupations (for example, patients, clients, passengers, students) influence how people in these industries think about their customers?

8.   How would TQ and the resource dependence perspective differ in describing the quality and effectiveness of a state university?

9.   Can you think of a situation in which customers are not important to the success of an organization?

10.   How should an organization go about deciding who its customers are? Identify the customers of a university, a government agency, and a movie producer.

CASES

The Case of the Missing Reservation

Mark, Donna, and their children, along with another family, traditionally attended Easter brunch at a large downtown hotel. This year, as in the past, Donna called and made a reservation about three weeks prior to Easter. Because half the party consisted of small children, they arrived 20 minutes prior to the 11:30 reservation to assure being seated early. When they arrived, however, the hostess said that they did not have a reservation. The hostess explained that guests sometimes failed to show and that she would probably have a table available for them before long. Mark and Donna were quite upset and insisted that they had made a reservation and expected to be seated promptly. The hostess told them, "I believe that you made a reservation, but I can't seat you until all the people on the reservation list are seated. You are welcome to go to the lounge for complimentary coffee and punch while you wait." When Mark asked to see the manager, the hostess replied, "I am the manager," and turned to other duties. The party was eventually seated at 11:45, but was not at all happy with the experience.

The next day, Mark wrote a letter to the hotel manager explaining the entire incident. Mark was in the MBA program at the local university and taking a course on total quality management. In the class, they had just studied issues of customer focus and some of the approaches used at the Ritz-Carlton Hotel, a 1992 Baldrige Award winner. Mark concluded his letter with the statement, "I doubt that we would have experienced this situation at a hotel that truly believes in quality." About a week later, he received the following letter:

We enjoy hearing from our valued guests, but wish you had experienced the level of service and accommodations that we strive to achieve here at our hotel. Our restaurant manager received your letter and asked me to respond as Total Quality Lead.

Looking back at our records we did not show a reservation on the books for your family. I have addressed your comments with the appropriate department head so that others will not have to experience the same inconveniences that you did.

Thank you once again for sharing your thoughts with us. We believe in a philosophy of "continuous improvement," and it is through feedback such as yours that we can continue to improve the service to our guests.

Discussion Questions

1. Were the hostess's actions consistent with a customer-focused quality philosophy? What might she have done differently?
2. How would you have reacted to the letter that Mark received? Could the Total Quality Lead have responded differently? What does the fact that the hotel manager did not personally respond to the customer tell you?

Pro Fasteners, Incorporated

Pro Fasteners of San Jose, California, has been particularly innovative in building quality customer-supplier relationships.[58] Inspired by such books as Crosby's *Quality Without Tears* and quality-oriented companies such as Nordstrom, President Steve Braccini conceived of a radical new role for his company, which provides industrial hardware and components to the electronics industry.

In the late 1980s, many of Pro's customers were making the kinds of changes we have discussed, such as buying from fewer suppliers and using long-term contracts. They were asking more of their suppliers, including a commitment to keep them stocked with their product, quality guaranteed. Braccini realized that his customers were really saying they didn't want to have to worry about their parts inventory and that Pro Fasteners could do a better job of managing it than they could—and at a lower cost to boot. As Braccini put it, "Suddenly, the customer could cut his in-house staff. He'd have no purchasing costs, no receiving costs, no quality-assurance costs."

With this vision of being excruciatingly close to the customer came some significant management and organizational challenges for Pro Fastener. They would need to learn to anticipate customer needs. They would have to be on the cutting edge of quality. They would need the computer power to keep track of hundreds of thousands of parts. Most important, they would need committed and adaptive people in the organization to pull this off.

Using teams, among other methods, Pro Fastener has made a great deal of progress in turning the quality vision into reality. One team found a way to ship

100 percent correct parts with 100 percent on-time delivery to Applied Materials, a major customer. Another team responded to customer complaints about setting up credit with a $100 "courtesy account" that can be opened immediately, with no credit check. Hundreds of similar changes have transformed the company, particularly its relationships with customers.

The changes did not come easily. Employees often wondered whether Braccini knew what he was doing. His wife and partner was especially concerned about the amount of responsibility that was given to associates. Braccini created an employee quality group called the Continuous Improvement Council (CIC), which eventually decided to kick all of the managers off the quality teams. If a new style of organization was being born, the labor pains were awful.

However, the quality CSRs Pro Fasteners has developed have paid off in a big way. Despite a recession, the company's sales rose 20 percent between 1989 and 1992, and the company won more than 50 quality awards during this period. Overall, as one purchasing agent puts it, "They're the best." What else could you ask for in a supplier?

Discussion Questions

1. How does Pro Fasteners illustrate the principles of customer-supplier relationships discussed in this chapter?
2. If the company had failed in this attempt to change the nature of its business, what would have been the likely causes?
3. What role can information systems play in managing customer-supplier relationships?

Lands' End: The Secrets of Success

Lands' End, a popular and very successful catalog company, recently shared with customers the secrets of its success. The following are some of the things they had to say:[59]

Here at Lands' End, in the heartland of America, we still believe the customer comes first. . . . There are four basic ways we put the customer first. We hope you'll take a few minutes to read about them. Then decide if you'd like to be treated that way yourself.

1. **Make your merchandise as good as you can.** Our goal has always been to make our clothing and accessories as good as they could possibly be. By adding back features others have taken out over the years. By using the finest fabrics available. By inspecting the finished goods by eye to make sure they measure up.

2. **Always, always price it fairly.** It's our policy to mark up products modestly, just enough to give us a fair profit and to give you a terrific value. Admittedly, we have a few advantages. We're direct merchants with no middlemen taking a bite out of the profits. We don't spring for glitzy,

budget-busting advertising. . . . Our main headquarters is in Dodgeville, Wisconsin, surrounded by cornfields (no kidding).

3. **Make it a snap to shop for, 24 hours a day.** Our store never closes. We're open around the clock every day of the week to accommodate the varied schedules and different time zones of our customers. . . . Should you have detailed questions, we'll hook you up with one of our Specialty Shopper operators. They're our elite corps—the best of the best—able to answer any questions you might have about styling, fit, color matching, and more.

4. **Guarantee it. Period.** We strive for perfection, but sometimes a flawed product slips through. The color may be a shade too dark. A button may break. A seam may unravel. In those cases, we beg your tolerance and offer you one final protection. If at any time you are not completely satisfied, return the item for a full refund or exchange. And please, never feel bad about sending something back. We'd rather a truckload of returns than one dissatisfied customer.

Discussion Questions

1. How is Lands' End practicing total quality in its products and services?
2. How would the experience of purchasing a shirt through a catalog company differ from purchasing the same shirt from a department store? Could they both represent high quality?

ENDNOTES

1. Reported in "Total Quality Management and Competitiveness" by G. Pouskouleli, *Engineering Digest*, December 1991, pp. 14–17. The Japanese response is based on a story in the *Toronto Sun* by S. Ford, April 25, 1983, p. 6.
2. This idea has been promoted by Richard J. Schonberger in his book, *Building a Chain of Customers*. New York: The Free Press, 1990.
3. Arthur R. Tenner and Irving J. DeToro, *Total Quality Management: Three Steps to Continuous Improvement*. Reading, Mass.: Addison-Wesley, 1992, p. 197.
4. David Kirkpatrick, "Breaking Up IBM," *Fortune*, July 27, 1992, pp. 44–58.
5. Patricia Sellers, "Companies That Serve You Best," *Fortune*, May 31, 1993, pp. 74–88.
6. The Forum Corporation, *Customer Focus Research*, Executive Briefing, Boston, 1988.
7. Sources: Southwest Airlines home page, http://iflyswa.com; Richard S. Teitelbaum, "Where Service Flies Right," *Fortune*, August 24, 1992, pp. 117–118; and Kevin Freiberg and Jackie Freiberg, *NUTS! Southwest Airlines' Crazy Recipe for Business and Personal Success*, Austin, TX: Bard Press, 1996.
8. 1998 Criteria For Performance Excellence, Malcolm Baldrige National Quality Award. Gaithersburg, Md.: National Institute of Standards and Technology, United States Department of Commerce.
9. Tim Minahan, "What Makes a Supplier World-Class," *Purchasing*, Vol. 125, No. 2, August 13, 1998, pp. 50–61.
10. Justin Martin, "Are You as Good as You Think You Are?" *Fortune*, September 30, 1996, pp. 142–152.
11. Valerie Reitman, "Toyota's Fast Rebound after Fire at Supplier Shows Why It's Tough," *Wall Street Journal*, May 8, 1997, p. 1.
12. As seen in Dear Abby column by Abigail Van Buren. Dist. by Universal Press Syndicate. Reprinted with permission. All rights reserved.

13. We are indebted to David Waldman for this insight.

14. As seen in Dear Abby column by Abigail Van Buren. Dist. by Universal Press Syndicate. Reprinted with permission. All rights reserved.

15. J.M Juran, *Juran on Leadership for Quality: An Executive Handbook.* New York: The Free Press, 1989.

16. James H. Drew and Tye R. Fussell, "Becoming Partners with Internal Customers," *Quality Progress,* Vol. 29, No. 10, October 1996, pp. 51–54.

17. John Carlisle, quoted in Tenner and DeToro, *Total Quality Management.*

18. Richard C. Whitely, *The Customer-Driven Company, Moving from Talk to Action.* Reading, Mass.: Addison-Wesley, 1991. p. 7.

19. Robert D. Buzzell and Bradley T. Gale, *The PIMS Principles: Linking Strategy to Performance,* New York: The Free Press, 1987.

20. Marriott's approach to gathering information from customers is discussed in detail in Whiteley, *The Customer-Driven Company.*

21. See Benson P. Shapiro, V. Kasturi Rangan, and John J. Sviokla, "Staple Yourself to an Order," *Harvard Business Review,* July–August 1992, pp. 113–122.

22. Byron J. Finch, "A New Way to Listen to the Customer," *Quality Progress,* Vol. 30, No. 5, May 1997, pp. 73–76.

23. Based on Houghton Award Application 1992, U.S Precision Lens, Inc.

24. Whiteley, *The Customer-Driven Company.*

25. Quoted in "Could AT&T Rule the World?" by David Kirkpatrick. *Fortune,* May 17, 1993.

26. "Quality '93: Empowering People With Technology," advertisement, *Fortune,* September 1993.

27. Whiteley, *The Customer-Driven Company.*

28. Whiteley, *The Customer-Driven Company.*

29. Dick Schaaf,"Complex Quality: AMP Rings Up Service Success," *Quality Imperative,* September 1992, pp. 16–26.

30. "Focusing on the Customer," *Fortune,* June 5, 1989, p. 226.

31. Based on "Arts Groups Try to Keep the Customer Satisfied" by Owen Findsen and Cliff Radel, *Cincinnati Enquirer,* February 7, 1993.

32. These practices are based on *The Deming Route to Quality and Productivity* by William W. Scherkenbach (Rockville, Md.: Mercury Press, 1988) and on *Juran on Leadership for Quality* by Joseph M. Juran (New York: The Free Press, 1989).

33. Larry Kishpaugh, "Process Management and Business Results," presentation at the 1996 Regional Malcolm Baldrige Award Conference, Boston, Massachusetts.

34. This idea has long been championed by Deming. See the discussion of his 14 points in chapter 2.

35. For a discussion of these two points, see David N. Burt, "Managing Suppliers Up to Speed," *Harvard Business Review,* July–August 1989, pp. 127–135.

36. Tenner and DeToro, *Total Quality Management.*

37. John R. Emshwiller, "Suppliers Struggle to Improve Quality as Big Firms Slash Their Vendor Rolls." *Wall Street Journal,* August 16, 1991, B2.

38. Patrick J. McMahon, "Supplier Involvement," chapter 9 in *The Improvement Process* by H. James Harrington (New York: McGraw-Hill, 1987).

39. Texas Instruments Defense Systems & Electronics Group, Malcolm Baldrige Application Summary (1992).

40. Mike Lovitt, "Responsive Suppliers Are Smart Suppliers," *Quality Progress,* June 1989, pp. 50–53.

41. McMahon, op. cit.

42. This point is discussed by Randall S. Schuler and Drew L. Harris in *Managing Quality: The Primer for Middle Managers,* Reading, Mass.: Addison-Wesley, 1992.

43. McMahon, op. cit.

44. McMahon, op. cit.

45. Juran, *Juran on Leadership for Quality.*

46. Schuler and Harris, *Managing Quality.*

47. W.W. Scherkenbach, *The Deming Route to Quality and Productivity.* Washington, D.C: CEEP Press, 1986, p. 131.

48. AT&T Corporate Quality Office, *Supplier Quality Management: Foundations,* 1994, p. 52.

49. This example is discussed by David N. Burt in "Managing Suppliers Up to Speed," *Harvard Business Review*, July–August 1989, pp. 127–135.

50. The section on Granite Rock is based on "The Changemasters" by John Case, *INC.* , March 1992, pp. 58–70.

51. Cynthia A. Lengnick-Hall, "Customer Contributions to Quality: A Different View of the Customer-Oriented Firm," *Academy of Management Review*, Vol. 21, No. 3, 1996, pp. 971–824.

52. C. Gersuny and W.R. Rosengren, *The Service Society*, Cambridge, Mass.: Schenkman Press, 1973.

53. Lengnick-Hall, "Customer Contributions to Quality: A Different View of the Customer-Oriented Firm."

54. Jeffrey Pfeffer and Gerald R. Salancik, *The External Control of Organizations: A Resource Dependence Perspective*, New York: Harper & Row, 1978.

55. Ibid, pp. 257–258.

56. Pfeffer and Salancik, *The External Control of Organizations*, p. 94.

57. See, for example, David W. Johnson and Frank P. Johnson, *Joining Together: Group Theory and Group Skills*, Englewood Cliffs, N.J.: Prentice-Hall, 1975; Max H. Bazerman and Roy J. Lewicki (eds.), *Negotiating in Organizations*. Beverly Hills: Sage Publications, 1983; M. Afzalur Rahim, "A Strategy for Managing Conflict in Complex Organizations," *Human Relations*, Vol. 38, No. 1, 1985, pp. 81–89.

58. The material on Pro Fasteners is based on "Quality with Tears" by John Case, *INC.*, June 1992, pp. 82–93.

59. Lands' End Direct Merchants. Reprinted with permission.

5

Designing Organizations
for Quality

CHAPTER OUTLINE

In 1950 Deming drew the following picture on a blackboard for a handful of Japanese executives:

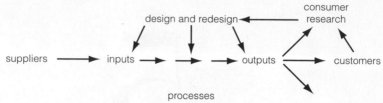

Reprinted from *Out of the Crisis* by W. Edwards Deming by permission of MIT and The W. Edwards Deming Institute. Published by MIT, Center for Advanced Educational Services, Cambridge, MA 02139. Copyright © 1986 by The W. Edwards Deming Institute.

Many people see this as simply a diagram of a typical production system that is linked to customers and suppliers. Visionaries in the practice of TQ see this as a new model of an organization chart.

Many organizations implementing total quality have found it necessary to reconfigure the structures of their organizations. This chapter discusses the changes in organization design necessary to achieve total quality. The chapter will

- describe the functional structure, the most common structure used at the plant or business unit level;
- show how many aspects of the functional structure stand in the way of quality and what changes are necessary to create organization structures that support TQ;
- provide several examples of how firms are making substantial changes in their organizations in order to implement TQ; and
- compare organizational design from a TQ point of view to more conventional perspectives.

THE FUNCTIONAL STRUCTURE

In the functional structure shown in Figure 5.1 on page 172, the organization is divided into functions such as operations and maintenance, each of which is headed by a manager. The title of these managers is often "director" in small organizations and "vice president" in larger ones. In function-oriented organizations, communication occurs vertically up or down the chain of command, rather than horizontally across functions.

Functional structures provide organizations with a clear chain of command and allow people to specialize in the aspect of the work for which they are best suited. They also make it easy to evaluate people based on a narrow but clear set of responsibilities. For these reasons, functional structures are common in both manufacturing and service organizations at plant and business unit levels.

Problems with the Functional Structure

Despite its popularity, the functional structure is designed primarily for the administrative convenience of the organization, rather than for providing high-quality service to customers. From a TQ point of view, the functional structure has several inadequacies.

FIGURE 5.1 FUNCTIONAL STRUCTURE FOR A MANUFACTURING COMPANY

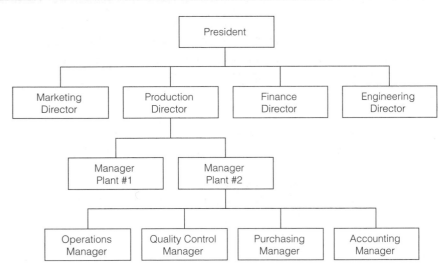

The Functional Structure Separates Employees from Customers

Few employees in the functional organization have direct contact with customers or even a clear idea of how their work combines with the work of others to satisfy customers. The functional structure tends to insulate employees from learning about customer expectations and their degree of satisfaction with the service or product the firm provides. Being insulated from customers encourages in workers a narrow conception of their responsibilities. This is often expressed in statements such as "It's not my job" or "I just work here." Even when such employees want to help customers, they often have such a limited understanding of how their organizational system works that they are unable to do so. This often results in demotivated workers and poor quality work.

Most of us have experienced this phenomenon when we call a large organization trying to get help and get switched to several different people before (if we're lucky) finding someone willing and able to help us. If our needs as customers relate to the product or service as a whole, but the knowledge and responsibilities of anyone with whom we deal relate only to their function, we are doomed to disappointment.[1]

More seriously, the functional structure promotes the idea that "the boss" is the customer the employee must satisfy. Of course, the boss trying to satisfy the next-level manager, and so on. If the chain ended at the customer, the structure might work, but this is generally not the case. Managers in functional organizations are usually rewarded for satisfying functional goals, such as meeting design deadlines and limiting manufacturing costs, rather than for providing value to customers.

Because functional organizations focus on vertical reporting relationships, many observers refer to departments in these organizations as "chimneys" or "silos." As Myron Tribus describes it, "The enterprise is viewed as a collection of separate, highly specialized individual performers and units. . . . Lateral connections are made by intermediaries close to the top of the provinces."[2]

Paul Allaire, Xerox's chairman and CEO, presided over a massive restructuring of the corporation. He describes the company's problems with the functional organization and its new approach as follows:

> We were an extremely functional organization. If you were in manufacturing, you strived to make manufacturing as good as possible—and only secondarily to make the businesses that manufacturing affected work well. The same was true for sales, R&D, or any other function. . . .
>
> We [now] want people who can hold two things in their heads at the same time, who can think in terms of their individual organizations but also in terms of the company as a whole. Our architecture won't work if people take a narrow view of their jobs and don't work together.[3]

The Functional Structure Inhibits Process Improvement

No organizational unit has control over a whole process, although most processes involve a large number of functions. This is because the breakup of the organization into functions is usually unrelated to the processes used to deliver a product to the customer. This structure is likely to create complex, wasteful processes, as people do things in one area that must be redone or undone in another.

For example, some organizations maintain a group of engineers whose sole responsibility is to redesign products so they can be manufactured effectively. The engineers who design the products in the first place worry only about product performance, not manufacturability. (For another example of problems in coordinating design and manufacturing, see the case "Barriers, What Barriers?" at the end of this chapter.) Worse yet, if one function tries to improve its part, it may well make things worse (more wasted time and effort, more cost) for another part of the process. In this environment, continuous process improvement doesn't stand a chance.

Richard Palermo, a vice president for quality and transition at Xerox, explains the problems with functional structures in terms of "Palermo's law," which states: "If a problem has been bothering your company and your customers for years and won't yield, that problem is the result of a cross-functional dispute, where nobody has total control of the whole process." The corollary to Palermo's law? "People who work in different functions hate each other."[4]

Functional Organizations Often Have a Separate Function for Quality, Called Quality Control or Quality Assurance

This may send a message to the rest of the organization that there is a group dedicated to quality, so it's not their responsibility. Furthermore, it breaks the feedback loop that informs employees that their work needs to be improved.

The QC department is generally responsible for collecting and maintaining quality statistics, which may not seem as valid to the departments actually doing the work.[5]

This arrangement obviously stands in the way of continuous process improvement. Organizations pursuing TQ often retain their quality assurance departments, but these units act more as coaches or facilitators to employees, rather than as the group with primary responsibility for quality.

In summary, the functional organization compromises total quality in several ways: It distances people from customers and insulates them from customer expectations. It promotes complex and wasteful processes and inhibits process improvement. It separates the quality function from the rest of the organization, providing people with an excuse for not worrying about quality. The next section discusses some remedies for the quality problems caused by the functional structure.

REDESIGNING ORGANIZATIONS FOR QUALITY

One of Deming's 14 points is to "break down barriers between departments" because "people in various departments must work as a team."[6] This slogan captures in a nutshell what the TQ philosophy entails for organizational design. People cannot contribute to customer satisfaction and continuous improvement if they are confined to functional prisons where they cannot see customers or hear their voices. Some of the more effective ways to break down these barriers are to focus on processes, recognize internal customers, create a team-based organization, reduce hierarchy, and use steering committees.

Focus on Processes

According to AT&T, a **process** is how work creates value for customers.[7] Common business processes include acquiring customer and market knowledge, fulfilling customer orders, purchasing, developing new products or services, strategic planning, production or service delivery, distribution, research and development, information management, performance measurement, and training, to name just a few. Processes that drive the creation of products and services, are critical to customer satisfaction, and have a large impact on the strategic goals of an organization are generally considered **core processes** of a business. **Support processes** are critical to the operation of a business but generally do not add direct value to the product or service. AT&T Consumer Communication Services, for example, defines its core processes as the network servicing process that addresses engineering, provisioning, and maintenance of the AT&T Worldwide Intelligent Network; the customer servicing process that guides customers to CCS employees for operator call completion, sales inquiries and assistance, billing inquiries, and account inquiries or billing adjustments; and the account management and billing process that manages the systems and interfaces for over 85 million customer accounts. Support processes include information and software services, human resources, public relations,

---

Chili, Spaghetti, and Cheese: It's the Process That Counts

You probably would not expect that a regional chain of small chili restaurants takes a formal view of process management, but Gold Star Chili, Inc., based in Cincinnati, Ohio, does just that. The company operates more than 100 regional locations (most of which are franchised; the remaining are company restaurants or are co-owned). The Gold Star menu is based on a unique, "Cincinnati-style" chili recipe—the basic "3 way" is a plate of spaghetti, topped with chili that is flavored with a proprietary blend of spices from around the world, followed by finely shredded cheese. (Visit the company's Web site: www.goldstarchili.com.)

Figure 5.2 shows a process-based organization of the company. Three core processes link the operation of the company to its customers and other stakeholders:

1. franchising,
2. restaurant, and
3. manufacturing/distribution.

Sustaining these core processes are various support processes, such as research and development, human resources, accounting, purchasing, operations, training, marketing, and customer satisfaction. Even restaurant operations are viewed from a process focus. Key processes such as Cash Register, Steam Table, Drive-Thru, Tables, Bussers, and Management are designed to ensure that customer needs are served in a timely manner. Prior to opening each restaurant, training sessions ensure that these processes are performed correctly and according to company standards.

---

law, regulatory, finance, marketing, and network security. A process such as order entry might be considered a core process for one company (for example, a direct mail distributor) but a support process for another (for example, a custom manufacturer). In general, core processes are driven by *external* customer needs while support processes are driven by *internal* customer needs. A process focus is not just for large companies like AT&T (see the box on Gold Star Chili).

Process management involves designing processes to develop and deliver products and services that meet the needs of customers, providing daily control so they perform as required, and continually improving the processes. Figure 5.3 (see page 180) compares a process focus to a functional focus. Nearly every major activity within a business involves some form of cross-functional cooperation. A process perspective links all parts of an organization and increases employee understanding of the entire system, rather than focusing on only a small part. In addition, it helps managers to recognize that problems arise from processes, not people.

FIGURE 5.2 GOLD STAR CHILI, INC., ORGANIZATION

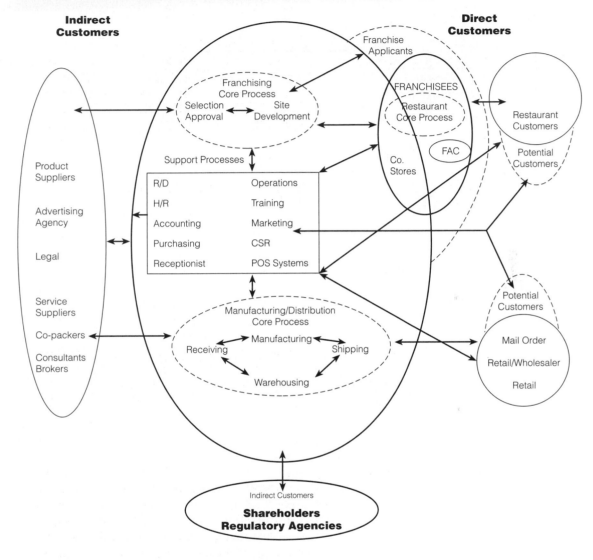

Recognize Internal Customers

One way organizations can promote quality and teamwork is to recognize the existence of "internal customers." An internal customer is another person or group within the organization who depends on one's work to get their work done. For example, machine operators in a manufacturing plant are customers of maintenance; if maintenance does not do its job well, the machines will not produce quality products (or perhaps not any products at all).

In a university, professors and students are customers of the audiovisual staff, who provide and maintain overhead projectors and VCRs. In a restaurant,

FIGURE 5.3 PROCESS VERSUS FUNCTION

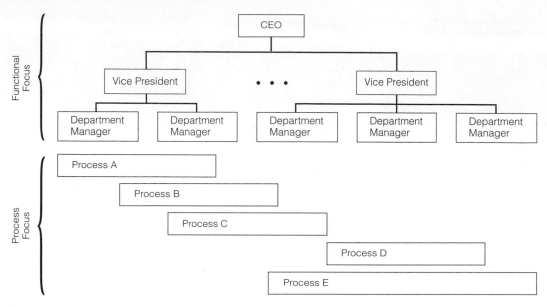

the servers are internal customers of the kitchen staff, because the servers' ability to serve appetizing food in a timely manner to customers depends on the kitchen. In Figure 5.4, product design is the internal customer of both research and development and marketing, manufacturing is the customer of product design and purchasing, and sales is the customer of manufacturing. Although not shown in the diagram, all of these departments are customers of staff groups such as human resources and finance.

Richard Schonberger, a noted consultant and writer on manufacturing and quality, has taken the internal customer idea one step further by arguing that organizations should be designed as "chains of customers." That is, customer-supplier links should be forged, one at a time, from the organization's suppliers all the way to its external (real) customers.[8] Motorola used this idea in its approach to designing and managing processes:

1. Identify the product or service: What work do I do?
2. Identify the customer: Who is the work for?
3. Identify the supplier: What do I need and from whom do I get it?
4. Identify the process: What steps or tasks are performed? What are the inputs and outputs for each step?
5. Mistake-proof the process: How can I eliminate or simplify tasks? What *poka-yoke* (mistake-proofing) devices can I use?
6. Develop measurements and controls, and improvement goals: How do I evaluate the process? How can I improve further?

FIGURE 5.4   INTERNAL CUSTOMERS IN A MANUFACTURING COMPANY

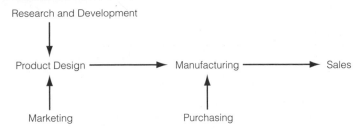

By linking customers and suppliers together at the individual level, the nature of cross-functional processes becomes clearer. Eventually, everyone can better understand their role in satisfying not only their internal customers, but also the external customers.

Promoting the idea of internal customers does not change the organization's structure so much as it changes the way people think about the structure. Rather than focusing on satisfying their immediate supervisor (vertical), people begin to think about satisfying the next person in the process (horizontal), who is one step closer to the ultimate customer. In a pizza delivery business, the people who deliver the pizzas are internal customers of the people who make them, who in turn are customers of the order-takers. Satisfying internal customers first is the best way to satisfy the external customer. An unusual customer-supplier relationship was uncovered at Oregon State University (see box on page 182).

Some managers resist the idea of internal customers, arguing that the only customers people should worry about are the ones who pay the bills. But for those employees who never come near a "real" customer, a focus on internal customers helps them to help those who do. Of course, this only works if the needs expressed by internal customers are in fact closely related to their ability to satisfy actual customers. A certain amount of trust that this is the case is necessary for the system to work.

A good example of creating links between internal customers and their suppliers is provided by an event at AMP Incorporated, a global electronic connector company. Sales engineers visited two of AMP's manufacturing plants and cooked a barbecue lunch for production workers. After lunch, the sales engineers introduced themselves, talked about their customers, and displayed some of the end products, such as power tools, into which the connectors made at the plant are placed. One production associate's reaction was, "I sometimes felt that we made millions of these parts and they simply dumped them in the ocean after we shipped them out. Now I know where most of them go."[9]

Create a Team-Based Organization

As more and more companies accept the process view of organizations, they are structuring the quality organization around functional or cross-functional

Where's the Paperwork? Quality Improvement at Oregon State[10]

Oregon State University was among the first universities to embrace TQ. In 1990, faced with state budget cuts and trying to improve the quality of its operation, Oregon State began the process of quality improvement. Like many schools, it focused first on improving administrative areas.

The physical plant was among the first areas singled out for quality improvement. Specifically, the group that did repair and remodeling at the university tackled the time it took to complete a work order, which its internal customers identified as the number one problem with the service they were receiving. When the group began to address the problem, they found that the average time to complete a job was 195 days, just over six months.

None of people who actually did the work could believe the entire process took so long, since individually each knew that their work lasted only a few days or weeks. In attempting to understand why it took so long, the group set up a flowchart of the process they used in their work.

They discovered that a woman in another group received their work orders first, and it took 10 days for the paperwork to make its way to the repair and remodeling group. Group members approached the woman and asked what she did with the paperwork during the time she kept it. She did her job and she did it well, exactly as she had been instructed, she told them. What exactly had she been told to do? When the paperwork arrives, put it aside and after 10 days, send it on to the repair and remodeling group!

As it turned out, there had been a time when the group had had trouble getting the material delivered for their jobs. Having no success in expediting the flow of material, they simply slowed down the flow of paperwork, so they would have a head start on the job when the paperwork arrived. Eventually the problems with material delivery were resolved, but no one had remembered to undo the 10-day waiting period. Since the paperwork was held by another functional group, no one in repair and remodeling had a broad enough view of the process to see what was going on.

Sometimes process improvement is hard work. But in this case the repair and remodeling group could get off to a fast start by immediately knocking 10 days off their time!

teams, each of which has the responsibility to carry out and improve one of the organization's core processes.[11] Mark Kelly provides an example of an organizational structure based on teams in *The Adventures of a Self-Managing Team*.[12] The building blocks of the Clear Lake Plant organization are process-based teams. Tasks that transcend processes (such as innovation and safety) are handled in task teams made up of members drawn from each of the process teams. This organization is depicted in Figure 5.5. (Compare this to the functional organization in Figure 5.1 to get an idea of the size of the changes we are talking about.)

FIGURE 5.5   ORGANIZATIONAL STRUCTURE OF THE CLEAR LAKE PLANT

Other team-based organizations revolve around customers, as shown in Figure 5.6. Another example is that of GTE Directories, shown in Figure 5.7. In this organizational structure, the management board leads the quality effort, meeting twice each month to discuss and review management and quality issues. Quality is implemented through various teams: core business process team, cross-functional coordinating committee, regional management councils, major business process management teams (PMTs), Malcolm Baldrige National Quality Award (MBNQA) teams, and quality improvement teams. The regional management councils identify and address key regional issues; the cross-functional coordinating committee reviews major proposals for consistency with the strategic plan and business priorities. Such team-based organization structures spread the ownership, and the accountability, for quality throughout the organization. The "quality department" serves as an internal consulting group, providing advice, training, and organizational development to the teams. Clearly, each organization needs to create a structure that meets its unique needs.

Depending on the size of the organization and the nature of the processes, teams may include everyone who contributes to a given process or only a representative subset. Similarly, the teams may meet continuously on a crash basis until their new process design is complete, after which they may meet periodically or on an ad hoc basis. For example, Solectron Corporation, a two-time Baldrige recipient, has a customer focus team for each customer that includes personnel from quality, manufacturing management, project engineering, sales, production control, test engineering, and a project buyer and program manager.

This approach eliminates many of the problems with the functional structure. By bringing together everyone associated with a process, practices that are wasteful or compromise quality become much easier to identify and eliminate. If a team has responsibility for an entire process, they don't have to worry that

FIGURE 5.6 TEAM-BASED ORGANIZATIONAL CHART

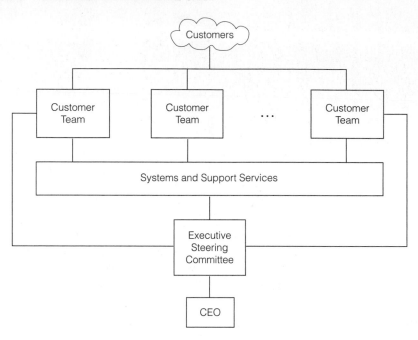

their improvement efforts will be undermined—intentionally or unintentionally—by the actions of another group.

Using processes as a grouping method can create substantial improvement in organizations by allowing people to see and change procedures they couldn't see or change in the functional structure. As Robert Brookhouse, mem-

FIGURE 5.7 GTE DIRECTORIES MANAGEMENT STRUCTURE

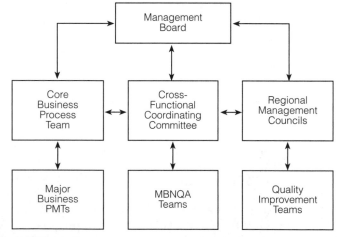

Courtesy of GTE Directories Corporation.

ber of a process organization at Xerox, puts it, "When you create a flow [Xerox's term for process organization], you find where you're wasting time, doing things twice. And because we own the entire process, we can change it."[13]

This is not to suggest that changing to a process-based organization is simple or easy. On the contrary, it takes a lot of thought, because it means essentially taking the organization apart and putting it back together again. As Robert Knorr and Edward Thiede describe it:

> The restructuring should begin by defining each process in terms of its operations, information, and skill needs. . . . Process definition also answers key questions about the lines of integration needed among processes and functions, such as who must interact and when? What changes are needed in upstream processes to accommodate the needs of those downstream, and vice versa?[14]

Reduce Hierarchy

A third type of structural change that often results from a focus on internal customers and the creation of process teams is a reduction in the number of hierarchical layers in the organization. Several levels of middle management are often eliminated. (Of course, if an organization is designed for quality from its inception, those levels are not there in the first place.) This reduction in middle management is also facilitated by advances in information systems that have taken over many of the information summarization and transmission roles formerly played by middle managers.

When organizations eliminate non-value-added activities and empower frontline workers to improve processes, managers have less supervision and coordination to do. An additional benefit of such "flatter" organizations is improved communication between top managers and frontline employees.

This is not to say that flattening organizational structures is without its drawbacks. People—sometimes many people—lose their jobs. This is not only a significant disruption in the lives of the individuals and communities affected, but also a loss of their experience to the organization. Furthermore, the morale of the people who remain in the organization may suffer. For all of these reasons, organizations should approach flattening with an attitude of caution and concern.

Use Steering Committees

A fourth type of structural change associated with TQ is the creation of a high-level planning group responsible for guiding the organization's quality efforts. Such *steering committees*, *quality councils*, or *quality improvement teams* are a key part of many firms' quality improvement efforts and an important part of the quality recommendations of both Juran and Crosby.

According to Juran, the role of the quality council is to "launch, coordinate, and institutionalize annual quality improvement."[15] In the Crosby system, the

FIGURE 5.8   CUSTOM RESEARCH INC. LEADERSHIP SYSTEM

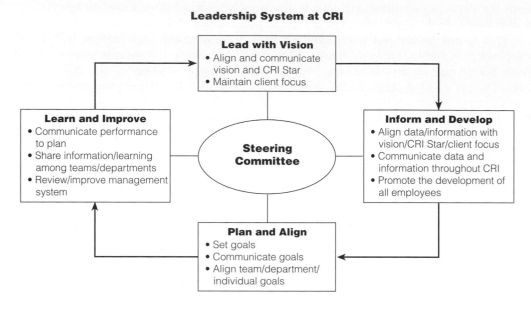

quality improvement team (QIT) sets annual quality objectives for the organization. In general, steering committees act as a focal point for quality in the organization. Such groups provide a means of demonstrating and increasing the organization's commitment to quality, as well as a mechanism for coordinating the efforts of various organizational units.

At Custom Research Inc., for example, a four-person steering committee is the center of the leadership system (see Figure 5.8). The steering committee sets the company directions, integrates performance excellence goals, and promotes the development of all employees, all revolving around a 5-pointed "CRI Star"—a logo that emphasizes the role of people, processes, requirements, relationships, and results in achieving "surprise and delight" for customers. Steering committee members interact with associates frequently and review overall company performance daily. They meet formally each month to evaluate performance and identify areas for improvement.

The AT&T Network Operations Group has several quality councils: an executive quality council, vice president quality councils, director quality councils, and division/district manager quality councils, all of which are networked together. Quality councils assume many responsibilities, such as incorporating total quality principles into the company's strategic planning process and coordinating the overall effort. At AT&T, the quality council is characterized by four essential elements:[16]

- *Leadership:* promoting and articulating the quality vision, communicating responsibilities and expectations for management action, aligning the business management process with the quality approach, maintaining high visibility for commitment and involvement, and ensuring that businesswide support is available in the form of education, consulting, methods, and tools.

- *Planning:* planning strategic quality goals, understanding basic customer needs and business capabilities, developing long-term goals and near-term priorities, formulating human resource goals and policies, understanding employees' perceptions about quality and work, ensuring that all employees have the opportunity and skills to participate, and aligning reward and recognition systems to support the quality approach.
- *Implementation:* forming key business process teams, chartering teams to manage and improve these processes, reviewing improvement plans, providing resources for improvement, enlisting all managers in the process, reviewing quality plans of major organizational units, and working with suppliers and business partners in joint quality planning.
- *Review:* tracking progress through customer satisfaction and internal measures of quality, monitoring progress in attaining improvement objectives, celebrating successes, improving the quality system through auditing and identifying improvement opportunities, planning improvements, and validating the impact of improvements.

Although many firms use only top managers in such groups, Portman Equipment Company—an industrial equipment sales, service, and rental company—uses people from all types of jobs. Richard Buck, Portman's vice president for quality, argues that the presence of frontline associates in the committee has made a big difference in the decisions the group has made:

> We have general managers, we have some supervisory people, and we have some hourly people. It was our decision in forming a steering committee to break precedence from every company we've studied that used only executives on the steering committee. We opted to break that pattern and listen to the voices of all of our people as we formulate our plans. I think it's one of the better decisions we've made. And looking back on decisions we have made in the steering committee, I think there's good evidence that some of our decisions would not have been the same if we did not have representation from hourly people. I think as managers we tend to learn to think the way managers think, . . . having hourly people gives us a different perspective. We see a broader picture and it's been good for our quality initiative.[17]

ORGANIZATIONAL DESIGN FOR QUALITY IN ACTION

Promoting the concept of internal customers, forming process teams, reducing hierarchy, and creating steering committees all facilitate quality. This section presents examples of organizations that use these ideas to ensure or improve quality in their operations. One example is from Puerto Rico, another from Japan, and a third from California.

General Electric Bayamón

Located near San Juan, Puerto Rico, GE Bayamón produces surge protectors that keep power stations and electric lines from being zapped by lightning. Bayamón is the newest high-performance workplace designed by Philip Jarrosiak, human resources manager for capacitor and power protection operations at GE.[18]

Bayamón's approximately 190 employees are structured into three levels: the plant manager, 15 "advisers," and the hourly workers. According to Jarrosiak, a traditionally structured plant would have twice as many managers. The hourly workers are divided into teams of about 10 people, each of which has responsibility for a process such as shipping and receiving. Team members represent all parts of a process, so that team decisions take into consideration a wide variety of views and needs. The advisers act as resources for the teams, becoming active only when a team needs help.

To prepare them for such extensive responsibility, workers at Bayamón are given a great deal of training in such areas as machine maintenance, quality control, business practices, and English. The more workers learn, the more they are paid. Workers rotate through the plant's four work areas every six months, so they bring a broad vision of how the factory operates to their teams.

The design for quality at Bayamón seems to be paying off. In just one year, the plant exceeded the productivity of similar plants by 20 percent, and its productivity continues to increase.

Toyota

Far to the east, many Japanese companies are organized in accordance with *kaizen*, the philosophy of continuous improvement.[19] Underlying kaizen is the belief that a great number of small improvements over time will create substantial improvement in organizational performance.

Although Japanese organizations practicing kaizen often maintain their functional structure, they superimpose on it a cross-functional management structure charged with continuous improvement of quality, cost, and ability to meet schedules (Figure 5.9). Each year top management articulates goals for improvements of cross-functional activities, which the kaizen management structure is designed to attain. Recently such efforts have been broadened in some Japanese organizations to include employee morale.

The relationships among competitive success, cross-functional goals such as quality, and the line organization are explained by Shigeru Aoki, senior managing director at Toyota:

> The ultimate goal of a company is to make profits. Assuming this is self-evident, then the next "superordinate" goals of the company should be such cross-functional goals as quality, cost, and scheduling (quantity and delivery). Without achieving these goals, the company will be left behind by the competition because of inferior quality, will find its profits eroded by higher costs, and will be unable to deliver the

FIGURE 5.9 KAIZEN ORGANIZATIONAL STRUCTURE

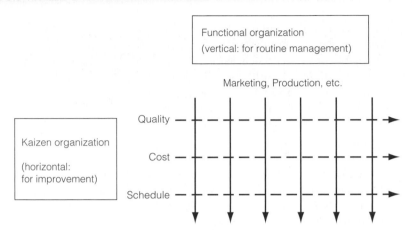

products in time for customers. If these cross-functional goals are realized, profits will follow. Therefore, we should regard all the other management functions as existing to serve the three superordinate goals. . . . These auxiliary management functions include product planning, design, production, purchasing, and marketing, and they should be regarded as secondary means to achieve QCS [quality, cost, and scheduling].[20]

The committees that devise cross-functional goals at Toyota are composed of heads of departments concerned with a particular goal. The director of quality assurance, for example, heads the cross-functional quality committee. The heads of design and manufacturing also play leading roles in this committee, because their departments are expected to play leading roles in achieving quality goals. It then becomes the job of each function to work toward achieving the goals that the committee has established. In this manner, Toyota and other Japanese companies with similar structures retain the advantages of the functional structure while orienting managers and other associates toward customer-focused, cross-functional goals such as high quality.

The San Diego Zoo[21]

With $75 million in revenues, 1,200 employees, and 5 million visitors annually, the Zoological Society of San Diego (a.k.a. the San Diego Zoo) is a force to be reckoned with in the animal world. Even during the recession of the early '90s, the zoo (and its Wild Animal Park) managed to increase attendance. Its overall objectives include recreation, education, and conservation.

One of the reasons for the zoo's success may be its reorganization. In the old system, the animals were organized by species (*phascolarctos cinereus*) and the humans by functions (*homo sapiensbeancounterus*). In fact, the humans were divided into 50 different departments, each of which played a role in the care and feeding of either animals, customers, or both. This led to a somewhat sterile and unrealistic environment for everyone involved. For example, a groundskeeper confessed to occasionally sweeping a cigarette butt from the path under a bush, so it would become the gardener's responsibility instead of his own. In the new organization, the animals are grouped into bioclimatic zones that mirror their natural habitats. Gorilla Tropics groups the animals normally found in an African rain forest, while Tiger River recreates the environment of a jungle in Asia.

The humans haven't been forgotten in the new zoo design. They are now organized into teams, each of which has responsibility for one of the bioclimatic zones. The team that runs Tiger River includes specialists in mammals and birds, as well as maintenance and construction personnel. Although turf was jealously guarded in the old organization, team members are now learning one another's skills and cooperate in making improvements that transcend the old functional boundaries. As the teams have taken over responsibility for activities that were previously the prerogatives of management, managers have been freed up to find ways to bring more people to the zoo. (As in any organization with a high level of fixed costs, maintaining a consistently high level of revenues is crucial to its survival.)

COMPARISON TO ORGANIZATIONAL DESIGN THEORY

This section compares the total quality view of organizational design with the viewpoint from organization theory. Topics discussed are structural contingency theory and the institutional theory of organization structure.

Structural Contingency Theory

The structural contingency model, which originated in the 1960s, is the dominant view of organizational design in the management literature. According to this view, the two principal types of organization structure are mechanistic (centralized, many rules, strict division of labor, formal coordination across departments) and organic (decentralized, few rules, loose division of labor, informal coordination across departments).[22] These structures are described in detail in most management and organizational theory textbooks. The structural contingency model holds that there is no "one best way" to organize and that the choice between mechanistic and organic structures should be a function of certain contingencies, most often characteristics of the organization's environment and technology.

The choice between mechanistic and organic structures is usually seen as a function of uncertainty. Organizations face a great deal of uncertainty if their environments are complex and changing and if the technology they use in creating their products is not well understood. The microcomputer industry is a good example of this type of industry. The contingency model says that organizations facing uncertainty should adopt an organic structure. On the other hand, organizations that experience little uncertainty—their environments are simple and stable, and their technology is well understood—are seen as needing a mechanistic structure.

The rationale for these recommendations is that organic organizations are better able to process the information necessary to deal with a complex environment and uncertain technology. They are also more flexible and can adapt to the changing circumstances associated with an unstable environment. However, this information processing and adaptive capacity comes at the expense of efficiency and control. Although mechanistic organizations may not be able to accomplish uncertain tasks or to change rapidly, they are better suited for accomplishing straightforward tasks in a predictable environment. The mechanistic organization will accomplish such tasks quite reliably, with little danger of employees engaging in costly experiments to see if there is a better way to do the job. The organic organization sacrifices reliability for flexibility.

Clearly a quality-oriented organization practicing continuous improvement cannot afford to freeze its processes by using a mechanistic structure. Most organizations practicing total quality move in the direction of organic structures. The number of levels in their hierarchy decreases, teams are created, and employees are given the authority (and even the responsibility) to develop new and better ways of accomplishing their tasks.

Coordination also tends toward the informal, as people who are interdependent are able to coordinate their work on a personal basis without the interference of a bureaucratic hierarchy. The relatively broader jobs in a TQ company give employees a better sense of how their work contributes to customer satisfaction, whether their customers are internal or external.

John Akers, former CEO of IBM who presided over a substantial reorganization of his company, stated that "Every reorganization solves some problems and creates some problems."[23] Are problems created by the adoption of organic type TQ organizational designs? It is too early to tell. Few organizations are more than a few years into TQ, so there is not enough of a track record on which to judge. Even fewer, however, have reverted from a TQ-type design to a more mechanistic design, and more organizations all the time are adopting a design that features internal customers, process teams, broad employee responsibilities, and quality steering committees. This indicates that such structures are seen as viable and necessary by an increasing number of managers and organizations.

How can the "one best way" approach of the quality movement be justified in light of organization theory's historical endorsement of a contingency approach to design? It may be that few industries and technologies are simple and stable enough for a mechanistic design to operate effectively. A second possibility is that TQ designs have capacities for producing efficiencies unanticipated in the old mechanistic-organic distinction. Once the improvement of a particular process has reached the point where it is impractical to search for further gains, teams may establish the process as their standard and attempt to recreate it perfectly each time without the involvement of their managers. In other words, efficiencies would be created through different methods than those used in mechanistic firms.

A third possibility is that TQ-oriented firms pay a price in efficiency for their organizational structures, but that the superior quality of their products more than makes up for the higher prices that a lack of efficiency entails. Such firms would be unlikely to compete effectively in markets, such as textiles, where price is the overriding competitive factor.

A final possibility is that firms structured to achieve quality are paying a price for inefficiency that is not offset by their advantages. In this case such structures are not viable in the long run. This possibility does not seem to be the case, based on the limited information currently available.

Institutional Theory

Structural contingency theory, like most organizational design theories, is based on the assumption that organizations choose structures to help them perform better—provide high quality, low costs, and so forth. Institutional theory, on the other hand, holds that organizations try to succeed by creating structures that will be seen as appropriate by important external constituencies—customers, other organizations in the industry, government agencies, and so on.[24]

According to institutional theory, an aspect of organizational structure need not contribute to organizational performance to be worthwhile. If the adoption of a certain structure helps the organization to be seen as legitimate in the eyes of those who have power to determine the organization's fate, then it is worthwhile. For example, many businesses have departments devoted to achieving environmental goals. Whether these departments help achieve these goals is debatable, but the existence of such departments helps to promote the legitimacy of these organizations as being concerned about the environment.

From an institutional theory standpoint, it is important to ask whether quality-oriented organization designs that include steering committees and extensive use of teams are actually intended to promote quality or are merely a means of legitimizing the organization as a progressive, quality-conscious organization. Little evidence has been generated to suggest that such structures demonstrably improve performance, yet they continue to be adopted in huge numbers by organizations in all sectors of the economy.

In some settings, the adoption of quality-oriented structures is motivated primarily by institution concerns. For example, any company that wishes to compete in Europe must be certified as complying with the ISO 9000 quality standards. Suppliers to American automobile producers must also have elaborate quality programs in place. To continue to receive accreditation, hospitals in the United States must show progress in implementing continuous quality improvement (CQI).

Thus, institutional theory provides another way of thinking about the rapid proliferation of quality-oriented structures in organizations. Although some organizations may be primarily seeking higher performance through the adoption of teams and steering committees, others may be primarily seeking the approval of important constituencies.

SUMMARY

Problems with the functional structure, such as overly complex processes and a narrow focus for individuals, have led many quality-oriented organizations to abandon this structure. New structures feature internal customers, process teams, less hierarchy, and quality steering committees. Although the widespread use of quality-oriented organic structures may be inconsistent with structural contingency theory, more companies are restructuring their organizations for quality. Some companies are adopting quality-oriented structures to appear legitimate in the eyes of important groups in their industry.

REVIEW AND DISCUSSION QUESTIONS

1. What are the advantages and disadvantages of the functional structure? How does a process focus overcome some of the disadvantages?
2. What are the major types of structural change exhibited by organizations pursuing total quality?
3. Think back to an experience you have had with poor customer service from an organization. Whom did you blame for it? Do you know anything about the design of the organization involved? Do you think it was the fault of the individual(s) involved or could the problem have resulted from a poorly designed system? Would what you have learned in this chapter change your reaction to receiving poor quality service? How?
4. What are the core processes in a restaurant? a video rental store? a department store? How could these organizations be redesigned around these processes? What barriers would need to be overcome to accomplish this?
5. Find an organizational chart for your college or university. Is it primarily functional or process focused? What advantages or problems do you see with this organizational structure?
6. How does the organizational structure of Gold Star Chili reflect Deming's view of a production system?
7. Explain how a focus on internal customers and a team-based organization supports the process view of organizations.
8. Richard Palermo of Xerox was quoted in *Fortune* as saying that "people in different functions hate each other." Allowing for some exaggeration due to dramatic license, do you find this to be true? Talk to several people in a functional organization, and ask them about their feelings for people in other functions. How would you explain the variation in attitudes? If you were assigned to try to solve the problem of bad feelings between departments, how would you begin?

9. Could total quality be effective in a company with a mechanistic structure? How would it work?
10. Do you feel that the institutional theory of structure is a good description of why organizations choose quality-oriented organization designs? Why or why not?

 CASES

Barriers? What Barriers?

The general manager of an elevator company had a common problem: He was utterly frustrated with the lack of cooperation between the mechanical engineers who designed new elevators and the manufacturing engineers who determined how to produce them in the factory. The mechanical engineers would often completely design a new elevator without any consultation from the manufacturing engineers and then expect the factory to somehow figure out how to build it. (This is known as "throwing it over the wall" to manufacturing.)

Often the new products were difficult or nearly impossible to build, and their quality and cost suffered as a result. The designs were usually sent back to the mechanical engineers (often more than once) for engineering changes to improve their manufacturability. While design and manufacturing played volleyball with the design, customers were forced to wait—often for months—for deliveries.

The general manager knew that if the two sets of engineers would simply communicate early in the design process, many of these problems could be eliminated before they occurred. At his wits' end, he found a large empty room in the facility and had the mechanical and manufacturing engineers working on the next product moved into the room, one group on one side and one on the other. Certainly if all they had to do to communicate was to walk from one side of the room to the other, communication would improve.

The manager relaxed somewhat, feeling that his problem had finally been solved. Upon returning to the new home of the engineers a few weeks later, he was in for a big surprise. The two sets of engineers had finally learned to cooperate! They had cooperated in building a wall of bookcases and file cabinets right down the middle of the room, effectively separating the large room into two separate offices, so they could continue as before.

Discussion Questions

1. What principles of total quality are illustrated or violated in this case?
2. Why do people feel such strong allegiance to their functional departments?
3. What could the general manager have done to improve the communication and the quality of the designs?

The British Post Office

The post office in Britain has undertaken a restructuring to improve the quality of service it provides.[25] Under the old organization, delivery of the mail and counter services were both handled through functional departments. At the local level, it was found that head postmasters were giving a great deal more attention to delivery, given its day-to-day urgency, than to counter service.

Upon reorganization, three new divisions were created: Royal Mail Letters, Royal Mail Parcels, and Post Office Counters, Ltd. By undertaking a focused set of customers and processes, each of these organizations has been able to reduce overhead and shorten the chain of command. In addition, responsibility for decision making has been placed much closer to the customer, and customers of each of the various post office services have an organization specifically charged with responding to their needs.

The corporate functional departments that remain, such as information technology, charge the divisions for their work. Periodic checks are made to ensure that the quality and costs of their service are comparable to what could be obtained outside the organization. Eventually these departments are expected to become full-fledged profit centers, so that the divisions are not burdened with subpar in-house suppliers.

Discussion Questions

1. Should the application of total quality be any different in a government agency than in a private organization?
2. What internal customer relationships have been created in the new organization?
3. Do you feel that the new organization will promote improved quality?

Legal Sea Foods

Legal Sea Foods operates several restaurants and fish markets in the Boston area. Their standards of excellence mandate that they serve only the freshest, highest-quality seafood. They guarantee the quality by buying only the "top of the catch" fish daily. Although Legal Sea Foods tries to make available the widest variety every day, certain species of fish are subject to migratory patterns and are not always present in New England waters. Weather conditions may also prevent local fishermen from fishing in certain areas.

Freshly caught fish are rushed to the company's quality control center where they are cut and filleted in an environmentally controlled state-of-the-art facility. All shellfish comes from government certified beds and are tested in an in-house microbiology laboratory for wholesomeness and purity. They even have special lobster storage tanks so that all lobsters are held under optimum conditions in clean, pollution-free water. Every seafood item is inspected for quality eight separate times before it reaches the table.

At Legal Sea Foods' restaurants, every meal is cooked to order. While servers make every effort to deliver all meals within minutes of each other, they will not jeopardize the quality of an item by holding it beneath a heat lamp until the entire order is ready. The service staff is trained to work as a team for better service. More than one service person frequently delivers food to a table. When any item is ready, the closest available person serves it. Customer questions can be directed to any employee, not just the person who took the initial order.

Discussion Questions

1. What are the major processes performed by Legal Sea Foods?
2. How does a process focus and the company's organizational design support their goal of serving only the freshest, highest-quality seafood?

ENDNOTES

1. An interesting perspective on this problem is provided by Benson P. Shapiro, V. Kasturi Rangan, and John J. Sviokla in "Staple Yourself to an Order," *Harvard Business Review*, July–August 1992, pp. 113–122.

2. Myron Tribus, "Total Quality in Education," unpublished manuscript, Hayward, Calif.: Exergy, Inc.

3. Quoted from "The CEO as Organizational Architect: An Interview with Xerox's Paul Allaire" by Robert Howard, in *Harvard Business Review*, September–October 1992, pp. l06–121.

4. Thomas A. Stewart, "The Search for the Organization of Tomorrow," *Fortune*, May 18, 1992.

5. J.M. Juran, *Juran on Leadership for Quality: An Executive Handbook.* New York: The Free Press, 1989.

6. W.E. Deming, *Out of the Crisis.* Cambridge, Mass.: MIT, Center for Advanced Educational Services, 1986.

7. *AT&T's Total Quality Approach*, AT&T Corporate Quality Office, 1992, p. 6.

8. R.J. Schonberger, *Building a Chain of Customers.* New York: The Free Press, 1990.

9. Jerry G. Bowles, "Leading the World-Class Company," *Fortune*, September 21, 1992.

10. Based on "TQM—Quality with Reduced Resources," a talk given by Dr. Edwin Coate, vice president for finance and administration, Oregon State University, presented via teleconference by Cuyahoga Community College, September 9, 1992.

11. Jeannie Coyle, "Aligning Human Resource Processes with Total Quality," *Employment Relations Today*, Vol. 18, No. 3, Fall 1991.

12. Mark Kelly, *The Adventures of a Self-Managing Team*, Raleigh, N.C.: Mark Kelly Books, 1990.

13. Stewart, "The Search for the Organization of Tomorrow."

14. Robert O. Knorr and Edward F. Thiede, Jr., "Making New Technologies Work," *Journal of Business Strategy*, Vol. 12, No. 1, pp. 46–49.

15. Juran, *Juran on Leadership for Quality*.

16. AT&T Quality Steering Committee, *Leading the Quality Initiative*, AT&T Bell Laboratories, 1990, pp. 13–14.

17. Interview with Richard Buck.

18. Based on Stewart, "The Search for the Organization of Tomorrow."

19. M. Imai, *Kaizen: The Key to Japan's Competitive Success*, New York: McGraw Hill, 1986.

20. Imai, *Kaizen*, p.128.

21. Based on Stewart, "The Search for the Organization of Tomorrow."

22. This version of the contingency model comes from T. Burns and G.M. Stalker, *The Management of Innovation.* London: Tavistock, 1961.

23. Quoted in D. Hellriegel, J.W. Slocum, and R.W. Woodman, *Organizational Behavior*, 5th ed., St. Paul, Minn.: West Publishing Company.

24. See J.W. Meyer and B. Rowan, "Institutionalized Organizations: Formal Structure as Myth and Ceremony," *American Journal of Sociology*, Vol. 83, 1977, pp. 340–363, or W.R. Scott, "The Adolescence of Institutional Theory," *Administrative Science Quarterly*, Vol. 32, 1987, pp. 493–511.

25. Based on R.M. Tabor, "Planning for Postal Services," *Long Range Planning*, Vol. 23, No. 5, 1990, pp. 91–96.

6

Total Quality and Organizational Change

CHAPTER OUTLINE

Psychologists suggest that individuals go through four stages of learning:

1.   Unconscious incompetence: You don't know that you don't know.
2.   Conscious incompetence: You realize that you don't know.

3. Conscious competence: You learn to do, but with conscious effort.
4. Unconscious competence: Performance comes effortlessly.

Many companies in the United States languished in stage 1 until receiving a wake-up call in the 1980s with regard to quality. Unfortunately, as many organizations move into stage 2, they tend to shoot the messenger and refuse to accept the state of incompetence. To move from stage 2 to stage 3, organizations must change. Lewis Lehr, former CEO of 3M Corporation, once observed, "Our successes of the past are no guarantee of the future. Perhaps our biggest need at 3M is for people who are uncomfortable without change."[1]

Organizational change is fundamental to total quality; indeed, there can be no quality without it. Anyone concerned with managing an organization dedicated to quality must understand what types of change are necessary in such an organization and how to manage them. This chapter explores cultural change, continuous improvement, and reengineering—the most important types of organizational change necessitated by TQ. Quality-related change in organization structure and employee responsibilities are discussed in other chapters. This chapter will

- explain the importance of organizational change to TQ,
- identify the types of changes necessary for quality,
- provide examples of firms undertaking these changes, and
- explain how the TQ perspective on organizational change relates to organization theory.

THE IMPORTANCE OF CHANGE

For organizations committed to pursuing total quality, change is a way of life. Organizational change is needed in implementing TQ and constantly thereafter. In the initial stage, an effort must be mounted to begin to change the culture of the organization. Unless the organization establishes a culture based on customer satisfaction, continuous improvement, and teamwork, TQ will be little more than "just another one of management's programs." Indeed, this is often the cause of failure of TQ initiatives.

Once TQ is under way in an organization, continuous improvement efforts will relentlessly create changes in product designs, standard operating procedures, and virtually every other aspect of the organization. One important aspect of continuous improvement is reengineering, in which the organization reexamines and redesigns its operating processes to provide higher quality at lower cost.

Why are these changes necessary? The major reason is that customer expectations continuously evolve. Features or services that delight customers one year may be taken for granted the next, and products that customers find acceptable one year may be perceived as substandard the next. Competition continues to raise the standard for quality, and organizations must keep up. (See the box "Quality Never Goes Out of Style.")

Quality Never Goes Out of Style[2]

In 1853 a young German immigrant named Strauss took a 17,000-mile trip on a clipper ship from New York around South America to San Francisco. He intended to set up shop selling dry goods to people lured to California by the gold rush. By the time he reached San Francisco, however, he had sold all the goods he brought except for some canvas for tents.

The miners told him he should have brought pants instead of canvas to sell, because most pants fell apart too quickly while they dug for gold. The enterprising young Strauss immediately took the heavy brown canvas to a tailor and created the world's first pair of jeans. Those "pants of Levi's" (Strauss's first name) were so popular that he quickly sold all of his canvas and switched to a heavy serge fabric made in Nimes, France ("serge de Nimes," eventually shortened to "denim"). When the new fabric was treated with indigo dye, it attained its familiar deep blue cover.

Levi never liked the term "jeans" so he called his pants "waist-high overalls." In fact, his company did not use the term—derived from the French word "genes" for a type of cotton trousers—until long after his death.

Levi noticed that miners often complained that the weight of gold nuggets was causing their pockets to tear. Always looking for ways to improve the quality of his pants, Levi and tailor Jacob Davis patented in 1873 the innovation of riveting pocket corners to add strength. By the 1930s, Levi's were worn by everyone from cowboys to school children. The rivets, much appreciated by miners, caused the company problems with other customers, which they quickly addressed. In 1937, the company covered the rivets on the rear pockets in response to complaints that they scratched both saddles and school desks. The rivet at the base of the fly was removed by executive order after company president Walter Haas crouched a little too close to a roaring campfire for a little too long and discovered what the cowboys had been complaining about.

The popularity of Levi's jeans surged again in the 1950s when actor James Dean (unfortunately no relation to the author) wore them in the movie *Rebel Without a Cause*. Today, Levi's jeans are sold in more than 70 nations. The company says that they are made with "the choicest fabric, the strongest thread, first-class buttons, rivets, and snaps, precise sewing and careful inspection." The jeans carry a "Levi's promise" card guaranteeing customer satisfaction. With this history of continuous improvement in response to customer needs, it's no wonder that, as the company's slogan puts it, "quality never goes out of style." Nevertheless, quality may face stiff competition, as Levi's has encountered recently from designer jean manufacturers and the Gap.

When *USA Today* was first published, its use of color and graphics was exceptional. In short order, however, newspapers copied these features so widely that exclusive use of black and white on the front page began to look old-fashioned. Any organization that focuses on meeting a fixed set of quality goals will quickly find itself trampled into the dust by competitors racing to keep up with customers. As one Xerox executive stated, "Quality is a race without a finish line."

Change is also required because processes tend to become unnecessarily complicated over a period of time, even when they are initially designed in a sensible manner. Each new person working on a process adds a wrinkle or two until, eventually, a monster has been created.

CULTURAL CHANGE

Culture is the set of beliefs and values shared by the people in an organization. It is what binds them together and helps them make sense of what happens in their company (see the box "The Eastman Way"). Cultures can vary dramatically between one company and another. In some firms, raw ambition is taken for granted, while in others subordination of one's own agenda to the good of the organization is expected. Some companies create a status hierarchy reminiscent of the court of Louis XIV, while others downplay status differences.

Culture is a powerful influence on people's behavior; not very long ago most employees at IBM would never wear anything other than a white shirt, while most people at Apple Computer wouldn't be caught dead in one. Culture has such power because it is shared widely within an organization and because it operates without being talked about, indeed, often without even being thought of.

Organizations are in some ways like a circle of high school friends who share strong beliefs about which activities, people, and music are okay and which are not. A new employee who did something that violated the culture might be told, "That's just not how we do things around here." The employee could be forgiven both for the error and for being perplexed at what was wrong, because the rules of culture are often not written down and must be deciphered.

Despite its intangibility, one can learn about an organization's culture in a number of ways. How people dress and how they address one another provide clues. The layout of offices, plant floors, and lounges may also reveal what is important in the organization. For example, do managers but not employees have reserved parking spots? Do offices have doors? Are there any private offices? Culture is expressed in the stories and jokes people tell, in how they spend their time at work, in what they display in their offices, and in a thousand other large and small ways. Culture is also reflected by the management policies and actions that a company practices. Therefore, organizations that believe in the principles of total quality are more likely to successfully implement the practices. Conversely, actions set culture in motion. Behavior leads people to think in certain ways. Thus, as total quality practices are used routinely within an organization, its people learn to believe in the principles, and cultural changes can occur.

From this description, it should be clear why firms deciding to pursue total quality need cultural change. If the TQ effort is inconsistent with the organizational culture, it will be undermined. For example, employees in a company in

The Eastman Way[3]

Eastman Chemical Company recognizes that people create quality; this is embodied in a philosophy known as the Eastman Way. The Eastman Way describes a culture based on key beliefs and principles of respect, cooperation, fairness, trust, and teamwork. Developing such a culture depends not only on learning how to recognize and reward behavior, but also understanding the processes and procedures that work against achieving corporate goals.

The wake-up call came in the late 1970s when a key customer told the company that their product was not as good as their competitor's and indicated that if things did not change, Eastman would lose business. Eastman's first realization was that customer feedback was essential to survival. In 1983, the company developed a quality policy and soon after began training in statistical process control, flow-charting, and other basic tools. Production employees were encouraged to post their quality results, both good and bad. As one employee stated, "You are asking all of us to post all of our mistakes. How will these things be used?" This clash between the traditional hierarchical, disciplinary organizational culture and the open, honest and trusting environment demanded by TQ led to the Eastman Way, which is as follows:[4]

Eastman people are the key to success. We have recognized throughout our history the importance of treating each other fairly and with respect. We will enhance these beliefs by building upon the following values and principles:

Honesty and integrity. We are honest with ourselves and others. Our integrity is exhibited through relationships with co-workers, customers, suppliers, and neighbors. Our goal is truth in all relationships.

Fairness. We treat each other as we expect to be treated.

Trust. We respect and rely on each other. Fair treatment, honesty in our relationships, and confidence in each other create trust.

Teamwork. We are empowered to manage our areas of responsibility. We work together to achieve common goals for business success. Full participation, cooperation, and open communication lead to superior results.

Diversity. We value different points of view. Men and women from different races, cultures, and backgrounds enrich the generation and usefulness of these different points of view. We create an environment that enables all employees to reach their full potential in pursuit of company objectives.

Employee well-being. We have a safe, healthy, and desirable workplace. Stability of employment is given high priority. Growth in employee skills is essential. Recognition for contributions and full utilization of employees' capabilities promote job satisfaction.

Citizenship. We are valued by our community for our contributions as individuals and as a company. We protect public health and safety and the environment by being good stewards of our products and our processes.

Winning attitude. Our can-do attitude and desire for excellence drive continual improvement, making us winners in everything we do.

which status is jealously guarded will feel uncomfortable participating on an equal basis in team meetings with individuals from three different levels of management. People who share the belief that stability is the source of business success will be skeptical about continuous improvement. In situations like these, TQ is like an organ transplanted to a poorly matched donor and will be rejected.

Elements of a Total Quality Culture

The organizational culture needed to support TQ is one that values customers, improvement, and teamwork. In an organization with a TQ-friendly culture, everyone believes that customers are the key to the organization's future and that their needs must come first. If two employees are having a conversation and a customer enters the shop, the conversation ends until the customer is served.

In a culture supportive of TQ, people expect their jobs to change due to improvements dictated by customer needs. They are always looking for better (faster, simpler, less expensive) ways to do things. "Because that's the way we've always done it" is not a valid reason for doing anything. The culture of improvement is exemplified by the Levi Strauss and Eastman Chemical stories.

Employees in a quality-oriented culture instinctively act as a team. If someone is away from her desk and her phone rings, another employee will answer it rather than leave a customer hanging. Organizations where a focus on customers, continuous improvement, and teamwork are taken for granted have a good chance of succeeding at total quality. Most organizations do not have such a culture prior to exposure to TQ; some degree of cultural change is necessary.

These elements, along with several others, are reflected clearly in the Malcolm Baldrige National Quality Award Criteria for Performance Excellence. The criteria are built upon a set of "core values and concepts":

- customer-driven quality,
- leadership,
- continuous improvement and learning,
- valuing employees,
- fast response,
- design quality and prevention,
- long-range view of the future,
- management by fact,
- partnership development,
- company responsibility and citizenship, and
- results focus.

These values provide a good summary of the cultural elements necessary to sustain a total quality environment.

The existence of a set of cultural values necessary for successful TQ does not mean that all quality-oriented organizations will have the same culture. Many aspects of culture differ greatly from one quality-oriented company to another. Company personnel may prefer to communicate in person or in writing; they may serve smoked salmon and champagne or a bushel of crabs and a keg of beer at the company picnic; they may wear uniforms, grey flannel suits, or jeans. As long as they hold the core values of TQ, quality can find a home in their organization.

How Organizational Culture Is Changed

How can a company change its culture to be more consistent with quality? As with most aspects of TQ, it begins with leadership (see the box "A Sincere Belief and Trust in People" on page 204).[5] Leaders must articulate to employees the direction in which they want the company to go. They must set an example by expressing TQ values in their own behavior and by recognizing and rewarding others who do the same. The efforts of a foundry's new leadership team to establish the values of continuous improvement and teamwork are described by the quality director, whose efforts had been frustrated under the old regime:[6]

> They brought in a people-oriented environment. They made the environment conducive to change and tried to get to the point where employees felt safe to make change. Before, you did what the boss told you to do, and if you didn't you're probably going to get fired. Now we have some coaches in place and facilitators, and they want the ideas from the employees, and it's a hell of a lot easier with their input.

A great deal of the effort leaders expend in cultural change is devoted to communication. Employees company-wide must be informed of the new values and practices desired. Any early successes of the new approach must also be publicized. This is not always easy, especially when the company's employees are geographically dispersed. In attempting to change the culture at Southern Pacific Lines, railroad executives held 125 "town meetings" at sites where employees worked, sometimes in groups as small as 5 to 10.[7]

In promoting a new culture, leaders must personally practice behaviors associated with the new culture. This provides a role model for employees and symbolizes management's sincerity about the new approach. When the Indian soap company, Godrej Soaps, tried to initiate continuous improvement, workers were reluctant to unwrap defective soaps to see how mistakes could be avoided in the future. When informed of this, the managing director said he would go into the plant to unwrap the soaps. As it turned out, he didn't need to do it. When workers heard that the top manager was willing to do this kind of work, they agreed to do it themselves.[8]

None of this should be interpreted to mean that cultural change is easy. On the contrary, it is very difficult, takes several years to complete, and often fails.[9] One reason for the difficulty is resistance by middle management. Managers resist change because it creates more work for them when they often feel over-burdened and disrupts the steady flow of work in the organization.[10]

Getting on board for a change in culture requires managers to acknowledge that the current approach is somehow lacking, despite any of their previous

A Sincere Belief and Trust in People[11]

One powerful example of the importance of cultural change is the case of Wainwright Industries, a 1994 Baldrige winner. During the 1970s and 1980s, Wainwright lost millions in sales. Operations slowed to three days a week; and tensions grew between employees and management. Recognizing the problem lay with management, the CEO made some radical changes. Workers were called "associates," and everyone was put on salary. Associates are paid even if they miss work and still receive time-and-a-half for overtime. The company has maintained over 99 percent attendance since this change. Managers shed their white shirts and ties, and everyone from the CEO down wears a common uniform, embroidered with the label *Team Wainwright*.

A team of associates developed a profit-sharing plan, whereby everyone receives the same bonus every six months. Everyone has access to the privately held company's financial records. In addition, all reserved parking spaces were removed and walls—including those for the CEO's office—were replaced with glass. Customers, both external and internal, are treated as partners with extensive communication.

The most striking example of change occurred when one worker admitted accidently damaging some equipment, even though most workers were afraid to report such incidents. The CEO called a plant-wide meeting and explained what had happened. Then he called the man up, shook his hand, and thanked him for reporting the accident. Accident reporting increased from zero to 90 percent, along with suggestions on how to prevent them.

Wainwright's culture can be summed up as *a sincere belief and trust in people*. One measure of Wainwright's success is that the number of implemented suggestions per person per year exceeds 50, while the previous benchmark that Wainwright identified (Milliken) was 15!

statements to the contrary. They also may be afraid that they will not be able to perform effectively in the new culture.

Often reward systems get in the way of cultural change and must be adjusted for the new culture to take hold. In many companies, telephone operators are rewarded for the speed with which they process calls, rather than for how completely they satisfy the customers who call. Unless this type of reward system is changed, management's pleas to increase customer satisfaction will fall upon deaf ears. Willingness to make such changes indicates management's commitment to the new culture.

Making the New Culture Permanent

Due to the difficulty of cultural change, leaders must work to ensure not only that change is initiated, but that the new culture becomes a permanent part of the organization. Managers can take a number of paths to this destination:[12]

1. Make involvement in TQ a required part of people's responsibilities. Making it voluntary implies that it is less important than things that are required.
2. Use the existing organization to implement TQ. Special task forces and committees can disband; TQ should be part of the permanent organization.
3. Make sure everyone spends at least one hour a week working on quality issues. Enforcing this rule gets people used to the idea of devoting time to quality and keeps other priorities from crowding out TQ.
4. Change the measurement and information systems.[13] Without appropriate measurements and information systems, quality cannot become part of the fabric of the organization. AT&T Universal Card Services, a 1992 winner of the Baldrige Award, spent $20 million on computer workstations to provide customer support personnel with easy access to detailed card member information.

Cultural Change in Action

Many organizations have attempted to change their cultures to become more responsive to customer needs. Boeing is a good example of a company in a difficult competitive situation that has undertaken this task.[14] Boeing has been a fixture in the aerospace industry since Bill Boeing built his first airplane—a single-engine seaplane—in 1916. Boeing's planes were heavily involved in World War II, with almost 7,000 produced by Boeing and another 13,000 produced by other manufacturers using Boeing designs. In modern times, approximately half the commercial jets in the world have been produced by Boeing; the company contributes substantially to the U.S. balance of trade by exporting planes.

Not content to rest on its corporate laurels, however, Boeing was among the early leaders of the quality movement in the United States, implementing quality circles in 1980. (Quality circles are groups of workers who meet for an hour or so each week to work on quality problems. They were a forerunner of total quality efforts in many companies.)

Managers at Boeing quickly recognized, however, that the corporate culture would need to be changed if quality efforts were to be successful, and they began a process to do so. This process consisted of five steps:

1. Identify norms that currently guide behaviors and attitudes.
2. Identify the behaviors necessary to make the organization successful for tomorrow.
3. Develop a list of new norms that will move the organization forward.
4. Identify the culture gaps—the difference between the desired norms and actual norms.
5. Develop and put in place an action plan to implement the new cultural norms. These new norms will replace the old ones, and this transition will be monitored and enforced.

Boeing backed up this commitment to cultural change with a great deal of training, surveying of employees and customers, and executive commitment. Today the company faces tremendous challenges, including a decline in demand for military aircraft, competition from Airbus Industries (the European airplane consortium), and a very weak global market for jets. Its quality-oriented culture, however, based on customers, continuous improvement, and teamwork, should help it to stay competitive for years to come. As Boeing's John Black reflected:

> This process of continuous improvement, to which we are committed, is not one that can suddenly be grafted onto a company. Every organization must make it their own. Top management leadership *must* be provided, and *all* management must be brought on board. Only when all the people are committed and the process is locked in for the long term, will it achieve the breakthrough that it is capable of providing for us—the key to economic success in the future.

CONTINUOUS IMPROVEMENT AND LEARNING

Continuous improvement (*kaizen* in Japanese) to provide quality to customers is essential to total quality. The TQ ideal is *not* to make a big splash by improving a system, only to mindlessly operate in the same "new and improved" manner for years to come. TQ-oriented organizations relentlessly improve their processes, products, and services, as well as their people (through training), day by day and month by month, over years and even decades.

The cumulative effect of hundreds or thousands of small improvements creates dramatic change in performance. This is not to say that breakthroughs do not occur; they certainly do, especially in the early phases of TQ. To use football as a metaphor, the successful practice of TQ is not reflected in the glamour of the occasional "long bomb," it consists of grinding out improvements "one yard at a time."

Consider the chart in Figure 6.1, which shows the result of attempts by a foundry to reduce its production of scrap (products rejected due to poor quality) over three years. Several points about continuous improvement are illustrated by this chart.

- The average amount of scrap declined each year, from approximately 9.5 in the first year to 6.5 in the second year and to 3.5 in the third year.
- Not only the level but also the variation from month to month declined each year. Compare the wild variation in the first year to the relative stability of the third.
- Even when quality efforts had not been undertaken, the company occasionally got lucky and produced good quality. It took the foundry two years to produce a month as good as the first month of the first year. Obviously, the first-year first-month was a fluke, as scrap was 50 percent higher the next

FIGURE 6.1 SCRAP REDUCTIONS IN A FOUNDRY OVER THREE YEARS

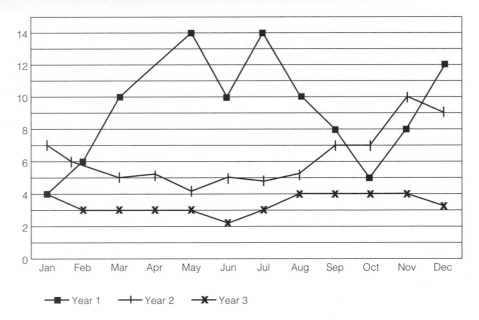

— ■ — Year 1   — + — Year 2   — ✗ — Year 3

month! The philosophy of continuous improvement was captured very well by the quality manager who said, "We're nowhere near where we ought to be, but we're getting better. And we're going to be better tomorrow."

Continuous improvement is difficult to achieve without creating a "learning organization," a term popularized by MIT professor Peter Senge. He defines the learning organization as

> an organization that is continually expanding its capacity to create its future. For such an organization, it is not enough merely to survive. "Survival learning" or what is more often termed "adaptive learning" is important—indeed it is necessary. But for a learning organization, "adaptive learning" must be joined by "generative learning," learning that enhances our capacity to create.[15]

Senge repeatedly points out, "Over the long run, superior performance depends on superior learning." The concept of organizational learning can be thought of as the process of moving through the four stages of learning that we described at the very beginning of this chapter. Effective learning requires an understanding and integration of many of the concepts and principles that are part of the TQ philosophy.

Continuous Improvement and Learning in the Baldrige Award

Continuous improvement and learning is a core concept in the Malcolm Baldrige National Quality Award criteria. The guidelines state:

Achieving the highest levels of performance requires a well-defined and well-executed approach to continuous improvement and learning. The term "continuous improvement" refers to both incremental and "breakthrough" improvement. The term "learning" refers to adaptation to change, leading to new goals and/or approaches. Improvement and learning need to be "embedded" in the way a company operates. Embedded means improvement and learning: (1) are a regular part of daily work; (2) seek to eliminate problems at their source; and (3) are driven by opportunities to do better, as well as problems that must be corrected. . . . Improvement and learning include: (1) enhancing value to customers; (2) developing new business opportunities; (3) reducing errors, defects, waste, and related costs; (4) responsiveness and cycle time performance; (5) productivity and effectiveness in the use of all company resources; and (6) improving the company's performance in fulfilling its public responsibilities and service as a good citizen.[16]

The Baldrige Award seeks evidence of evaluation and improvement cycles in nearly every category of the criteria. The award itself sets an example by continually improving the nature of the award criteria and the application process each year.

How Continuous Improvement Is Practiced

The most important ingredient for continuous improvement is one we have already discussed: an appropriate organizational culture (see the box "The Law of Quality"). If everyone in the organization understands and believes in the importance of continuous improvement, the rest is a question of technique. If not, no techniques will do the job.

Given the large number of possible areas in an organization that could be improved, setting priorities is crucial. There are several ways to do this. Many organizations rely on customer input and feedback to help set their priorities.[17] For example, if late deliveries are the most common customer complaint, continuous improvement efforts should be directed at reducing delivery times. Often customers cannot see inside the organization to identify the root causes of problems, so some additional sorting out is generally necessary.

The time-honored tradition of the suggestion system has taken on a new life under TQ to serve this purpose. At Portman Equipment Company, an employee who sees an improvement opportunity fills out a Proposal for Change form, which initiates the formation of a team to attack the issue.[18] At AT&T Universal Card Services, employees contribute an average of 4.6 suggestions per year, half of which are implemented.[19] This rate of suggestions, large compared to most American firms, is still dwarfed by the number of suggestions contributed in some Japanese firms.

The Plan-Do-Study-Act (PDSA) cycle discussed in chapter 3 provides the basic process for continuous improvement. An operation is examined to identify potential areas for improvement. Techniques such as check sheets and Pareto charts are used to prioritize problems. Then steps are taken to improve

---

The Law of Quality[20]

Implementing a continuous improvement process in most law firm cultures can be difficult. This is partly because lawyer's compensation is directly linked to the number of hours they bill; many don't see themselves being able to devote time to a quality initiative, even though, in the long run, such a program would likely streamline their processes and give them more time. In a culture with many individual habits and idiosyncrasies, standardizing processes and procedures can be difficult, if not impossible.

Nevertheless, some firms have made remarkable progress. The 130-lawyer firm of Mays & Valentine in Richmond, Virginia set up quality improvement teams. A short survey was mailed to clients to find out where the firm stood with its external customers. At the same time, an internal survey was administered to the entire firm to determine whether the firm's culture was receptive to the TQ philosophy. The firm's executive committee carefully selected the mission and objectives for each team. Based on the survey results, the areas they chose for improvement were attorney responsiveness and accessibility to clients, the firm's copying operations, and the use of alternative billing methods. The resulting changes included new standards for responsiveness to clients, which were made firm policy; a new branch office telephone system; outsourcing copy center operations to Xerox; and new measurements for administrative systems, such as computer performance, turnover rate, central fax operations, speed of billing, complaints, and collection rates.

Not only has service improved, but employees are more satisfied because they are asked for their input and encouraged to suggest ways to improve effectiveness.

---

the operation, and the results of the change are studied. This leads to further action, and the cycle continues indefinitely.

This is somewhat similar to the familiar problem-solving model:

1. specify the problem,
2. identify causes of the problem and determine which are most serious,
3. develop a list of potential solutions,
4. analyze the potential benefit of the solutions and choose one, and
5. implement the solution.

An important difference, however, is that with a continuous improvement mindset, step 5 leads directly back to step 1, unless the operation is now flawless.

Eastman Chemical, profiled in an example earlier in this chapter, uses seven steps for accelerated continuous improvement.

1. *Focus and pinpoint*—"Focus" is about getting everyone on the same page with regard to goals; "pinpoint" is about specifying in measurable terms what is expected.

2. *Communicate*—Communication is done companywide by publicizing key result areas, the vision, and the mission statement so employees can answer the questions: What is being improved? Why is it important to the customer, to the company, and to me? What has the management team committed to do to help? And What, specifically, is the company asking me to do?

3. *Translate and link*—Teams translate the companywide objectives into their own language and environment.

4. *Create a management action plan*—Management creates a plan with specific actions to reach a goal, including metrics to measure success. Each team member is asked to know what tasks need to be done, why they are important, and what the team's role is in getting them done.

5. *Improve processes*—Teams use a six-step problem-solving process.

6. *Measure progress and provide feedback*—Eastman is adamant about the importance of unambiguous, visual feedback to employees and appropriate measures of performance. Eastman's rules include:

    • Feedback should be visual, frequent, simple, and specific.
    • The baseline performance should be shown for comparison.
    • The past, current period, and goals should be posted.
    • The best-ever score should be posted.
    • A chart should be immediately understandable.
    • A good scorecard allows comments and annotations.

7. *Reinforce behaviors and celebrate results*—Eastman reinforces that learning the leads to positive results by encouraging teams at celebrations to answer the questions: What did you do? Why did it work? Why is it important for the customer, the company, and the team? How did the team accomplish its achievement?

Eastman points out that its formula cannot be blindly followed by others but must be adapted to the specific corporate culture. Nevertheless, the human principles are universal.

Continuous improvement efforts can be directed at a number of different types of improvement. For example, changes could result in work being done more easily, more accurately, faster, at lower cost, more safely, and in a way that provides greater customer satisfaction.[21] Thinking about continuous improvement in this way makes it clear how many opportunities for improvement exist in almost any system. How many operations are there that couldn't be improved on even one of these dimensions?

Persistence is important in pursuing continuous improvement. Not only will small changes in operations take some time to add up to any serious improvement, but they are often disruptive when first implemented. According to the late Japanese manufacturing expert, Shigeo Shingo:[22]

Since improvement . . . demands new procedures, a certain amount of difficulty will be encountered. . . . Initially, new methods will be difficult. Old procedures, however, are easy just because they are familiar. . . . As long as it is unfamiliar, even an improved procedure will be more difficult and will take more time than the old procedure. . . . Thus, no improvement shows its true worth right away; . . . 99 percent of all improvement plans would vanish without a trace if they were to be abandoned after only a brief trial.

Like the cultural change that motivates it, continuous improvement is difficult to sustain. Perhaps the "if it's not broke, don't fix it" mentality is too deeply embedded our culture. In any case, many organizations that wish to embrace continuous improvement have not been able to do so successfully, as indicated by the findings of a recent survey of American manufacturing firms by the National Center for Manufacturing Science (NCMS):

Japan, Germany, and other industrialized nations recognize the continuous improvement process as crucial to world-class manufacturing. But industrial leaders responding to the NCMS survey admit they have a spotty track record in this area. For example, half of those responding say they have no continuous improvement plan in place. . . . Nearly 40 percent of the respondents also indicated that suggestions from continuous improvement team members are not regularly implemented.[23]

Continuous Improvement in Action

An increasing number of companies have begun to convert to the continuous improvement philosophy. One unusual example of this idea in practice is provided by the Walt Disney Company.[24] The 1992 opening of Euro Disney near Marne la Vallee, France, brought to four the number of parks operated around the world by the Walt Disney Company. Disneyland, the original, opened in 1955 in Anaheim, California. Disney World, in Orlando, Florida, opened in 1971 and was expanded in 1982 to include Epcot Center and later MGM Studios Theme Park and again in 1998 to include Animal Kingdom. Tokyo Disneyland, Disney's first overseas park, opened in 1983.

Disney faced a difficult challenge in bringing its American style of fun to the French people, who are often ambivalent at best about American cultural imperialism. The opening of Euro Disney (now renamed Disneyland Paris) was not without problems, as Disney faced labor disputes over its personal appearance policies, such as no facial hair, and substantial difficulties with getting construction work done on time and under budget. The company anticipated and tried to defuse any cross-cultural difficulties through an exchange of hundreds of European and American managers.

One major advantage Disney had in establishing its European park was its ability to learn from its past successes, as well as its past mistakes. When the original park was opened in Anaheim, its 185 acres were quickly surrounded by hotels and restaurants that competed with Disney's own. This mistake was not repeated in Orlando, where Disney bought 28,000 acres (much of which is still unused), nor in France.

Disney built six hotels for the opening of Euro Disney, far more than would be immediately needed. Why? The company had dragged its heels in building hotels in Florida, allowing competitors to become established. Almost unbelievably, the plans for Euro Disney (to be completed in 2017) call for an additional 4,000 hotel rooms, a retail and industrial park, and even 8,000 private homes.

When one thinks of continuous improvement, processes that are repeated every hour, day, or week come to mind. However, Disney has applied continuous improvement to the process of park design, which it has practiced only about every 10 years!

REENGINEERING

Reengineering (also known as process redesign) is focused on "breakthrough" improvement to dramatically improve the quality and speed of work and to reduce its cost by fundamentally changing the processes by which work gets done. Reengineering is often used when the improvements needed are so great that incremental changes to operations will not get the job done. Ten percent improvements can be created by tinkering, but 50 percent improvements call for process redesign.

The irony of reengineering is that, once the new process is in place, people often feel that the new way of operating is so much better, they should have thought of it long ago. Another common reaction is "Why did we ever do it like that in the first place?" The answer is often, "That's the way we've always done it." GE Chairman Jack Welch compared his company to a 100-year-old attic, which has collected a lot of useless junk over the years. Process redesign (called *workout* in GE jargon) is the process of cleaning all the junk out of the attic.[25]

Often the old ways of doing things were a function of administrative, rather than customer-centered, thinking. In one plant, a product was boxed and wrapped to be sent from one side of the plant to the other, only to be unwrapped and unboxed. Why? Because the two parts of the plant were separate profit centers, and the first had to "sell" the product to the second! If a process is driven by an administrative logic such as cost accounting or functional specialization, it is ripe for reengineering.[26]

The importance of process redesign to quality improvement can be seen in Figure 6.2, based on the work of Professor Asbjorn Aune of Norway.[27] Process is what connects customer expectations to the products or services they receive. It is what ensures (or fails to ensure) that products meet or exceed customer expectations.

Principles of Process Redesign

Waste is the enemy of effective processes. Reducing waste of any kind encompasses both TQ and just-in-time practices and is a central theme in Japanese

Figure 6.2 The Key Role of Process

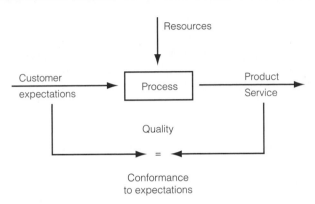

manufacturing management. Poor processes waste time, money, material, effort, and customer goodwill. Redesigning processes to reduce waste is, at this point at least, more an art than a science. Every process redesign is unique, but the general principles of redesign include:[28]

1. *Reduce handoffs*—Every time a process is handed from one person or group to another, errors can occur. (Think of passing the baton in a relay race.) Time is often wasted as one group waits for the other to finish or needs to consult with the first group before continuing.

2. *Eliminate steps*—The best way to save time on a step is to not do it at all. If the step does not add value to the product or service or make the product more attractive to customers, stop doing it. In manufacturing organizations, moving, storing, and inspecting products rarely add value. These steps should be eliminated wherever possible.

3. *Perform steps in parallel rather than in sequence*—Unless one operation cannot be done until another is finished, why not do them both at once? Many organizations operate like two people doing the dishes, where one washes all the dishes that will fit in the drainer, then calls the other to dry them. When the drying is done, the dryer calls the washer back in and leaves again. Stupid? Yes, but that's the way they've always done it.

4. *Involve key people early*—The point of this is to avoid doing things over when key people do not give their input until the process is under way. For years, manufacturing companies have had their engineers design entire products before consulting the manufacturing engineers who will have to build them. The manufacturing engineers would then suggest a number of changes that the designers would reluctantly incorporate into their designs. Many firms recently have changed this process to allow early involvement of manufacturing.[29] This is one of the most common forms of process reengineering and is consistent with the TQ principle, "Do it right the first time!"

Reengineering in Action

The improvements created by reengineering are often amazing and provide impressive testimony to the power of the method. A case in point is the changes made in processing applications at Mutual Benefit Life. In the old days, Mutual Benefit Life (MBL) processed its applications like every other insurance company.[30] An application went through up to five departments, 19 people, and 30 steps. Under this system, the hour or so of work associated with an application took between 5 and 25 days to complete!

MBL's president believed that customer service had to be improved and decreed a 60 percent improvement in productivity. The team assigned to produce this improvement realized that this goal could not be achieved by cosmetic changes; a complete process redesign was in order.

The new arrangement trashed the existing system of departments and job descriptions and created the new role of "case manager." Case managers have complete responsibility for applications—from reception to completion—and work quite autonomously. They can operate in this manner due to the support of computer workstations that run an expert system (a program that provides advice based on the knowledge and experience of experts) and other programs. With this support, even a case manager of limited experience can make good decisions. In unusually tough situations, case managers can still call senior underwriters or physicians for advice.

The benefits of the new process are impressive. Applications can now be processed in as few as four hours and on average take only two to five days. Case managers now can process twice as many applications as the previous system, despite the fact that the number of field office positions has been reduced by 100.

Like many other management approaches, reengineering has suffered from criticism that its results have not lived up to its promises. Often, such criticism is a backlash to the hype generated by the approach's advocates and the cottage industries they create. But like any other approach, managers must understand how to implement it properly. As one MBL manager stated,

> The bottom line is that reengineering is like so many other management methodologies—it can only be effective when implemented in conjunction with sound strategies for improving overall corporate performance. This means that effective reengineering efforts align and leverage cost-reduction and process-improvement efforts with the strategies, structures, technologies and people of the organization.

QUALITY-ORIENTED CHANGE AND ORGANIZATION THEORY

A large amount of research and writing in organization theory (OT) focuses on organization change. This section compares the TQ perspective on organization change to this literature. Given the amount of work in this area, we can only identify a few of the major ideas in the literature on organization change and show how they relate to total quality. Organizational behavior and organization theory textbooks generally have at least one chapter on organization change, which can be consulted for further details on this research.

The following sections compare TQ to organization theory in terms of the reasons for change, the source of change, the nature of change, the difficulty of change, and how to manage change. Our overall conclusion is that, despite some differences in focus, the research on change conducted by organization theorists is a rich source of information for those embarking on the changes required by total quality.

The Reason for Change

The reason behind TQ-oriented change is quality improvement for customer satisfaction. This has not been a major focus of the OT literature on change, which has focused primarily on changes intended to improve productivity and/or improve job satisfaction. Of course, many quality-oriented changes may improve productivity or job satisfaction, but that isn't usually their main objective.

The Source of Change

The source of most change considered in OT is top management. In general, top management responds to changes in the organizational environment, such as increased competitiveness or declining demand. This parallels the cultural change aspect of TQ. In fact, the OT literature on change is most relevant to cultural change, as opposed to continuous improvement or process redesign.

Types of Change

The types of changes considered in OT theories partially overlap with TQ-oriented changes. In particular, OT theories that deal with changes in values and norms are relevant to the transformations associated with cultural change in TQ. Other types of change featured in OT theories, such as the introduction of new technology, are not as directly relevant to TQ. (Reengineering, however, often involves the application of some type of information technology.)

Furthermore, the changes discussed in the OT literature tend to differ in two important ways from TQ-oriented change. First, they tend to be limited in scope, usually to one or two departments, and even to only a few aspects of the work of these departments. Second, they tend to be limited in duration, with the idea being to get the change over with and get on with organizational life. This may apply to cultural change (and to some extent to process redesign), but it is very different from continuous improvement. Indeed, the management of continuous change over a long period of time has not been addressed often by OT research and presents a clear opportunity for research.

One of the earliest studies of organization change was conducted by Coch and French in a Virginia factory that produced pajamas.[31] In this study, a change in procedure was made in three different ways. In one group, the workers themselves devised the change. In a second group, workers appointed representatives who devised the change. In a third group, the new system was imposed on the workers by management.

The study found that the change was much more successful in the more participative groups; this study is often cited as support for the need for employee participation in organizational change. What is interesting from a TQ perspective is that it is a study of process redesign and, in the participative groups at least, of process redesign initiated by the people actually doing the work. Thus it anticipates by 40 years the kinds of changes that have become commonplace among firms practicing total quality. True to the limits in the thinking at the time, however, the improvement was a one-shot deal. Continuous improvement was an idea whose time had not yet come.

TQ and the OT literature agree on the difficulty of successfully changing organizations and on the fact that "resistance to change" is often the underlying problem. OT research has made significant progress in identifying why organization members resist change and even in identifying various methods for dealing with this problem.[32] Resistance is at least as likely to come from managers as from lower-level employees.

The whole idea of resistance, however, flows from a concept of change mandated by top management. Managers or workers are unlikely to resist a process change that they themselves have devised. For such changes, the literature on resistance to change seems off the mark.

Perhaps the literature on population ecology provides a more helpful perspective on the difficulty of organizational change in the TQ context.[33] From this perspective, worker resistance is not to blame for the difficulty of change. Rather, the structures and systems that management has created are at fault. For example, the hierarchical organization structure of most firms makes it difficult for them to adapt effectively to environmental changes such as the evolution in customer demand. This idea is consistent with Deming's theory that problems are more often related to system imperfections than to worker inability or lack of motivation.

Population ecology theorists generally argue that the difficulty of changing structures, authority, reward systems, and so forth, renders most organizations unsuccessful in their change efforts. Writers on TQ often have commented on the major impediments such structures and systems create but have gone on to identify ways in which such obstacles can be removed. This difference in prognosis should not mask the fundamental agreement between the ecological OT perspective and TQ on the importance of structural and systemic impediments to change.

From the ecological perspective, change in a set of similar organizations often comes about by ineffective organizations going out of business and being replaced by new ones, rather than by changing from ineffective to effective. Clearly both processes occur. Many organizations that did not provide the quality customers demanded are no longer with us, while others (Xerox is an excellent example) have managed to transform themselves in order to survive. Needless to say, the battle between transformation and extinction continues to be fought every day in many firms throughout the world.

Many of the principles for managing change derived from the OT literature apply directly to total quality change. Some of these principles are as follows:

1. *It is necessary to "unfreeze" people's attitudes and behavior before they can be changed.*[34] This principle, a staple of the OT understanding of change, relates directly to TQ. Before organizations can change in the direction of practicing TQ, people must see why the current approach is inappropriate or incomplete and what problems of competitiveness and customer dissatisfaction this causes. Cultural change in TQ is often the vehicle for unfreezing behavior.

2. *Change can only succeed with effective leadership.* One early proponent of this view was Thomas Bennett.[35] Bennett identified the need for leaders to deal with the emotional aspects of the change for subordinates, the need for clear goals, and the importance of logical problem-solving processes. These and other aspects of the leader's role identified by OT theorists clearly are relevant to TQ.

3. *Change agents must manage interdependence.* Few things in organizations—for example, jobs or technology—can be changed without affecting other things—structures or processes. Many OT theorists of change recognized this fact and based their theories on the need to identify and manage the interdependence among organizational phenomena.[36] This applies directly to process redesign and is consistent with Deming's emphasis on organizations as systems.

4. *Effective change must involve the people whose jobs are being changed.* This point was noted in reference to the Coch and French study. Although a variety of rationales for the importance of participation have been advanced, its significance for reducing resistance is an article of faith among organization change theorists.[37] This is probably the point of greatest overlap between OT and TQ. The "participation" and "involvement" championed by OT theorists as much as 50 years ago have become so widely accepted in industry that they have evolved into today's concepts of "empowerment" and "self-management."

5. *Refreezing is needed to make gains permanent.* Research in OT has concluded that steps are needed to lock in the changes that have been made.[38] This point has not been lost upon the TQ community, as many organizations are now becoming concerned about maintaining, as opposed to creating, change. Many of the recommendations of the OT literature, especially the need to monitor and revise change efforts continually, are quite relevant to TQ.

SUMMARY

Organizational change and learning are fundamental to total quality. The three most important types of change practiced in TQ are cultural change, continuous improvement, and process redesign. Cultural change, which makes the other two types of change possible, depends on leadership and the creation of systems to make the changes permanent.

Continuous improvement often involves suggestion systems and operates on the principle that major improvements can come from the accumulation of many small changes. Process redesign is a type of improvement in which breakthroughs are made by fundamentally changing the way work gets done. The organization theory literature on change, despite some differences in focus, provides a number of observations and recommendations that are relevant to managing quality-oriented change.

REVIEW AND DISCUSSION QUESTIONS

1. Briefly describe the three kinds of organizational change practiced in total quality efforts.
2. You probably have, unfortunately, heard the term "dysfunctional family" in news stories about our society. What might the term "dysfunctional corporate culture" mean?
3. Describe the culture of an organization you have worked in or are familiar with. What is valued in this culture? Do you think this culture provides fertile ground for total quality? Why or why not?
4. Will an organization's culture be the same throughout or will it vary from department to department? Why?
5. How do the values stated in "The Eastman Way" promote a total quality culture?
6. Find and examine five Internet Web sites for large corporations. What do these sites tell you about the company's culture?
7. Download the latest version of the Baldrige criteria from the NIST Web site www.quality.nist.gov and discuss how the core values and concepts underlying the Baldrige criteria are reflected in each category of the criteria.
8. Managers can enforce rules about what people do and say at work. But can they enforce a culture? If yes, how can they do it? If no, what does this say about the limits of managers' ability to ensure quality?
9. How could you apply continuous improvement methods to the job of being a student?
10. Can you think of any company that has been successful for a long time without improving its product? What conditions have made this possible?
11. How could you improve your process for studying for an exam? Getting to class on time? Cleaning your room or apartment?
12. What principles of process redesign are illustrated by the Mutual Benefit Life story? Can you discern other principles not listed in the chapter from this case?

CASES

The Yellow Brick Road to Quality[39]

In the film *The Wizard of Oz*, Dorothy learned many lessons. Surprisingly, managers can learn a lot also. For each of the following summaries of scenes in the film, discuss the lessons that organizations can learn in pursuing change and a TQ culture.

A. Dorothy was not happy with the world as she knew it. A tornado came along and transported her to the Land of Oz. Dorothy's house was dropped by the tornado on the Wicked Witch of the East, killing the witch. "Ding, dong, the witch is dead!" rang throughout Munchkinland, but Dorothy had enraged the dead witch's sister. Dorothy only temporarily lost her home support provided by family back in Kansas. All is not good, however, in the Land of Oz. Dorothy's problem is to find her way home to Kansas. Her call to action was precipitated by a crisis—the tornado that transported her to an alien land.

B. In the throes of a Kansas tornado, Dorothy is transported to an unfamiliar land. Immediately, she realizes her world is different, and the processes and people she encounters are different, yet they bear some similarity to her Kansas existence. She is lost and confused and uncertain about the next steps to take. She realizes she is in a changed state—the Land of Oz—and must devise a plan to get home.

C. Dorothy is a hero for killing the Wicked Witch of the East. Glinda the Good Witch sends Dorothy on her way to meet the Wizard of Oz who will help her get back to Kansas. The Wicked Witch of the West tries to get Dorothy's newly acquired ruby slippers, but to no avail. Dorothy and Toto leave for Oz via the Yellow Brick Road. Along the way, they are joined by Scarecrow, Tin Man, and Lion. Through their teamwork, they provide mutual support to endure the vexing journey. They overcome many risks and barriers, including the sleeping poppy field, flying monkeys, and a haunted forest on the way to Oz.

D. Dorothy and her entourage finally reach Oz and meet the Wizard. Rather than instantly granting their wishes, the Wizard gives them an assignment—to obtain the Wicked Witch's broom. They depart for the West.

E. Charged with the task of obtaining the broom, Dorothy and company experience several encounters with near disaster, including Dorothy's incarceration in the witch's castle while an hourglass counts the time to her death. In a struggle to extinguish the Scarecrow's fire (incited by the Wicked Witch), Dorothy tosses a bucket of water, some of which hits the Witch and melts her. Dorothy is rewarded with the broomstick and returns to Oz.

F. Returning to Oz, the group talks with the Wizard, expecting him to help Dorothy return to Kansas. After defrocking the Wizard, they find out he does not know how. The Wizard tries to use a hot-air balloon to return and accidentally leaves Dorothy and Toto behind upon takeoff. Glinda arrives and helps Dorothy realize she can return to Kansas on her own with the help of the ruby slippers.

G. Dorothy awakens from her dream and experiences a new understanding and appreciation for her home and family in Kansas: "Oh, Auntie Em, there's no place like home."

The Machine That Didn't Change the World[40]

Mike Weaver, president of Weaver Popcorn Company of Van Buren, Indiana, had always believed that if the customer was not happy with an order, the only thing to do was to take it back. "No sale is complete if the customer isn't satisfied," the Reverend Ira E. Weaver, company founder and Mike's grandfather, was fond of saying. What if the order was 280,000 pounds of popcorn (use your imagination), and what if it was in Tokyo, and what if it was worth $70,000? "Let's bring it back," Weaver told Pat Vogel, the company's export manager, when awakened with the bad news around midnight one evening in October 1985.

The refusal of the order by Shintoa Koeki Kaisha Ltd., on the basis of excess impurities, was a hard kernel to swallow for Weaver the man and Weaver the company. Both had regarded the order from Japan as an indication of the company's ability to sell popcorn to anybody, anywhere. How could the company recover its quality image in the face of such an embarrassment?

A few months later, trucks pulled up to the Weaver plant bearing $1 million worth of high-speed optical scanners. The new machines would subject anything passing beneath their electronic eyes to a cold-hearted inspection, dooming to the trash heap any weed seeds, dirt clods, and soybeans trying to pass themselves off as popcorn. Goodbye foreign particles. Goodbye irate customers. Hello quality!

However, continuous improvement seldom occurs in big bangs and rarely can be accomplished simply by buying new technology. These were the quality lessons learned by Weaver in the months and years after the new equipment was installed. Although the machines couldn't solve Weaver's quality problems, they certainly made people more aware of them. Questions were raised about virtually every aspect of the operation, including the raw materials, the tools, and the people.

Things came to a head when, during a quality meeting, Marty Hall from processing informed the group that all the talk about quality was total bull as long as Weaver was accepting popcorn that was way out of spec, for example in moisture content. Aware that the outgoing product cannot be good if the incoming raw materials are not, Hall believed that the quality efforts to date were useless.

This sparked dramatic changes in Weaver's operations. Mike Weaver began to give vastly increased responsibility for quality to people in the plant. The resigning plant manager was replaced by seven team leaders from the plant floor. Employees were brought into the process of hiring, even for managers.

Hundreds of minor changes have been made by employees now sensitized to the importance of quality, which has been steadily improving. The lesson? According to Mike Weaver, "With the machines there, everybody began to see that it takes so much more than machines. Nothing has a greater impact on the quality of the corn than these people." As Mike's grandfather might have added, "Amen."

Reprinted with permission, *Inc. Magazine* (May 1990). Copyright © 1990 by Goldhirsh Group, Inc., 38 Commercial Wharf, Boston, MA 02110.

Discussion Questions

1. Would you have made the same decision as Mike Weaver to bring back the popcorn from Japan? Why or why not?
2. Did the optical scanners turn out to be a good idea?
3. Did the fact that Weaver is a family-owned business make a difference in how Mike Weaver thought about quality? Can the same attitude be created in shareholder-owned companies?
4. What elements of the company had to change for the quality of the popcorn to improve?
5. Can quality ever be completely automated so that people don't make any difference?

Reject Rate Reduction at the Reserve Bank of India[41]

The National Clearing Cell (NCC), Madras, is a division of the Reserve Bank of India responsible for check-clearing operations in the Madras area. Check clearing has been computerized since 1987 and involves running checks on a high-speed reader-sorter system (HSRSS) driven by a mainframe computer. The checks customers cash at their banks that are drawn on other banks are presented to the Clearing Cell, which captures the data on the HSRSS, sorts the checks on the basis of the drawee bank and branch code, and prints out a number of reports, including the clearing settlement.

The HSRSS reads the Magnetic Ink Character Recognition (MICR) code on the band at the bottom of the check. The first fields on the MICR line (serial, route, account, transaction codes) are preprinted, and the amount field is encoded after the customer presents the check to the bank. Checks that are improperly encoded or of poor quality are rejected by the HSRSS; they must be manually sorted and their data manually entered. Banks get back their checks in two lots, one fully sorted by branch and transaction code by the HSRSS, and the other that still must be sorted by branch and transaction code by the bank.

The quality of the entire operation hinges on the reject rate on the HSRSS, and this most important quality parameter was found to be very high, around

10 percent. The banks complained that they were receiving too many rejected checks and were left with a lot of tedious, labor-intensive, and costly work to do after the NCC process was complete. The manual handling of the rejected checks meant possible errors in both data entry and sorting, which often resulted in reconciliation differences among banks. Also, the banks pay a penalty on every item if their reject rate exceeds 3 percent.

The controlling authorities pointed out several times to the manager of NCC, M.R. Srinivasan, that the reject rate was too high and that customers were unhappy that the benefits of shifting to computerized processing had not been realized. Srinivasan explained to his authorities that the high reject rate of checks at Madras was due to the peculiarity of checks presented there and pointed out the high proportion of bank drafts from other places. In short, the blame was shifted elsewhere.

After about a year of this, the manager decided to look inward to try to improve performance and chose one of his shifts-in-charge, Kaza Sudhakar, to do the job. It was felt that the high reject rate was due to poor tuning of the HSRSS equipment. The engineers fine-tuned the equipment and cleaned the entire operations area to eliminate all traces of dust. This reduced the reject rate by only 1 percent. The NCC then issued a series of instructions to the banks to help them improve the encoding of their checks, but this did not help much.

NCC then embarked upon a project to inspect all of the checks presented by the banks and to separate and repair the bad checks. This reduced the reject rate by 2 percent, but at a tremendous time and labor cost. This approach was abandoned, and it was decided to review where the NCC had gone wrong.

The clerks receiving the checks pointed out that the process started at the banks where the checks are encoded. This meant that the solution would have to involve nearly 800 branches of 50 banks in and around Madras! But the potential benefits were great, so the NCC decided to go ahead. Five officers were allotted 10 banks each, with the assignment to train the banks' encoding staff. The first two months of the project produced negligible results, but as more and more banks were trained, the reject rate fell to 4.5 percent!

The banks were advised to continue the training on an ongoing basis, to train every new operator, and to designate an officer to ensure that only quality checks are presented to NCC. The banks were also invited to visit the clearing facilities so they could understand the importance of encoding to the entire clearing operation. Although these steps had resulted in dramatic improvement, the reject rate still exceeded the international standard of 3 percent.

The NCC team once again reviewed the process with people from the banks, who pointed out that most of their checks had five fields preprinted on them; the banks merely encoded the amount field. The banks felt they were paying for the poor quality of the preprinting done by the check printers.

The printers were invited to the NCC and asked to send a proof batch of 100 checks before printing a run, which often numbered in the millions. The NCC promised to run the proof batch on the HSRSS and deliver a report to the printer within half an hour. Some agreed to proof their checks, others did not. Subsequent study showed that banks whose printers had proofed their checks had a reject rate of less than 1 percent! This shifted the balance in favor of checking proof batches, and soon all of the printers were doing so. The overall reject rate for the clearing operation was now around 2 percent, which proudly measured up to any international standard.

The benefits of this improvement were many. NCC manpower devoted to manual entry and sorting could be dramatically reduced and redeployed to other areas in need of personnel. The banks were happy to receive almost all of their checks fully sorted by the HSRSS, and reconciliation differences among the banks were reduced to negligible levels. Banks also could redeploy their manual sorting and reconciliation staff, which had tremendous financial implications for them.

Srinivasan initiated measures to standardize all the procedures that enabled the achievement of low reject rates. The staff was even rotated to see if the standards could be met independent of personnel, and this was accomplished. Regular meetings were arranged with the banks to solicit feedback on the clearing operations and to elicit suggestions for further improvement.

NCC's quality project became truly total in dimension, involving thousands of employees in 800 bank branches in Madras. It had the full support of the top management and the newly empowered operating staff. One lesson taken from the project was that no operation could be improved just by tuning up the equipment until the people connected with the operation are also tuned up (trained). The improvement has to be continuous, without accepting defeat at any stage. Perhaps the most important lesson is that a project that started aimed solely at better customer service ended up producing substantial cost savings, without a conscious effort in that direction.

Discussion Questions

1. How does the role of technology in improving quality in this case differ from the Weaver Popcorn case?
2. How would you draw the customer-supplier chain (explained in chapter 4) that goes through the clearing operation?
3. How many different approaches to quality improvement were attempted by the National Clearing Cell? Which were the most effective?

ENDNOTES

1. Quoted in E.F. Cudworth, "3M's Commitment to Quality as a Way of Life," *Industrial Engineering*, July 1985.

2. Based on *Everyone Knows His First Name* by Levi Strauss & Company.

3. Adapted from Weston F. Milliken, "The Eastman Way," *Quality Progress*, Vol. 29, No. 10, October 1996, pp. 57–62. Reprinted with permission of Eastman Chemical Company.

4. Source: "To Be the Best," Eastman Chemical Company publication ECC-67, January 1994. © 1996 American Society for Quality. Reprinted with permission.

5. For a more detailed look at leadership's role in total quality, see chapter 9.

6. Interview with Richard Garula.

7. J.M. Delsanter, "On the Right Track," *TQM Magazine*, March/April 1992, pp. 17–20.

8. Kiron Kasbekar and Namita Devidayal, "Improvement Is Not All Smooth Sailing," *Times of India*, January 8, 1993.

9. Dan Ciampa, *Total Quality: A User's Guide to Implementation*, (Reading, Mass.: Addison-Wesley, 1992), cautions about trying to change culture.

10. Several reasons for managerial resistance to change are outlined by J.M. Juran in *Juran on Leadership for Quality*, New York: The Free Press, 1989.

11. Gregory P. Smith, "A Change in Culture Brings Dramatic Quality Improvements," *Quality Observer*, January 1997, pp. 14–15, 37.

12. These suggestions are taken from G.R. Pieters, "Behaving Responsibly," *TQM Magazine*, Vol. 2, No. 2, March/April 1992, pp. 25–29.

13. Ciampa, *Total Quality*.

14. Based on John R. Black, "Boeing's Quality Strategy: A Continuing Evolution," *Quest for Competitiveness*, Y.K. Shetty and V.M. Buehler (eds.), Wesport, Conn.: Quorum Books, 1991.

15. Peter M. Senge, *The Fifth Discipline: The Art and Practice of the Learning Organization*, New York: Doubleday Currency, 1990, p. 14.

16. 1998 Criteria for Performance Excellence, Malcolm Baldrige National Quality Award.

17. See chapter 4 for a discussion of various ways to get ideas from customers.

18. Interview with Richard Buck, vice president for quality, Portman Equipment.

19. B.A. Reeve, "What's In It for Me?," *Universe*, AT&T newsletter special report, July 1992.

20. Adapted from Nancy Blodgett, "Law Firm Pioneers Explore New Territory," *Quality Progress*, April 1996, pp. 90–94.

21. Based on chapter 14 in *Continuous Improvement in Operations:A Systematic Approach to Waste Reduction*, Alan Robinson (ed.), Cambridge, Mass.: Productivity Press, 1991.

22. S. Shingo, *The Sayings of Shigeo Shingo: Key Strategies for Plant Improvement*, Cambridge, Mass.: Productivity Press, 1987, p.l 52.

23. "U.S. Manufacturers Give Themselves a 'C,' Admit They Have Substantial Work to Do," *Focus*, National Center for Manufacturing Sciences, January 1993, p. 4.

24. Based on Cheri Henderson, "Monsieur Mickey," *TQM Magazine*, September/October 1992, pp. 220–224.

25. N. Tichy and R. Charan, "Speed, Simplicity, and Self-Confidence: An Interview with Jack Welch," in J. Gabarro (ed.). *Managing People and Organizations*, Boston: Harvard Business School Publications, 1992.

26. Robinson, *Continuous Improvement*.

27. Reprinted from "Total Quality Management: Time for a Theory?" Paper presented at the EOQ Conference in Prague, 1991, by Asbjorn Aune.

28. These principles are based on Richard C. Whiteley, *The Customer-Driven Company: Moving from Talk to Action*, Reading, Mass.: Addison-Wesley, 1991.

29. See J.W. Dean, Jr., and G.I. Susman, "Organizing for Manufacturable Design," *Harvard Business Review*, January–February 1989.

30. This example is taken from Michael Hammer, "Reengineering Work: Don't Automate, Obliterate," *Harvard Business Review*, July–August 1990, pp. 104–112.

31. L. Coch and J.P. French, "Overcoming Resistance to Change," *Human Relations*, Vol. 1, 1948, pp. 512–532.

32. For a summary of this material, see J.P. Kotter and L.A. Schlesinger, "Choosing Strategies for Change," in J.J. Gabarro (ed.), *Managing People and Organizations*. Boston: Harvard Business School Publications, 1992, pp. 395–409.

33. See, for example, H.A. Aldrich, *Organizations and Environments*. Englewood Cliffs, N.J.: Prentice-Hall, 1979.

34. K. Lewin, "Forces behind Food Habits and Methods of Change," *Bulletin of the National Research Council #108*, 1947, pp. 35–65. See also E. Schein, "Organizational Socialization and the Profession of Management," *Industrial Management Review*, 1968, pp. 1–16.

35. See Thomas R. Bennett III, *Planning for Change*, Washington, D.C.: Leadership Resources, 1961.

36. See, for example, Harold J. Leavitt, "Applied Organization Change in Industry: Structural, Technical, and Human Approaches," in W.W. Cooper, H.J. Leavitt, and M.W. Shelly (eds.) *New Perspectives in Organizational Research*, New York: Wiley, 1964.

37. For an interesting (and now classic) discussion of this issue, see P.R. Lawrence, "How to Deal with Resistance to Change," *Harvard Business Review*, May/June 1954.

38. See Schein, "Organizational Socialization," *Industrial Management Review*. See also, P.S. Goodman and J.W. Dean, Jr., "Creating Long-Term Change," in P.S. Goodman (ed.), *Change in Organizations*. San Francisco: Jossey-Bass, 1983.

39. Reprinted from David M. Lyth and Larry A Mallak, " 'We're Not in Kansas Anymore, Toto' or Quality Lessons from the Land of Oz," *Quality Engineering*, Vol. 10, No. 30, 1998, pp. 579–588, by courtesy of Marcel Dekker, Inc.

40. Reprinted with permission of *Inc. Magazine*, Goldhirsh Group, Inc., 38 Commercial Wharf, Boston, MA 02110 (http://www.inc.com). *The Machine That Didn't Change the World* (Excerpt), *Inc. Magazine*, May 1990. Reproduced by permission of the publisher via Copyright Clearance Center, Inc.

41. This case was written especially for this book by Kaza Sudhakar, Officer, Reserve Bank of India, Madras.

III

Total Quality and Organizational Behavior

CHAPTER

7

Quality Teamwork

CHAPTER OUTLINE

No matter what you are trying to do, teams are the most effective way to get the job done.

—Donald Peterson, former CEO, Ford Motor Company[1]

A **team** is a small number of people with complementary skills who are committed to a common purpose, set of performance goals, and an approach for which they hold themselves mutually accountable.[2] Teams are ubiquitous in our world—the Denver Broncos, Navy SEALS, the Tokyo String Quartet, the cast of *ER*, and Jeff Gordon's pit crew, to name just a few. Teams also are a central facet of total quality. Although many types of teams exist in organizations pursuing TQ, the concept of teamwork is widespread and a key contributor to TQ success in just about any setting. Chapter 5 introduced teams as an aspect of quality-oriented organizational design. This chapter will

- explain the importance of teams in TQ,
- identify the different types of teams used in TQ,
- explain some of the factors associated with the successful use of teams,
- give examples of effective teams in action, and
- relate the use of teams in TQ to organizational behavior theories.

Teamwork for Fun and Profit at Motorola[3]

Dina Trinidad is a mold operator at a Motorola semiconductor plant in Manila, Philippines. When she had worked for Motorola for over 17 years—and had never left her native country— the company sent her and 11 of her co-workers to a posh resort in Scottsdale, Arizona for five days as part of Motorola's Total Customer Satisfaction (TCS) team competition. The workers made a presentation to top executives and were treated like royalty. This competition helps to renew emphasis on team processes, recognize and reward outstanding team performance, reaffirm the environment for continuous improvement, demonstrate the power of focused team effort, and communicate the best team achievements throughout the company.

Some 5,000 teams take part in preliminary contests in each of Motorola's business units, and one to five teams from each region move forward to the worldwide finals. With names such as the Green Tray Packers, Document Doctors, and Irish Risky, teams are awarded points in seven categories: project selection (tied to Motorola's key initiatives), teamwork (participation and contributions), analysis analytical tools (leading to root causes and solution identification), remedies that are (consistent with analysis and creative), results, institutionalization (sustainable improvement over time), and presentation (clear and concise). One team saved $1.8 million in 1996 by reducing polyimide delamination for electronic circuits by 85 percent; another increased production capacity for cellular phone production by 50 percent in just eight weeks; and the winning team's efforts were expected to save over $6 million in one year.

For Dina Trinidad, the competition only reinforced the feeling that Motorola values its employees. She says, like others, she will treasure every one of her TCS memories: "The experience emphasized even more the value of each individual in the company. It's worth remembering time and again—even forever."

THE IMPORTANCE OF TEAMS IN TQ

Teams are everywhere in TQ organizations: at the top and bottom and in every function and department in between. For instance, Corning Telecommunications Products Division, a 1995 Baldrige recipient, has employee-designed work teams, customer account teams, market teams, new product development teams, and manufacturing operation teams. Why are there so many teams? Teamwork enables various parts of the organization to work together in meeting customer needs that can seldom be fulfilled by employees limited to one specialty. The TQ philosophy recognizes the interdependence of various parts of the organization and uses teams as a way to coordinate work.

TQ organizations recognize that the potential contributions of employees are much greater than in the traditional organization, and teams are an attempt to take advantage of this potential. Further, the competitive environment of modern business requires flexible, fast reaction to changes in customer demands or technological capacity. Teams can provide the capacity for rapid response. During the past few years, many companies have gone public with stories of their successful teams as well as sharing their recognition efforts (see the box on Motorola on page 230). Managers are always looking for ideas that produce results, and teams certainly fall squarely within this category.

TYPES OF TQ TEAMS

TQ uses so many different types of teams that sometimes it is difficult to tell one from another. Some common types of teams include:

- *Steering committees (or quality councils)*—management teams that lead an organization and provide direction and focus.
- *Problem-solving teams*—teams of workers and supervisors that meet to address workplace problems involving quality and productivity, or ad hoc teams with a specific mission.
- *Self-managed teams*—teams of people who work together every day, who study and improve their processes, and who are empowered to make and control their own decisions.
- *Virtual teams*—teams whose members communicate by computer, take turns as leaders, and jump in and out as necessary. Virtual teams are beginning to play an increasingly important role because of the Internet and electronic communication.

Steering Committees

Most organizations practicing total quality have a steering committee, called a **quality council** by Juran and a **quality improvement team** by Crosby.[4] Steering committees are responsible for establishing policy for TQ and for guiding the implementation and evolution of TQ throughout the organization. The top manager of the organization is usually on the steering committee, as is the manager with overall responsibility for quality—for example, the vice president/director of total quality.

The steering committee may meet fairly often when a TQ effort is getting started but usually meets only monthly or quarterly once things are under way. This group makes key decisions about the quality process—how quality should be measured and what structures and approaches should be used to improve quality. The steering committee also periodically reviews the status of TQ and makes adjustments to ensure customer satisfaction and continuous improve-

Quality Circles in Japan: Still Unbroken

Quality circles were among the first Japanese management practices used in the United States. When visiting Japan in the 1970s, American managers noticed groups of workers meeting to address quality problems. The managers recognized this as a practice that could easily be copied, and they returned home to institute it in their own companies. Quality circles (QCs) took off in the United States as the Japanese management mania peaked, and firms like Lockheed and Westinghouse reported early successes with QCs. The movement boomed in the early 1980s as most large American companies introduced the practice.

The bloom was soon off the rose, however, as firms found themselves devoting a lot of time and attention to QCs and receiving relatively little in return. There were a number of reasons for the lack of results. Employees were only encouraged to work on quality problems during their meetings (usually about an hour a week) and spent the rest of their week just "doing their job." Supervisors were often not involved in the program and were indifferent, if not downright hostile, to it. Perhaps the biggest problem was that QCs were "just a program," cut off from and often opposed to the way the organization usually worked. Managers preached about the importance of quality work during their QC events, but when crunch time came, their attitude was, in the words of one QC member, "If it doesn't smoke, ship it!"

Not surprisingly, companies started to disband their QC programs, which were soon dismissed as just another passing fad. In the context of the current interest in total quality, many managers look back on QCs as essentially a false start on the road to quality. It is interesting in this light to note that many Japanese companies still operate QCs and that they are seen as a critical part of the total quality control (TQC) effort in these companies.[5]

According to the Japanese Union of Scientists and Engineers, 5.5 million workers take part in 750,000 circles. Managers as well as frontline employees are involved, and the circles are considered a normal part of working life, rather than a "program." In fact, QCs often work to achieve the objectives set in the kaizen process (see chapter 5), which puts them in the mainstream of TQC activity. Some organizations provide monetary incentives for suggestions provided by circles, and employees in some firms make dozens of suggestions per year. It appears that the mistake made in the U.S. introduction of quality circles was not in introducing them, but in not taking them seriously.

ment. In general, the steering committee has overall responsibility for the progress and success of the TQ effort.

As TQ is becoming more integrated within organizations, the notion of a separate steering committee dedicated to TQ is disappearing. As discussed in chapter 5, TQ efforts are often led by the executive management team, which acts both as a quality council and a business leadership team.

Problem-Solving Teams

The second, and probably most common, type of team used in TQ is the problem-solving team. As the name implies, problem-solving teams work to improve quality by identifying and solving specific quality-related problems facing the organization. Such teams are sometimes referred to as *corrective action teams*, or *quality circles* (see box on page 232), although many organizations have created their own names for them. Two basic types of problem-solving teams are departmental and cross-functional.

Departmental Problem-Solving Teams

These teams are limited in membership to employees of a specific department and are limited in scope to problems within that department. Such groups typically meet once a week for one to two hours and progress through a standardized problem-solving methodology. First they identify a set of problems and select one to work on. Then they collect data about the causes of the problem and determine the best approach to solving it. (Often this will entail using many of the techniques described in chapter 3.)

If the solution does not require any major changes in procedures or substantial resources, the group frequently can implement its own solution. If this is not the case, group members will make a presentation to some level of management, requesting approval for their solution and the resources to implement it. These teams typically remain relatively intact as they address a number of problems in succession.

The problems that such teams work on can be quite diverse. A team of hourly workers at U.S. Steel's Gary Works has solved a number of crippling quality problems, helping to reduce the amount of steel rejected by automotive customers by 80 percent.[6] A team of service technicians at an equipment rental company simplified the form used to perform preventive maintenance, saving the company considerable time in the process. A team of people from the "resort" department at FedEx improved the process of package sorting, which created savings in labor costs and helped to avoid the cost and embarrassment of having to send overnight packages via commercial airlines.[7]

Cross-Functional Teams

Cross-functional teams are not unique to total quality—they are commonly used in new product development, for example—but they are increasingly becoming a mainstay of quality programs. These teams are similar in many ways to the departmental teams just discussed: They receive training in problem solving, identify and solve problems, and either implement or recommend solutions.

The differences are that members of cross-functional teams come from several departments or functions, deal with problems that involve a variety of functions, and typically dissolve after the problem is solved. For example, a cross-functional team in a brokerage might deal with problems in handling questions from clients. The issues raised would not be limited to stocks, bonds, or mutual funds, so people from all of these areas would be involved.

Cross-functional teams make a great deal of sense in an organization devoted to process improvement, because most processes do not respect functional boundaries. If a process is to be comprehensively addressed, the team addressing it cannot be limited, by either membership or charter, to only one function. To be effective, cross-functional teams should include people from several departments: those who are feeling the effects of the problem, those who may be causing it, those who can provide remedies, and those who can furnish data.[8]

One cross-functional team made up of nurses, dieticians, and other nursing unit and food services staff addressed the problem of patients receiving their dinners late. This problem was quite aggravating to patients, but if it had been addressed by only the nursing unit, ignorance or apathy in the food services

---

Gravedigging in New York[9]

Have you ever sent a letter only to have it returned as "undeliverable" by the post office? How about 7,000 undeliverable pieces of mail every week? This was the problem faced by New York Life Insurance Company. Most of the mail being returned was notices to people that their premiums were due, so a great deal of revenue was being lost. In fact, the company estimated the problem to be costing them as much as $80 million.

The team formed to attack this problem became known as the Gravediggers because of their relentlessness in "digging up" addresses so premium notices could be delivered. The 18-member team, whose members were drawn from around the nation, met via teleconference once or twice a week. Following total quality principles, the team began by looking for the root causes of undeliverable mail. Some of the most common were (1) policyholders who forgot to notify New York Life when they moved, and (2) long addresses that did not fit into the window on the mailing envelope.

The Gravediggers instituted a number of corrective measures to deal with the problem. They created units in each of the company's service offices to find addresses and keep company records up to date, they worked out a deal with the post office to forward mail and provide the company with corrected addresses, and they used a more elaborate mail-sorting system with bar codes. Early results found that the volume of returned mail was reduced by more than 20 percent, and the postal service provided the company with 61,000 correct addresses in a nine-month period. In fact, the Gravediggers are among the most successful teams in the history of New York Life's total quality effort.

department would most likely have been blamed. Had the problem been addressed by food services, nursing would likely have been blamed. In either case, little would have been accomplished. A cross-functional team was required to unravel the complex scheduling and delivery issues associated with the problem.

Similarly, a cross-functional team at New York Life Insurance Company addressed the problem of returned mail. This was crucial for the company, because if policyholders do not receive their premium notices, New York Life does not get paid (see box on page 234).

Self-Managed Teams

The third type of team used in Total Quality is the **self-managed team (SMT)**, also known as a self-directed team or autonomous work group. Although self-managed teams have been used for decades, their popularity has increased in recent years, due in part to their use in TQ. Unlike problem-solving teams, SMTs replace rather than complement the traditional organization of work. In place of a first-level supervisor and a set of employees with narrowly defined jobs is a set of associates (a term increasingly used for employees) with broad responsibilities, including the responsibility to manage themselves. In the absence of a supervisor, SMTs often handle budgeting, scheduling, setting goals, and ordering supplies. Some teams even evaluate one another's performance and hire replacements for departing team members.

A team in an automotive manufacturing plant placed an advertisement in the classified section of their local newspaper that read in part:

> Our team is down one good player. Join our group of multiskilled Maintenance Associates who work together to support our assembly teams. . . . We are looking for a versatile person with . . . ability to set up and operate various welding machinery . . . willingness to work on detailed projects for extended time periods, and general overall knowledge of the automobile manufacturing process. . . . You must be a real team player, have excellent interpersonal skills, and be motivated to work in a highly participative environment.[10]

This ad illustrates many of the differences between SMTs and the traditional organization of work for nonmanagerial employees. For example, members of such teams are expected to actually work as a team, rather than just perform their own jobs capably. Their knowledge must be broad rather than narrow, their skills interpersonal as well as technical. For example, as part of a self-directed restaurant team at a Ritz-Carlton hotel, employees frequently arrive before the maître d' to set up. If a server calls in sick, employees take responsibility for a replacement. Servers are also closely involved in planning menus with chefs.[11] In short, members of such teams are more like managers than employees in the traditional sense, hence the term self-managed teams. SMTs have resulted in improved quality and customer service, greater flexibility, reduced costs, faster response, simpler job classifications, increased employee commitment to the organization, and the ability to attract and retain the best people.[12]

Virtual Teams

Virtual teams are groups of people who work closely despite being geographically separated. Their primary interaction is through technologies such as telephone, fax, shared databases, the Internet, e-mail, and videoconferencing. Virtual teams are becoming important because of increasing globalization and the need to bring diverse talents and expertise to complex projects and customize solutions to meet market demands. For example, a product design team in the United States can hand off its work to another team in Asia or Australia, resulting in an almost continuous work effort that speeds up development time considerably. However, challenges include language, culture, and style differences and the lack of social relationships that can lessen team commitment.[13]

EFFECTIVE TEAMWORK

Teams are the main structure of many TQ organizations.[14] Thus, effective teamwork is critical to a successful TQ effort. If teams are not effective, TQ processes will suffer. Steering committees will choose poor directions and policies for the organization; departmental and cross-functional problem-solving teams will choose inappropriate problems or won't be able to solve the problems they identify; and self-managed teams will not be able to fulfill the promise of an empowered, creative workforce.

This section explores what it takes for teams to be effective in a TQ environment. Although the relative importance of these factors will vary from one type of team to another, they generally apply to any type of team found in TQ organizations. As you read this section, consider the ideas in light of your own experiences, rewarding or otherwise, on teams. If you are currently on a team, you may identify some ideas for improvement.

Criteria for Team Effectiveness

There are several criteria for team effectiveness. First, the team must achieve its goals of quality improvement. A steering committee must move the TQ effort ahead; a problem-solving team must identify and solve important problems; a self-managed team must operate and improve a set of production or service processes.

Second, teams that improve quality performance quickly are more effective than those that take a long time to do so. One of the strengths of teams is their potential for rapid adaptation to changing conditions. A team that takes a long time to accomplish anything is losing the potential benefits of having problems solved sooner and is consuming a greater-than-necessary amount of resources, including the time devoted to team meetings. In short, it is inefficient.

Third, the team must maintain or increase its strength as a unit. Think of the team as representing an asset—a quantity of human capital—beyond that represented by its individual members. This additional human capital is based on the ability to understand and adjust to one another's work styles, the development of an effective set of routines, the growth of trust among team members, and so on. A team that remains intact over a period of time preserves and enhances this human capital. A team that solves an important problem but has such miserable relations that it dissolves, does not. It may make a contribution to the TQ effort, but it squanders a considerable amount of human capital in the process.

Fourth, the team must preserve or strengthen its relationship with the rest of the organization. With apologies to John Donne, "no team is an island," especially in the TQ environment. A team that accomplishes its goals at the cost of alienating others in the organization violates the TQ spirit of teamwork and compromises its ability to perform successfully in the future, when the collaboration of others may well be needed.

An effective team—whether it be a steering committee, problem-solving team, or self-managed team—must improve quality within a reasonable time frame and strengthen working relationships both inside and outside the team.

Team Membership

Like any system, teams cannot function effectively without high-quality input. The most important elements of team processes are the team members themselves. Managers need to understand why people do and do not join teams. People participate on teams for many reasons:[15]

- They want to be progressive in making decisions that affect their work.
- They believe that being involved in teams will enhance their potential for promotion or other job opportunities.
- They believe that teams will be privy to information that typically is not available to individuals.
- They enjoy the feeling of accomplishment and believe that teams provide greater possibilities.
- They want to use team meetings to address personal agendas.
- They are genuinely concerned about the future of the organization and feel a sense of obligation to help improve it.
- They enjoy the recognition and rewards associated with team activity.
- They find teams to be a comfortable social environment.

Likewise, many people refuse to join teams for reasons such as outside commitments, fear of embarrassment, an overwhelming workload, mistrust of management, fear of failure or losing one's job, or simply an "I don't care" attitude. True leaders need to develop strategies for dealing with these issues.

To be effective, team members must be representative of the departments or functions related to the problem being addressed. For example, a steering committee made up of members from one part of the organization would be insufficiently representative of the organization to be effective. Representation is particularly important for cross-functional teams.

One study of cross-functional organizational design teams suggests that *team skills*, as well as a clear purpose and expectations, are significant predictors of team performance.[16] Team members must possess the necessary technical knowledge to solve the problem at hand. This may mean understanding metallurgy for a team in a steel mill or understanding credit approval for a team in a bank. All members need not share the same knowledge, and in fact team members are often selected on the basis of specialized knowledge, but all of the appropriate technical bases must be covered for the team to be effective.

Effective teams must have members with problem-solving skills. These include problem diagnosis and data collection, as well as the ability to use TQ tools such as fishbone diagrams, histograms, and so on. Most organizations provide training in such techniques to people as they form teams.

Finally, teams must also have members with strong interpersonal skills. The critical importance of interpersonal skills is demonstrated by the following passage from a book on self-managed teams:

> We often hear experienced team leaders and members make remarks like this one: "I'll take someone with a good attitude over someone with just technical skills any day. I can train technical skills." With further prodding, we usually discover that they are really talking about interpersonal skills. . . . Because these qualities can be difficult to detect in a casual selection process, they are often overlooked in the pursuit of apparent, more objectively measured technical skills.[17]

What is meant by interpersonal skills? Think of people who are easy to work with in a group. They are good listeners and do not ignore or downgrade someone else's ideas in order to promote their own. They try to understand other people's positions, even when they do not agree with them. They offer help to other group members, rather than waiting to be asked. They are willing and able to communicate their opinions, ideas, and any information that needs to be shared. They can deal with conflict without turning it into a personal issue. Finally, they are willing to share credit for accomplishments with other members of the group, rather than trying to keep the limelight for themselves.[18] If you have worked on a team with people who possess even most of these skills, you are lucky indeed!

Team Processes

Many processes are undertaken within TQ teams, including quality planning, problem selection and diagnosis, communication, data collection, and implementation of solutions. Team processes are not fundamentally different from other processes, such as assembling an electronic device, taking a patient's vital signs, or preparing coq au vin. The customers of all these processes can be identified, their elements can be placed in a flowchart, steps that do not add value can be removed, and their quality can be improved continuously.

Most people, however, are not accustomed to thinking of group processes in this manner. This may be why group meetings are often long and boring and why so many people try to escape committee assignments and avoid committee meetings like the plague. A willingness to tolerate poor-quality group processes has no place in organizations practicing total quality. This section identifies a few of the processes used in teams and provides some ideas about how teams can use them to operate effectively.

Problem Selection

One of the processes undertaken at least occasionally by most teams and frequently by problem-solving teams is the choice of problems or issues on which to work. This process can be particularly difficult for newly empowered employees, who are more accustomed to being told what to do than they are to establishing their own agenda. New teams are often tempted to select the biggest, most glaring problem in sight that has been haunting them for years. Selecting such problems—called "world hunger" problems in TQ jargon—is usually a mistake.

New teams generally are not skilled enough to solve massive problems, and a failure to address such a visible problem successfully may be difficult for the team to overcome. It makes more sense for a team initially to select a problem of moderate importance and difficulty and to move on to more complex and difficult problems when the team is better established. This approach is more likely to lead to successful solutions, which will build momentum for each team and for the quality effort as a whole.

Another common problem among new teams is that they select problems that are not associated—at least in management's eyes—with important business or quality issues. When given a voice for the first time, many teams ask for things they have been denied in the past, such as a better lunch area or break room. Although managers often consider such behavior an indictment of quality teams, it is in fact an indictment of management itself. It is unrealistic to expect employees to focus on business issues when managers have not taken seriously employee requests for adequate facilities. In fact, it is better for issues such as these to be worked out prior to initiating a team-based quality effort, rather than allowing them to undermine such efforts.

The selection of "trivial" problems by teams may also indicate that management has not done an effective job of sharing information about the business with team members. If they truly understand the nature of the important problems faced by the organization, teams are much more likely to choose worthwhile issues on which to work.

Problem Diagnosis

After problems to be addressed are identified, their causes must be ascertained. Thus, a second critical process in TQ groups is problem diagnosis, the process by which the team investigates potential causes of problems to identify potential solutions. Juran refers to this step as the "diagnostic journey" and explains that it consists of three parts:

1. understanding the symptoms (for example, a process out of control),
2. theorizing as to causes (for example, preventive maintenance neglected), and
3. testing the theories (for example, reviewing preventive maintenance records to see if they relate to the problems experienced).

Many teams want to bypass problem diagnosis and begin problem solving as soon as possible, usually because they mistakenly believe that the problem's causes are obvious. Teams that spend more time diagnosing problems have been shown to be much more effective than those that proceed immediately to solutions. Spending time pinning down the sources of problems is consistent with the TQ principle of decision making based on facts and reduces the potential for what are sometimes called "type 3 errors"—solving the wrong problem. Training in methods of diagnosis and analysis is important for team effectiveness.

Work Allocation

Another important process is the allocation of work within the team. Many teams approach this process haphazardly, assigning tasks to the next in line or the first person who volunteers. Assigning tasks is one of the keys to team effectiveness and should not be taken so lightly.[19] Each team member has certain skills and will perform well on tasks that use those skills and not so well on tasks that use other skills. The team needs to assign people tasks that will utilize their skills to the greatest extent possible.

Imagine a women's college basketball team that consists of some tall women who are excellent rebounders and inside shooters and some shorter (vertically challenged?) women who are skilled ball handlers and outside shooters. This team will be much more successful if the coach takes the time to assess the skills of each player and assigns them to the position where they can best help the team.

When explained in this context, the point is obvious, but you would be amazed at how many teams have the tall members bring the ball down the floor and pass to the short members underneath the basket! Differences in status within the group can be a problem if team members in higher positions are assigned the more glamorous roles, even when others are more qualified to fulfill them.[20] The status problem is particularly acute in organizations that have very high- and very low-status members, especially when (as in medicine) these differences are institutionalized in society. The vice president of quality at one hospital described a team with this problem:

> We had an emergency room physician who was a disaster. He was very much the old school expert, and he was not about to be egalitarian in his approach. This created a lot of problems for that team. In spite of

that, we were able to achieve some success with that team, but it was, I'm sure, limited. If there was one factor [that hurt us], it was probably his impact on the team.

Communication

Communication is a key process for any team attempting to improve quality. Steering committees communicate priorities to employees. Members of problem-solving teams communicate among themselves and to their internal and external customers. For example, problem-solving teams often have to present their recommendations to management. Self-managed teams have similar communication needs and often must communicate effectively across shifts.

Three times every day in thousands of hospitals, mines, and manufacturing plants, teams of nurses, miners, and machine operators explain to the next shift what has happened in the last eight hours and what needs to be done in the next. The quality of this communication can dramatically affect the performance of the team on the next shift.

The communication process can be improved by carefully assigning people to key communication tasks and by training people in communication. We spend so much time communicating in our daily lives that we sometimes forget that skills such as listening and asking questions are vital to effective communication.

Communication within and across teams can also be enhanced by using a variety of media. Many TQ teams use electronic mail and fax machines but also benefit from such low-tech media as posters and graphs posted on the walls. As with many team processes, any specific recommendations are less important than the general idea of recognizing communication as a process that consists of a series of steps that can be improved.

Coordination

Another key process is coordinating the team's work with other teams and departments in the organization. Maintaining good relationships outside the team is one criterion of team effectiveness. However, researchers have often found a tendency among teams to turn inward, believing that their own needs, ideas, and plans are more valid than those of "outsiders." Ironically, the more cohesive the team becomes, the greater the likelihood of this occurring.[21]

Such a tendency is antithetical to TQ, but it is a danger faced by virtually all groups. Teams can try to overcome this problem by keeping their customers in mind and using customer satisfaction as the yardstick against which ideas and plans are measured. Remaining aware of the need to improve team processes should also guard against the tendency to downplay the potential contributions of non–team members, as outsiders are often the source of ideas for improvement that team members have overlooked.

Finally, good communication should also help to coordinate work with other teams and departments. The likelihood of following a path that works against the needs or plans of other groups will be diminished if teams communicate with other groups early and often. Tools such as quality function deployment and affinity diagrams, discussed in chapter 3, can be used to enhance such communication.

In a sense, quality-oriented process improvement and problem solving are a minefield for the unsuspecting team. Whenever changes are made in an organization, vested interests are challenged. By carefully managing the coordination process, teams will reduce the potential for unnecessary conflict with groups outside the team and will greatly enhance their potential for long-term effectiveness.

In summary, team processes can be improved just like any other process. Several key processes that are candidates for improvement are problem identification and diagnosis, work allocation, communication, and coordination of work with other teams and departments.

Organizational Support

However skillful the team, they will find it hard to be successful unless their efforts are supported by the organization in general and by management in particular. Organizational support is the foundation for effective teamwork. Management must provide the following if a TQ team is to be successful.

First, management must issue a clear charge to the group; that is, a description of what the group is and is not expected to do. This is often called a *team charter*. Many teams have wasted a great deal of time and energy on issues that they later found they were not authorized to pursue. Management's guidance as to the quality priorities of the organization is crucial, especially in the early stages of a team's work. Several organizational researchers have found that team performance improved for teams with charters and clear expectations.[22]

Second, human resource management (HRM) systems often must be adjusted. Conventional HRM systems may be barriers to effective teamwork that will undermine TQ if not changed.[23] The need for enhanced training is particularly acute, as team members must be brought up to speed on the various types of skills necessary for effective teamwork.

Performance appraisal and reward systems are also a concern. Many of these systems are designed to reward individual effort or the attainment of functional goals, rather than teamwork. Numerous research studies over the past several decades have pointed out the problems and pitfalls of performance appraisals.[24] Many legitimate objections can be made:[25]

- They tend to foster mediocrity and discourage risk taking.
- They focus on short-term and measurable results, thereby discouraging long-term planning or thinking and ignoring important behaviors that are more difficult to measure.
- They focus on the individual and therefore tend to discourage or destroy teamwork within and between departments.
- The process is detection oriented rather than prevention oriented.

- They are often unfair, since managers frequently do not possess observational accuracy.
- They fail to distinguish between factors that are within the employees' control and system-determined factors that are beyond their control.

This can greatly undermine teamwork and can be fatal to the team if not addressed. Imagine a class project in which each student was graded on the quality of his or her part, rather than on the quality of the project as a whole, and you will have the general idea of the impact of inappropriate reward systems.

The RIT/*USA Today* Quality Cup[26]

The RIT/*USA Today* Quality Cup Competition, established in 1991, recognizes teams that make significant contributions to the improvement of quality in their organization. The competition is conducted as a cooperative academic-industry effort between the College of Business at the Rochester Institute of Technology and *USA Today*. Team awards are presented in six categories:

- education,
- government,
- health care,
- manufacturing Industry,
- service Industry, and
- small Businesses with fewer than 500 employees.

Each year, up to three teams are honored in each of the six categories. The winning team receives a handcrafted pure silver Quality Cup that sits atop a white marble cylinder with a sterling silver disk at its base. Quality Cup winners and finalists are recognized at a ceremony at *USA Today* Headquarters near Washington, D.C., and also receive recognition in special pages of *USA Today*.

One of the 1998 winners was a team from Allied Signal Aerospace. They resolved a problem of unacceptable faults in a valve on the Airbus-300 aircraft. It was among the top 10 reasons for flight delays and cancellations. Valve manufacturer Allied Signal had tried nine times since 1974 to correct the problems when it decided to look at the entire system. The team spent days in the hangars where American Airlines performs its most comprehensive inspections, allowing the engineers to see what happens when a fault light comes on. One discovery was that in a typical fix, the existing valve would be replaced with a spare because it takes only minutes. But by tracking each $37,500 valve that had been removed, the team found that many of them didn't need to be replaced. Judge Chuck Blevins of Blevins Harding Group noted, "This shows that a group, given the right environment, can become very creative and effective." More information can be found at the Web site, www.qualitycup.org.

Performance appraisals are most effective when they are based on the objectives of the work teams that support the organization.[27] In this respect, they act as a diagnostic tool and review process for individual, team, and organizational development and achievement. The performance appraisal can also be a motivator when it is developed and used by the work team itself. Team efforts are harnessed when team members are empowered to monitor their own workplace activities. In a TQ culture, quality improvement is one of the major dimensions on which employees are evaluated. Xerox, for instance, changed its performance review criteria by replacing traditional measures such as "follows procedures" and "meets standards" to evaluating employees on the basis of quality improvement, problem solving, and team contributions. Many companies use peer review, customer evaluations, and self-assessments as a part of the appraisal process.

Selection processes may also be changed in conjunction with TQ implementation. Companies like Procter & Gamble seek entry-level college graduates who understand total quality principles. They specifically want their new employees to think in terms of creating quality and value for consumers, to understand their customers and needs, and to work toward results despite obstacles. The members of self-managed teams often take much of the responsibility for hiring people for their team. Human resource professionals should play a consultative role in such efforts, however, to make sure that selection is done in a fair and legal manner.

Third, management must provide the team with the resources necessary to be successful. These include a place and time to meet and the tools to get the job done. Human resources are also important: Management should avoid moving people on and off teams frequently, as this can disrupt teamwork and send a message that quality and teamwork are really not a high priority for the organization.

Fourth, when teams make a proposal, management must respond swiftly and constructively. It is not realistic to expect that every quality improvement proposal made by a team will be implemented. For those proposals that cannot be implemented, management owes the team a reasonable explanation as to why it is not feasible and some guidance as to how the proposal might be modified so that it would be acceptable. Few experiences are as demoralizing to quality teams as making an elaborate, reasoned presentation, only to be met with deafening silence from management. This was one of the problems that undermined quality circle programs. It is less of a problem for self-managed teams that generally have broad authority to implement their own solutions.

For those proposals that are accepted, some form of recognition for the team is in order. At the Ritz-Carlton, team awards include bonus pools and sharing in the gratuity system. Many companies have formal corporate recognition programs, such as IBM's Market Driven Quality Award for outstanding individual and team achievements in quality improvement, or the Xerox President's Award and Team Excellence Award. Solectron rewards groups by buying entire divisions lunch and bringing in ice cream for the entire plant.

Often the most effective forms of recognition are symbolic, such as a citation or picture in the company newspaper.

TEAMWORK IN ACTION

This section provides two examples of quality teamwork: one a problem-solving team in a general hospital (a winner of the RIT/*USA Today* Quality Cup Competition—see box on page 243), and the other an unusual instance of teamwork in a Baldrige Award winner. As you read these minicases, reflect on whether the teams are effectively practicing the team processes we have discussed.

A Team with a Transparent Problem[28]

Have you ever had tests done in a hospital and wondered why it takes so long to get the results back? So did the employees and managers in the radiology department at Sentara Norfolk General Hospital in Norfolk, Virginia. Although everyone associated with the process felt they were working as fast as they could, performing and reporting the results of an X-ray or CAT scan was taking three days on average (72.5 hours, to be precise). A nine-person team was formed to address the problem, and they vowed to cut the time down to 24 hours.

The first step was to focus the team on the process, rather than on individual performance, and to create a sense of teamwork that would override the differences in status that sometimes hamper the work of medical professionals. Pat Curtis, head of cardiac nursing, was chosen as the team's facilitator, partially for her recognized skills but also because she was from outside radiology and had no formal authority over team members.

Although the team met infrequently, the members had plenty of work to do between meetings, mostly on collecting information. Using techniques associated with Norfolk General's CQI effort (Continuous Quality Improvement, as TQ is often known in health care), the team identified 40 steps in the X-ray process and 50 possible causes of delay, only a few of which were causing most of the problems. Rather than waiting for a grand changeover at the culmination of their work, the team made improvements to the process as they discovered them. This was greatly facilitated by the cross-functional representation and the presence of managers on the team. As one member put it, "Folks who could effect change were part of the decision making."

None of the changes the team made was particularly dramatic. Curtis helped the nursing department to reduce errors such as forgetting to note whether patients would need stretchers or oxygen. X-ray technologists began to walk developed films to the next person in the process, rather than waiting for the internal mail service to move them. Fourteen of the 40 steps were redesigned out of the process.

The results were clearly dramatic. The average time to process an X-ray dropped to 13.8 hours, an 81 percent improvement! This achievement was impressive enough to win the team an RIT/*USA Today* Quality Cup for team accomplishment in the not-for-profit category. Physicians in the hospital report that the faster availability of diagnostic information is helping them to improve their own processes, and other companies and government agencies in the Norfolk area are looking to the hospital for help with their own quality improvement challenges.

The team has responded to its success with a renewed commitment to continuous improvement. The introduction of a CD-based digital system to replace tapes for dictating physician comments is expected to cut the time down to 11 hours. The team's new goal? Eight hours.

The Birth of Teamwork at Globe Metallurgical[29]

Globe Metallurgical, with plants in Beverly, Ohio, and Selma, Alabama, was the first small-company winner of the Malcolm Baldrige National Quality Award. Considering the problems the company has faced, it is lucky to be operating, let alone winning awards. As with many companies, its quality and teamwork principles first crystallized under a great deal of pressure.

On October 8, 1986, Globe's unionized workforce went out on strike over differences with management concerning pay and work rules, such as which workers can perform what jobs. In a small town like Beverly, a strike is a very big deal, with lifetime friendships and even family relationships at stake. There was even some violence as suppliers and people working through the strike tried to cross the picket lines.

During the strike, work usually done by union workers was performed by salaried workers and managers on 12-hour shifts, seven days a week. Although this was no doubt an exhausting routine, it provided an opportunity for people to learn a number of lessons about teamwork and continuous improvement. In the words of Arden Sims, chief executive of Globe:

> The strike was a time of great stress but also a time of great progress. We experimented with everything. . . . Our objective was to find the most efficient way to run the furnaces, with no constraints on how we did it. . . . We were operating in a very fast continuous improvement mode. Every day, people would suggest ways to improve the operation of the furnaces or [other processes]. I kept a pocket notebook, and if I saw something, I'd jot it down and discuss it with the team over coffee or during a meal. I filled a notebook every day.
>
> As we made more and more changes and as we settled into the routine of running the plant, it became evident that we didn't need first-line supervisors. We could produce the product more effectively if everyone just worked together cooperatively—welders, crane operators, furnace operators, forklift drivers, stokers, furnace tappers, and tapper assistants.[30]

What Globe had discovered, without using the name, was self-managed teams. The experiments undertaken during the strike resulted in dramatic improvements in efficiency for the company's operations. Unfortunately for the union employees, many of them never returned to the new-and-improved company, which had learned to operate with many fewer people. It is ironic that the high degree of teamwork exhibited by the management team during the strike was only possible because of a breakdown of teamwork between management and the union, which ultimately led to a substantial reduction in union workers in the company.

COMPARISON TO ORGANIZATIONAL BEHAVIOR THEORIES

Little conflict exists between the use of teams in TQ and theories of organizational behavior, but there are differences in emphasis. Along with social psychology and sociology, organizational behavior (OB) is the source of much of what is known about groups or teams. Since there is no separate tradition of research or thinking about groups within TQ, virtually all of the practices and recommendations ultimately derive from conventional (or unconventional) management theory.

Research knowledge about groups is most heavily emphasized in organizational development (OD), the branch of the organizational sciences that deals with changing and improving organizations. Most team-based practices in TQ come from OD. Some of these practices, such as the nominal group technique, are based on research in organizational behavior or social psychology, others are not.

Teams are actually a subset of the organizational behavior/social psychology concept of groups. All teams are groups, but not all groups are teams. Compare our definition of a team as "people working together to achieve a goal" to the following definition of a group: "A number of persons who communicate with one another often over a span of time, and who are few enough in number that each person may communicate with all the others."[31] Clearly we ask more of our teams than we do of our groups! Organizational behavior has traditionally focused on workgroups, people who work together in the same function. Theory has addressed why some groups are more cohesive or productive than others and whether groups are likely to support or undermine organizational goals.

The specific types of teams used in TQ efforts are also derived from OB research. Self-managed teams are a modern version of semiautonomous work groups, which were championed for use in underground coal mines by researchers from Britain's Tavistock Institute more than 40 years ago.[32] Similarly, cross-functional teams have been discussed within OB for many years as a way to integrate work across interdependent functions.[33]

Much of the knowledge from OB research on groups has not yet been absorbed into TQ thinking in a widespread manner, but it probably should be. This includes the research on the relative advantages of homogeneous and heterogeneous groups, which appears to be relevant to effective team building.

Research has shown that homogenous groups (those in which members are similar in age, race, gender, experience, and so on) are better suited to well-defined, familiar tasks, where the emphasis is on efficient production. Heterogeneous groups, on the other hand, are better at tasks that require creative thinking. This implies that teams used in TQ efforts generally should be quite diverse, due to the heavy emphasis on creativity and fresh thinking in the tasks they face. Based on this research, managers selecting people for teams should make heterogeneity their goal.

Research also suggests that cultural values play a role in an employee's support of, or resistance to, self-managed teams.[34] This is particularly important as companies expand globally. (Motorola and Eastman Kodak, for example, each have operations in more than 50 countries.) People from collectivistic cultures—those who value the welfare of the group more than the individual, such as South Korea, China, and Sweden—appear to have more of the skills and attitudes that lead to the acceptance of SMTs. In contrast, people in individualistic cultures like the United States have more of a tendency to resist SMTs. The success of SMTs is therefore related to the extent to which organizations manage culture-based resistance. Practitioners should consider using selection systems in each country to obtain employees having those values most compatible with SMT requirements and should adopt SMTs that mesh with the cultural values of the country.

SUMMARY

Four types of teams are used in TQ efforts: steering committees, problem-solving teams (both departmental and cross-functional), self-managed teams, and virtual teams. Teams allow organizations to focus on customer needs and to deal with interdependence across functions and processes.

Team effectiveness consists of achieving quality goals in a timely manner and strengthening relationships both within the team and between the team and the rest of the organization. Teams will be effective to the extent that their members have the appropriate technical and interpersonal skills and are able to manage team processes, such as problem selection and communication.

Teams cannot be effective without organizational support, especially the provision of resources. Although the use of teams in TQ efforts is broadly consistent with traditional organizational behavior theories, teamwork is more heavily emphasized within TQ.

REVIEW AND DISCUSSION QUESTIONS

1. In the quote that introduces the chapter, Donald Peterson claims that teams are the best way to accomplish any kind of work. Do you agree? Why or why not?

2. Petronius, a Roman satirist, noted back in 66 A.D: "We trained hard—but it seemed that every time we were beginning to form up into teams, we

would be reorganized. I was to learn later in life we tend to meet any new situation by reorganizing, and a wonderful method it can be for creating the illusion of progress while producing confusion, inefficiency, and demoralization." What implications does this quote have for modern managers?

3. What are the similarities and differences among the types of teams used in TQ?

4. Discuss possible ideas for how managers might deal with individuals who refuse to join teams for the following reasons: outside commitments, fear of embarrassment, an overwhelming workload, mistrust of management, fear of failure or losing one's job, and an "I don't care" attitude.

5. Think of a team that you are on or have been on recently. How does it stack up against the criteria for quality teamwork? What specific steps could be used to improve the performance of your team? How could TQ techniques be used to improve team processes?

6. Identify a problem in some area of your work, school, or home life. What are the symptoms of the problem? What is the obvious cause? Now think harder about the causes of the problem. (Try to spend 10 minutes doing this.) Do other causes come to mind? How would your solution result in better problem diagnosis?

7. How did the team at Norfolk General Hospital illustrate the effective teamwork practices discussed in the text?

8. If self-managed teams can succeed without active intervention from managers, what—if anything—does this imply about the traditional roles of management (to plan, organize, and control) in organizations? Should a new set of roles be identified for such situations?

9. Do you think that the current popularity of teams in organizations is a fad or a fundamental change in the way we manage organizations? Why?

10. Are teams absolutely necessary for total quality to be successful? Sketch out a plan for a total quality effort that does not involve teams.

CASES

Makin' Waves at Siemens[35]

Here is a summary of a quality improvement project conducted by a team at Siemens Energy Automation and presented in the 1997 Ohio Manufacturers' Association Case Studies in Team Excellence Competition.

The Makin' Waves team is a continuous improvement team from the Siemens facility located in Urbana, Ohio. The Urbana facility is a supplier plant to the Siemens plant in Bellefontaine. We supply molded plastic, stamping, and plating support to the Bellefontaine plant. The Makin' Waves team is from the plastics department. Our team has been functioning for four years and has completed many highly successful projects. The team consists of two press operators, one product repairperson, one janitor, and one quality assurance person, all from the plastics department. We also included a supervisor from the E-Frame circuit breaker line in Bellefontaine, who was added at the beginning of this project as a representative of our stakeholders and to provide valuable input.

Our team began this project by looking into ideas for a project from the Corrective Action System and the Value Improvement Program. Our project started out as a way to reduce the negative effect caused by the poor appearance of the E-Frame breaker. Upon investigating the problem we discovered that we could actually eliminate the operation that was causing the negative appearance. We decided to make our project the elimination of the washing operation station in the production of the E-Frame plastic case.

The E-Frame breaker case is molded in a compression press. The problem begins during the trimming and filing processes that are done after the part is removed from the mold. The plastic contains fiberglass, which becomes a fine dust that adheres to the part. To eliminate the dust, the parts are put through a washing operation. This process uses a conveyor system to carry the parts through a water spray cleaning system. The problem with this process is that the finish comes out looking spotty and with some fiberglass particles still adhering to the parts themselves.

Our customers on the E-Frame breaker line had written Corrective Actions against this procedure because of the poor appearance and the dust still being present on the parts. They were experiencing problems with the fiberglass and were having to wear gloves to protect their hands.

Through data collection we realized that this operation takes 6,831 man-hours a year at a labor cost of over $96,000. Yet after the washing process, the parts still were not clean and had a negative appearance that was not acceptable. We took the top five part numbers and charted the clean versus the dirty parts. We found that 97 percent of the parts did not meet customer standards and that our customers were having to add a rework operation to keep the E-Frame line going!

We set a goal to eliminate the washing operation by May 1997. In order to have this happen we needed to find a better process to take its place. We did a fishbone analysis to outline the causes of the problem and followed up with a root cause analysis to eliminate any causes that did not pertain. We brainstormed for possible solutions, producing five possible alternatives to the washing operation. They were

- constant air flow,
- shop vacuum,
- deflashing parts,
- ionizer (mouse trap), and
- air hose at press.

We tested and evaluated each solution, working with both the operators in the plastics department and our customers on the breaker line. As a result of our evaluation, we found that an air hose at the press was the best solution. We instructed the operators that after the parts were filed, they should be blown free of all fiber particles. Because they were not being washed with water, this would eliminate the spotty appearance of the parts. We set up direct communication with our customers to make sure that this process was eliminating the problem permanently. Their feedback showed that they were satisfied with the new process and that there was not a problem with either the fiberglass or the appearance of the parts. We then took the findings and recommended that the washing operation be eliminated and replaced by an air hose at the press. We communicated to quality assurance that the job instructions should be updated to include our new process so that supervisors and operators would be trained on the new process at the end of their safety meetings. We then went to the scheduler and had the washing process eliminated from the system. After this was accomplished and there was still favorable feedback from the customers, we pulled the plug on the washing operation altogether.

Our goal as a team was to eliminate the washing operation and we accomplished this goal. There were other benefits attached to the project:

- $98,000 cost reduction in labor and maintenance,
- additional 136 square feet of valuable floor space freed up,
- improved delivery to customer,
- improved teamwork between customer and supplier,
- open communication with customer,
- elimination of a rework operation,
- improved quality to the consumer, and
- improved safety and health of operators.

Discussion Question

1. Based on the Makin' Waves team's project summary, discuss why this team was effective, using the concepts developed in this chapter.

A Self-Managed Cheese-Making Team[36]

Monday at 6 A.M., the Green team relieves the Silver team for a 12-hour shift at the R.G. Bush plant of Schreiber Foods. Schreiber is the second-largest producer of cheese in America, and the 53 employees at the Bush plant (near Tempe, Arizona) are responsible for making bulk cheese that is further processed into finished products by other plants. The Bush plant is extremely efficient, producing about one million pounds of cheese each week, due to both advanced production control technology and the use of self-managed teams. In addition to the Green and Silver teams, there are also Red, Blue, maintenance, support, and management teams.

The process that the six-member Green team has just assumed responsibility for includes condensing, evaporating, filling, packing, and palletizing operations. As the shift begins, the designated communicators from the two teams discuss a potential pH problem that was identified overnight. Two team members take their places in the process control room in front of a bank of computer screens, switches, and meters. They check the performance of the process over the past few hours and consult a schedule for preventive maintenance. The other three team members are in the barrel room today and will be performing manual labor: making cardboard barrels, filling them with cheese, and placing them on pallets.

The team members rotate among these tasks, including the communicator job, which is the closest thing to a designated team leader at the plant. Team members have taken over the functions of team advisers, nonteam personnel who guided the teams until they were no longer needed. At this plant, the practice of job rotation is seen as more important than having the most qualified person in a job at all times: Larry is the most technically qualified person on the team, but today he is filling barrels with cheese.

The team addresses a number of problems during its shift. The computer screen alerts Tim in the control room to a problem with an evaporator. He calls Tony, who escapes from the barrels for a few minutes to find and clean out a clogged check valve. Later, the pH problem reappears; it is now so low that it is out of specification. To make matters worse some burned cheese has been detected. The evaporator must be shut down for cleaning, and the team takes the maintenance team's advice to perform a more extensive cleaning that has to be done soon anyway.

The team wants to get the process back on line as soon as possible because the evaporator shutdown costs the company money, and the out-of-spec cheese is reflected in the team's incentive payout. After a filter is replaced and the cleaning completed, the process is ready to roll.

While the team works, they are literally surrounded with information. A three-foot-long electronic sign updates them on various aspects of performance, including conformance, production, and customer complaints. A bulletin board is crammed with information on raw material consumption, the incentive system, and so on. Wrapped around the control room is a banner that exhorts them to "Do it right the first time."

Green team members communicate constantly. Beyond their daily job communication, they have a monthly team meeting to discuss goals, problems, schedules, and whatever else needs to be covered. There are also corrective action team meetings, communicators' meetings, and incentive meetings. Members understand all of the meetings as the price of empowerment and teamwork but feel that the sacrifice is better than letting management make all the decisions.

The team recently had its first experience with firing a member, which was particularly hard because he was a friend and a teammate. They had hired him because of his technical ability, despite past problems with attendance. They did everything they could to keep him, but the attendance problems continued, and the team felt he was letting them down.

Ted, the newest member of the Green team, summarizes the team's feeling about self-management:

> When I got here, I knew that this was just up my alley. I don't need a boss looking over my shoulder, because I know how to do the work. It never made sense to me to see grown-ups standing around watching

other grown-ups do their jobs. I could see it if you were 14 years old. But I'm an adult, and Schreiber respects that.

Discussion Questions

1. Outline what a day at work would be like in a cheese plant that utilized a more conventional organization—no teams, foremen, many job classifications. How would this differ from the day the Green team at Schreiber's Bush plant experienced? What are the advantages and disadvantages of the two arrangements?
2. In the text it was argued that team members should be assigned to the work that they do best. Yet in the Green team case, team members rotated through all jobs regardless of their skills. Do you think this is a good idea? Why or why not?
3. What would a manager's job be like in this kind of plant? Would you want to work as a manager there?

ENDNOTES

1. Quoted in John Hillkirk, "New Award Cites Teams with Dreams," *USA Today*, April 10, 1992.
2. Jon R. Katzenback, and Douglas K. Smith, "The Discipline of Teams," *Harvard Business Review*, March/April 1993, pp. 111–120.
3. Adapted from Leigh Ann Klaus, "Motorola Brings Fairy Tales to Life," *Quality Progress*, June 1997, pp. 25–28.
4. J.M. Juran, *Juran on Leadership for Quality: An Executive Handbook*, New York: The Free Press, 1989; and P.B. Crosby, *Quality is Free: The Art of Making Quality Certain*, New York: McGraw-Hill, 1979.
5. The information on quality circles in Japan is from B.G. Dale and J. Tidd, "Japanese Total Quality Control: A Study of Best Practice," *Proceedings of the Institution of Mechanical Engineers*, Vol. 205, No. 4, pp. 221–232.
6. James R. Healey, "U.S. Steel Learns from Experience," *USA Today*, April 10, 1992.
7. Martha T. Moore, "Hourly Workers Apply Training in Problem Solving," *USA Today*, April 10, 1992.
8. Juran, *Juran on Leadership for Quality*.
9. Based on Jerry G. Bowles, "Leading the World-Class Company," *Fortune*, September 21, 1992.
10. Richard S. Wellins, William C. Byham, and Jeanne M. Wilson, *Empowered Teams: Creating Self-Directed Work Groups That Improve Quality, Productivity, and Participation*, p. 21. San Francisco: Jossey-Bass, 1991.
11. Wanda Savage-Moore, "Self-Directed Work Team Series: Part II of a Two-Series Interview with Ritz-Carlton," *Quality Observer*, March/April, 1998.
12. Ron Williams, "Self-Directed Work Teams: A Competitive Advantage," *Quality Digest*, November 1995, pp. 50–52.
13. Jane E. Henry and Meg Hartzler, "Virtual Teams: Today's Reality, Today's Challenge," *Quality Progress*, May 1997, pp. 108–109.
14. P. Alexander, M. Biro, E.G. Garry, D. Seamon, T. Slaughter, and D. Valerio, "New Organizational Structures and New Quality Systems," in J.P. Kern, J.J. Riley, and L.N. Jones (eds.), *Human Resources Management*, Milwaukee: ASQC Quality Press, 1987, pp. 203–268.
15. Michael Jaycox, "How to Get Nonbelievers to Participate in Teams," *Quality Progress*, March 1996, pp. 45–49.
16. Eileen M. Van Aken and Brian M. Kleiner, "Determinants of Effectiveness for Cross-Functional Organizational Design Teams," *Quality Management Journal*, Vol. 4, No. 2, 1997, pp. 51–79.

17. Wellins et al., *Empowered Teams*, p. 147.

18. Partially based on Wellins et al., *Empowered Teams*, and H.J. Harrington, *The Improvement Process: How America's Leading Companies Improve Quality*, New York: McGraw-Hill, 1987.

19. This point is based on a model developed by I. Steiner in his book *Group Process and Productivity*, New York: Academic Press, 1972.

20. The problems of differential status in groups are discussed by Alvin Zander in *Making Groups Effective*, San Francisco: Jossey-Bass, 1982.

21. The classic statement of this problem is by Irving Janis in his book *Groupthink*, 2nd ed., Boston: Houghton-Mifflin, 1982.

22. Van Aken and Kleiner, op. cit.

23. Wellins et al., *Empowered Teams*. See also S.A. Snell and J.W. Dean, Jr., "Integrated Manufacturing and Human Resource Management: A Human Capital Perspective," *Academy of Management Journal*, August 1992, pp. 467–504.

24. Douglas McGregor, "An Uneasy Look at Performance Appraisal," *Harvard Business Review*, September/October 1972; Herbert H. Meyer, Emanuel Kay, and John R.P. French, Jr., "Split Roles in Performance Appraisal," *Harvard Business Review*, January/February 1965; Harry Levinson, "Appraisal of What Performance?" *Harvard Business Review*, January/February 1965; A.M. Mohrman, *Deming Versus Performance Appraisal: Is There a Resolution?* Los Angeles: Center for Effective Organizations, University of Southern California, 1989.

25. John F. Milliman and Fred R. McFadden, "Toward Changing Performance Appraisal to Address TQM Concerns: The 360-Degree Feedback Process," *Quality Management Journal*, Vol. 4, No. 3, 1997, pp. 44–64.

26. RIT/*USA Today* Quality Cup Web site, www.qualitycup.org, and Levy, Doug. "Manufacturing Winners Teamed to Trouble-Shoot Valve Problem," *USA Today*, May 1, 1998, 4B.

27. Stanley M. Moss, "Appraise Your Performance Appraisal Process," *Quality Progress*, November 1989, 60.

28. Based on Kevin Anderson, "X-ray Processing Time Cut 81%," *USA Today*, April 10, 1992.

29. Based on Bruce Rayner, "Trial-By-Fire Transformation: An Interview with Globe Metallurgical's Arden C. Sims," *Harvard Business Review*, May–June 1992, pp. 117–129.

30. Ibid.

31. G.C. Homans, *The Human Group*, New York: Harcourt, Brace, and World, 1959, p. 2.

32. E. Trist and K.W. Bamforth, "Some Social and Psychological Consequences of the Long Wall Method of Coal-Getting," *Human Relations*, Vol. 4, No. 1, 1951, pp. 3–38.

33. For example, J.E. McCann and J.R. Galbraith, "Interdepartmental Relations," in P.C. Nystrom and W.H. Starbuck (eds.), *Handbook of Organizational Design, Vol. 2: Remodeling Organizations and Their Environments*, New York: Oxford University Press, 1981.

34. Bradley L. Kirkman and Debra L. Shapiro, "The Impact of Cultural Values on Employee Resistance to Teams: Toward a Model of Globalized Self-Managing Work Team Effectiveness," *Academy of Management Review*, Vol. 22, No. 3, 1997, pp. 730–757.

35. Courtesy of Siemens Energy and Automation Distribution Products Division.

36. Wellins et al., *Empowered Teams*, chapter 4.

8

Empowerment and Motivation

Chapter Outline

In 1988, Takeo Miura of Hitachi Corporation made the following statement to a group of senior U.S. business executives:

> We are going to win and the industrial West is going to lose out; there's nothing much you can do about it, because the reasons for your failure are within yourselves. . . . With your bosses doing the thinking while the workers wield the screwdrivers, you're convinced deep down that this is the right way to run a business. For you, the essence of management is getting the ideas out of the heads of the bosses and into the hands of labor. We are beyond the Taylor model: Business, we know, is so complex and difficult that survival for firms . . . depends on the day-to-day mobilization of every ounce of intelligence.[1]

Miura threw down the gauntlet to American business: Bring the brainpower of your entire organization to the competition or prepare to lose permanently. In the years since this challenge was issued, American firms have begun to undertake the process of employee empowerment. This chapter will

- explain what is meant by empowerment,
- explain the importance of empowerment to quality,
- identify the principles of successful empowerment,
- provide examples of firms practicing empowerment, and
- link empowerment to theories of motivation.

INTRODUCTION TO EMPOWERMENT

Empowerment means giving someone power—granting the authority to do whatever is necessary to satisfy customers and trusting employees to make the right choices without waiting for management approval. By empowering employees, organizations drive decision making down to its lowest possible level. Managers in many companies have found that giving people throughout the organization the power to make a difference contributes greatly to providing quality products and services to their customers.

Examples of empowerment abound. Workers in the Coors Brewery container operation give each other performance evaluations and even screen, interview, and hire new people for the line. At Motorola, sales representatives have the authority to replace defective products up to six years after purchase, a decision that used to require top management approval. Hourly employees at GM's antilock brake system plant in Dayton, Ohio, can call in suppliers to help solve problems, and they manage scrap, machine downtime, absences, and rework. At Globe Metallurgical, hourly group leaders take care of business on the weekends; no supervisors are needed. FedEx empowers employees to "do everything humanly possible to get the job done and to satisfy customers." See the box on UPS for a good example.

Empowerment is a natural extension of employee involvement concepts such as worker participation in decision making. In some companies empow-

Stuff Happens[2]

Jim Kelly, UPS chairman and CEO, recounted an example of empowerment in a speech at Rutgers University:

At UPS, we've got thousands of heroes every day. Not the kind that make headlines, but the kind that do make a difference.

For instance, there's the story of an account executive who took responsibility for a damaged parcel that was packed incorrectly. This particular parcel was a rare numbered art print sent by an elderly homebound couple in Florida to their son in Wisconsin.

The print was valued at $350, but it had much greater emotional value. It was a beautiful limited edition of an elk in a forest, and the couple sent it as a best wishes offering to their son who raised elk on his farm.

It arrived in Wisconsin badly damaged. The elderly couple was devastated. However, our account executive in Wisconsin wanted to help.

A wildlife art collector himself, he knew that most artists keep a couple of extra unnumbered prints around for such misfortunes. He contacted the artist in Florida, and had a new print renumbered and shipped back to Wisconsin. He then personally delivered it to the delighted son. The son was impressed. His parents were overjoyed.

The point is, one of our people took a lot of initiative and responsibility for a problem he didn't even directly cause. He took a bad situation and turned it into a customer-for-life situation.

erment is used as the umbrella term for increasing employee involvement in decision making. Empowerment is more than another term for involvement, however. It represents a high degree of involvement in which employees make decisions themselves and are responsible for their outcomes. This is a more radical change than having employees merely participate in managers' decisions, even when they are given some influence (see Figure 8.1).

For empowerment to occur, managers must undertake two major initiatives:[3]

- identify and change organizational conditions that make people powerless, and
- increase people's confidence that their efforts to accomplish something important will be successful.

The need to do both of these implies that organizational systems often create powerless employees and that these systems must be changed first. Examples of systems in need of change are those that specify who can (and cannot) make certain types of decisions and systems of standard operating procedures (and who can override them). Even when systems are changed to permit empowerment, individuals who have lived under those systems are not readily able to

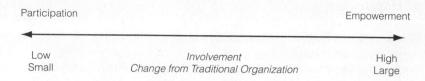

FIGURE 8.1 CONTINUUM OF EMPLOYEE INVOLVEMENT PRACTICES

Participation   Empowerment

Low   *Involvement*   High
Small   *Change from Traditional Organization*   Large

operate in an empowered manner. The other need in empowering people is to deal with the psychological aftereffects of powerlessness by convincing people that they are in fact able to "make a difference."

Empowerment is an application of the teamwork principle of total quality, embodying "vertical" teamwork between managerial and nonmanagerial personnel. If employees are given important responsibilities—and the authority that goes along with them—it is more realistic to describe their relationship with management as teamwork than it would be in a hierarchical system. After all, people can hardly be seen as team members if they only execute decisions made by others.

The need to empower the entire workforce in order for quality to succeed has long been recognized, even if it is only recently coming into practice. Five of Deming's 14 points relate directly to the notion of empowerment.

Point 6:   Institute training.
Point 7:   Teach and institute leadership.
Point 8:   Drive out fear. Create trust. Create a climate for innovation.
Point 10: Eliminate exhortations for the workforce.
Point 13: Encourage education and self-improvement for everyone.[4]

Juran wrote that "ideally, quality control should be delegated to the workforce to the maximum extent possible."[5] Empowerment resembles Juran's concept of "self-control." For employees to practice self-control, they must know their unit's goals and their actual performance and have a means for changing performance if the goals are not being met.[6] Although it is a difficult struggle, organizations are increasingly meeting these conditions.

One survey found that more than 40 percent of the largest U.S. corporations are moderate to high users of employee involvement practices such as empowerment.[7] Manufacturing, especially in the chemical and electronics industries, has tended to empower employees more than service organizations, although the financial services industry has taken a leading role.

Empowerment has even played a role in such business successes as the Ford Taurus program.[8] Employee ideas were responsible for reducing the number of different welding guns on the assembly line from three to one and for developing a standard screw size for use in the car's interior plastic moldings. Although these changes may not sound very dramatic, a Ford executive estimated that such ideas often are worth more than $300,000 each.

The objective of empowerment is "to tap the creative and intellectual energy of everybody in the company, not just those in the executive suite, . . . to provide everyone with the responsibility and the resources to display real leadership within their own individual spheres of competence."[9] In the quote that introduced this chapter, Takeo Miura took American managers to task for ignoring the creative and intellectual energies of the workforce.

The traditional treatment of employees by American managers led W. Edwards Deming to plead with managers to drive out fear—defined as "feeling threatened by possible repercussions as a result of speaking up about work-related concerns."[10] Today managers in quality-oriented companies, hampered by decades of policies encouraging employees to keep their ideas to themselves, struggle to find ways to encourage employees to take responsibility for their work.

THE IMPORTANCE OF EMPOWERMENT

Empowerment is important primarily because it improves organizational performance. A recent survey of 55,000 workers by the Gallup Organization found that four employee attitudes, taken together, correlate strongly with higher profits:[11]

- Workers feel they are given the opportunity to do what they do best every day.
- They believe their opinions count.
- They sense their fellow workers are committed to quality.
- They've made a direct connection between their work and the company's mission.

Everyone in an organization is an asset, albeit an asset whose value is not automatically realized. If money is put into a closet instead of a bank, it will not gain interest. Employees who are put into jobs that are like being in a closet (in the dark, isolated) similarly will not provide value to the organization.

Giving employees responsibility for their own work has led to improvements in quality, productivity, motivation, customer service, and morale, as well as in the speed of decision making.[12] The benefits of empowerment have become obvious to many managers, such as Art Wegner, president of Pratt & Whitney, a producer of jet engines:

> If I try to make a lot of decisions with the goal of reducing costs by 30 percent, I'm not likely to understand all the issues very well. But if you get everybody—all those people in the organization—asking themselves "How am I going to get 30 percent of the costs out of there?", the power of that is unbelievable.[13]

Although empowerment is relevant for all aspects of organizational performance, it plays a special role in quality improvement. Total quality requires people to make real changes in the way work is done and relies upon in-depth understanding of the current system. Only employees involved in the system day to day possess such an understanding, which is why so many managers see employee involvement as an integral part of total quality. As one survey concluded, "Employee involvement . . . may be viewed as creating the organizational context needed to support quality improvement processes."[14]

The importance of empowerment to total quality is underlined by its inclusion in the Malcolm Baldrige National Quality Award Criteria for Performance Excellence. In category 5, Human Resource Focus, the criteria specifically seek information about "how work processes are designed and managed to encourage individual initiative and self-directed responsibility." The criteria explain:

> The basic aim of such design should be to enable employees to exercise discretion and decision making, leading to flexibility, innovation, knowledge and skill sharing, and rapid response to the changing requirements of the marketplace.[15]

Beyond its impact on quality and other aspects of organizational performance, empowerment also leads to greater levels of satisfaction among the workforce.[16] This plays a special role in TQ, insofar as Deming speaks of the right of employees to enjoy their work and claims that there should be more joy in the workplace.

Although enhancing people's enjoyment of their work is a worthwhile goal in itself, empowered employees give faster and friendlier service to customers as well.[17] This is not much of a surprise, as we have all been victimized at some point by surly employees who decided to take their organizational powerlessness out on us. Employee satisfaction is related to customer satisfaction.

Companies, such as Disney, that excel at customer service have long been aware of this relationship. Disney cast members, as those who work at Disneyland and Disney World are called, are treated with special care. For example, before the Star Tours attraction opened, it was previewed by cast members and their families for four nights. The cast members who tried it received free dinners. Social events for cast members are also held, including Minnie's Moonlight Madness, an after-hours treasure hunt.[18]

It's not just "being nice" to employees that leads them to provide better customer service. The continuous improvement of organizational processes removes many hassles that produce disgruntled employees, who in turn produce dissatisfied customers. As Hal Rosenbluth, president of Rosenbluth Travel puts it, "By maintaining an enjoyable, bureaucracy-free work environment, one that encourages innovative thinking, . . . and honest communication, people are freed to concentrate solely on the needs of the clients."[19] The relationship between empowerment and quality is summarized in Figure 8.2.

PRINCIPLES OF EMPOWERMENT

Although many organizations have undertaken the journey toward empowerment, many have become lost along the way. Empowerment may sound

FIGURE 8.2 HOW EMPOWERMENT LEADS TO QUALITY

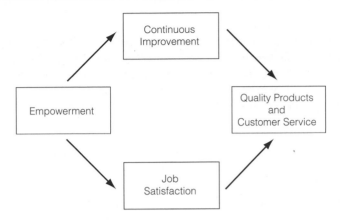

easy, but there is a lot more to it than telling employees they are (poof!) empowered, like the Fairy Godmother's transformation of Cinderella before the ball. A number of principles are involved in successfully giving power to employees.

Empower Sincerely and Completely

It should go without saying that empowerment must be done sincerely. It cannot be done superficially. To gain its benefits, managers must empower for its improvement value, not for its public relations value. As Dan Ciampa, a consultant with expertise in empowerment puts it:

> Simply bringing employees together once a month and exhorting them to work harder to achieve the business's objectives is not enough. A process is needed that enables them to make significant improvements in their own work area that help meet the business imperatives in a way that will satisfy the needs of the individual employee.[20]

Furthermore, nothing could be worse for employees than to be told they are responsible for something, only to be jerked back at the first sign of trouble or uncertainty. Managers must think long and hard before making the commitment to empowerment—once done, it can't be done halfway. Semi-empowerment just doesn't work.

This does not mean that there should be no limits. On the contrary, managers must be clear on exactly what responsibility and authority rests with employees. Questions such as "What procedures can we change?" and "How much money can we commit?" must be answered ahead of time. Finally, managers must be willing to wait for results—miracles do not happen overnight.[21]

All You Need Is Trust[22]

Texas Nameplate Company (TNC), a small (less than 70 people), privately held firm founded in 1946, makes nameplates, the small metal tags with etched lettering that get riveted to refrigerators, computers, high-pressure values, and military equipment. When serious work started on reducing nonconformances through statistical process control in 1992, total nonconformances amounted to about 15–18 percent of billing—a significant amount of lost profit. Improvement activities were able to drive that rate down to 3.7 percent by 1997, in an industry that averages around 10 percent. But Dale Crownover, the company president wasn't happy.

TNC started a gainsharing plan that distributed bonuses equally to all employees, beginning with nonconformance rates of less than 5 percent. Results are posted daily. By the end of 1997, TNC employees whittled nonconformances down to 1 percent. In January 1998, in an attempt to further carve away at the problem, TNC did away with its quality control department. In the first month following that move, which Crownover said was part of the company's strategic plan, nonconformances were cut in half.

Quality improvement now comes through DOIT—Daily Operation Innovation Team—which consists of supervisors who meet every other week to discuss accomplishments and opportunities for further improvements. They are charged with sharing information discussed at meetings with their employees. "People on the floor can figure out what's happening and make adjustments the fastest," says Troy Knowlton, company operations manager. He added that they are quick to help out when one person is having a problem; they know what's at stake. "People listen to peers more than supervisors. We tried that for 45 years, and it didn't work. We have found the value of letting people do the work, with management providing the guidance."

Not surprisingly, in 1998 TNC became the smallest company ever to win a Baldrige Award.

Establish Mutual Trust

As Juran put it, "The managers must trust the workforce enough to be willing to make the delegation, and the workforce must have enough confidence in the managers to be willing to accept the responsibility."[23] Trust is not created just by saying you trust someone; it must be backed up by actions (see the box on Texas Nameplate). For management, this might mean granting employees access to information, such as their personnel files, and resources, such as the quality improvement budget.[24]

In one plant utilizing self-managed teams, trust was symbolized by giving each new employee a key to the plant, a highly unusual practice.[25] The ultimate issue for many employees, however, is job security. They must trust that management will not take advantage of productivity increases to cut the workforce, in effect working themselves out of a job. Firms embarking upon employee involvement activities often make explicit commitments to this effect to employees.[26]

Provide Employees with Business Information

For empowerment to succeed, it must focus on making the organization more competitive.[27] Empowerment can contribute to organizational performance only if employees have access to the necessary information about the business and its performance. Information about the employees' department or other subunit is particularly necessary, because this is the level of performance they can affect. Sharing business information with employees relates directly to quality, customer service, and competitiveness.[28] At DuPont's Delaware River plant, for example, management shares cost figures with all workers.[29] By sharing this information, management believes that workers will think more for themselves and identify with company goals. Globe Metallurgical regularly conducts small group meetings with all employees to review financial performance. To help employees make decisions on issues affecting production, a department manager at Texas Eastman Chemical (a division of Eastman Company) supplied operators with a daily financial report that showed how their decisions affected the bottom line. As a result, department profits doubled in four months, and quality improved by 50 percent as employees began suggesting cost-saving improvements.[30]

In the absence of appropriate information, empowered employees may squander their power on problems that are not very important. As Peter Senge put it, "Empowering the individual where there is a relatively low level of alignment [between organizational and employee goals] worsens the chaos and makes managing . . . even more difficult."[31]

The criticism of misplaced goals was often leveled at earlier employee-involvement efforts, such as quality circles. Although managers formerly blamed employees for having the wrong priorities, sophisticated managers today recognize that they are responsible for providing employees with the information necessary to develop educated priorities.

Ensure That Employees Are Capable

"You can't empower incompetence," says one manager. If employees are going to take on important organizational responsibilities, they must be prepared to do so. To operate in an empowered, TQ environment, employees must possess not only technical skills (including statistics), but also interpersonal and problem-solving skills (see the box on Starbucks). Unfortunately, many people entering the workforce today lack even the most basic skills in reading and math, let alone these relatively advanced skills.[32]

Employee capability can be ensured through selection and training processes. Unless the human resource processes are adapted to provide capable employees, empowerment cannot succeed, and management's worst nightmares will be realized. Unfortunately, many employees are not trained in these areas, which helps explain the mixed results many organizations have had with empowerment.[33]

A Corning Glass plant in Erwin, New York, exemplifies this principle.[34] The union agreed to replace 21 different jobs with one "specialist" job. Employees were placed in teams and given broad authority over production scheduling and the division of labor. Did a bright new day dawn at Erwin? Not exactly. Conflict and confusion went up, and productivity went down. Plant manager Gary Vogt concluded: "We took steps to empower people, but the desired outcomes were not reached because we had not prepared them." An elaborate training program was created, and workers now become certified for the various tasks in the operation through testing. The promise of empowerment is now being fulfilled, and quality and productivity have increased.

Rosenbluth Travel, on the other hand, has made substantial investments in providing the kind of employees needed for an empowered, quality-oriented workforce.[35] Extensive research has led to tests that predict the likely success of applicants for such positions as corporate reservationist, based on personality type and skill repertoire. When individuals are hired, they attend a two-day orientation session at corporate headquarters, where they are immersed in the

---

Spilling the Beans: Secrets of Starbucks' Success[36]

Starbucks Coffee, which grew from a small Seattle retailer to a national phenomenon, can be found in cities and airports across America, as well as up in the friendly skies. Its consistency and precision stem from its employee training program. All "partners," as employees are called, complete five classes during their first six weeks with the company, including "Brewing the Perfect Cup," "Coffee Knowledge," and "Customer Service." All partners have to memorize and practice the rules. Milk must be steamed to at least 150° F. but never more than 170° F. Every espresso shot must be pulled within 23 seconds—or tossed. Trainers demonstrate how to wipe oil from the coffee bin, open a giant bag of beans ("In a sanitary manner! You never put your hand in there!"), and clean the milk wand on the expresso machine ("It's like blowing a little boy's nose"). They demonstrate how to fill sacks with coffee and affix a sticker exactly one-half inch over the Starbucks logo. Practicing on lattes, the trainer cries out "Fabulous foam! It's okay to practice in your stores. Pull 10 shots and dump 'em. And what does it taste like when the milk in your latte is 190° F? Be a mad scientist behind the bar . . . you'll understand why customers complain."

Three guidelines (Star Skills) govern interpersonal relations: maintain and enhance self-esteem, listen and acknowledge, and ask for help. Throughout the training partners are encouraged to share their feelings about selling, about coffee, about working for the company. They also learn relaxation techniques so they can focus on the cappuccinos, to take personal responsibility for the cleanliness of the coffee bins—even when it's someone else's job, and to treat partners respectfully and do the right thing when one of them spills a gallon of milk.

company's philosophies and values and begin to understand the company's concept of customer service. (This point is illustrated by the corporate officers serving the new associates afternoon tea on the second day.) This is just the beginning of training, however. Reservationists must successfully complete up to 320 hours of classroom instruction, which focuses on the mechanics of reservations and how to provide quality service.

Don't Ignore Middle Management

A well-known principle of organization theory popularized by Deming is that organizations are systems. When changing one part of an organization, it is necessary to consider the effects of the change on other parts of the system. Thus, managers must consider how empowering lower-level employees will affect middle managers. If the needs and expectations of middle managers are ignored, empowerment will be confusing at best and disastrous at worst. One manager described the situation with middle managers in his company like this:

> We pretty much promoted people because of their technical knowledge, not their management skills. Therefore we have a group of people in supervisory positions who aren't people oriented; they don't know how to get the ideas and the solutions and better ways of doing things out of their people. And they are not receptive to employee-involvement programs, they are not receptive to too much change in their lives; they feel comfortable in this doing role rather than a coaching or facilitator's role. So therefore we have to train these people to think differently and manage their departments from a management point of view rather than a doer's point of view. . . . It's the middle management transition from the old style of management to today's new style of management that's the problem, that stops companies from getting where they need to be as fast as they need to get there.

Among the roles for middle managers in organizations with empowered workforces are[37]

- maintaining focus on the organization's values,
- managing solutions to system-level problems (those that involve many functions and departments), and
- acting as teachers and coaches.

It's tempting to think of middle managers faced with empowerment efforts as dinosaurs, rapidly becoming extinct because the world has changed too quickly for them. However, remember that most middle managers are a product of their organizations and have attained their level of success in an environment that rewarded different things than are needed from managers now. Given a new set of instructions from top management, backed up by new performance appraisal criteria, many (but far from all) managers will be able to make the necessary transition.

Change the Reward System

Rarely can substantial organizational change be created without changing the reward system. The reward system includes all of the rewards that employees receive, as well as the criteria for distributing these rewards. An organization is to its reward system like a boat is to its anchor: unless the reward system is changed, the organization may drift a little bit in one direction or another, but it won't get very far.

It is hard to specify exactly what kinds of reward system will be needed to complement empowerment. Some of the practices common to organizations utilizing employee involvement include pay-for-skills, in which employees' pay increases as they learn new job-relevant skills, and profit sharing, in which employees receive bonuses related to the profits of their organization.[38] Nor should intrinsic rewards be overlooked: A picture in the company newsletter or an evening of celebration upon a major accomplishment may be of tremendous value to employees who have seldom received any recognition in the past. In fact, a Conference Board survey found that noncash recognition for hourly/ production workers was found to be effective to "great/some extent" by 84 percent of business units in contrast to only 63 percent for cash recognition.[39]

EMPOWERMENT IN ACTION

We present two examples of how empowerment is practiced followed by some observations as to its lack of universal appeal.

Semco

Semco is a machinery manufacturer in Brazil, with sales of over $30 million per year.[40] Semco's president, Ricardo Semler, practices three-pronged empowerment with his 800-person workforce: sharing power, sharing information, and sharing profits. Semler believes that empowerment saved the company from failure in the 1980s, so it is not surprising that he is a firm believer in the connection between empowerment and organizational performance.

The company is divided into units, called cells, of 150 people or less; when a unit reaches this size, it is subdivided. The 11 layers of management that the firm had in the 1970s have been reduced to three. Important decisions at Semco are made by self-managed cross-functional teams, which set their own working hours, strategies, and even salaries. Great care is taken to make sure that these decisions are based on the best information available, by making timely and accurate financial and performance data available to the teams at all times.

To reward its associates for the unusual amount of responsibility they assume for running the company and to keep them focused on the overall performance of the firm, bonuses are distributed based on corporate profits. The teams have responsibility for allocating the bonuses, and they usually do it on an equal basis. In general, Semco appears to have firmly embraced the principles of empowerment.

The Ritz-Carlton Hotel Company

"Ladies and gentlemen serving ladies and gentlemen." That's how Horst Schulze, president of Ritz-Carlton, describes customer service in his company.[41] Although in some companies the emphasis on customers might seem to diminish the importance of employees, Ritz-Carlton has found a way to treat both groups with dignity and respect. Its efforts in this direction were rewarded with a Malcolm Baldrige National Quality Award.

Living out the ideal of respect for both customers and employees requires some subtle compromises. Many guests, whose schedules are very demanding, want breakfast delivered to their rooms within 30 minutes after it is ordered. However, chefs work at different paces, and not all menu items can be prepared within this time. The solution was to offer only certain items with a half-hour guarantee and to provide time ranges for others, so that different chefs can work in their preferred manner. In this way both customers and chefs are satisfied.

One way Ritz-Carlton empowers employees is by giving them authority to commit company funds when needed to satisfy customers. The company is experimenting with giving front-desk employees authorization to spend up to $2,000 and sales managers $5,000 to ensure customer satisfaction. Schulze dramatizes the importance of employees when he introduces himself to them: "My name is Horst Schulze. I'm president of this company; I'm very important. [Pause.] But so are you. Absolutely. Equally important." Employees' feeling of importance may be responsible for a turnover rate that is less than half the industry average.

Ritz-Carlton relies heavily on employees' suggestions for quality improvement. Their goal is to have twice as many employee complaints as customer complaints—the rationale being to resolve problems before customers experience them. Sometimes managers have to take a deep breath before implementing employee suggestions. Schulze himself received a proposal from a room service waiter to spend $50,000 to implement a recycling program. The company's commitment to empowerment was sufficient to make the investment, which has really paid off: Weekly garbage pickups have been reduced by two days, and Ritz-Carlton now sells its cardboard and paper, rather than paying someone to take it away. The changes save $80,000 a year, so the initial investment was quickly paid back.

When Empowerment Doesn't Work

Beverly Reynolds thought she wanted to be an empowered worker.[42] But after nine months at an Eaton Corporations plant, she left for another job. Though she liked the idea of being her own boss, she hated the headaches that came with it—fixing broken machines and having to learn a wide variety of jobs. Many workers prefer the old-style approach with narrowly defined tasks and find that an empowered organizational culture is simply not for them. Saturn Corporation, for instance, found that many job candidates from old-style

General Motors plants just couldn't adjust to a new style of work. This provides a big challenge to organizations to recruit the right people at the outset.

Other efforts at empowerment have failed because of the inability of management to understand and implement it properly. Among the reasons for failure are:[43]

- Management support and commitment is nonexistent or not sustained .
- Empowerment is used as a manipulative tool to ensure employees complete tasks and assignments without giving them any real responsibility or authority.
- Managers use empowerment to abdicate responsibility or task accountability, accepting accolades for successes and assigning fault to others for failure.
- Empowerment is deployed selectively, segmenting the workforce into those who are empowered and those who are not.
- Empowerment is used as an excuse to not invest in training or employee development.
- Managers fail to provide feedback and do not recognize achievements.

These problems can be avoided by applying the principles discussed earlier in this chapter.

EMPOWERMENT AND THEORIES OF MOTIVATION

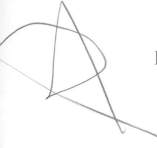

The TQ approach to managing employees in general, and empowering them in particular, is quite consistent with organizational behavior (OB) theory. In fact, most of TQ thinking about empowerment and motivation is derived, directly or indirectly, from OB theory. Managers' willingness to accept these ideas and put them into practice, however, has been greatly increased by incorporating these ideas into the total quality package.

A few examples should serve to make our point. The idea that quality problems are usually attributable to management-created systems rather than employee motivation was proposed by organizational psychologist Chris Argyris.[44] Rensis Likert described an organizational system he called "System IV," which featured empowered work groups and cross-functional teams. Douglas McGregor developed the well-known "Theory Y" approach to managing employees, which is based on the assumption that people wish to do a good job and emphasizes that people in organizations should make decisions for themselves. These are the fundamental principles of the TQ approach to managing people, but they were developed decades ago by theorists concerned with reconciling the psychological needs of people and the economic needs of businesses.

The TQ philosophy is also consistent with several more recent theories of work motivation. This means that implementing TQ should result in increased employee motivation, because the kinds of changes that TQ represents are among those that theories say will result in increased effort on the job. Specifically, the following sections discuss the TQ approach in terms of job characteristics theory, acquired need theory, and goal-setting theory. The theories themselves are not described in detail, as they are covered in OB and management textbooks. Here they are compared to total quality practices.

Job Characteristics Theory

The job characteristics theory (JCT) states that people will be more motivated to work and more satisfied with their jobs to the extent that their jobs possess certain core characteristics: skill variety, task identity (doing a meaningful unit of work), task significance, autonomy, and feedback. If jobs do not have such characteristics—that is, involve few skills and give workers little control over what they do—most employees are likely to be unmotivated and dissatisfied.[45]

In general, we would expect TQ to increase the motivating potential of jobs through increases in the foregoing task characteristics. In fact, TQ practices resemble some of the steps recommended by job design experts for making jobs more motivating. For example, getting people involved in problem solving and other quality improvement activities should increase both the variety of skills they use in their jobs and their perception of doing a meaningful unit of work. Empowerment should increase the degree of autonomy people feel they have in doing their work. Focusing their efforts on increasing customer satisfaction should increase people's perception of the significance of their roles in the organization.

Three factors have been identified that will influence the way people react to jobs that have high levels of the task characteristics: knowledge and skill, growth-need strength, and satisfaction with contextual factors.[46] Knowledge of how to do one's job should be enhanced by the training that often accompanies TQ and empowerment. Growth-need strength, on the other hand, is rooted in people's personalities and is unlikely to be affected by TQ. Satisfaction with contextual factors (company policies, working conditions) may increase with implementation of TQ, as various groups in the organization make improvements to satisfy internal customers. This means that TQ is likely not only to increase the levels of task characteristics that people find motivating, but also to change two of the three factors that influence how people react to these characteristics, in such a way that they are more likely to find such jobs motivating.

Acquired Needs Theory

Another perspective on employee motivation states that people are motivated by work that fulfills their needs. The need for achievement, the need for affiliation, and the need for power have been the subjects of extensive research.[47] People who have a strong need for achievement will work hard to reach a high standard of excellence. The need for affiliation refers to the desire to have close relationships with other people, for example as part of a team. The need for power is the desire to have influence over one's environment and the people in it.

How will the implementation of TQ, including empowerment practices, influence people who are motivated by these needs? Since research has not addressed this question, we can only speculate. The need most likely to be fulfilled by participation in TQ is the need for affiliation. The most obvious way this would occur is through the formation of self-managed or cross-functional teams. TQ promotes close relationships between people in the same or different subunits and even in different organizations in the customer-supplier chain.

The connection between TQ and the need for achievement is a bit murkier. Effective utilization of TQ should allow organizations to achieve higher levels of performance in such areas as quality and customer satisfaction, but these achievements are likely to come through team, rather than individual, efforts. Thus the opportunity to participate in such efforts is likely to motivate people with high achievement motivation only if they can see the relationship between their own work and team performance and feel a sense of achievement on that basis.

TQ and empowerment are likely to be motivating for employees with a high need for power. In fact, employees with a high need for power are likely to be quite frustrated with traditional organizations that give them little influence. Empowerment, if it follows the principles described in this chapter, should go a long way toward reducing this frustration and provide newfound motivation for individuals with a high need for power.

However, empowerment can be a double-edged sword. Middle managers whose subordinates are being empowered may feel that their own needs for power are less fulfilled under TQ. This need not occur, as empowerment of lower-level employees should be accompanied by finding new and fulfilling roles for middle managers. Many organizations will not be able to accomplish this, however, and even if they do, a certain number of middle managers with a high need for power will miss the old "command and control" type of organization.

Goal-Setting Theory

The central insight of goal-setting theory is that people whose goals are clear will work more quickly, perform better, and generally be more motivated than people who lack clear goals. A great deal of research has been performed on goal-setting theory, and it generally supports the theory's predictions. According to the theory, goals will motivate people when the goals are specific and difficult and people accept them as their own.[48]

How does goal-setting theory relate to total quality in general and empowerment in particular? This connection has not been the subject of research, but we can offer some conjecture about it. One likely link between empowerment and goal-setting is the goal-acceptance aspect of the theory. Although there has been some debate about this among scholars, it seems that people who set their own goals (as in empowerment) are likely to be more motivated by them than are people whose goals are set by others (as in the traditional organization). People who set their own goals may also find that their goals are clearer (to them, at least).

The principle that goals should be specific and difficult can be related to total quality and empowerment. In general, the principle of continuous improvement leads to fairly difficult goals. In traditional management, when an acceptable level of performance is reached, people simply try to maintain it. Under TQ, an acceptable performance level would be a stepping-stone to further improvements. Therefore, the difficulty of goals would be enhanced by TQ.

One wonders whether this compromises the long-run specificity of goals. Continuous improvement is a noble ideal, likely to spur heroic efforts in many cases. When, if ever, is the goal reached? Can workers be motivated by a goal of eternal improvement or must milestones be placed along the way to maintain motivation and enthusiasm? Perhaps as organizations gain more experience with TQ, such questions will be answered. Given the increasing importance of continuous improvement for competitiveness, organizations will need to find ways to motivate employees for sustained improvement in order to be economically viable in the twenty-first century.

Summary

Empowerment—giving people real authority in their work—is being practiced by an increasing number of organizations. Empowerment improves quality by allowing people to use their resources to address quality problems and by changing conditions that lead to poor customer service. Empowerment is not simple, but it can be successful if a number of principles are followed. These principles include developing trust between managers and employees and sharing business information widely within the organization.

Companies as diverse as Semco of Brazil and the Ritz-Carlton hotel chain have found that empowerment provides important competitive advantages. The doctrine of empowerment evolved from behavioral science concepts and is consistent with several organizational behavior theories, including job characteristics theory, acquired needs theory, and goal-setting theory.

Review and Discussion Questions

1. What is employee empowerment? What do you see as the most important barriers to employee empowerment?
2. Have you ever experienced fear in the workplace? What impact did it have on your performance? Is a little bit of fear a good thing for motivating performance?
3. Are there circumstances in which employee empowerment would hurt rather than improve quality? Why would this occur?
4. What risks does an organization face in empowering its employees?
5. How will employees know when they are empowered?
6. What sort of performance appraisal process would be appropriate for empowered workers in a total quality company?
7. Which of the principles of empowerment do you think is most important? Why?

8. Have you ever received exceptional service from an empowered employee? What happened? How did you react to it?

9. In what ways do Semco and Ritz-Carlton exemplify the principles of empowerment?

10. What can managers do to mitigate the risks of failure associated with empowerment?

11. Which theory of motivation do you see as most consistent with empowerment? Why?

12. Philip Atkinson tells the story of a government agency that fired up its employees to do great things with a wilderness training experience.[49] One young man, upon his return to work, noticed some parking spaces owned by the organization in a busy part of the city. The spaces were always free and could be rented for a substantial sum. The young man made a proposal to do so, but it was rejected out of hand. Undeterred, he rented the spaces himself, only to find that there was no mechanism to deposit the checks into corporate accounts. Eventually, the young man left the company to work for one in which people's ideas were taken more seriously, and initiative was valued. How does this story illustrate the principles of empowerment discussed in this chapter?

CASES

The Case of the Stranded Traveler

One of the authors traveled to Texas to attend a meeting. Before leaving home, he made a reservation to be picked up by a shuttle company (one with operations in several cities) and taken to his hotel, about one-half hour from the airport. The company's promotional materials strongly recommended securing reservations, as this would ensure "priority service." He was instructed to call the shuttle service once inside the terminal. He was told on the phone where to wait, what the sign on the van would say, and that it would pick him up within about 10 minutes. He was happy to hear that the van would be arriving soon, because it was raining and unseasonably cool, even for February, and it had been a long flight.

After 20 minutes, although many of the company's vans had passed by, the van with the correct destination sign still had not arrived. One of the company's drivers pulled over and asked the traveler which van he was waiting for. The driver radioed the dispatcher, who told him that the correct van would be there momentarily.

After another 15 minutes, another of the company's vans pulled over, but it was still not the right one. The woman driving this van asked the traveler which van he was waiting for and, after hearing the story, also radioed the dispatcher. She requested and received permission to change her route to take the traveler to his hotel.

The traveler relaxed in the back seat of the van, believing that his experience with "priority service" was almost over. As it became increasingly clear that the van was not leaving the airport, but was circulating among the terminals, the traveler asked the driver what was going on. She said that drivers were not allowed to leave the airport with fewer than three passengers. She had requested permission to drive the traveler immediately to his hotel to make up for the inconvenience he had suffered, but the request was denied. The driver apologized and said she would take him directly to the hotel if it were up to her.

After another 10 minutes or so cruising the terminals, a couple boarded the van. The driver requested permission to leave the airport, and this time permission was granted. Fortunately, one of the passengers knew a good route to the hotel, because the driver was not very familiar with this destination.

As the traveler got out of the van, the driver continued to apologize for the poor service he had received from the company and gave him the name of a manager to call to complain. Like most people in this situation, the traveler did not call the manager, but quietly resolved never to use this company's services when visiting this or any other airport.

Discussion Questions

1. In what ways did the shuttle company fail to provide quality service?
2. Were the dispatcher's decisions appropriate?
3. How would you change the company's policies to improve quality?
4. What are the lessons about empowerment from this case?

IBM Rochester[50]

Empowerment was concept a foreign to the traditional culture at IBM, but IBM's Rochester, Minnesota, facility (which produces AS/400 business computers and won a Baldrige Award in 1990) was one of the first to practice it. One particular incident occurred on a weekend. A woman in the plastics area was putting together some parts for a storage file. To do this, she had to attach a vendor-supplied part to an IBM-manufactured part. In the process, she noticed that the color of the vendor-supplied parts didn't exactly match the color of the IBM-manufactured parts. It wasn't too much of a mismatch, since the parts were basically just two shades of gray. But it didn't seem right to her, so she took it upon herself to stop the production line. She called over one of her peers to look at the parts, and, together, they agreed that the parts didn't seem right. They decided to call an engineer at home and ask him to come in and check the parts. He came in and looked at them. Although he couldn't see anything wrong with the parts, he agreed to run some tests. As it turned out, the women had been right. The parts were bad. Something in the vendor's process had changed, ever so slightly. The net result of that change was that the parts would have passed all of IBM's tests and worked fine in the device for a while. But then, one of the chemicals in the parts would have outgassed and created a film on the hard disk. That film would have caused the hard disk to crash. The customer would have lost data, and the disk would have to have been replaced. It would have been very costly for IBM and the customer. Those women catching that problem saved IBM enough money to cover their entire training bill for a year.

Discussion Questions

1. What types of management practices and culture might have contributed to the decisions these women made?
2. How might job characteristics theory apply to this case?

 ENDNOTES

1. Quoted in David Ulrich and Dale Lake, "Organizational Capability: Creating Competitive Advantage," *Academy of Management Executive*, Vol. 5, No. 1, 1991, pp. 77–92.

2. Brad Stratton, UPS: Its Long-Term Design Delivers Quality Millions of Times Each Day," *Quality Progress*, October 1998, pp. 37–38.

3. J.A. Conger and R.N. Kanungo, "The Empowerment Process: Integrating Theory and Practice," *Academy of Management Review*, Vol. 13, No. 3, 1988, pp. 471–482.

4. Phillip A. Smith, William D. Anderson, and Stanley A. Brooking, "Employee Empowerment: A Case Study," *Production and Inventory Management*, Vol. 34, No. 3, 1993, pp. 45–50.

5. J.M. Juran, *Juran on Leadership for Quality: An Executive Handbook*, New York: The Free Press, 1989, p. 264.

6. Juran, *Juran on Leadership for Quality*, pp. 147–148.

7. E.E. Lawler, S.A. Mohrman, and G.E. Ledford, *Employee Involvement and Total Quality Management*, San Francisco: Jossey-Bass, 1992.

8. Richard C. Whiteley, *The Customer-Driven Company: Moving from Talk to Action*, Reading, Mass.: Addison-Wesley, 1991.

9. M.J. Kiernan, "The New Strategic Architecture: Learning to Compete in the Twenty-First Century," *Academy of Management Executive*, Vol. 7, No. 1, 1993, p. 14.

10. Kathleen D. Ryan and Daniel K. Oestreich, *Driving Fear Out of the Workplace*, San Francisco: Jossey-Bass, 1991.

11. Linda Grant, "Happy Workers, High Returns," *Fortune*, January 12, 1998, p. 81.

12. Lawler, Mohrman, and Ledford, *Employee Involvement*; Dan Ciampa, *Total Quality: A User's Guide for Implementation*, Reading, Mass.: Addison-Wesley, 1992.

13. Quoted in Whiteley, *The Customer-Driven Company*, p. 180.

14. Lawler, Mohrman, and Ledford, *Employee Involvement*, p. 105.

15. Malcolm Baldrige National Quality Award Criteria for Performance Excellence, 1998, p. 27.

16. Lawler, Mohrman, and Ledford, *Employee Involvement*, p. 60.

17. Lawler, Mohrman, and Ledford, *Employee Involvement*, p. 60.

18. Brad Stratton, "How Disneyland Works," *Quality Progress*, July 1991, pp. 17–30.

19. Hal F. Rosenbluth, "Have Quality, Will Travel," *TQM Magazine*, November/December 1992, pp. 267–270.

20. Dan Ciampa, *Total Quality: A User's Guide for Implementation*, Reading, Mass.: Addison-Wesley, 1991.

21. Lawler, Mohrman, and Ledford, *Employee Involvement*, p. 51.

22. Adapted from Brad Stratton, "Texas Nameplate Company: All You Need Is Trust," *Quality Progress*, October 1998, pp. 29–32.

23. Juran, *Juran on Leadership for Quality*, p. 277.

24. A.R. Tenner and I.J. DeToro, *Total Quality Management: Three Steps to Continuous Improvement*, Reading, Mass.: Addison-Wesley, 1992.

25. Mark Kelly, *The Adventures of a Self-Managing Team*, Raleigh, N.C.: Mark Kelly Books, 1990.

26. Lawler, Mohrman, and Ledford, *Employee Involvement*, p. 47.

27. Ciampa, *Total Quality*.

28. Lawler, Mohrman, and Ledford, *Employee Involvement*, p. 60.

29. "Changing a Culture: DuPont Tries to Make Sure That Its Research Wizardry Serves the Bottom Line," *Wall Street Journal*, March 27, 1992, A5.

30. Robert S. Kaplan, "Texas Eastman Company," Harvard Business School Case, No. 9-190-039.

31. Peter M. Senge, *The Fifth Discipline: The Art and Practice of the Learning Organization*, New York: Doubleday Currency, 1990.

32. See *America's Choice: High Skills or Low Wages!*, National Center on Education and the Economy's Commission on the Skills of the American Workforce, National Center on Education and the Economy, 1990.

33. Lawler, Mohrman, and Ledford, *Employee Involvement*, p. 16.

34. Based on Ronald Henkoff, "Companies That Train Best," *Fortune*, March 22, 1993, pp. 62–75.

35. Rosenbluth, "Have Quality, Will Travel," *TQM Mazagine*, Vol. 2, No. 5, pp. 267–270.

36. Jennifer Reese, "Starbucks: Inside the Coffee Cult," *Fortune*, December 9, 1996, pp. 190–200.

37. Based on Jack Johnson and Jack T. Mollen, "Ten Tasks for Managers in the Empowered Workplace," *Journal for Quality and Participation*, December 1992, pp. 18–20.

38. Lawler, Mohrman, and Ledford, *Employee Involvement*, p. 20.

39. The Conference Board, "Innovative Reward and Recognition Strategies in TQM," Report Number 1051, 1993, p. 15.

40. The information on Semco is from Matthew J. Kiernan, "The New Strategic Architecture: Learning to Compete in the Twenty-First Century," *Academy of Management Executive*, Vol. 7, No. 1, pp. 7–21. See also R. Semler, "Managing Without Managers," in J.J. Gabarro (ed.), *Managing People and Organizations*, Boston: Harvard Business School, 1992.

41. Based on Cheri Henderson, "Putting on the Ritz," *TQM Magazine*, November/December 1992, pp. 292–296.

42. Timothy Aeppel, "Not All Workers Find Idea of Empowerment As Neat As It Sounds, *Wall Street Journal*, September 8, 1998, A1, A13.

43. Sharafat Khan, "The Key to Being a Leader Company: Empowerment," *Journal for Quality and Participation*, January/February 1997, pp. 44–50.

44. This discussion of organizational behavior theory's contribution to TQ thinking is based on J.J. Riley, "Human Resource Development: An Overview," in J.P. Kern, J.J. Riley, and L.N. Jones (eds.), *Human Resources Management*, Milwaukee: ASQC Quality Press, 1987.

45. Job characteristics theory is described in J.R. Hackman and G.R. Oldham, *Work Redesign*, Reading, Mass.: Addison-Wesley Publishing Company, 1980.

46. Hackman and Oldham, *Work Redesign*.

47. D.C. McClelland, *Assessing Human Motivation*, Morristown, N.J.: General Learning Press, 1971. See also D.C. McClelland and R.E. Boyatzis, "Leadership Motive Pattern and Long-term Success in Management," *Journal of Applied Psychology*, 1982, pp. 67, 737–743.

48. Edwin Locke, "Toward a Theory of Task Performance and Incentives," *Organizational Behavior and Human Performance*, Fall 1968, pp.167–189. For a more recent treatment of goal setting, see Mark E. Tubbs and Steven E. Ekeberg, "The Role of Intentions in Work Motivation: Implications for Goal-Setting Theory and Research," *Academy of Management Review*, January 1991, pp. 180–199.

49. Philip Atkinson, "Leadership, Total Quality, and Cultural Change," *Management Services*, Vol. 35, No. 6, 1991, pp. 16–19.

50. Joseph H. Boyett, Stephen Schwartz, Laurence Osterwise, and Roy Bauer, *The Quality Journey: How Winning the Baldrige Sparked the Remaking of IBM*, New York: Penguin Books USA, 1993.

CHAPTER

9

Quality Leadership

Chapter Outline

Motorola's former CEO, Bob Galvin, made a habit of making quality the first item on the agenda of executive staff meetings—and leaving the meeting before discussion of financials. His actions spoke louder than words: If quality was taken care of, financial performance would follow. His leadership guided Motorola to become one of the first winners of the Malcolm Baldrige National Quality Award.

Leadership is fundamental to management and organizational behavior and is on just about everyone's short list of prerequisites for organizational success. Thus, it is not surprising that leadership plays a crucial role in the total quality organization. Virtually every article and book about quality emphasizes leadership. "Teach and institute leadership" is one of W.E. Deming's 14 points. Leadership is the first category in the Malcolm Baldrige National Quality Award, and it is recognized as the "driver" of successful quality systems. Indeed, leadership is seen by many quality experts as the *sine qua non* (if you don't have it, you have nothing) of TQ. As two quality experts put it, "Without management leadership, quality and productivity will result only as fortunate accidents."[1] This chapter will

- discuss the importance of leadership for quality,
- describe the role of leaders in pursuing total quality,
- provide some examples of leaders who have inspired their organizations to attain very high quality in businesses as disparate as raising chickens in Maryland and making noodle soup in Japan, and
- compare the TQ view of leadership to several prominent leadership theories.

THE ROLES OF A QUALITY LEADER

Why is leadership so important to quality? Leaders establish plans and goals for the organization. If the plans and goals do not include quality or, worse yet, are antithetical to quality, the quality effort will die. Leaders help to shape the culture of the organization through key decisions and symbolic actions. If they help to shape a culture that puts convenience or short-term benefits over quality, quality will die. Leaders distribute resources. If resources are showered on programs that cut short-term costs while quality is starved for resources, quality will die. This list could go on. Virtually everything an organization needs to succeed in meeting its customers' expectations—goals, plans, culture, resources—can either be helped or hurt by leaders. With this in mind, let us examine in more detail the roles that managers play in a total quality company.

Many writers and managers have tried to define what a manager must do to be an effective quality leader. Edwin L. Artzt was chairman of Procter & Gamble, one of the nation's oldest and most successful companies and one of the earliest to emphasize quality. He believes:

> To lead quality—and I'm talking about leaders at every level in an organization—means providing the clear strategic choices, the guiding principles, and the disciplined application to continually improve and reinvent ourselves . . . and to do that with a focus on the good of the whole.[2]

The criteria for the Malcolm Baldrige National Quality Award also dwell heavily on leadership. Here is what the Baldrige examiners look for:

> A company's senior leaders need to set directions and create a customer orientation, clear and visible values, and high expectations. . . . The leaders need to ensure the creation of strategies, systems, and methods for achieving excellence and building knowledge and capabilities. The strategies and values should help guide all activities and decisions of the company. The senior leaders need to commit to the development of the entire workforce and should encourage participation, learning, innovation, and creativity by all employees. Through their personal roles in planning, communications, review of company performance, and employee recognition, the senior leaders serve as role models reinforcing the values and expectations and building leadership and initiative throughout the company.[3]

A final overview of the concept of quality leadership comes from Dan Ciampa, president and chief executive officer of Rath & Strong, a consulting group specializing in total quality:

> The mandate is to inspire, to invoke commitment, to enable employees to form a different concept of the organization in which they believe deeply, and to change without being threatened.[4]

Underlying the concept of quality leadership in general, and these three quotes in particular, are some clear imperatives for managers who aspire to quality leadership. First, they must establish a vision. Second, they must live the values. Third, they must lead the improvement efforts. Let's examine each of these in turn.

Establish a Vision

A **vision** is a vivid concept of what an organization could be. It is a striking depiction of possibilities, of potential. It is a dream, both in the sense of being desirable and in the sense of being a long way from the current reality, but it is not an "impossible dream." A vision should be clear and exciting to an organization's employees. It should be linked to customers' needs and convey a general strategy for achieving the mission. For example, PepsiCo states, "We will be an outstanding company by exceeding customer expectations through empowered people, guided by shared values." Alcoa's vision is stated as: "Alcoa is a growing worldwide company dedicated to excellence through quality—creating value for customers, employees, and shareholders through innovation, technology, and operational expertise. Alcoa will be the best aluminum company in the world, and a leader in other businesses in which we choose to compete."

To be quality leaders, managers must establish a vision for and in their organization. "Establishing" a vision implies both the intellectual and emotional work of conceiving the vision and the interpersonal and managerial work of communicating the vision to the organization and leading employees to embrace it.

Quality-oriented visions have inspired some of the most dramatic corporate success stories in business history. IBM was founded on the idea of exceptional customer service and fair treatment of employees. Federal Express (now called FedEx) sought what, at the time, was seen as almost inconceivable speed and reliability in the package delivery market. Apple Computers wanted to make computing accessible to the masses.[5] These visions were creative, captivating, and, most of all, achievable. (For more examples, see the box on page 280.)

Jane Carroll, president of The Forum Corporation, Europe/Asia, emphasizes the visionary role of leadership for quality, which she calls focus. She believes that most managers do not understand the need for a quality vision and their personal involvement in establishing it:

> In our experience, very few CEOs have a real sense of what their role is in the quality improvement process. It goes far beyond simply being a cheerleader and handing out an occasional award. Top management has to provide the proper focus for the organization. This is not something that can be delegated.[6]

Putting together a vision is hard work, but quality leaders do not have to do it alone. They can draw upon the talents and imagination of all the members of their organizations in developing their vision. In fact, in many organizations, people are walking around with "mini-visions" of their own, that sound like "if only we could [do something they have been told can't be done], things would be so much better around here." The raw material for a vision may be all around leaders in the organization. The first step may be simply listening for it. Leaders who are open to the ideas of people throughout the organization will be much better prepared to develop a vision that people will accept.

In the current competitive environment, if a given organization is not pursuing a customer-oriented vision, competing organizations probably are and are planning to use their vision to win over the competition's customers (or are already doing so). This is why a quality vision is such a crucial first step in quality leadership. An organization with no vision about how to create long-term customer loyalty has little chance of survival. (Unless, of course, it's a monopoly.)

The second part of establishing a vision is instilling it in all the members of the organization. This will be a lot easier if many people were involved in the first part of the process, and the leader doesn't act like Moses coming down the mountain with the stone tablets. When Corning Glass instituted a quality vision, Chairman Jamie Houghton introduced it to employees at all

A World of Vision

Visit most any major corporate Web site and you will find a vision statement. Some are short; some are long, but all focus on competitive leadership. Here is just a sampling:

State Farm Insurance Our vision for the future is to be the customer's first and best choice in the products and services we provide. We will continue to be the leader in the insurance industry and we will become a leader in the financial services arena. Our customers' needs will determine our path. Our values will guide us.

Bell Atlantic Our vision is to be the leading wireless provider in each market we serve. We use our domestic market presence to achieve maximum scale advantages and invest selectively in international properties where we can use our management expertise to create value.

CIGNA . . . we intend to be the best at helping our customers enhance and extend their lives and protect their financial security. Satisfying customers is the key to meeting employee needs and shareholder expectations, and will enable CIGNA to build on our reputation as a financially strong and highly respected company.

AMR We will be the global market leader in air transportation and related information services. That leadership will be attained by: Setting the industry standard for safety and security. Providing world-class customer service. Creating an open and participative work environment which seeks positive change, rewards innovation and provides growth, security and opportunity to all employees. Producing consistently superior financial returns for shareholders.

U.S. West We will be the leader in providing telecommunications solutions that make the lives of our customers better, easier, and hassle free. And deliver to them applications that communicate, educate, entertain and inform.

Goodyear Goodyear ranked by all measures as the best tire and rubber company in the world, and returning to our position as the industry's undisputed world leader by the end of the year 2000.

Texas Instruments . . . to become a premier electronics company providing world leadership in digital solutions for the networked society—a society transformed by personalized electronics, all speaking the same digital language, all able to communicate anytime, anywhere.

levels in countries all over the world. Communication is vitally important. A leader who is able to present the vision in an intriguing way has an advantage in trying to capture the imagination of the people in the organization, according to Francis Adamson, manager of quality engineering/TQM at Heinz U.S.A.:

> The ability to fascinate is one of the most powerful tools of the charismatic leader. Leaders can use it to weave a fabric of commitment

throughout the organization. This is the empowering function of the leader: allowing everyone to buy into the vision.[7]

Live the Values

Pursuing the quality vision commits the organization to living by a set of values, such as devotion to customers, continuous improvement, and teamwork. A manager who hopes the organization will embrace and live by these values must live them to the utmost. As former Procter & Gamble Chairman and CEO Edwin Artzt puts it, "Leaders of the best companies profoundly believe in, and promote, the core values of customer-focused quality."[8] By "walking the talk," leaders serve as role models for the whole organization. Many CEOs lead quality training sessions, serve on quality improvement teams, work on projects that do not usually require top-level input, and personally visit customers. For example, senior managers at Texas Instruments Defense Systems and Electronics Group (now Raytheon Systems Company) led 150 of 1,900 cross-functional teams. At Custom Research, Inc., the top four senior leaders ensure that employees have the responsibility, training, and information they need to do their jobs through empowering everyone to do what it takes to serve clients. They work with nine other senior people to set strategy and make middle managers the real leaders.

When dramatic organizational changes are taking place, people in organizations are very sensitive to any sign of hypocrisy. A leader can undermine 100 hours of speeches with one decision that reveals his or her commitment to quality values to be superficial. This is not just a symbolic issue: Harvard's David Garvin found in a study of the air conditioner industry that the quality of a firm's products was strongly related to the quality values expressed by management.[9]

Managers' actions can symbolize their commitment to quality-oriented values in many concrete ways. For example, they can attend training programs on various aspects of quality, instead of just sending others. They can practice continuous improvement in processes they control, such as strategic planning and capital budgeting. Perhaps most importantly, they can provide adequate funding for quality efforts, so TQ will not be the "poor cousin" to other business issues.[10]

Virtually every management team that has staged a major quality turnaround has recognized this need to "walk," not just "talk," quality. In looking back on the return to financial success from near bankruptcy of his company, Harley Davidson's Ron Hutchinson stated:

> We realized that, if we really wanted to communicate to our people a change in the company's direction and approach, what we needed to do as senior managers was demonstrate that we were going to live by a new set of rules.

Lead Continuous Improvement

Beyond establishing a vision for the organization and expressing quality values through their decisions and actions, quality-oriented leaders must lead the continuous process improvement efforts that are the meat and potatoes of total quality management. All of the vision and values in the world are worthless if the organization does not continuously make strides to improve its performance in the eyes of customers. Visions of world-class quality and competitiveness can only be achieved if an organization keeps finding ways to do things a little better and a little faster. Leaders must be at the center of these efforts.

Managers are sometimes reluctant to take an active role in the organization's improvement efforts for fear of dominating or undercutting their newly empowered workers. Like many aspects of management, this is a question of balance, but it is a mistake for managers to remain uninvolved in process improvement efforts. Harry Levinson and Chuck DeHont, quality leaders at Sierra Semiconductor, have thought about this dilemma and concluded:

> It is often perceived, incorrectly, that management should never specify how problems should be solved, that to do so would be considered improper delegation. What is actually true is that managers who set no rules for how problems should be solved have abdicated their leadership roles.[11]

There are a number of ways for managers to lead continuous improvement, and which ones make the most sense will depend on the specific organization. One option already mentioned is for leaders to lead by example, by working continuously to improve the processes that they control. For some of these processes, organizational members are among the customers, which gives management the opportunity to model the behaviors associated with obtaining and acting upon customer input.[12] For example, streamlining the capital budgeting procedure by speeding up the process and eliminating non-value-added activities would provide powerful examples for people to emulate.

A second way managers can lead process improvement is to help organization members prioritize processes to work on. Here managers can take advantage of their knowledge of the "big picture" and suggest avenues of improvement that are likely to have big payoffs in terms of quality improvement and customer satisfaction. This point was underscored in a recent statement by Gerhard Schulmeyer, president and CEO of Asea Brown Boveri, a multinational company headquartered in Germany:

> It doesn't help simply to encourage everybody to work harder. The issue is to take a fresh look at the problems and concentrate our efforts on core processes that have the largest leverage in improving our position in the market.[13]

A third way is to inspire people to do things they do not believe they can do. Motorola set aggressive goals; to reduce defects per unit of output in every operation by 100fold in four years and to reduce cycle time by 50 percent each year. One of Hewlett-Packard's goals is to reduce the interval between product concept and investment payback by one-half in five years. The 3M Company seeks to generate 25 percent of sales from products less than two years old. To promote such "stretch goals," leaders provide the resources and support to meet them, especially training.

Of course, managers leading process improvement bear some responsibility for educating all their associates as to how the various processes within the company fit together. If this is done effectively, organization members eventually will be able to set their own priorities for process improvement.

Managers also can lead this effort by removing barriers to success in process improvement.[14] Barriers may consist of a nettlesome standard operating procedure or a recalcitrant manager in a key position. Without leadership from management, such barriers may undermine efforts at process improvement. Of course, in dealing with such barriers, managers must continue to operate in a manner consistent with quality values. For example, managers who balk at changes must be treated with respect and their reservations considered seriously, even if they are eventually overruled.

One final way for managers to lead process improvement is to keep track of improvement efforts, to encourage them, and to provide recognition when key milestones are reached. Solectron managers, for example, recognize and reward groups for exceptional performance. Besides monetary awards, Solectron often buys lunch for an entire division or brings in ice cream for the whole corporation. One top manager of our acquaintance makes it a practice always to be present for such recognition ceremonies. If he cannot attend, the ceremony is rescheduled. By doing this, the manager accomplishes several things at once: He shows his sincere interest in the process, he provides reinforcement for those people working to make key changes, and he lets his subordinates know that it is not acceptable to make excuses for missing quality-related functions. (For an additional and unusual example of leadership for continuous improvement, see the box on Tampopo on page 284.)

QUALITY LEADERSHIP IN ACTION

Some of the best examples of leadership come from Baldrige Award winners. In this section we describe some of the leadership activities of two winning companies, Solectron Corporation (the first repeat winner) and Armstrong World Industries Building Products Operations.

Solectron Corporation[15]

Solectron was founded in 1977 in San Jose, California. Dr. Winston Chen, the first CEO, established the entrepreneurial foundation for the company's leadership system. He focused all employees on:

Tampopo: The Quest for the Perfect Noodle Soup[16]

Like many aspects of organizations, the nature of leadership is changed dramatically by TQ. Moving beyond a command and control mentality, leaders in a TQ organization help their associates to provide better products and services to customers. This style of leadership is personified by Goro, a truck driver and noodle expert who in the film *Tampopo* helps Tampopo in her quest to create the perfect noodle soup. An unlikely blend of Western and samurai movie cliches, *Tampopo* is at the same time a parody and a virtual road map for continuous quality improvement.

Goro and his friend Guntu meet Tampopo when they stop in at the Lai Lai noodle stand for a quick bite. When Goro tells a drunken customer that Tampopo's noodles are mediocre, he gets taken outside and beaten up, a fate that (metaphorically at least) awaits many leaders who publicly state that the status quo is not good enough. But Tampopo is wise enough to accept Goro's judgment on the poor quality of her noodles and asks for his help.

One of Goro's first suggestions is to study her customers as they enter the shop, so she can adjust her service to their needs. Tampopo soon begins to recognize that quality noodle soup involves a lot more than just cooking. She closes her shop until further notice and devotes herself to elevating the quality of her noodle business. In a scene reminiscent of *Rocky*, Tampopo (now in a sweat suit) runs through the park, with Goro following on a bicycle. She then practices lifting pots of boiling water, working to reduce her soup production time below three minutes.

The next step is to learn from the competition. The nearby shop Goro and Tampopo visit first is full, demonstrating that customers are there if only Tampopo is good enough. In the second shop, the cooks talk to each other too much and forget people's orders. In the third, the cook's motions are elegant, with no wasted motion. In the fourth, a busy place by a rail station, the cook must keep track of many orders at once. Tampopo shows her progress by rattling off all the orders that have been given. At the fifth shop, the broth is so good that Goro and Tampopo stoop to spying to try to duplicate the recipe. By the sixth, the owners see what is going on and kick them out, but Tampopo tells them they have nothing worth stealing: Their dough sat out too long, their pork is overcooked, and their soup tasteless.

Although this noodle benchmarking tour greatly improves the quality of Tampopo's soup, she recognizes that it is not yet good enough. Help then comes from an unlikely source, an old friend of Goro's living in a hobo camp where everyone is a gastronome. He takes them to yet more restaurants, including one where they rescue a man from choking. The man lends them his chauffeur, who, against all odds, is also a noodle expert, and takes them to even more restaurants. (The quest for quality can be exhausting, and in this case pretty rough on the waistline.) In the shop with the best-tasting noodles, Tampopo has to trick the proprietor into divulging his process: "These noodles are not as good as usual, perhaps you did not let them sit long enough." "I left them overnight, as usual," he growls, and so on until Tampopo has the entire recipe.

At this point, Goro and Tampopo's other advisors urge her to reopen her shop, now renamed after her. The drunken customer from her old shop turns out to be a contractor and decorator, who remodels the shop for efficiency and attractiveness. Tampopo herself also gets remodeled, as she drops her dumpy old outfit for a new chef's uniform. The transformation is remarkable.

Still the quest for improvement continues. The experts tell Tampopo that her soup "lacks profundity" and suggest adding spring onions. Although the other elements are nearly perfect, there is nothing to distinguish it, no unexpected element to delight customers and exceed their expectations. With the spring onions added, she tries again. The experts drink her soup to the bottom. Success! Soon customers are swarming to her new shop, and Goro and the others drift away, as Tampopo no longer needs them. A cycle of quality leadership is complete, and Goro rides off into the sunset.

- the needs of the customer,
- the improvement of quality in manufacturing processes,
- the challenge of providing a reasonable return to shareholders, and
- the responsibility to do what it takes to satisfy the customer.

Dr. Chen also developed a set of basic values, (the Solectron Beliefs), to use as the model for behavior for all employees. These are:

Customer First—The customer is our first priority, and it is our constant objective to satisfy customer requirements on time with zero defects. We do this by strengthening partnership relationships and providing products and services of the greatest value through innovation and excellence.

Respect for the Individual—We recognize the importance of listening to every employee. We emphasize employee dignity, equality, and growth.

Quality—Customers are entitled to products and services that meet their expectations and specifications. It is our goal to execute with excellence and exceed customer expectations.

Supplier Partnership—We emphasize partnership, communication, and measurement.

Business Ethics—Honesty, integrity, and dependability are the corner-stones of all successful relationships. We believe we must conduct our business with uncompromising integrity.

Shareholder Value—We optimize business results through continuous improvement.

Social Responsibility—It is our objective to be an asset to our community.

In 1988, Dr. Koichi ("Ko") Nishimura joined Solectron as chief operating officer. Dr. Nishimura's objective was to develop and sustain an infrastructure and management system that would meet the challenge of a 30 percent annual growth rate, while maintaining profit levels, improving levels of customer satisfaction, and providing growth opportunities for employees.

Solectron's vision is to be the best electronics design and manufacturing service company in the world. In 1989, Dr. Nishimura adopted the Malcolm Baldrige National Quality Award Criteria as the foundation and framework for Solectron's business and leadership system. To accelerate the compliance of Solectron's leadership system and company-wide processes to the Baldrige criteria, Ko suggested that Solectron should enter the award process to get examiner feedback on how they could improve. Since 1989, the company's leadership group under Dr. Nishimura, who is now Solectron's chairman, president, and CEO, has been using the Baldrige criteria, including both external and internal assessments, to drive business excellence. The Baldrige road map has helped Solectron to grow and thrive, resulting in an average compound annual growth rate in excess of 50 percent.

Ko taught the leadership team that their job is to manage the business to ensure the needs of all stakeholders are addressed. Ko coaches the leadership team to live the Solectron Beliefs. The Solectron Beliefs have been in place for many years and have been reaffirmed year after year. Ko emphatically states that if behavior does not reflect the Solectron Beliefs, then they need to change behavior, not the beliefs.

Ko Nishimura and the senior leadership team drive the annual planning process for the corporation. The process includes developing the long-range plan (LRP), the annual operating plan (AOP), and the annual improvement plan (Hoshin). Senior leaders continuously review company performance. Key performance reviews include:

- Each site manager monitors operational, quality, business, supplier, and customer data daily.
- Performance to strategic and annual plans is reviewed by the CEO every month and then collectively reviewed at the bimonthly general managers' meeting. All region presidents, site general managers, and corporate vice presidents attend and present status and results.
- Ko Nishimura travels to each site every quarter to review performance in detail. These reviews allow line managers and employees to make presentations to the CEO. Ko reinforces the company's commitment to customers, shareholders, and employees in these meetings. He also facilitates internal communication between sites.
- Site general managers conduct quarterly informational meetings for employees. They review quarterly business results, developments with key customers, and the status of important strategic initiatives. These meetings are also used to recognize contributions of employees and employee teams.
- The results of an annual customer executive survey are reviewed in detail at general managers' meetings. These data re-analyzed for both near-term ac-

tions and longer-term capability enhancement. Critical issues are integrated into action plans and are reviewed during the CEO's site visits.

Solectron is focused on satisfying customers' requirements on a global basis, with facilities in North America, Europe, and Asia. The firm has grown both by setting up "greenfield" locations and by buying facilities from customers. Ko Nishimura manages Solectron as an entrepreneurial company. Ko has set up a Business Conduct Guide that defines the individual responsibilities for conducting business in the highest ethical manner. This guide drives home the point that the Solectron Beliefs are the principles for running the company. Solectron is also proactively involved with various government and regulatory groups to help in shaping policy. Among various recognitions for its environmental approaches, Solectron California was awarded a "special recognition" by the San Francisco Bay Area's Peninsula Conservation Center Foundation for its environmental, pollution prevention, and recycling programs.

Armstrong Building Products Operations[17]

Reporting to the Executive Office of Armstrong World Industries, Inc., the Building Products Operations (BPO) Quality Leadership Team, consisting of the president and direct reports, leads and manages all aspects of Armstrong's U.S. ceilings business. In 1990, as a result of an internal self-assessment against the 1989 Baldrige criteria, BPO leaders reorganized to improve customer focus and satisfaction, forming the BPO General Management Team (GMT). The purpose of this reorganization was to more formally define and execute a leadership system within BPO. Its focus: improving customer satisfaction, financial performance, and capabilities across functional lines.

In January 1994, BPO aligned key support services into the operation to better communicate and integrate their values and expectations for employees, customers, and shareholders. Shortly thereafter, the BPO GMT reorganized into the BPO Quality Leadership Team (QLT), which now includes the key support staff leaders as well as the leaders of the five value-adding functions. The purpose of the QLT is "to ensure that the values, goals, and systems are in place to guide the sustained pursuit of customer value and operational performance improvement."

The leadership system that the QLT has developed and refined to drive for business excellence includes the following specific roles and responsibilities:

- The QLT creates quality values and sets rational stretch goal expectations for BPO.
- Management-led Quality Improvement Teams extend the leadership system to each location and focus on customer requirements and continuous improvement.
- The QLT uses the Baldrige criteria to assess performance. Based on Baldrige feedback, QLT members are assigned specific areas in which to develop and implement action plans to capitalize on their strengths and address opportunities for improvement.

- The QLT keeps refining the BPO planning process to create an integrated strategic management process aimed at delivering value and satisfaction to customers, employees, and shareholders.
- QLT members and many other employees systematically participate in various Customer advisory committee meetings, national customer conventions, and conversations with customers to communicate and reinforce BPO's quality values.
- The QLT refines relationships with BPO's channel customers.
- QLT members conduct and participate in a wide variety of education, training, benchmarking, and capability development.
- QLT members communicate and reinforce their values to a long list of stakeholders outside of Armstrong.

The foundation of BPO's values is Armstrong's operating principles; the ethics behind them date from the company's beginnings in 1860. The company's operating principles have been unchanged since they were first set to paper in 1960, on Armstrong's 100th anniversary. They are the roots of the firm's quality values and are discussed with all new employees on their first day. The operating principles are:

- to respect the dignity and inherent rights of the individual human being in all dealings with people;
- to maintain high moral and ethical standards and to reflect honesty, integrity, reliability, and forthrightness in all relationships;
- to reflect the tenets of good taste and common courtesy in all attitudes, words, and deeds; and
- to serve fairly and in proper balance the interests of all groups associated with the business—customers, stockholders, employees, suppliers, community neighbors, government, and the general public.

The QLT (and the former GMT) has been very successful in leading changes in culture, organizational structure, and levels of performance. This has been achieved through an ever-improving understanding of the dynamics of markets, competitors' performance, and drivers of business results. The QLT meets twice per month to review, evaluate, and manage performance against the strategic plan. All QLT members review their functional action plan performance a minimum of once per quarter and at the QLT semiannually. They manage performance daily. The president and other QLT members review plants' action plans with each manufacturing plant during semiannual plant quality and service review meetings and global plant managers meetings. Every year, the president and the quality manager meet with each plant's Quality Improvement Team solely to review the plans and progress of its quality improvement process. Each member of the QLT conducts individual employee performance reviews each year. Members of the QLT actively participate in BPO's annual quality council meetings, where Quality Improvement Team leaders come together to review their strengths and areas for improvement. The QLT reviews the company's strategic management process annually. QLT members use a variety of systematic approaches to evaluate and improve the effectiveness of their personal and collective leadership. These include employee feedback, performance reviews, Baldrige assessments, and benchmarking.

In 1990, Armstrong's quality managers developed Armstrong's 14 Actions, based upon the quality philosophy of Philip Crosby. In 1994 the 14 actions were refined again to improve the company's approaches and bring in new methods and systems, such as capability development. The refined 14 actions are:

1. *Leadership*—Demonstrate understanding, commitment, and resolve to improve quality in all areas of the organization.
2. *Quality Improvement Teams*—Plan, implement, and evaluate the organization's quality improvement activities.
3. *Customer Satisfaction*—Ensure that the systems to improve quality, and actions to change our culture, focus on our markets and customers.
4. *Planning and Goal Setting*—Establish specific targets and assess progress.
5. *Awareness:* Increase awareness of the importance of quality improvement among all employees.
6. *Education and Training*—Provide employees with the education required to effectively participate in improvements.
7. *Measurement*—Know if we are meeting our customers' requirements. Understand and communicate current performance.
8. *Process Improvement*—Identify all major business processes in the organization, establish ownership, and clarify improvement priorities.
9. *Opportunities for Improvement*—Provide a system for all employees that encourages, communicates and recognizes improvement ideas.
10. *Supplier Quality Management*—Involve Armstrong suppliers in our efforts to improve quality and achieve customer satisfaction.
11. *Recognition*—Encourage, recognize, and reward participation in improvement activities.
12. *Quality Councils*—Periodically bring leaders together to share information and set direction.
13. *Benchmarking*—Provide a disciplined approach for comparing the performance of our processes against best-in-class criteria.
14. *Assessment*—Evaluate the organization's performance against recognized standards.

Principles, values, and plans are communicated and reinforced throughout the entire organization. They are communicated by BPO's senior management during presentations at management meetings, Team Expos, crew meetings, and talks with customers, suppliers, and community neighbors. Behavior is reinforced by linking variable compensation to these values through business strategies. Over 90 percent of all BPO manufacturing employees are part of the company's Gainsharing Plan, which compensates plant employees (hourly and salaried) for improvements in safety, quality, productivity, and customer service. All other BPO employees are rewarded through the Salaried Employees' Bonus Plan. 1994's record results in sales and profitability resulted in Armstrong BPO's highest-ever payout in both plans.

TQ AND LEADERSHIP THEORY

There are a great number of theories of leadership, and we can only discuss the relationship of TQ to a few of them. This section outlines some of theories that seem to relate most closely to TQ and compares them to the TQ view of leadership.

Consideration and Initiating Structure

In a series of studies done several decades ago at Ohio State University, researchers tried to identify the behaviors associated with effective leadership. These studies concluded that many of these behaviors could be captured by two dimensions: consideration and initiating structure.

Consideration (also known as socioemotional orientation) means taking care of subordinates, explaining things to them, being approachable, and generally being concerned about their welfare. *Initiating structure* (also known as task orientation) means getting people organized, including setting goals and instituting and enforcing deadlines and standard operating procedures. Research indicates that, although different situations require different leadership behaviors, over a period of time most organizational units will require both types of leadership in order to be successful.[18]

One apparent difference between this classic view of leadership and the TQ view is that the classic view emphasizes leadership at the work group level, whereas the TQ view deals with the more global level of organizations or major subunits. Writers on TQ leadership have focused less on lower-level leaders, perhaps due to the emphasis on self-management at those levels.

Despite these differences, consideration and initiating structure are not irrelevant for organizations pursuing TQ. Such organizations recognize the importance of employees for the success of their quality efforts and for their performance in general. Thus, leaders certainly need to be considerate of employee needs. Consideration of employees minimizes their frustration and allows them to focus on customer service and continuous improvement. In a TQ environment, consideration is not done in a paternalistic manner, emphasizing the power of leaders over subordinates. On the contrary, people are treated as respected associates.

Initiating structure is appropriate in the TQ environment, but it may be accomplished differently than in the traditional organizational setting. Traditionally, leaders were responsible for the whole gamut of activities associated with initiating structure—setting goals, establishing deadlines, enforcing rules, and so on. In organizations striving for empowerment, many of these activities are taken over by employees.

The discussion of leadership for TQ suggests that quality leadership consists more of setting a direction for people by establishing a vision and identifying values. By leading continuous improvement efforts, leaders establish priorities for activities throughout the organization. Such activities provide the necessary context for employees to initiate structure for themselves.

The Roles of Managers

One well-known model, advanced by Henry Mintzberg, categorizes the work of managers into 10 roles. Although this is a model of managerial roles, rather than leadership per se, it is useful to explore how roles may change as managers attempt to practice total quality leadership.

There are interpersonal roles (figurehead, leader, and liaison), informational roles (monitor, disseminator, spokesperson), and decisional roles (entrepreneur, disturbance handler, resource allocator, and negotiator).[19] Each of these roles is likely to be played by managers practicing total quality, although the relative importance of the roles, and the ways in which they are played, may differ from more traditional organizations.

The figurehead role, which involves the ceremonial or symbolic tasks of managers, is certainly played in TQ organizations. A manager presiding at a recognition ceremony for a team's quality accomplishments is fulfilling this role. The leadership role is obviously important for TQ-oriented managers, but the directing and controlling aspects of this role are downplayed. The liaison role—dealing with customers, suppliers, and others—is still played, but it also is fulfilled to an increasing extent by employees, as an outgrowth of their empowerment.

In a TQ environment, managers play informational roles, but non-managerial personnel are more involved in these activities, rather than looking to managers as the source of all information. Employees involved in benchmarking, for example, play an important part in monitoring and disseminating information. Although top managers play an important role as spokespersons, in TQ this role also is increasingly shared with people throughout the organization. By now, probably hundreds if not thousands of non-managerial personnel have stepped up to the microphone to share their teams' accomplishments with the world.

Many of the behaviors leaders use to initiate and support a TQ program are characterized by the entrepreneurial role, one of the decisional roles. In this role, managers try to improve their organization by identifying problems and instituting processes to solve them. The disturbance-handler role—in which leaders resolve conflicts among subunits—should be diminished, at least in the long run, as people take on a more holistic view of the organizational mission. The resource allocator role continues to be key, as TQ will not succeed unless leaders are unswerving in their commitment of resources to continuous improvement and customer satisfaction. Finally, the negotiator role still is played, but it is different, as companies try to create long-term, win-win arrangements with suppliers, unions, and customers.

The Mintzberg model attempts to describe the behavior of managers, not to prescribe what they should do. It also attempts to capture the broad scope of managerial activities across many types of organization. For this reason it is difficult to compare it directly to the more limited, but explicitly prescriptive, content of the TQ leadership model. Nevertheless, the comparison is instructive in linking this discussion to the mainstream management literature on leadership: Managers in TQ settings play some roles (entrepreneurial) more than other managers, other roles (disturbance handler) less often, and still others (leader) differently.

Transformational Leadership Theory

Another model that can be compared to the TQ approach is Transformational Leadership Theory.[20] According to this model, leaders who wish to have a major impact on their organizations must take a long-term perspective, work to stimulate their organizations intellectually, invest in training to develop individuals and groups, take some risks, promote a shared vision and values, and focus on customers and employees as individuals.

The transformational leadership model dovetails with leadership for TQ. Many of its aspects (emphasis on vision and focus on customers and employees as individuals) are right out of the TQ playbook, while others are generally consistent with TQ. For instance, Deming emphasized the need for managers to have "constancy of purpose"—to pursue diligently the long-term goal of remaining competitive through continuous improvement processes. They should also communicate an appealing vision that emphasizes continuous improvement, teamwork, and customer service in order to inspire followers. Moreover, managers can act as role models by taking a personal interest in activities geared toward improving processes and customer relationships.[21]

It would be tempting to say that all managers in TQ organizations should be transformational leaders, but this is unrealistic and probably unwise. It is not realistic because few, if any, organizations have such a concentration of transformational leaders. It is not wise because such a concentration would likely breed more chaos than quality. An organization pursuing TQ needs both those who establish visions and those who are effective at the day-to-day tasks needed to achieve them.[22] These "transactional leaders" play an important role in promoting total quality.

Management and Leadership

A recent treatment of leadership by John Kotter compares the concept of leadership to the concept of management.[23] According to this view, management is needed to create order amid complexity, and leadership is needed to stimulate the organizational change necessary to keep up with a changing environment. This view avoids the simplistic ideas that management is somehow trivial, generally unnecessary, and should be replaced by leadership and that the same person cannot practice both management and leadership.

Kotter differentiates leadership from management by contrasting the activities central to each. While management begins with planning and budgeting, leadership begins with setting a direction. Direction setting involves creating a

vision of the future, as well as a set of approaches for achieving the
promote goal achievement, management practices organizing and .
while leadership works on aligning people—communicating the visio.
developing commitment to it. Management achieves plans through control.
and problem solving, whereas leadership achieves its vision through mo.
vating and inspiring.

Kotter's view of leadership similar to transformational theory dovetails
with our depiction of quality leadership. Both focus on developing and communicating a vision. Kotter's view of inspiring resembles our discussion of
giving people values to embrace and then making sure the leader is practicing
them.

The idea of aligning people is consistent with the idea of empowerment,
because it gives people a goal, then leaves them to move in that direction. Our
description of the role of leaders in continuous improvement is more hands on
than Kotter's description, perhaps suggesting that some management behaviors will continue to be important to leaders in total quality organizations.

SUMMARY

Quality leadership is clearly important for a company trying to practice total
quality. Much of what managers can do to promote TQ can be summarized by
three processes: establishing a vision, living the values, and leading improvement. David Kearns's leadership of Xerox (see the case at the end of this
chapter) is but one example that demonstrates that these processes are not just
abstractions, but actually capture the behavior of real leaders whose companies
have experienced considerable success with quality. These leadership processes
overlap with several theories of leadership, particularly Transformational
Leadership Theory.

REVIEW AND DISCUSSION QUESTIONS

1. What three processes must leaders undertake to promote total quality in
   their organizations?
2. Take a few minutes and try to conceive of a total quality vision for an
   organization with which you are familiar. Suppose you choose your university. What would your vision be? Think of all the customers of the university. Now think of what would make them ecstatic about the service
   the university is providing for them. As a customer, what would delight
   you? Would this also delight your current or future employer? How
   about the taxpayers (if you are in a public university or college) or the
   school's benefactors?
3. State some examples in which leaders you have worked for have exhibited leadership practices discussed in this chapter. Can you provide
   examples for which they have not?

4. Most of the talk on leadership for quality focuses on top managers. What can middle and first-level managers do to promote quality in their organizations? How does this differ from the role of top management?

5. John Young, president and CEO of Hewlett-Packard, summarized the role of the CEO in quality improvement in the following recommendations.[24]

   a. Dramatize the importance of quality to the organization.

   b. Establish agreed-upon measures of quality.

   c. Set challenging and motivating goals.

   d. Give people the resources and information needed to do the job.

   e. Reward results.

   f. Keep an attitude that high quality is not only desirable, but possible.

   How do these recommendations differ from those given in this chapter? Are they really different or do they capture the same ideas in different words?

6. Prior to its 1999 revision, the Baldrige criteria define the *leadership system* as "how leadership is exercised, formally and informally, throughout the company—the basis for and the way that key decisions are made, communicated, and carried out. It includes structures and mechanisms for decision making, selection and development of leaders and managers, and reinforcing values, practices, and behaviors." What are some attributes of an effective leadership system? How would you design one for an organization?

7. William Scherkenbach, a quality expert and Deming disciple, states:[25]

   If management is to improve their organization, they must change the process. This means that they cannot accept conference room promises, but must work directly with their people on the process, the how and the why. During this period of transition, everyone must be willing to learn. . . . No one is too senior to be involved in the how.

   Do you agree or disagree? Why?

8. What aspects of an organization's culture or structure could keep managers from leading effectively?

9. Sir John Harvey-Jones, head of Britain's Imperial Chemical Industries from 1982 to 1987, once commented, "The task of leadership is really to make the status quo more dangerous than launching into the unknown."[26] Do you think this statement represents a good approach to total quality leadership? Why or why not?

10. Compare the leadership practices of Solectron and Armstrong BPO. How do these practices relate to the concepts developed in this chapter? What differences and similarities can you point to?

CASES

David Kearns and the Transformation of Xerox[27]

David Kearns, former chairman and CEO of Xerox, provides an excellent example of leadership for quality. Xerox's problems in the early 1980s were legion and typical of American manufacturers facing serious foreign competition for the first time. Xerox discovered to its horror that Japanese companies were able to sell copiers in the United States for roughly what it cost Xerox to build them. Its former lion's share of the copier market had dwindled to a paltry 8 percent. Even at the time, Xerox was hardly complacent: Productivity was increasing by as much as 7 or 8 percent every year. Kearns calculated that gains closer to 18 percent a year were needed to catch Xerox's competitors.

About this time, Kearns read Philip Crosby's book *Quality Is Free*. He invited Crosby to address Xerox's management. Kearns's pleas for change initially were resisted by a management team who said they were already doing everything they could. This led Kearns to tell his managers that trying to change Xerox was like "pushing a wet noodle." It was time for more drastic action.

In 1983 the top management team at Xerox designed a new approach to quality that was dubbed "Leadership through Quality." The central principle of the new approach was that quality would be defined as customer satisfaction, not internal standards. If customers were not satisfied, quality had not been attained. A second principle was to focus on processes, not just outcomes. In the past, poor outcomes were an occasion to blame someone and to hammer into them the importance of doing better. This was replaced with an approach that focused on examining the process that had created the outcome and improving it.

In order to operate according to these principles, a number of specific practices were undertaken. Xerox is perhaps best known for its extensive use of benchmarking—a process of comparing your operations to the best practices of other companies. The company's approach is to benchmark against the best, in whatever industry it is found. Xerox has benchmarked its billing processes against American Express and its distribution processes against L.L. Bean.

To demonstrate their commitment to these principles, Kearns and his management team were the first to undergo the newly devised quality training. They then became the teachers for the next level of management, and training flowed throughout the organization in this manner. In a move that represented a major departure from tradition, each senior manager was made responsible for taking calls from customers one day a month. Xerox managers still interrupt their meetings to take such calls.

Although Kearns's efforts were crucial to this process, he believes that leadership must (and in this case did) come from other sources as well, including the Amalgamated Clothing & Textile Workers, the union representing Xerox's production employees:

We've also learned that it's important to have union leaders as deeply committed to the quality process as management. A strong and enlightened union leadership shared management's vision and understood that changes had to be made if there was to be a future for all Xerox employees. We shared each other's trust.[28]

Xerox's competitive resurgence was dramatic. Market share, revenues, and profits all have recovered substantially. In 1989 Xerox became one of the first winners of both the Baldrige and Canadian National Quality Award. Kearns believes that "Xerox is probably the first American company in an industry targeted by the Japanese to regain market share without the aid of tariffs or government help."[29] Despite the recovery and the awards, however, Kearns has not abandoned the principle of continuous improvement:

We take great satisfaction in winning these awards, but the fact is that we're far from finished with our drive to improve. We have learned that the pursuit of quality is a race with no finish line. We see an upward and never-ending spiral of increased competition and heightened customer expectations.[30]

David Kearns was succeeded as Xerox's chairman in 1991 by Paul Allaire and began working within the U.S. Department of Education to bring the quality perspective to America's schools.

Discussion Questions

1. How did David Kearns fulfill the roles of a quality leader at Xerox?
2. Is Kearns's approach broadly applicable, or would different approaches be needed in other settings?
3. Kearns began a practice of having senior managers personally take phone calls from customers with problems. Call the president of an organization of which you are a customer and report a quality or service problem you are experiencing. Will the president take the call? Will the president or someone else return your call? (If you get to talk to someone, congratulate them on their responsiveness and be as constructive as possible in describing your problem.)

The Power of Leadership Teams[31]

When the top management group at Georgia Power Company's Plant Hammond decided to become a team, everyone was quite sure that they were already a team and worked pretty well together. The top leadership group in early 1995 was 10 people from three management levels and two individual contributors. The management style was much the same as they had been using for many years in the utility industry and was characterized by an emphasis on the chain of command for most decisions—with the important ones made by one or two people. Information and business results were communicated on a "need to know" basis. For the most part, each department operated and made decisions independently.

This management style served the utility business well, given its business requirements. The business was relatively predictable and structured with a regulated rate of return, regional market protection, and 100 percent control of access to its own distribution facilities. A watershed development, however, occurred in the early 1990s—a move toward deregulation. This demanded fundamental changes in the way Plant Hammond operated and managed its resources.

In the early 1990s, the plant had reduced the number of employees by about one third, resulting in fewer management levels and fewer managers in those levels. In early 1995, the parent organization, Southern Company, implemented a transformation process to improve the plant's ability to compete. This transformation process required an emphasis on business results at all levels and creation of an organization culture that could deal with uncertainty and competition.

As the plant manager considered the requirements for the future, he determined that the structure, processes, and culture of the plant would need to change. Therefore, top management must change how it operated, broadening capabilities at all levels. Processes were needed to manage decision making risk and gain consensus on direction. A new organizational structure was one of the early steps in their transformation. The structure provided an "outside in" focus—identifying the operations function as the primary internal customer—and grouped plant activities into several functional areas.

However, plant management knew that simply changing the boxes on an organization chart was not sufficient for real change. In the summer of 1995, the plant manager and nine other employees took their first step toward becoming a team when they came together at a facilitated off-site meeting. They clarified individual roles and responsibilities on this new team and began developing team relationships. They agreed that the role of each leadership team member should be one of "shared responsibilities with a functional focus." Top managers at the plant could no longer make decisions from only their own departments' view. In fact, managers were required to consider the impact of their decisions—not only on the total plant, but also on the total operating system of the Southern Company.

Each member took on the responsibility to champion specific transformation activities for the leadership team. The team began to have regular one-day session meetings where they discussed and made decisions on strategic and operational issues. This management team took a key developmental step in 1996 by setting expectations for their behavior and presenting them to their organizations during reviews of the 1996 plant strategic plan. Putting these expectations "on the record" built incentives to act accordingly.

The team found several tools be helpful in its operation and development. One was a *common work plan* that served multiple purposes: (1) to ensure integration of their efforts and to track team results; (2) to establish member accountability; (3) to facilitate the delegation of traditional plant manager tasks;

and (4) to act as a catalyst for surfacing strategic issues. Each team member—or members—took responsibility for accomplishing particular parts of the work plan. The team also used various assessment instruments to understand and deal with the individual styles of team members. Each team member discussed his or her assessment in an open forum. As a result, members made commitments for change and support. Each team member also formulated his or her own development plan based on these and other assessments.

Since one of the plant's strategies was to improve the capabilities of the management team, the team worked with an outside consultant to identify strengths and weaknesses. The consultant observed each of the team members in work situations and provided specific personal feedback and suggestions over an extended period of time. Each team member reviewed his or her assessment with the group and asked for reactions and recommendations. The consultant also provided feedback on group processes and worked in concert with an internal consultant to improve teamwork processes.

Discussion Questions

1. What lessons do you think the company learned about transforming its leadership system to a team-based organization?
2. What conditions do you think are necessary for management teams to become "real teams" and not just a grouping of independent functional managers who cooperate with each other?
3. What challenges do leadership teams like these face?

Crosby's Quality Nightmare

An example of what is not needed in a quality leader is provided by Philip Crosby in *Quality Is Free.*[33] Crosby goes to visit his old pal Ernest Dinsmore, manager of the Flagship Hotel, to see how a real hotel is run "from the inside." Crosby's arrival at the hotel is a comedy of errors: He dashes inside through a cloudburst as the doorman watches safely from the door. He has to wait several hours for his room to be made up, then has to climb the stairs because the elevator is broken. To top things off, his car is towed from in front of the hotel.

Dinsmore dismisses these problems as "growing pains" and takes Crosby on a tour of the guts of the hotel. The maids are gathered in one room arguing because, due to a shortage of vacuum cleaners, those on the upper floors cannot vacuum until those on the lower floors are finished. Dinsmore decrees, Solomonlike, that henceforth the rooms will be vacuumed only every other day, first the bottom floors, then the top. This way there will be enough vacuum cleaners to go around. Another dispute, this time among the bellmen, is also handled by Dinsmore. The tips, which seem to be getting lower all the time, will all be given to the bell captain, who will distribute them according to the effort he feels people are exerting. When Crosby remarks on the number of room service trays laying in the hallway, Dinsmore tells him that guests don't mind, because it reminds them that room service is available.

After this madness, the hotel restaurant appears to Crosby an oasis of quality and efficient service. They are promptly seated, drinks quickly appear, and the promises of an attractive menu are fulfilled as wonderful presentations emerge from the kitchen. This oasis turns out to be a mirage, because Dinsmore wants to "improve" the operation. Although most hotels lose money on their restaurants, this one was making about 10 percent net profit. It was obvious to Dinsmore that by raising prices and cutting back on the help, it could be turned into a real money machine.

At their farewell meeting, Dinsmore discusses the difficulty of finding people willing to do quality work and complains about the falling standards of today's workers. A few months later, Crosby learns that the Flagship has been closed and Dinsmore has been offered a position running a chain of motels. He hopes Crosby can be his guest at one of them sometime soon. Crosby says he "can hardly wait."

Discussion Questions

1. In what specific ways did Ernest Dinsmore fail to fulfill the roles of a quality leader?
2. What advice would you give him on how to start improving the quality of the service in his new hotel?

ENDNOTES

1. Harry J. Levinson and Chuck DeHont, "Leading to Quality," *Quality Progress*, May 1992, pp. 55–60.
2. Quoted in Jerry G. Bowles, "Leading the World-Class Company," *Fortune*, September 21, 1992.
3. 1998 Award Criteria, Malcolm Baldrige National Quality Award Criteria for Performance Excellence, p.40.
4. Dan Ciampa, *Total Quality: A User's Guide for Implementation*, Reading, Mass.: Addison-Wesley Publishing Company, 1992. p. 115.
5. These examples are from A.R. Tenner and I.J. DeToro, *Total Quality Management*. Reading, Mass: Addison-Wesley, 1992.
6. Quoted in Bowles, "Leading the World-Class Company."
7. F.B. Adamson, "Cultivating a Charismatic Quality Leader," *Quality Progress*, July 1989, pp. 56–57.
8. Quoted in Bowles, "Leading the World-Class Company."
9. D. Garvin, "Quality Problems, Policies, and Attitudes in the United States and Japan: An Exploratory Study," *Academy of Management Journal*, Vol. 29, No. 4, 1986, pp. 653–673.
10. These and other means of demonstrating commitment to TQ values were suggested by Tenner and DeToro, *Total Quality Management*.
11. Levinson and DeHont, "Leading to Quality," p. 56.
12. See P. Richards, "Right-side-up Organization," *Quality Progress*, October 1991, pp. 95–96.
13. Quoted in Bowles, "Leading the World-Class Company."
14. This idea is discussed in Howard S. Gitlow and Shelly J. Gitlow, *The Deming Guide to Quality and Competitive Position*, Englewood Cliffs, N.J.: Prentice-Hall, 1987.
15. Adapted from Solectron Malcolm Baldrige National Quality Award Application Summary, 1997.
16. Based on James C. Spee, "What the Film *Tampopo* Teaches about Total Quality Management." *Tampopo* is directed by Juzo Itami and stars Nobuko Miyamoto and Tsutomu Yamazaki, 1987 Itami Productions. Available on Republic Pictures Home Video in Japanese with English subtitles.
17. Adapted from Armstrong Building Products Operations Malcolm Baldrige National Quality Award Application Summary, 1995.

18. R. House and M. Baetz, "Leadership: Some Generalizations and New Research Directions," in B.M. Staw (ed.), *Research in Organizational Behavior*, Greenwich, Conn.: JAI Press, 1979, p. 359.

19. Henry Mintzberg, *The Nature of Managerial Work*, New York: Harper & Row, 1973.

20. B.M. Bass, *Leadership and Performance beyond Expectations*, New York: The Free Press, 1985. This discussion is based on David A. Waldman, "A Theoretical Consideration of Leadership and Total Quality Management," *Leadership Quarterly*, Vol. 4, 1993, pp. 65–79. See also J. Conger and R. Kanungo, "Toward a Behavioral Theory of Charismatic Leadership in Organizational Settings," *Academy of Management Review*, October 1987, pp. 637–647.

21. David A. Waldman, "The Contributions of Total Quality Management to a Theory of Work Performance," *Academy of Management Review*, Vol. 19, No. 3, pp. 510–536.

22. Philip Atkinson, "Leadership, Total Quality and Cultural Change," *Management Services*, June 1991, pp. 16-19.

23. J.P. Kotter, "What Leaders Really Do," in J.J. Gabarro (ed.), *Managing People and Organizations*, Boston: Harvard Business School Press, 1992, pp. 102–114.

24. John A. Young, "The Quality Focus at Hewlett-Packard," *Journal of Business Strategy*, Vol. 5, No. 3, 1985, pp. 6–9.

25. William W. Scherkenbach, *The Deming Route to Quality and Productivity*, Washington, D.C.: CEEPress Books, George Washington University, 1986, p. 139.

26. Quoted in Sir John Harvey-Jones, Harvard Business School Case 9-490013, p. 8.

27. This case is based on David Kearns, "Leadership through Quality," *Academy of Management Executive*, Vol. 4, No. 2, 1990, pp. 86–89; "A CEO's Odyssey Toward World-Class Manufacturing," *Chief Executive*, September 1990; and Alan C. Fenwick, "Five Easy Lessons," *Quality Progress*, December 1991.

28. Kearns, "Leadership through Quality," p. 88.

29. Kearns, "Leadership through Quality," p. 88.

30. Kearns, "Leadership through Quality," p. 88.

31. Adapted from Billie R. Day and Michael Moore, "Plugging Into the Power of Leadership Teams," *Journal for Quality and Participation*," May/June 1998, pp. 21–24.

32. Philip B. Crosby, *Quality Is Free*, New York: McGraw-Hill, 1979.

P A R T

IV

Total Quality and Strategic Management

C H A P T E R

10

Total Quality and Competitive Advantage

CHAPTER OUTLINE

Competitive advantage denotes a firm's ability to achieve market superiority over its competitors. In the long run, a sustainable competitive advantage provides above-average performance. A strong competitive advantage has six characteristics:[1]

1. It is driven by customer wants and needs. A company provides value to its customers that competitors do not.
2. It makes a significant contribution to the success of the business.
3. It matches the organization's unique resources with the opportunities in the environment. No two companies have the same resources; a good strategy uses them effectively.
4. It is durable and lasting and difficult for competitors to copy. A superior research and development department, for example, can consistently develop new products or processes to remain ahead of competitors.
5. It provides a basis for further improvement.
6. It provides direction and motivation to the entire organization.

Since each of these characteristics relates to quality, quality can be an important means of gaining competitive advantage. This chapter focuses on how total quality contributes to competitive advantage. This chapter will

- discuss the role of quality in cost leadership and differentiation, the two principal sources of competitive advantage;
- relate quality to the achievement of competitive advantage;
- describe the importance of quality in meeting customer expectations in product design, service, flexibility and variety, innovation, and rapid response; and
- discuss the importance of results measurement in focusing strategy.

SOURCES OF COMPETITIVE ADVANTAGE

The literature on competitive strategy suggests that a firm can possess two basic types of competitive advantage: low cost and differentiation.[2]

Cost Leadership

Many firms gain competitive advantage by establishing themselves as the low-cost leader in an industry. These firms produce high volumes of mature products and achieve their competitive advantage through low prices. Such firms often enter markets that were established by other firms. They emphasize achieving economies of scale and finding cost advantages from all sources. Low cost can result from high productivity and high capacity utilization. More importantly, improvements in quality lead to improvements in productivity, which in turn lead to lower costs. Thus a strategy of continuous improvement is essential to achieve a low-cost competitive advantage.

Lower costs result from innovations in product design and process technology that reduce the costs of production and from efficiencies gained through meticulous attention to operations. This approach has been exploited by many Japanese firms. Japanese companies adopted many product innovations and process technologies that were developed in the United States. They refined the

You Can't Fool All of the People All of the Time

The problems with focusing on costs at the expense of quality are illustrated by the case of the Schlitz Brewing Company.[3] In the early 1970s, Schlitz, the second largest brewer in the United States, began a cost-cutting campaign. It included reducing the quality of ingredients in their beers by switching to corn syrup and hop pellets and shortening the brewing cycle by 50 percent.

In the short term, it achieved higher returns on sales and assets than Anheuser-Busch (and the acclaim of Wall Street analysts). *Forbes* magazine stated, "Does it pay to build quality into a product if most customers don't notice? Schlitz seems to have a more successful answer." But customers do recognize inferior products. Soon after, market share and profits fell rapidly. By 1980 Schlitz's sales had declined 40 percent, the stock price fell from $69 to $5, and the company was eventually sold.

designs and manufacturing processes to produce high-quality products at low costs, resulting in higher market shares.

To achieve cost leadership for high-volume products, companies use a variety of approaches:[4]

- Early manufacturing involvement in the design of the product both for make-versus-buy decisions and for assurance that the production processes can achieve required tolerances.
- Product design to take advantage of automated equipment by minimizing the number of parts, eliminating fasteners, making parts symmetric whenever possible, avoiding rigid and stiff parts and using one-sided assembly designs.
- Limited product models and customization in distribution centers rather than in the factory.
- A manufacturing system designed for a fixed sequence of operations. Every effort is made to ensure zero defects at the time of shipment. Work-in-process inventory is reduced as much as possible, and multiskilled, focused teams of employees are used.

A cost leader can achieve above-average performance if it can command prices at or near the industry average. However, it cannot do so with an inferior product (see the box about Schlitz Brewing Company). The product must be perceived as comparable with competitors' products, or the firm will be forced to discount prices well below competitors' prices to gain sales. This can cancel any benefits that result from cost advantage.

Differentiation

To achieve differentiation, a firm must be unique in its industry along some dimensions that are widely valued by customers. It selects one or more attributes that customers perceive as important and positions itself uniquely to meet those needs. As a result, it can command premium prices and achieve higher profits. Juran cites an example of a power tool manufacturer that improved reliability well beyond that of competitors.[5] Field data showing that the differences in reliability resulted in significantly lower operating costs were publicized, and the company was able to secure a premium price.

However, a firm that uses differentiation as its source of competitive advantage cannot ignore cost. It must achieve a cost position on a par with its competitors and reduce costs in all areas that do not affect differentiation.

These issues apply to services as well. For example, Marriott's Fairfield Inn was designed to appeal to business travelers who wanted clean, comfortable rooms at inexpensive prices. Within this market, they are focused on cost leadership. On the other hand, the Ritz-Carlton hotels (acquired by Marriott several years ago) focus on differentiation (exceptional personal attention, twice-a-day housekeeping service, and special amenities such as bathrobes and rooms with bay windows) and can command premium prices.

THE IMPORTANCE OF QUALITY TO COMPETITIVE ADVANTAGE

The role of quality in achieving competitive advantage was demonstrated by several research studies during the 1980s. PIMS Associates, Inc., a subsidiary of the Strategic Planning Institute, maintains a data base of 1,200 companies and studies the impact of product quality on corporate performance.[6] PIMS researchers have found that

- Product quality is the most important determinant of business profitability.
- Businesses offering premium-quality products and services usually have large market shares and were early entrants into their markets.
- Quality is positively and significantly related to a higher return on investment for almost all kinds of products and market situations. PIMS studies have shown that firms with products of superior quality can more than triple return on sales over products perceived as having inferior quality.
- A strategy of quality improvement usually leads to increased market share but at a cost in terms of reduced short-run profitability.
- High-quality producers can usually charge premium prices.

General Systems Company, a prominent quality management consulting firm, has found that firms with TQ systems in place consistently exceed industry norms for return on investment. This is attributed to three factors:

1. TQ reduces the direct costs associated with poor quality.
2. Improvements in quality tend to lead to increases in productivity.
3. The combination of improved quality and increased productivity leads to an increase in market share.

FIGURE 10.1 QUALITY AND PROFITABLILITY

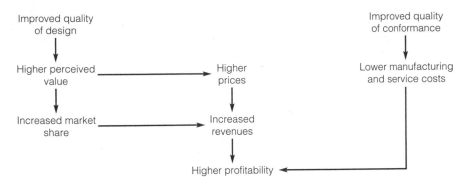

These findings, summarized in Figure 10.1, relate to both sources of competitive advantage—differentiation and low cost. The value of a product in the marketplace is influenced by the quality of its design. Improvements in performance, features, and reliability will differentiate the product from its competitors, improve a firm's quality reputation, and improve the perceived value of the product. This allows the company to command higher prices and achieve an increased market share. This, in turn, leads to increased revenues that offset the added costs of improved design.

Improved conformance in production leads to lower manufacturing and service costs through savings in rework, scrap, and warranty expenses. This viewpoint was popularized by Philip Crosby in his book *Quality Is Free.*[7] As Crosby states:

> Quality is not only free, it is an honest-to-everything profit maker. Every penny you don't spend on doing things wrong, over, or instead of, becomes half a penny right on the bottom line. In these days of "who knows what is going to happen to our business tomorrow," there aren't many ways left to make a profit improvement. If you concentrate on making quality certain, you can probably increase your profit by an amount equal to 5 percent to 10 percent of your sales. That is a lot of money for free.

The net effect of improved quality of design and conformance is increased profits.

Today, many consumers are basing their purchasing decisions on *value*. Value can be defined as quality relative to price. When organizations provide less perceived value than their competitors, they lose market share. This is what happened to U.S. automakers in the 1970s and 1980s. Thus, firms must focus their efforts at improving the quality of design and service as well as reducing costs. No longer can firms focus their quality efforts solely on defect elimination. Today, the absence of defects is a "given" rather than a distinctive source of competitive advantage. Both Deming and Juran stress the need for never-ending cycles of market research, improved product development and design, production, and sales.

QUALITY AND DIFFERENTIATION STRATEGIES

Competitive advantage is gained from meeting or exceeding customer expectations—the fundamental definition of quality. A business may concentrate on any of several quality-related dimensions in order to differentiate itself from its competition. These key dimensions are

- superior product design,
- outstanding service,
- high flexibility and variety,
- continuous innovation, and
- rapid response.

Traditional management strategists advocated focusing on a single dimension. However, as consumers become more demanding, firms can no longer compete along only one dimension. Pursuing a strategy of total quality helps improve all of these dimensions. The following sections discuss these approaches to differentiation and the role of quality in each.

Competing on Superior Product Design

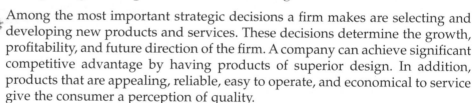

Among the most important strategic decisions a firm makes are selecting and developing new products and services. These decisions determine the growth, profitability, and future direction of the firm. A company can achieve significant competitive advantage by having products of superior design. In addition, products that are appealing, reliable, easy to operate, and economical to service give the consumer a perception of quality.

Basically, there are three types of products: custom products, option-oriented products, and standard products.[8] Custom products, generally made in small quantities, are designed to meet customers' specifications precisely. Two examples are a wedding gown and a machine tool designed to perform a specific, complex task. The production cost is relatively high and the assurance of quality requires careful attention at every step in the manufacturing process. Since custom products can only be produced upon demand, the customer must wait for the product to be made.

Option-oriented products are unique configurations of subassemblies that are designed to fit together. The customer participates in choosing the options to be assembled. A good example is a personal computer system in which the customer defines the types of processor, modem, memory configurations, and so forth. The subassemblies are made in relatively large quantities; therefore, costs are reduced, and quality is easier to achieve because of repetition. Since the manufacturer cannot anticipate all of the configurations a customer may desire, the customer sometimes must wait while the product is assembled to the desired configuration.

Standard products are made in larger quantities. Examples include radios, TVs, appliances, and most consumer goods found in department stores. The customer has no options to choose from, and quality is easiest to achieve because the product is made the same way every time. Since the manufacturer makes standard products in anticipation of customer demands, the customer will not have to wait for the product unless it is out of stock.

Standard products offer many advantages in terms of manufacturing efficiency, quality, and dependability. Mass production on fixed assembly lines yields high levels of productivity. Thus, standard products are the basis for cost leadership. With fewer different parts to purchase, make, and assemble, quality is generally improved because there is less chance for error. Schedules are more predictable, so dependability is improved. Standard products also simplify purchasing and customer service. Orders of components are more consistent, and shipments can be scheduled more frequently, resulting in lower inventories.

Marketing personnel are concerned with sales and how to respond correctly and successfully in the market. They prefer products to be customized to the individual needs of customers. Custom and option-oriented products can be produced to meet customer expectations, whereas standard products offer little flexibility in meeting changing customer needs. Customer expectations can be incorporated only in the design stages. However, this leads to manufacturing efficiencies. This inherent conflict between manufacturing and marketing must be addressed from a strategic perspective.

In the quick-service restaurant industry, similar strategic choices are made. McDonald's, for example, produces a standard product and achieves an advantage in terms of service delivery. Burger King and Wendy's, on the other hand, produce option-oriented products. Although their selection may be greater, these companies sacrifice speed of service. Neither the standard nor the option-oriented approach is necessarily better; each firm must decide what trade-offs must be made with each approach and select the approach that best fits their overall strategic focus.

Many products begin as custom products and, over time, become standard products. For instance, Henry Ford was one of the first to standardize production of the automobile. Later, however, consumers demanded more variety of options, and the American automobile evolved into the classic option-oriented product. Customers can now choose from dozens of colors, seat types, engines, transmissions, tires, and other options.

Many German and Japanese automobile manufacturers have chosen a strategy that limits the number of options. Few options exist, and some are installed by the dealer, rather than the manufacturer. This strategy provides a distinct cost advantage and enables the factory to achieve higher levels of productivity. Flexibility is achieved by offering several model variations of the same car and frequent design changes. The Japanese can produce as many as seven models on a single production line. (Most U.S. manufacturers' production lines are dedicated to a single model.)

The product design function that traditionally was concerned solely with technical aspects of the product must now be concerned with manufacturing and marketing issues. Product designers must match the right products with the continually changing variety of customer needs. This requires great flexibility. At the same time, costs must be minimized, which demands attention to the manufacturing process during the design stage.

The quality of a product's design is influenced by several quality dimensions:[9]

- *Performance*—the primary operating characteristics of the product: the horsepower of an engine or the sound quality of a stereo amplifier.
- *Features*—the "bells and whistles" of a product: antilock brakes or a CD player in an automobile or surround-sound options in an amplifier.
- *Reliability*—the probability of a product's surviving over a specified period of time under stated conditions of use: the ability of a car to start consistently in all types of weather and the lack of failure of electronic components.
- *Durability*—the amount of use one gets from a product before it physically deteriorates or until replacement is preferable: the number of miles one would expect from an automobile with normal maintenance.
- *Aesthetics*—how a product looks, feels, sounds, tastes, or smells: the sleekness of an automobile's exterior and the black "high-tech" look of modern stereo components, for example.

The Role of Total Quality in Product Design

A firm must focus on the key product dimensions that reflect specific customer needs. If these expectations are not identified correctly or are misinterpreted, the final product will not be perceived to be of high quality by customers. Considerable marketing efforts are needed to ensure that the needs are correctly identified.

The Malcolm Baldrige Award criteria emphasize the importance of systematic processes to design and improve products and services. The award application requires evidence of how customer requirements are translated into product requirements; how quality requirements are addressed early in the design process; how designs are coordinated and integrated with production and delivery systems; and how key process performance characteristics are selected based on customer requirements.

A total quality focus in product design requires significant investment in engineering to ensure that designs meet customer expectations. Quality engineering is concerned with the plans, procedures, and methods for the design and evaluation of quality in goods and services. Useful techniques of quality engineering include:

- *concurrent engineering*, in which engineering and production personnel jointly develop product designs that are both functional and easy to manufacture, thus reducing opportunities for poor quality;
- *value analysis*, in which the function of every component of a product is analyzed to determine how it might be accomplished in the most economical fashion;
- *design reviews*, in which managers assess how well the design relates to customer requirements and how it might be improved prior to releasing it to production; and
- *experimental design*, in which formal statistical experiments are applied to determine the best combinations of product and process parameters for high quality and low cost. All of these efforts involve a high level of teamwork.

Competing on Service

Until rather recently, companies viewed service as secondary in importance to manufacturing. However, next to the quality of the product itself, service is perhaps the greatest key to success and a key source of competitive advantage. This may be due to the fact that as the average level of product quality increases, consumers turn to service as the primary means of differentiating among competing firms.

The importance of service was recognized in the early 1980s because of the book *In Search of Excellence* by Tom Peters and Bob Waterman.[10] One of their key themes was that excellent companies share an obsession with service. How important is it? A 1985 Gallup poll on the quality of American products and services found that the vast majority of consumers believe that quality is determined by employee behavior, attitudes, and competence. They also believe—to an even greater degree—that poor service quality is due to the same set of factors. These attitudes hold true even today.

Service translates into dollars. Banking studies have found that 10 percent of customers leave each year,[11] and 21 percent of those leave because of poor service. Each customer contributes $121 per year in profit, and the cost to acquire a new customer is $150. If a bank has a base of 200,000 customers, this means that 4,200 will leave because of poor service. The arithmetic shows that the combined lost profit and replacement effort costs are more than $1 million. Similar studies in other industries have found a high correlation between customer retention and profitability.

Another important aspect of service is complaint resolution (an important criterion in the Baldrige Award). Research has shown that about 80 to 95 percent of unhappy customers (depending on the amount of loss) will purchase from a company again if their complaints are resolved quickly. This drops to around 20 to 45 percent if complaints are not resolved. Furthermore, of the majority of unhappy customers that do not complain at all, only about 10 to 40 percent will become repeat customers.

The Role of Total Quality in Service

Companies that have consistently provided superior service—such as IBM, FedEx, Nordstrom, and many others—have certain elements in common:[12]

1. They establish service goals that support business and product line objectives.
2. They identify and define customer expectations for service quality and responsiveness.
3. They translate customer expectations into clear, deliverable service features.
4. They set up efficient, responsive, and integrated service delivery systems and organizations.
5. They monitor and control service quality and performance.
6. They provide quick, but cost-effective, response to customers' needs.

These ideas are embodied in the Malcolm Baldrige Award criteria in the Customer and Market Focus category. Among the areas addressed in this category are:

- *Accessibility and Complaint Management.* This includes determining how the company provides access and information to enable customers to seek assistance, to conduct business, and to voice complaints; how the company determines customer contact requirements, deploys them to all employees who are involved in meeting the requirements, and evaluates and improves customer contact performance; and how the company ensures that complaints are resolved effectively and promptly, and that they are aggregated and analyzed for use throughout the company.
- *Relationship Building.* How the company builds loyalty, positive referral, and relationships with customers.

Much of the total quality concept is devoted to empowering frontline employees to provide the services that satisfy and exceed customer expectations. Because service usually occurs in direct contact with the customer, the attention to the human resource is critical. Most of this book focuses on these issues.

Competing on Flexibility and Variety

Flexibility is the capacity of a production system to adapt successfully to changing environmental conditions and process requirements. *Variety* refers to the ability to produce a wide range of products and options. Companies that can change product lines more rapidly in the face of changing consumer demands and that exploit new technologies can gain a competitive advantage in certain markets.

Many firms use flexibility and variety as a competitive weapon. Some firms provide custom service on complex systems for low-volume customers and markets. They must be excellent at product design and responsiveness to customers. Other firms do little innovation themselves but take product designs from customers and produce custom products on a low-volume basis. Both types of firms must have considerable flexibility in their production operations to produce low volumes and customized products. High quality is a must, as is delivery on schedule.

While the quality gap between U.S. and Japanese products narrows, many Japanese firms are focusing their strategies on flexibility and variety—more and better product features, factories that can change product lines quickly, expanded customer service, and continually improving new products. For instance, Toshiba's computer factory assembles nine different word processors on the same production line and 20 varieties of laptop computers on another.[13] The flexible lines guard against running short of a hot model or overproducing one whose sales have slowed.

Nissan describes its strategy as "five anys": to make anything in any volume anywhere at any time by anybody. Nissan's high-tech Intelligent Body Assembly System can weld and inspect body parts for any kind of car, all in 46 seconds. As U.S. automakers think about dropping entire car lines, Nissan is gearing up to fill market niches with more models.

The value of flexibility and variety was illustrated by the "Honda-Yamaha war" in 1981. Honda, whose supremacy in motorcycles was being challenged by Yamaha, responded by introducing 113 new or revamped models in 18 months. Yamaha could only manage 37 model changes and finally announced that it was content to be number two.

The Role of Quality in Flexibility and Variety

The ability to develop the right products depends on a clear customer focus and determination of customer expectations. As these change, the company must be able to respond quickly. Being close to the customer is essential.

Equally important is the ability of different functions and groups of employees to work together as teams in designing and operating the type of production systems that require continuous change and improvement. In fact, the Baldrige criteria seek evidence on how companies ensure "flexibility, rapid response, and learning in addressing current, and changing, customer, operational, and business requirements" in the Human Resource Focus category. Good supplier relations, a key issue in total quality, are also critical as designs and volumes change.

Competing on Innovation

Many firms focus on research and development as a core component of their strategy. Such firms are on the leading edge of product technology, and their ability to innovate and introduce new products is a critical success factor. Product performance, not price, is the major selling feature. When competition enters the market and profit margins fall, these companies often drop out of the market while continuing to introduce innovative new products. These companies focus on outstanding product research, design, and development; high product quality; and the ability to modify production facilities to produce new products frequently.

As global competition increases, the ability to innovate has become almost essential for remaining competitive. National Cash Register, for example, clung to outdated mechanical technologies for years, while competitors developed innovative new electronic systems. The lack of innovation nearly destroyed the company.

Today leading companies do not wait for customers to change; they use innovation to create new customer needs and desires. At 3M, for example, every division is expected to derive 25 percent of its sales each year from products that did not exist five years earlier. This forces managers to think seriously about innovation. Such a spirit of continuous improvement not only will result in new products, but also will help managers to create better processes that improve quality.

The Role of Quality in Innovation

The Malcolm Baldrige Award criteria explicitly state that invention, innovation, and creativity are important aspects of delivering ever-improving value to customers and maximizing productivity. Innovation and creativity are crucial features in company competitiveness and can be applied to products, processes, services, human resource development, and overall quality systems. The award criteria encourage innovation through several means:

- The criteria are nonprescriptive. They encourage creativity and breakthrough thinking because they channel activities toward the organization's purpose and are not focused on following specific procedures.
- Customer-driven quality emphasizes the "positive side of quality"— enhancement, new services, and customer relationship management. Success with the positive side of quality depends heavily on creativity, more so than on steps to reduce errors and defects that rely on well-defined techniques.
- Human resource focus stresses employee involvement, development, and recognition and encourages creative approaches to improving employee effectiveness, empowerment, and contributions.
- Continuous improvement and learning are integral parts of the activities of all work groups. This requires analysis and problem solving everywhere within the company. Emphasis on continuous improvement encourages change, innovation, and creative thinking in how work is organized and conducted.
- The focus on future requirements of customers encourages companies to seek innovative and creative ways to serve their patrons.

Competing on Time

In today's fast-paced society, people hate to wait. Time has come to be recognized as one of the most important sources of competitive advantage. The total time required by a company to deliver a finished product that satisfies cus-

Domino's Pizza Changed the Rules[14]

Tom Monaghan, founder of Domino's Pizza, determined that customers ordering home-delivered pizza wanted their pizzas quickly because they were usually hungry when they ordered. He also understood that people anticipated having their pizzas delivered anywhere from 20 minutes to two hours after placing their orders. This wide variation in delivery was acceptable because people had been conditioned to accept that there were no other options available. Since fast, consistent delivery was not an option, customers placed their pizza orders based only on taste and price. Monaghan changed all that by promising fast and consistent delivery—30 minutes or less—or it's free. Domino's exceeded customers expectations. Today, this "delighter/exciter" has become a satisfier, and consistently fast delivery is often the first criterion in the pizza-ordering decision process.

tomers' needs is referred to as the product lead time. This includes time spent on design, engineering, purchasing, manufacturing, testing, packaging, and shipping.

Short product lead times offer many advantages. First, they allow companies to introduce new products and penetrate new markets more rapidly. Being the first to market a new product allows a firm to charge a higher price, at least until competitive products are offered. For example, when first introduced, Kodak's Ektar film sold for 10 to 15 percent more than conventional film; Motorola's pocket-sized cellular telephone was 50 percent smaller than any competing Japanese product and sold for twice the price; and the Mazda Miata sold for up to $5,000 above sticker price.

Second, every month saved in development time can save a large company millions of dollars in expenses. Third, short lead times reduce the need to forecast long-term sales, allow more accurate production plans to be developed, and reduce inventory. Short lead times increase the flexibility of a company to respond to changing customer needs.

The Role of Quality in Time Competitiveness

The Malcolm Baldrige Award criteria emphasize the importance of reducing cycle times in all business processes. Success in competitive markets increasingly demands shorter cycles for new or improved product and service introduction. Also, faster and more flexible response to customers is a more critical requirement of business management (see the box on Domino's).

Major improvements in response time often require work organizations, processes, and paths to be simplified and shortened. To accomplish this, more attention needs to be paid to time performance. This can be done by making response time a key indicator for work unit improvement processes. Simplified processes reduce opportunities for errors, leading to improved quality.

Improvements in response time often result from increased understanding of internal customer-supplier relationships and teamwork. Cutting response time requires a significant commitment from all employees and leadership from top management. Such efforts must involve the entire organization and often require organizational redesign.

QUALITY STRATEGIES AND BUSINESS RESULTS

Baldrige Award winners have demonstrated that quality leads to competitive advantage and improved business performance. A 1991 General Accounting Office (GAO) study of Baldrige finalists explored four measurable areas of a company's operations that could demonstrate the impact of TQ practices on corporate performance:[15]

1. employee relations,
2. operating procedures,
3. customer satisfaction, and
4. financial performance.

In employee relations, significant improvements were realized in employee satisfaction, attendance, turnover, safety and health, and suggestions received. In operating procedures, favorable results were realized in reliability, timeliness of delivery, order-processing times, errors and defects, product lead time, inventory turnover, cost of quality, and overall cost savings. Overall customer satisfaction also improved, as customer complaints fell and customer retention rose. In the financial performance area, market share, sales per employee, return on assets, and return on sales all showed positive improvement for most companies.

The GAO developed a general framework for describing Total Quality and its effect on competitiveness (Figure 10.2.) The solid line shows how TQ processes lead to improved competitiveness, beginning with leadership dedicated to improving products and services, as well as quality systems. Improvements in these areas lead to customer satisfaction and benefits to the organization, both of which improve competitiveness. The dotted lines show the information feedback necessary for continuous improvement. The arrows in the boxes show the expected direction of the performance indicators.

A more recent survey of almost 1,000 executives conducted by Zenger Miller Achieve noted similar benefits from quality initiatives, including increased employee participation, improved product and service quality, improved customer satisfaction, improved productivity, and improved employee skills.[16]

Winners of the Malcolm Baldrige National Quality Award, which represent companies having the highest level of commitment to quality management, have achieved outstanding operational and financial results, some of which are:

FIGURE 10.2   GENERAL ACCOUNTING OFFICE FRAMEWORK

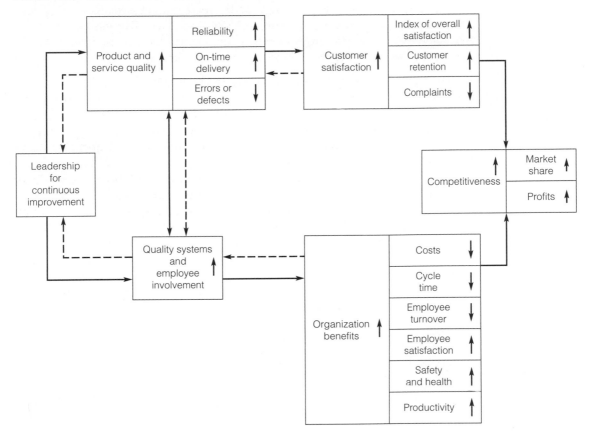

- Customer retention rates at ADAC Laboratories, a Silicon Valley–based maker of high-tech health care products, increased from 70 to 93 percent from 1990 to 1995. Defect rates at final inspection have fallen by about 40 percent.
- In 1992, Texas Instruments Defense Systems & Electronics Group had a 21 percent reduction in production cycle time with a 56 percent reduction in stock-to-production time.
- Armstrong World Industries Building Products Operations found that its cost-of-poor-quality index dropped by 37 percent, contributing $16 million in additional operating profit in 1994 alone. The company set industry safety records with more than 3 million hours without a lost-time injury, and made its highest-ever gainsharing and incentive payouts.
- Motorola's employee productivity improved 100 percent during the time period from 1988 to 1994—an annual compounded rate of 12.2 percent—through better design, continuous improvement in defect reduction, and employee education and empowerment.

- Solectron, by focusing on customer satisfaction, experienced average yearly revenue growth of 46.8 percent, and by focusing on process quality saw average yearly net income growth of 57.3 percent over five years.
- At Globe Metallurgical, from 1988 to 1992, exports grew from 2 percent to 20 percent of sales, while overall sales grew by 24 percent.

The Commerce Department annually tracks a hypothetical investment of $1,000 in common stock in each publicly traded winning company (or a proportional investment in winning subsidiaries of larger companies). Results consistently show that such an investment typically outperforms the S&P 500 by approximately 3 to 1. (Current results of this study may be found at the Baldrige Web site, www.quality.nist.gov).

Perhaps the most comprehensive study to date, which has garnered a lot of attention in the business press, is that of Hendricks and Singhal.[17] They compared over 400 firms that had won some type of quality award (such as Baldrige, a state award, or supplier awards) with a control group over a 10-year period. Statistical tests provided strong evidence that these firms outperformed the control group on operating income–based measures. The mean change in the operating income was 48 percent higher than that of the control sample. Evidence also showed that these firms did better on sales growth, as well as in growth of employment and total assets.

The Strategic Value of Business Results Measurement

Understanding the impact of quality strategies on business results, along with benchmarking results against competitors and industry leaders, has taken on increased importance in recent years. A supply of consistent, accurate, and timely information across all functional areas of business provides real-time information for evaluation and improvement of processes, products, and services to meet business objectives and rapidly changing customer needs—in short, to create and sustain a competitive advantage.

Most businesses have traditionally relied on organizational performance data based almost solely on financial or factory productivity considerations, such as return on investment, earnings per share, direct labor efficiency, and machine utilization.[18] Unfortunately, many of these indicators are inaccurate and stress quantity over quality. Today, many organizations create a "balanced scorecard" of measures that provide a comprehensive view of business performance. This often consists of five key categories (which reflect the Results category of the Baldrige criteria):

1. customer satisfaction measures,
2. financial and market performance measures,
3. human resource measures,
4. supplier and partner performance measures, and
5. organizational effectiveness measures that support company strategy.

These performance indicators span the entire business operation, from suppliers to customers, and from frontline workers to top levels of management.

Wainwright Industries, for example, aligns the company's business objectives with customers' critical success factors: price, line defects, delivery, and partnership. This alignment process prompted the development of five key strategic indicator categories: safety, internal customer satisfaction, external customer satisfaction, defect rate, and business performance. Within each category, Wainwright developed specific indicators and goals. For instance, for external customer satisfaction, they measure a satisfaction index and customer complaints monthly; for business performance, they track sales, capital expenditure, and market share for drawn housings.

Comparative information includes comparisons relative to direct competitors as well as best-practices benchmarking, either inside or outside of one's industry. Such information allows organizations to know where they stand relative to competitors and other leading companies, provides the impetus for breakthrough improvement, and helps them understand their own processes before they compare performance levels. For example, Corning Telecommunications Products Division (TPD) uses a competitive analysis process to gather publicly available data to analyze competitors' intentions and capabilities, including manufacturing capacity, cost, and cost of incremental capacity, and they determine product capability and quality through direct evaluation of competitors' products.

Leading companies employ a variety of statistical tools and structured approaches for analyzing data and turning it into useful information. Fuji-Xerox, a Japanese subsidiary of Xerox, uses a variety of statistical techniques, such as regression and analysis of variance, to develop mathematical models relating such factors as copy quality, machine malfunctions, and maintenance time to customer satisfaction results. Such approaches can uncover important cause-and-effect relationships. FedEx, for example, collects a lot of data using its automated systems and aggregates it into an internal process quality index and an external service quality index. They strive for internal measures to predict external measures. Companies need to ask the key question: How do overall improvements in product and service quality and operational performance relate to changes in company financial performance and customer satisfaction? Corning TPD aggregates data and information into key financial and business-level analyses that quantify the impact of decisions on financial and market performance. They examine relationships among quality, price, and image as they relate to attracting and retaining customers. They also quantify the relationships among process capability, people and process productivity, and unit costs.

A focus on strategic information management, while being a key element of a TQ strategy, has other benefits. A survey conducted by Wm. Schiemann & Associates found that measurement-managed companies are more likely to be in the top third of their industry financially, to complete organizational changes more successfully, to reach clear agreement of strategy among senior managers, to enjoy favorable levels of cooperation and teamwork among management, to undertake greater self-monitoring of performance by employees, and to have a greater willingness by employees to take risks.[19]

SUMMARY

Every business strives to achieve a competitive advantage. This is usually done through cost leadership or product/process differentiation that meets the needs and expectations of customers. Improved quality leads to lower costs and higher productivity, thus helping a firm to attain a cost leadership position. Similarly, differentiation strategies, such as superior product design, outstanding service, high flexibility and variety, continuous innovation, and rapid response, are driven and improved by attention to total quality.

Many studies have shown that quality influences financial performance and competitive position. Achieving competitive advantage through quality requires a good strategy and good implementation. The next chapter discusses these issues.

REVIEW AND DISCUSSION QUESTIONS

1. Explain how a total quality perspective can support the six characteristics of competitive advantage introduced at the beginning of the chapter.
2. Discuss the two basic types of competitive advantage. Can a company achieve both?
3. List 10 firms or businesses you have read about or have personal experience with. Describe their sources of competitive advantage and how you believe that quality supports (or does not support) their strategy.
4. Prepare a report (using sources such as business periodicals, personal interviews, and so on) profiling a company that competes on each of the major dimensions of differentiation discussed in the chapter. What aspects of their total quality approach support their strategic focus?
5. Think of a product or service you have purchased recently. What aspects of the product or service made it attractive?
6. What is the importance of total quality to achieving competitive advantage?
7. Explain how quality affects profitability.
8. Discuss the key quality dimensions of differentiation strategies.
9. Explain the differences among custom, option-oriented, and standard products.
10. How might the dimensions of product design (performance, features, reliability, durability, and aesthetics) discussed in this chapter be applied to services?
11. Describe one good and one bad service experience you have encountered. How did this change your perceptions of the company?
12. How are flexibility and variety sources of competitive advantage? What relationships do these dimensions have with quality?
13. What is the role of quality in innovation?

14. How can the tools of quality discussed in chapter 3 help in reducing cycle times?

15. Explain the General Accounting Office framework for TQ. Discuss specific cause-and-effect relationships of a total quality focus and the expected changes in performance indicators.

16. How might the principles of competitive advantage that we discussed be applied to the management of your college or university? How about a fraternity or student professional organization? What types of results measurements would be appropriate?

CASE

Case of the Rotary Compressor[20]

In 1981 market share and profits in General Electric's appliance division were falling. The company's technology was antiquated compared to foreign competitors. For example, making refrigerator compressors required 65 minutes of labor in comparison to 25 minutes for competitors in Japan and Italy. Moreover, GE's labor costs were higher. The alternatives were obvious: either purchase compressors from Japan or Italy or design and build a better model.

By 1983 GE had decided to build a new rotary compressor in-house and to commit $120 million for a new factory. GE was not a novice in rotary compressor technology; they had invented it and had been using it in air conditioners for many years. A rotary compressor weighed less, had one-third fewer parts, and was more energy efficient than the current reciprocating compressors. The rotary compresor took up less space, thus providing more room inside the refrigerator and better meeting customer requirements.

Some engineers argued to the contrary, citing the fact that rotary compressors run hotter. This is not a problem in most air conditioners, because the coolant cools the compressor. In a refrigerator, however, the coolant flows only one-tenth as fast, and the unit runs about four times longer in one year than an air conditioner. GE had problems with the early rotary compressors in air conditioners. Although the bugs had been eliminated in smaller units, GE quit using rotaries in larger units due to frequent breakdowns in hot climates.

GE managers and design engineers were concerned about other issues. Rotary compressors make a high-pitched whine, and managers were afraid this would adversely affect consumer acceptance. Managers and consumer test panels spent many hours on this issue. The new design also required that key parts work together with a tolerance of only 50 millionths of an inch. Nothing had been mass produced with such precision before, but manufacturing engineers felt sure they could do it.

The compressor they finally designed was nearly identical to that used in air conditioners, with one change. Two small parts inside the compressor were made out of powdered metal, rather than the hardened steel and cast iron used in air conditioners. This material was chosen because it could be machined to much closer tolerances, and it reduced machining costs. Powdered metal had been tried a decade earlier on air conditioners but did not work. The design engineers, who were new to designing compressors, did not consider the earlier failure important.

A consultant suggested that GE consider a joint venture with a Japanese company that had a rotary refrigerator compressor already on the market. The idea was rejected by management. The original designer of the air conditioner rotary compressor, who had left GE, offered his services as a consultant. GE declined his offer, writing him that they had sufficient technical expertise.

About 600 compressors were tested in 1983 without a single failure. They were run continuously for two months under elevated temperatures and pressures that were supposed to simulate five years' operation. GE normally conducts extensive field testing of new products; their original plan to test models in the field for two years was reduced to nine months due to time pressure to complete the project.

The technician who disassembled and inspected the parts thought they did not look right. Parts of the motor were discolored, a sign of excessive heat. Bearings were worn, and it appeared that high heat was breaking down the lubricating oil. The technician's supervisors discounted these findings and did not relay them to upper levels of management. Another consultant who evaluated the test results believed that something was wrong because only one failure was found in two years and recommended that test conditions be intensified. This suggestion was also rejected by management.

By 1986, only 2.5 years after board approval, the new factory was producing compressors at a rate of 10 per minute. By the end of the year, more than 1 million had been produced. Market share rose and the new refrigerator appeared to be a success. But in July 1987 the first compressor failed. Soon after, reports of other failures in Puerto Rico arrived. By September the appliance division knew it had a major problem. In December the plant stopped making the compressor. Not until 1988 was the problem diagnosed as excessive wear in the two powdered-metal parts that burned up the oil. The cost in 1989 alone was $450 million. By mid-1990, GE had voluntarily replaced nearly 1.1 million compressors with ones purchased from six suppliers, five of them foreign.

Discussion Questions

1. What factors in the product development process caused this disaster? What individuals were responsible?
2. How might this disaster have been prevented? What lessons do you think GE learned for the future?
3. On what basis was GE attempting to achieve a competitive advantage? How did they fail?

ENDNOTES

1. S.C. Wheelwright, "Competing through Manufacturing," in Ray Wild (ed.), *International Handbook of Production and Operations Management*, London: Cassell Educational, Ltd., 1989, pp. 15–32.

2. Michael E. Porter, *Competitive Advantage: Creating and Sustaining Superior Performance*, New York: The Free Press, 1985.

3. Bradley T. Gale, "Quality Comes First When Hatching Power Brands," *Planning Review*, July/August 1992, pp. 4–9, 48.

4. H. Lee Hales, "Time Has Come for Long-Range Planning of Facilities Strategies in Electronic Industries," *Industrial Engineering*, April 1985.

5. J.M. Juran, *Juran on Quality by Design*, New York: The Free Press, 1992, p. 181.

6. *The PIMS Letter on Business Strategy*, The Strategic Planning Institute, Number 4, Cambridge, Mass., 1986.

7. Philip Crosby, *Quality Is Free*, New York: McGraw-Hill, 1979.

8. Charles A. Horne, "Product Strategy and Competitive Advantage," *P&IM Review with APICS News*, Vol. 7, No. 12, December 1987, pp. 38–41.

9. David A. Garvin, "What Does Product Quality Really Mean?" *Sloan Management Review*, Vol. 26, No. 1, 1984, pp. 25–43.

10. Tom Peters and Bob Waterman, *In Search of Excellence*, New York: Harper & Row, 1982.

11. F.F. Reichheld and W.E. Sasser, Jr., "Zero Defections: Quality Comes to Services," *Harvard Business Review*, September–October, 1990.

12. Jeffrey Margolies, "When Good Service Isn't Good Enough," *Price Waterhouse Review*, Vol. 32, No. 3, New York: Price Waterhouse, 1988, pp. 22–31.

13. Thomas A. Stewart, "Brace for Japan's Hot New Strategy," *Fortune*, September 21, 1992, pp. 62–73.

14. Joan Uhlenberg, "Redefining Customer Expectations," *Quality*, September 1992, pp. 34–35.

15. U.S. General Accounting Office, "Management Practices: U.S. Companies Improve Performance Through Quality Effort," GA/NSIAD-91-190, May 1991.

16. "Progress on the Quality Road," *Incentive*, April 1995, p. 7.

17. Kevin B. Hendricks and Vinod R. Singhal, "Does Implementing an Effective TQM Program Actually Improve Operating Performance? Empirical Evidence from Firms that Have Won Quality Awards," *Management Science*, Vol. 43, No. 9, September 1997, pp. 1258–1274.

18. Robert S. Kaplan and David P. Norton, "The Balanced Scorecard—Measures that Drive Performance," *Harvard Business Review*, January/February 1992, pp. 71–79.

19. Laura Sturebing, "Measuring for Excellence," *Quality Progress*, December 1996, pp. 25–28.

20. Reprinted by permission of *The Wall Street Journal*, © 1990 Dow Jones & Company, Inc. All rights reserved worldwide.

CHAPTER

11

Strategic Planning and
Total Quality Implementation

CHAPTER OUTLINE

Quality as a Strategy
  Strategic Planning and the Baldrige Award
The Strategic Management Process
  Strategy Development
  Strategy Implementation
  Strategic Management in Action
TQ and Strategic Management Theory
Implementing a TQ Strategy
  Roles in Implementing a Quality Strategy
  Union/Management Relations
  Common Implementation Mistakes
  Strategies for Success
  Best Practices
Summary
Review and Discussion Questions
Cases

A firm has many options in defining its long-term goals and objectives, the customers it wants to serve, the products and services it produces and delivers, and the design of the production and service system to meet these objectives. *Strategic planning* is the process by which the members of an organization envision its future and develop the necessary procedures and operations to carry out that vision. *Strategy*—the result of strategic planning—is the pattern of decisions that determines and reveals a company's goals, policies, and plans to meet the needs of its stakeholders. An effective strategy allows a business to create a sustainable competitive advantage, as discussed in chapter 10. This chapter discusses the role of quality in strategy, and strategic issues of implementing total quality in organizations. This chapter will

- discuss quality as a generic business strategy,
- describe the role of quality in strategy formulation and implementation and introduce policy deployment as a means of implementation,
- explore the relationship between TQ and strategic management theory, and
- discuss approaches to implementing TQ strategies in organizations.

QUALITY AS A STRATEGY

The concept of strategy has different meanings to different people. Quinn characterizes strategy as follows:[1]

> A strategy is a pattern or plan that integrates an organization's major goals, policies, and action sequences into a cohesive whole. A well-formulated strategy helps to marshal and allocate an organization's resources into a unique and viable posture based on its relative internal competencies and shortcomings, anticipated changes in the environment, and contingent moves by intelligent opponents.

Formal strategies contain three elements:

1. goals to be achieved,
2. policies that guide or limit action, and
3. action sequences, or programs, that accomplish the goals.

Effective strategies develop around a few key concepts and thrusts that provide focus. The essence of strategy is to build a posture that is so strong in selective ways that the organization can achieve its goals despite unforeseeable external forces that may arise.

The traditional focus of business strategies has been finance and marketing. These parallel the two principal sources of competitive advantage discussed in chapter 10—cost and differentiation. Total quality leads to improvements in both areas. Therefore, quality can be viewed as a strategy in itself.

The role of quality in business strategy has taken two significant steps since 1980. First, many firms have recognized that a strategy driven by quality can lead to significant market advantages. Second, the lines between quality strategy and generic business strategies have become blurred to the point

Xerox 2000: Sustaining Leadership Through Quality

The introductory section of chapter 1 described the turnaround Xerox experienced by developing a strategy based on quality. The Xerox Leadership Through Quality strategy is built on three elements:

1. Quality Principles
   - Quality as the basic business principle for Xerox in its leadership position
   - An understanding of customers' existing and latent requirements
   - Products and services that meet the requirements of all external and internal customers
   - Employee involvement, through participative problem solving, in improving quality
   - Error-free work as the most cost-effective way to improve quality
2. Management Actions and Behaviors
   - Assuring strategic clarity and consistency
   - Providing visible supportive management practices, commitment, and leadership
   - Setting quality objectives and measurement standards
   - Establishing and reinforcing a management style of openness, trust, respect, patience, and discipline
   - Developing an environment in which each person can be responsible for quality
3. Quality Tools
   - The Xerox quality policy
   - Competitive benchmarking and goal setting
   - Systematic defect and error-prevention processes
   - Training for leadership through quality
   - Communication and recognition programs that reinforce leadership through quality
   - A measure for the cost of quality (or its lack)

Xerox updated the Leadership Through Quality approach that formed the basis for its successful turnaround.[2] In 1994, Chairman Paul Allaire outlined the strategy for Xerox 2000. Xerox used the term "reaffirmation strategy" to emphasize that the company stood firmly behind the basic Leadership Through Quality plan but that adjustments were needed to broaden the concept from basically a strategic approach to one that better integrated TQ into all aspects of daily business operations. Xerox identified two critical objectives: profitable revenue growth and world-class productivity.

Xerox uses more than 60 specific process improvement initiatives, employee involvement programs, and quality tools to manage its business. It also uses a range of business policies and approaches, quality intensification efforts, and benchmarking. These elements were integrated into Xerox 2000. To communicate this in a simple manner, Xerox created the Xerox Management Model, which addresses every aspect of work: planning, creating, leading, managing, changing, organizing, communicating, learning, and rewarding. A description of the mdoel's six categories follows.

1. *Management leadership.* Xerox management displays a customer focus, exhibits role model behavior, establishes clear long-term goals and annual objectives, establishes strategic boundaries, and provides an empowered environment to achieve world-class productivity and business results.

2. *Human resource management.* Xerox management leads, motivates, develops, and empowers people to realize their full potential. All employees are personally responsible for continuously learning and acquiring competencies required to achieve business objectives and to continuously improve productivity for customers and Xerox.

3. *Business process management.* Business processes are designed to be customer driven, cross functional, and value based. They create knowledge, eliminate waste, and abandon unproductive work, yielding world-class productivity and higher perceived service levels for customers.

4. *Information utilization and quality tools.* Fact-based management is led by line management. It is achieved through accurate and timely information and by the disciplined application and widespread use of quality tools.

5. *Customer and market focus.* Current, past, and potential customers define the business. Xerox recognizes and creates markets by identifying patterns of customer requirements. By anticipating and fully satisfying those requirements through the creation of customer value, Xerox achieves its business results.

6. *Business results.* Business results are determined by how well Xerox performs in the first five categories.

Allaire expects Xerox employees to use the model to define processes, individual roles, and responsibilities at regular operations reviews; for coaching and training employees; in management meetings; when introducing new business initiatives; for identifying internal benchmarks and best practices; and as the foundation for business assessments and certification. By using the strategy as its guide, Xerox is preparing its people to grow the company's business results, productivity, and quality performance.

where TQ principles are integrated into most businesses' normal business planning; that is, TQ is a basic operating philosophy (see the box on Xerox).

For most companies, integration of TQ into strategic business planning is the result of a natural evolution. For most new companies—or those that have enjoyed a reasonable measure of success—quality takes a back seat to increasing sales, expanding capacity, or boosting production. Strategic planning usually focuses on financial and marketing strategies.

As a company begins to face increasing competition and rising consumer expectations, cost-cutting objectives take precedence. Some departments or individuals may champion quality improvement efforts, but quality is not integrated into the company's strategic business plan. In the face of market crises, which many U.S. firms experienced in the 1970s and 1980s, top management begins to realize the importance of quality as a strategic operating policy. In many cases, however, quality is considered separate from financial and marketing plans. Companies that aspire to world-class status reach the highest level of evolution, where quality becomes an integral part of the overall strategic plan and is viewed as a central operating strategy.

Strategic Planning and the Baldrige Award

The Baldrige Award recognizes the importance of integrating total quality principles with overall business planning. The Strategic Planning category addresses strategic business planning and deployment of plans. It stresses that customer-driven quality and operational performance are key strategic business issues that need to be an integral part of overall company planning, and it emphasizes that improvement and learning must be integral parts of company work processes. The special role of strategic planning is to align work processes with the company strategic directions, thereby ensuring that improvement and learning reinforce company priorities.

The Strategic Planning category examines how companies

- understand the key customer, market, and operational requirements as input to setting strategic directions. This is to help ensure that ongoing process improvements are aligned with the company's strategic directions.
- optimize the use of resources, ensure the availability of trained human resources, and ensure bridging between short-term and longer-term requirements that may entail capital expenditures, supplier development, etc.
- ensure that deployment will be effective—that there are mechanisms to transmit requirements and achieve alignment on three basic levels: (1) company/executive level; (2) the key process level; and (3) the work-unit/individual-job level.[3]

It is important to understand that a broad emphasis on strategic planning in the Baldrige criteria evolved over the years as the notion of quality itself evolved in the business world from a technical function to a basic business philosophy.[4] The charter version of the Strategic Planning category in 1988 captured the essence of the model's narrow scope in its formative years. The category's title, Strategic Quality Planning, reflected the model's focused requirements for planning in the context of quality and customer satisfaction, but it paid little attention to other business aspects as part of the planning process. This early framework reflected the influence of the popular quality theorists. In particular, the Strategic Planning category's initial emphasis on planning for quality and on quality improvement through projects resembled Juran's approach.[5]

By 1990, the Strategic Planning category reflected the consolidation that would characterize the criteria's evolution. Examination items pertaining to planning functions and planning innovation were eliminated. The items began to distinguish between strategy process and strategy content. Item 3.1 specified assessment of external environment (customers and competitors) and of internal resources (process capabilities) as part of the strategic planning process.

The focus was still on planning related to quality, although this emphasis would soon change.

By 1992, the category's wording was further reduced. More importantly, the Strategic Planning category's scope began to broaden beyond the quality focus. Item 3.1 was renamed Strategic Quality and Company Performance Planning Process and Item 3.2 became Quality and Performance Plans. The corresponding areas to address required plans related to two different areas: the quality plans and the company's performance plans. The side-by-side appearance of these two sets of plans implied a relationship that justified their inclusion inside the same planning process. Two-to-five year projections of key performance measures were required by applicants. These projections needed to include relevant levels and trends of competitor or other benchmarking data. Efforts to relate quality planning to other relevant company plans continued with the 1993 revisions. Explicit reference to quality goals was reduced. Emphasis was on developing strategic plans for quality, customer satisfaction, and waste reduction.

The most significant effort to integrate quality planning with business planning occurred in the 1995 criteria revision. Most symbolic was the change in the category's title from Strategic Quality Planning to Strategic Planning. This change signaled a "major emphasis on business strategy as the most appropriate view-of-the-future context for managing performance." The integration of quality and operational issues with business planning became a dominant theme, with a focus on "performance," "competitive position," "customer-related," and "operational" themes.

The 1999 version is the most consolidated to date. Explicit references to quality planning have been eliminated (in fact, the term *quality* is conspicuously absent from the entire document). What remains is a generic framework for strategic business planning. One dimension of the framework addresses the process for developing strategy. The other dimension relates to how strategy is deployed. These changes reflect the criteria's evolution toward "comprehensive coverage of strategy-driven performance, addressing the needs of all stakeholders—customers, employees, stockholders, suppliers, and the public."

THE STRATEGIC MANAGEMENT PROCESS

Strategic planning helps leadership mold an organization's future and manage change by focusing on an ideal vision of what the organization should and could be 10 to 20 years in the future. In contrast, the term "long-range planning" may only mean one year in the future or the next budget submission in many organizations. Strategic plans are developed at the highest level of an organization and deployed throughout.

The strategic management process consists of two parts: *formulation* and *implementation*. Strategy formulation consists of defining the mission of the organization—the concept of the business and the vision of where it is headed; setting objectives—translating the mission into specific performance objectives;

and defining a strategy—determining specific actions to achieve the performance objectives. Implementation focuses on executing the strategy effectively and efficiently, as well as on evaluating performance and making corrective adjustments when necessary.

Strategy Development

The organization's leaders first must explore and agree upon the mission, vision, and guiding principles of the organization; these form the foundation for the strategic plan.

The *mission* of a firm defines its reason for existence. For example, Procter & Gamble states its mission ("purpose") as "We will provide products of superior quality and value that improve the lives of the world's consumers." A firm's mission guides the development of strategies by different groups within the firm. It establishes the context within which daily operating decisions are made, and it sets limits on available strategic options. In addition, it helps to make trade-offs among the various performance measures and between short and long-term goals.

The *vision* describes where the organization is headed and what it intends to be. (See chapter 9 for a discussion of vision from a leadership perspective.) Solectron's vision is simple: "Be the best and continuously improve." It is brief and memorable, inspiring and challenging, appeals to all stakeholders, and describes an ideal state.

The *guiding principles* direct the journey to a vision by defining attitudes and policies for all employees that are reinforced through conscious and subconscious behavior at all levels of the organization. FedEx states: "We will be helpful, courteous, and professional to each other and the public. We will strive to have a completely satisfied customer at the end of each transaction."

Not all companies clearly separate their mission, vision, and values. Milacron, for example, expresses them as "Milacron will be a global leader in industrial processes, offering products and services so clearly outstanding in terms of innovation, quality, delivery, and value that we are consistently the supplier of choice. We will be driven to FIND A BETTER WAY for our customers and provide growth opportunities for employees, suppliers, shareholders, while adhering to the business philosophy of Total Quality Leadership and our core values." It does not matter what you call them; what is important is that a company can articulate them and more importantly, commit to them.

Strategy development refers to a company's approach, formal or informal, for making or guiding business decisions, resource allocations, and company-wide management. The process typically takes into account customer and market requirements, the competitive environment, financial and societal risks, human resource capabilities and needs, technological capabilities, and supplier capabilities. This process might use models, market or sales forecasts, scenarios, analyses, business intelligence, and other tools to develop strategies to bridge the gap between where the organization is now and where it wants to be. Strategies might include new products, services, and markets; revenue growth;

FIGURE 11.1 STRATEGIC PLANNING PROCESS

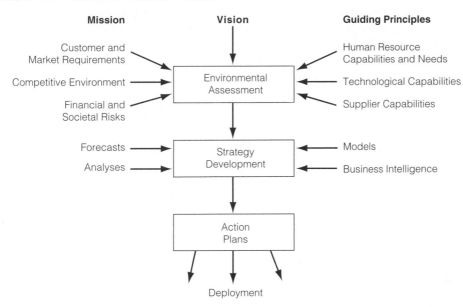

cost reduction; or global alliances. They might be directed toward making the company a preferred supplier, a low-cost producer, or a market innovator. (See chapter 10 for discussions of competitive advantage.)

Specific *action plans* derive from strategy. These clearly describe the things that need to be done, human resource plans and support, performance measures and indicators, and resource deployment. This process is summarized in Figure 11.1.

TQ and Strategy Development

Total quality can improve the strategy formulation process in several ways. First, it forces the organization to think in terms of its customers. Second, it places the expectation of leadership on senior management in developing and implementing the strategy. Third, the focus on measurement and objective reasoning introduces a reality check in determining the effectiveness of strategy and performance in meeting goals and objectives. Fourth, the focus on teamwork creates an expectation that everyone in the organization play a role in the formulation of the strategy. Finally, it supports the inclusion of quality as part of the fundamental strategy.

Strategy formulation is a process. Like any other process, it can be improved through the use of TQ methods (see the box "Searching for Strategy"). The final benefit of TQ in strategy formulation is the potential for improving this process each time it is undertaken. The aspects of this process that could be improved are forecasting future demand, assessing internal capabilities, and integrating internal and external perspectives into the planning process.

Searching for Strategy[6]

Xerox, Ford, Microsoft, Motorola, Hewlett-Packard, and other companies have used an approach called the Search Conference method to facilitate their strategic planning processes. A Search Conference is a participative event that enables a large group to collectively create a plan that its members will implement. Typically, 20 to 40 people from an organization work progressively for two or three days on planning tasks in large group plenary sessions. They develop long-term strategic visions, achievable goals, and concrete action plans. All of the work is conducted in self-managed teams that are responsible for the entire planning process. Even after the conference, those who created the plan are responsible for its implementation. This democratic approach gives those employees most affected by the change more control over direction setting and policy deployment.

Senior management cannot manipulate a Search Conference agenda to steer participants in some predetermined direction. Further everything that is discussed is public information. The intended result is to produce a committed group of knowledgeable people who have a deep understanding of the challenges confronting their organization, agreement about the ideals the strategy is supposed to serve, action plans that are aligned with those ideals, a social mechanism for participation, and a process for engaging the whole system in the strategy implementation. As one Xerox vice president reflected, "We used the output from the Search Conference teams in our annual planning process to develop our business strategy for the next three years. Our culture has engineered a big shift; we've moved the [unit's] members from being highly dependent on top-down planning to acting like entrepreneurs."

Strategy Implementation

Top management requires a method to ensure that their plans and strategies are successfully executed (the term "deployed" is frequently used) within the organization. The Japanese deploy strategy through a process known as *hoshin planning*, or policy deployment. *Hoshin* means policy or policy deployment. Policy deployment is a systems approach to managing change in critical business processes. It emphasizes organization-wide planning and setting of priorities, providing resources to meet objectives, and measuring performance as a basis for improving performance. Policy deployment is essentially a TQ-based approach to executing a strategy. King describes it eloquently:[7]

> Imagine an organization that knows what customers will want 5 to 10 years from now and exactly what they will do to meet and exceed all expectations. Imagine a planning system that has integrated [Plan, Do, Study, Act] language and activity based on clear, long-term thinking, a realistic measurement system with a focus on process and results, iden-

tification of what's important, alignment of groups, decisions by people who have the necessary information, planning integrated with daily activity, good vertical communication, cross-functional communication, and everyone planning for himself or herself, and the buy-in that results. That is hoshin planning.

With policy deployment, top management is responsible for developing and communicating a vision, then building organization-wide commitment to its achievement.[8] This vision is deployed by developing and executing annual policy statements (plans). All levels of employees actively participate in generating a strategy and action plans to attain the vision.

At each level, progressively more detailed and concrete means to accomplish the annual plans are determined. The plans are hierarchical, cascading downward from top management's plans. There should be a clear link to common goals and activities throughout the organizational hierarchy. Policy deployment provides frequent evaluation and modification based on feedback from regularly scheduled audits of the process. Plans and actions are based on analysis of the root causes of a problem, rather than only on the symptoms.

Planning has a high degree of detail, including the anticipation of possible problems during implementation. The emphasis is on improving the process, as opposed to a results-only orientation.

An example of policy deployment is provided by Imai:[9]

To illustrate the need for policy deployment, let us consider the following case: The president of an airline company proclaims that he believes in safety and that his corporate goal is to make sure that safety is maintained throughout the company. This proclamation is prominently featured in the company's quarterly report and its advertising. Let us further suppose that the department managers also swear a firm belief in safety. The catering manager says he believes in safety. The pilots say they believe in safety. The flight crews say they believe in safety. Everyone in the company practices safety. True? Or might everyone simply be paying lip service to the idea of safety?

On the other hand, if the president states that safety is company policy and works with his division managers to develop a plan for safety that defines their responsibilities, everyone will have a very specific subject to discuss. Safety will become a real concern. For the manager in charge of catering services, safety might mean maintaining the quality of food to avoid customer dissatisfaction or illness.

In that case, how does he ensure that the food is of top quality? What sorts of control points and check points does he establish? How does he ensure that there is no deterioration of food quality in flight? Who checks the temperature of the refrigerators or the condition of the oven while the plane is in the air?

FIGURE 11.2   HOSHIN PLANNING PROCESS

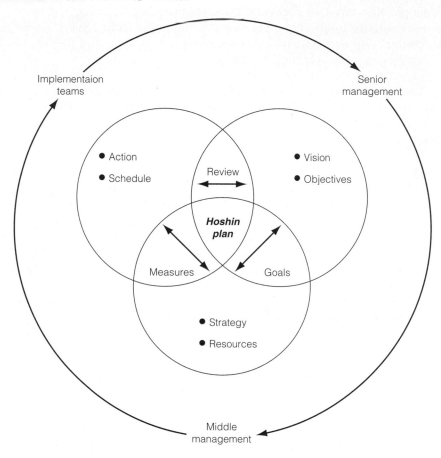

From *Hoshin Kanri: Policy Deployment for Successful TQM,* by Yoji Akao. [English translation] Copyright © 1991 by Productivity Press, P.O. Box 13390, Portland, OR 97213-0390; 800-394-6868. Reprinted by permission.

Only when safety is translated into specific actions with specific control and check points established for each employee's job may safety be said to have been truly deployed as a policy. Policy deployment calls for everyone to interpret policy in light of their own responsibilities and for everyone to work out criteria to check their success in carrying out the policy.

Figure 11.2 shows the general hoshin planning process. Policy deployment starts with the senior managers of the company. The senior managers establish the vision and core objectives of the company. An example of an objective might be "to improve delivery," which supports the long-term vision of "to be the industry leader in customer satisfaction." Middle management negotiates with senior management regarding the goals that will achieve the objectives. Goals specify numerically the degree of change that is expected. These should be challenging, but people should feel that they are attainable.

Strategies specify the means to achieve the goals. They include more specific actions to be taken. Middle managers are responsible for managing the resources to accomplish the goals. Middle management then negotiates with the implementation teams regarding the performance measures that are used to indicate progress toward accomplishing the strategies.

Measures are specific checkpoints to ensure the effectiveness of individual elements of the strategy. The implementation teams are empowered to manage the actions and schedule their activities. Senior management then uses a review process to understand both the progress of the implementation teams and the success of their planning system. The "new seven" management and planning tools described in chapter 3 are used extensively in the process.

Although policy deployment bears some similarity to management by objectives (MBO), an approach condemned by Deming, there are some important differences. First, typical MBO focuses on the performance of individual employees rather than on improvement of the organization as a whole. Attainment of objectives is closely tied to individual performance evaluation and rewards. This tends to promote actions that optimize individuals' gain, rather than that of the organization. Second, MBO objectives generally are not supportive of the company's vision but are set independently. Third, MBO is primarily used as a means of management control; in practice, most subordinates succumb to their supervisor's wishes. Finally, MBO objectives are often not used in daily work but are resurrected only during performance reviews. However, many different MBO approaches exist in the United States, and MBO is practiced differently in Japan. Many smaller organizations that have good internal communication have used MBO successfully.

Strategic Management in Action

In this section we provide some examples that illustrate the themes we have discussed about strategic planning.

Mission, Vision, and Values for the Stroh Brewery Company[10]

The Total Quality Management program at the Stroh Brewery Company is based on the belief that employees hold the key to achieving a comprehensive focus on Service-Quality—an organized concerted effort to add value to products, including those processes through which services are delivered—that will enable Stroh to meet and exceed the expectations of its customers. Service-Quality means more than a quality product. It is defined through customers' perception of value. The customer judges Stroh not just by the reliability of their basic product, but by the total experience of doing business with them. Every encounter with a company system or a company employee is a "moment of truth" when the customer will judge the Service-Quality efforts of Stroh. This philosophy is reflected in the company's strategic plan:

Vision

Our vision of The Stroh Brewery Company is one of a growing and prospering company with a dynamic and motivated organization providing our shareholders with reasonable return on their investment.

Mission

To achieve this vision, our mission is to produce, distribute, and market a variety of high-quality beers in a manner that meets or exceeds the expectations of our customers.

Values

Our company values provide a constant point of reference for all of our efforts and confirm our commitment to Stroh employees and to all of our customers. The core values of Quality, Integrity, and Teamwork will serve as the foundation upon which we will build success.

Quality. We seek to continuously improve the level of quality in all that we do. We pursue having the finest products, efficient production and distribution facilities, innovative marketing and sales programs, and totally supportive administrative policies and procedures. These efforts are directed at meeting or exceeding our customers' expectations—both inside and outside the company.

Integrity. We conduct all of our activities with integrity. We believe that the Stroh name stands for honesty and trust. We apply this belief to our relationship with all employees, our suppliers, wholesalers, and all others with whom we have business relationships. Our business activities will model our values, demonstrating that we are a responsible corporate citizen with a firm resolve to live up to our social and environmental responsibilities.

Teamwork. Teamwork is essential to our mutual success. Stroh employees are a valuable asset. Every employee is given respect and trust, regardless of position in the organization. All employees are encouraged to share their views and suggestions. It is through mutual respect, cooperation, and sharing of ideas with employees, suppliers, wholesalers, and retailers that the full potential of the company will be realized. We will fully support the submission and discussion of new ideas from all of our associates (employees, wholesalers, and suppliers). Commitment and innovation will be viewed as actions worthy of praise and recognition.

Strategic Planning at Corning TPD[11]

Corning's Telecommunications Products Division (TPD), whose primary product is optical fiber, has a three-stage planning system shown in Figure 11.3. This system consists of Strategy Development, in which new or updated strategy is determined; Planning, in which strategy is translated into Key

FIGURE 11.3 CORNING TPD STRATEGIC PLANNING PROCESS

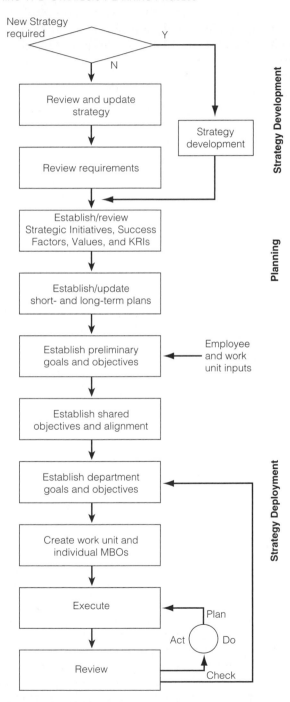

(KRIS = KEY RESULTS INDICATORS)

Strategic Initiatives and associated Critical Success Factors, as well as three-year and one-year plans to deploy the strategy; and Strategy Deployment, in which the company develops goals and objectives in alignment with the Key Strategic Initiatives for units, work groups, and individuals. Review and feedback ensure that planning remains effective despite changes in customer requirements and in the competitive environment.

TPD normally develops its strategy every other year and performs strategy review and update in the off-years. The process begins with the definition of external environment assumptions, including customer needs, competitors' positions, market projections, economic projections, and regulatory trends. These assumptions are then used to develop specific human resource, commercial, technology, and manufacturing functional strategies. TPD's business strategy is stated simply as

$$\text{Lowest Cost} + \text{Market Access} = \text{Success}$$

They derive key strategic initiatives directly from this statement. To ensure market success, they must achieve unparalleled customer satisfaction with end-user, cabler, and joint venture customers; select and effectively develop the right functional and geographic markets around the world; and be certain that they can afford to increase capacity to meet customer demand. To survive in the face of vigorous price competition and threatened backward integration and acquisition of customers, they must be the lowest-cost producer by a significant margin.

FIGURE 11.4 SOLECTRON CORPORATION'S STRATEGIC PLANNING PROCESS

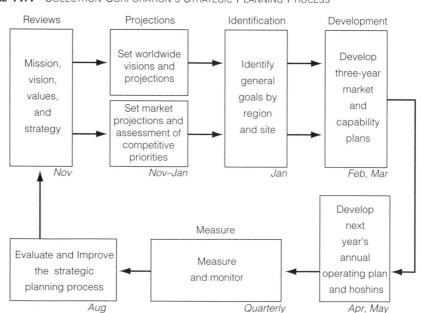

Hoshin Planning at Solectron[12]

Figure 11.4 shows Solectron's annual strategic planning process. The output of this process is an updated three-year long-range plan, annual operating plan, and annual improvement plan. In developing market projections, regional and site leaders and corporate staff develop their visions, business projections, and capability requirements. Account plans are developed for all customers. The corporate marketing group uses market and competitor information to assess risks. Information sources include industry tracking organizations, Solectron management and staff, and the 10-K reports of publicly held competitors. The marketing group also distills competitor data into a quarterly report to senior management to fine-tune projections for local markets. This process is followed by development of strategies, market targets, and financial targets for regions and sites. The plans for all regions are reviewed for alignment with the corporation as a whole. Next, one-year action plans are developed based on the three-year plan. Figure 11.5 shows the hoshin planning process that ties these

FIGURE 11.5 SOLECTRON CORPORATION'S HOSHIN PLANNING PROCESS

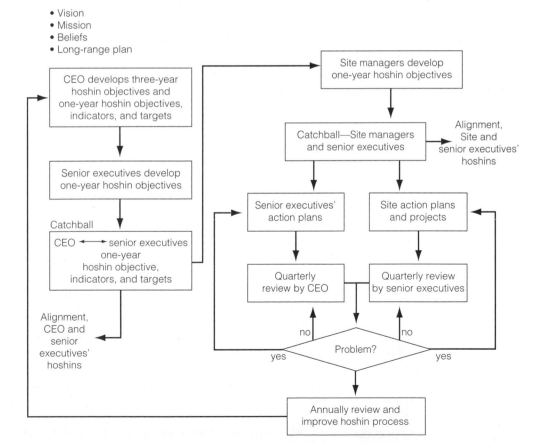

plans together. "Catchball" is a term used to describe the process of negotiating plans between organizational levels until agreement is reached on the feasibility of plans and the resources necessary to achieve them.

TQ and Strategic Management Theory[13]

The TQ perspective, as reflected in the Baldrige criteria, suggests several requirements for effective strategic planning:

- A definable approach for developing company strategy. The approach should consider factors related to the market environment, the competitive environment, risk, human resource capabilities, company capabilities, and supplier/partner capabilities.
- A clear company strategy with action plans derived from it, and human resource plans related to the action plans. Differences between short- and longer-range plans should be recognized and understood.
- An approach for implementing action plans. The approach should consider how the critical requirements for implementing action plans—including human resource plans, key processes, performance measures, and resources—will be aligned and deployed.
- An approach for monitoring company performance relative to the strategic plan.
- Projections of strategy-related changes in key indicators of company performance. These projections should include relevant comparisons to competitors or other benchmarks, and the assumptions used in the projections.

Strategic planning and deployment have been issues of management research for many years, and the conceptual literature in strategic management generally supports these requirements. For example, strategy as a deliberate, definable undertaking has constituted an essential element of classical strategic management frameworks developed by strategy scholars. However, the general usefulness of strategy making to enhanced performance has not been rigorously affirmed. Theoretical arguments, such as those presented by population ecologists, question the efficacy of planning, and findings from empirical studies that attempt to link strategic planning to performance have been inconclusive.

Three of the six factors that TQ perspectives suggest should make up strategy development—market environment, competitive environment, and company capabilities—pervade most classic work in strategy formulation. However, the other three factors—financial and societal risk, human resource capabilities, and supplier/partner capabilities—gain only indirect support from the strategy literature. The criteria's specification of human resource capabilities and supplier/partner capabilities appears somewhat redundant, since these factors are asset classes that can be appropriately filed under the "internal capabilities" factor.

The strategy literature sometimes refers to strategic plans as *strategic content*. The Baldrige criteria provide little detail as to what a strategy or an action plan should contain or the form it should take. Such a nonprescriptive stance fits the literature robustly, since strategy scholars have proposed many purposes and forms of strategy. Breaking down a strategy into action plans for effective implementation is a common notion among organization and strategy theorists. However, differentiating between short- and longer-term plans garners little direct literature support, although the notion can be indirectly linked to the general concept of dividing strategic goals into doable pieces.

Structure for implementing strategy, in the form of human resource plans, key processes, performance measures, and resources, must be aligned and deployed. Several strategy researchers have examined the role of managerial systems in strategy implementation, particularly systems connected to middle management.

Although the TQ perspective requires specification of how performance will be tracked, it addresses only indirectly the issue of control. Nevertheless, control has been a fundamental concept in management, dating back to Anthony's classic framework,[14] and the literature is replete with studies on managerial control systems. Perhaps the most compelling support for using performance measures in strategic management is related to the managerial control notion that measurements provide objective information that managers can use to judge how well the organization is performing in comparison to strategic targets and to signal the need for corrective action. Stating the assumptions behind strategic projections has some grounding in systems theory and some strategy development literature. Inclusion of competitive comparisons and other benchmarks in performance projections can be indirectly related to the requirement for industry and competitive scanning as part of strategy development.

IMPLEMENTING A TQ STRATEGY

A total quality strategy has several elements:[15]

1. a customer-focused vision,
2. a concept of the voice of the customer,
3. a way of learning from outstanding companies,
4. an expression of caring for employees,
5. a means of removing the barriers to achieving quality, and
6. a measurement plan.

These elements can be implemented in any organization, provided the organization has made a commitment to quality. Yet, many companies have experienced great difficulty in implementing total quality and even deciding *whether* to do it. This difficulty often results from some common misconceptions, such as TQ means doing lots of "things" like collecting data and organizing teams or that it only applies to large companies. A total quality strategy does, however, require significant changes in organization design, processes, and culture. Such broad change has been a stumbling block for many companies.

Companies make the decision to adopt the TQ philosophy for two basic reasons:

1. A firm reacts to competition that poses a threat to its profitable survival by turning to TQ.
2. TQ represents an opportunity to improve.

Most firms—even Baldrige Award winners—have moved toward total quality because of the first reason. Xerox, for example, watched its market share fall from 90 percent to 13 percent in a little over a decade; Milliken faced increased competition from Asian textile manufacturers; Zytec Corporation found itself in financial difficulties because of reliance on a single customer. While not facing dire crises, perceived future threats were the impetus for FedEx and Solectron. When faced with a threat to survival, a company effects cultural change more easily; under these circumstances, organizations generally implement TQ effectively. A company will generally have more difficulty gaining support for change when not facing a crisis. This reluctance is a reflection of the attitude "If it ain't broke, don't fix it." In such cases, a company might attempt to manufacture a crisis mentality to effect change.

The biggest dangers lie in the lack of complete understanding and the tendency to imitate others—the easy way out. Many of the experts and consultants have rewritten total quality management around their own discipline, such as accounting, engineering, human resources, or statistics. The "one best model" of TQ may not mesh with an organization's culture; most successful companies have developed their own unique approaches to fit their own requirements. Research shows that imitation of TQ efforts made by one successful organization may not lead to good results in another. Building and sustaining a TQ organization requires a readiness for change, the adoption of sound practices and implementation strategies, and an effective organization (see box).

Roles in Implementing a Quality Strategy

Senior management, middle management, and the workforce each has a critical role to play in the implementation process. Senior managers must ensure that their plans and strategies are successfully executed within the organization. Middle managers provide the leadership by which the vision of senior management is translated into the operation of the organization. In the end, it is the workforce that delivers quality and must have not only empowerment, but also a true commitment to quality for TQ to succeed.

Senior Management
Senior managers must ensure that the organization focuses on the needs of the customer. They must promote the mission, vision, and values of the company throughout the organization. Senior managers must identify the critical processes that need attention and improvement and the resources and trade-offs that must be made to fund the TQM activity. They must review progress and remove barriers to implementation. Finally, they must improve the pro-

"There is No Instant Pudding"[16]

This is one of Deming's more descriptive phrases in describing American managers' obsession with quick results. Quality takes time.

At Armstrong Building Products Operations, the evolution of quality has occurred in several phases since 1983:

Phase I (1983–1985)
- Commitment to try
- Philip Crosby system
- Quality improvement teams

Phase II (1985–1990)
- Process improvement
- Quality plans added to business plans
- Supplier quality management

Phase III (1989–1992)
- Vision clearly defined
- Empowered employees; flatter organization
- Use of Baldrige criteria for self-assessment

Phase IV (1991–1994)
- Product and service leadership
- Baldrige Award applications (1995 winner)
- Business results

Phase IV (1994–present)
- High performance change process
- "Nonnegotiable" business strategies
- Achieving value for employees, customers, shareholders

Similarly, ADAC Laboratories began its TQ approach in 1991 by benchmarking other leading organizations, forming a monthly quality committee, developing a commitment to customer satisfaction, investing in field service, and designing a new strategic planning process. In 1992, ADAC developed its vision, began weekly quality meetings, adopted the Baldrige criteria and conducted a self-assessment, and strengthened quality incentives and rewards. During 1993, the Baldrige criteria were widely deployed, benchmarking was performed in all areas, systematic and comprehensive training programs were started, and quality performance was monitored on a twice-weekly basis. In the next two years, policy deployment was introduced, the ADAC business approach was refined based on TQ and mutual learning principles, the company focused on people-value-added processes, breakthrough improvement became a priority, and ADAC pursued ISO 9000 registration. ADAC received the Baldrige Award in 1996.

cesses in which they are involved (strategic planning, for example), both to improve the performance of the process and to demonstrate their ability to use quality tools for problem solving.[17]

Middle Management

Middle management has been viewed by many as a direct obstacle to creating a supportive environment for TQ.[18] Middle managers are often seen as feeding territorial competition, stifling information flow, not developing and/or preparing employees for change, and feeling threatened by continuous improvement efforts. However, middle management's role in creating and sustaining a TQ culture is critical. Middle managers improve the operational processes that are the foundation of customer satisfaction; they can make or break cooperation and teamwork; and they are the principal means by which the workforce prepares for change.

Mark Samuel suggests that transforming middle managers into change agents requires a systematic process that dissolves traditional management boundaries and replaces them with an empowered and team-oriented state of accountability for organizational performance.[19] This process involves the following:

1. *Empowerment*—Middle managers must be accountable for the performance of the organization in meeting objectives.
2. *Creating a common vision of excellence*—This vision is then transformed into critical success factors that describe key areas of performance that relate to internal and external customer satisfaction.
3. *New rules for playing the organizational game*—Territorial walls must be broken, yielding a spirit of teamwork. One new approach is interlocking accountability, in which all managers are accountable to one another for their performance. The second is team representation, in which each manager is responsible for accurately representing the ideas and decisions of the team to others outside the team.
4. *Implementing a continuous improvement process*—These projects should improve their operational systems and processes.
5. *Developing and retaining peak performers*—Middle managers must identify and develop future leaders of the organization.

The Workforce

The workforce must develop ownership of the quality process. Ownership and empowerment gives employees the right to have a voice in deciding what needs to be done and how to do it.[20] It is based on a belief that what is good for the organization is also good for the individual and vice versa. At Westinghouse they define ownership as "taking personal responsibility for our jobs . . . for assuring that we meet or exceed our customers' standards and our own. We believe that ownership is a state of mind and heart that is characterized by a personal and emotional commitment to approach every decision and task with the confidence and leadership of an owner." Self-managed teams, discussed in chapter 7, are one form of ownership.

Ownership is prevalent among Baldrige winners. At Cadillac, for example, some teams have "cradle to grave" responsibility for products. Milliken employees are responsible for assigning team-member roles and electing team leaders; they are becoming involved in the initial employee selection decision. At Zytec, employees design many of their tools and workstations.

Training, recognition, and better communication are key success factors for transferring ownership to the workforce. With increased ownership, however, comes a flatter organization—and the elimination of some middle managers. Increased ownership also requires increased sharing of information with the workforce and a commitment to the workforce in good times and in bad. This might mean reducing stock dividends and executive bonuses before laying off the workforce during economic downturns. This is what Japanese companies do when the business climate turns south.

Union/Management Relations

A major stumbling block in implementing TQ in the United States has been the traditional adversarial relationship between unions and management.[21] For example, in 1986 General Motors introduced a team concept for quality improvement in Van Nuys, California, which passed a union membership vote with only 53 percent in support. Since then, the opposition has worked against the concept. In many cases, management must share the responsibility in working with unions as equal partners. Both union and management have important roles in TQ.

Labor's role is to recognize the need for changing its relationship with management and then to educate its members as to how cooperation will affect the organization. This includes what its members can expect and how working conditions and job security might change. Labor must carefully select members for such a program and have a positive attitude. TQ programs must be separated from collective bargaining.

Management must realize that it needs the skills and knowledge of all employees to improve quality and meet competitive challenges and must be willing to develop a closer working relationship with labor. Management must be ready to address union concerns and cultivate trust. Both sides should receive training in communication and problem-solving skills. Union and management should have equal representation on committees and have total trust and commitment. External consultants can play an important role as facilitators and mediators in such efforts.

Common Implementation Mistakes

A wide range of quality implementation strategies exist, many of which have serious pitfalls. For example, the general manager of a large defense electronics contractor unveiled a major program, then plunged into dealing with the unit's plummeting revenues and layoffs. Quality went nowhere. At Florida Power and Light, John J. Hudiburg drove hard to win the Deming Prize but created a large bureaucracy in which morale fell as workers and managers had to compile hundreds of pages of analysis. The new CEO reduced the scope of the quality effort. Alcoa's CEO scrapped the company's decade-long continuous improvement strategy, calling it a "major mistake," focusing instead on "quantum" improvements.[22]

Implementation of TQ is often attempted without a full grasp of its nature, and certain mistakes are made repeatedly. The most frequent errors are as follows:[23]

1. TQ is regarded as a program, despite rhetoric to the contrary.
2. Short-term results are not obtained. There may be no attempt to get short-term results, or management may believe that measurable benefits lie only in the distant future.
3. The process is not driven by a focus on the customer, strategic business issues, and senior management.
4. Structural elements in the organization (such as compensation systems, promotion systems, accounting systems, rigid policies and procedures, specialization and functionalization), and status symbols (such as offices and perks) block change.
5. Goals are set too low. Management does not shoot for stretch goals or use outside benchmarks as targets.
6. The organizational culture remains one of "command and control" and is driven by fear or game playing, budgets, schedules, or bureaucracy.
7. Training is not properly addressed. There is too little training of the workforce. Training may be of the wrong kind; for example, providing only classroom training without on-the-job reinforcement or focusing on the mechanics of tools and not on identifying problems.
8. The focus is mainly on products, not processes.
9. Little real empowerment is given and what is given is not supported in actions.
10. The organization is too successful and complacent. It is not receptive to change and learning and clings to the "not invented here" syndrome.
11. The organization fails to address three fundamental questions: Is this another program? What's in it for me? How can I do this on top of everything else?
12. Senior management is not personally and visibly committed and actively participating.
13. The use of teams to solve cross-functional problems is overemphasized to the neglect of individual efforts at local improvements.
14. The belief prevails that more data are always desirable, regardless of relevance—"paralysis by analysis."
15. Management fails to recognize that quality improvement is a personal responsibility at all levels of the organization.
16. The organization does not see itself as a collection of interrelated processes making up an overall system. Both the individual processes and the overall system need to be identified and understood.

Although this list is extensive, it is by no means exhaustive. It reflects the still immature development of TQ. TQ requires a new set of skills and learning, including interpersonal awareness and competence, team building, encouraging openness and trust, listening, giving and getting feedback, group participation, problem solving, clarifying goals, resolving conflicts, delegating and coaching, empowerment, and continuous improvement as a way of life.[24] The process must begin by creating a set of feelings and attitudes that lead to lasting values.

Strategies for Success

Studies of Deming Prize and Baldrige Award winners suggest that certain key practices contributed to their success:[25]

- Successful companies have a sharp focus on quality through planning. Deming Prize winners develop detailed, well-communicated plans and reinforce them by visual aids posted throughout the company. These firms have specific annual objectives, with frequent review of progress. Goals include both defensive goals (such as cost reduction) and offensive goals (such as building market share).
- Top management is heavily involved. Senior managers are personally involved in the process. It is not uncommon for the top executives to make numerous field visits to customers and divisions.
- Customer satisfaction is integrated across functions. Customer satisfaction drives the quality effort. Specific tasks and responsibilities are assigned to all departments. Many companies use techniques such as quality function deployment.
- Employee participation is high, especially among Deming Prize winners. As we discussed elsewhere in this book, suggestion systems have much greater importance in Japan than in the West. Training is steady and continuous and involves everyone in the company.

It's not rocket science.

Although some universal principles apply, a successful quality strategy needs to fit within the existing organization culture. This is why the Baldrige Award guidelines are nonprescriptive; there is no magic formula that works for everyone. At Zytec, for instance, Deming's 14 points were chosen as the cornerstone of the quality improvement culture. They established a Deming Steering Committee to guide the Deming process and champion individual Deming points and to act as advisors to three Deming Implementation Teams. Motorola, on the other hand, invited numerous consultants to propose quality plans, but in the end they decided to develop a quality program tailored to their specific needs.

One study of Baldrige winners concluded that each has a unique "quality engine" that drives the quality activities of the organization.[26] These are summarized in Figure 11.6. This is not to suggest that all other aspects of TQ are ignored; they are not. The quality engine customizes the quality effort to the organizational culture and provides a focus for all quality efforts.

FIGURE 11.6 QUALITY ENGINES OF BALDRIGE AWARD WINNERS

- **Market-Driven Quality**—Focus on customer needs early in the planning and design process (IBM Rochester)

- **Process Control**—Focus on defect prevention, such as six-sigma quality (Motorola)

- **Product Development**—Focus on integrating manufacturing and design and partnering with customers and suppliers (Cadillac)

- **Benchmarking**—Focus on competitive and best-in-class benchmarks (Xerox)

- **Technology**—Focus on using technology to speed processes and improve customer service (FedEx)

- **Employee Empowerment and Involvement**—Use self-managed teams and active participation of employees in all aspects of the business (Milliken)

- **Strategic Planning**—Involve cross-functional teams, customers, and suppliers in the planning process (Zytec)

- **Management by Data and Facts**—Focus on the use of measurements to track and improve quality (Westinghouse)

Best Practices

Imitation, while the sincerest form of flattery, may not always be the best strategy for TQ. In fact, it can actually hurt, wasting time and money on the wrong things. In 1992 the International Quality Study (IQS) published research results that provide a factual basis for this claim.[27] The study suggests that best practices depend on the current level of performance of a company. Two measures of performance are the ROA (return on assets—after-tax income divided by total assets) and VAE (value added per employee—sales less the costs of materials, supplies, and work done by outside contractors divided by the number of employees).

Low performers, those with less than 2 percent ROA and $47,000 VAE, can reap the highest benefits by concentrating on fundamentals. This includes identifying processes that add value, simplifying them, and improving response to customer and market demands. In addition, training and teamwork—particularly in resolving customer complaints—can lead to significant improvements. More advanced concepts, such as self-managed teams, take too much preparation and time to be worthwhile for these companies. Other suggestions include benchmarking competitors (rather than world-class companies), listening to the customer for ideas, selecting suppliers mainly for price and reliability, buying turnkey technology for reducing costs, and rewarding frontline workers for teamwork and quality.

Medium performers, those with ROA from 2 percent to 7 percent and VAE from $47,000 to $74,000, achieve the most benefits from meticulously documenting gains; further refining practices to improve value added per employee, time to market, and customer satisfaction; and encouraging employees at every level to find ways to improve their jobs. A separate quality assurance staff is recommended. These companies should emulate market leaders and selected world-class companies; use customer input, formal market research, and internal ideas for new products; select suppliers by quality certification, then price; find ways to use facilities more flexibly to produce a wider variety of products and services; and base compensation for workers and middle managers on contributions to teamwork and quality.

High performers, with ROA and VAE exceeding 7 percent and $74,000 respectively, gain the most from using self-managed teams and cross-functional teams that focus on horizontal processes, such as logistics and product development, and from benchmarking product development, distribution, and customer service against world-class firms. Additional training, except for new hires, is of limited value. In addition, new products should be based on customer input, benchmarking, and internal research and development. Suppliers should be chosen primarily for their technology and quality. Strategic partnerships should be considered to diversify manufacturing. Senior managers should be included in compensation schemes pegged to teamwork and quality. Finally, these firms should further refine practices to improve VAE, market response, and customer satisfaction.

Strangely, the IQS Best Practices Report has been interpreted by many in the news media as a criticism of TQ.[28] On the contrary, the results are the first significant effort to develop a prescriptive theory (back to Deming again) of TQ implementation, rather than relying on intuition and anecdotal evidence. We are now in a position to begin to understand how TQ can best be applied. The findings contradict the notion that there is one magic quick fix for quality. Rather, companies advance in stages along a learning curve and must design their TQ initiatives carefully to optimize their effect.

SUMMARY

Many organizations now recognize that quality is a viable strategy for achieving competitive advantage. Moreover, a total quality focus within an organization can make the strategic planning and implementation processes more effective, particularly if policy deployment principles are applied.

Successful implementation of TQ-based strategies depends on the commitment and involvement of all constituents: senior management, middle management, and the workforce, including union leadership. Doing so is not easy, and many mistakes can be made. However, we are continually learning what practices lead to successful strategies and implementation. This suggests that today's managers cannot cling to past practices but must constantly improve their approaches to meet competitive challenges.

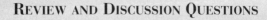

REVIEW AND DISCUSSION QUESTIONS

1. What is a strategy? What elements does a formal strategy contain?
2. What factors have led companies to pursue a strategy based on quality?
3. Research some of the background of recent Baldrige winners (see Table 2.2). How do they integrate quality into their business strategies? Discuss different approaches these firms use.
4. Discuss the process of strategy formulation. How can TQ improve this process?
5. Interview managers at some local companies to determine if their businesses have well-defined missions, visions, and guiding principles. If they do, how are these translated into strategy? If not, what steps should they take?
6. What is hoshin planning, or policy deployment? Explain how this approach is used in organizations.
7. What are the differences between policy deployment and management by objectives?
8. Does your university or college have a mission and strategy? How might policy deployment be used in a university setting?
9. Describe the roles of senior managers, middle managers, and the workforce in implementing a quality strategy.
10. How can TQ be implemented in unionized companies? What role should the union play?
11. Discuss the common implementation mistakes that many organizations make when trying to implement TQ.
12. For each of the common implementation mistakes cited in the chapter, develop a remedy or process for helping an organization to avoid them.
13. What strategies for success have been found to be especially useful in implementing TQ?
14. Do the results of the IQS Best Practices Report make sense? What might happen in companies that try to implement TQ practices that are beyond their abilities?

CASES

Stroh Brewery's Strategy[29]

The strategy of the Stroh Brewery Company (whose vision, mission, and values were introduced in this chapter) follows.

Strategy

In support of our vision and mission, the following strategies will be employed to achieve our Service-Quality goal. WE WILL:

Maintain a competitive brand portfolio that allows us to capture unique market opportunities and strive to realize the potential of our present brands and new product introductions. Our goal is to increase unit volume. This does not mean, however, that every brand will experience unit growth every year. We will manage each brand based on its long-term growth potential, its strategic relevance, and its relationship to the company's overall business strategy.

Invest heavily in the development of our human resources through orientation and training, which will enable our employees to make better decisions and to improve processes. We will hire individuals who have the job-related skills and abilities that support Stroh's Service-Quality mode of operation.

Develop and introduce line extensions, new brands, and new packages, seeking to create innovative breakthroughs. New products are a critical element to Stroh's overall success. We will develop new products with a sense of urgency while maintaining a commitment to sound product concepts, excellent sales execution, and appropriate marketing support.

Maintain a flexible approach in the balance between national and regional marketing and sales efforts. Although there are aspects of marketing our products that have relevance to all markets (e.g., national advertising), we will always to try to find ways to capitalize on regional strengths and opportunities.

Pursue opportunities to develop international markets. Our focus for the future extends to international markets where we believe there are significant opportunities to market our products both directly and in partnership with others.

Commit to maintaining the best distribution network in the industry along with our full support of the three-tier system. Our distribution system will function around the guiding principles of Service-Quality.

Strive to control production and administrative expenses, which allows us to provide the maximum funds to market our products. We will do this by constantly seeking ways to improve our method of completing tasks necessary to our business.

Consider acquiring assets to build synergies and to reduce production costs. The acquisition of additional brands, manufacturing facilities, and other businesses that will improve the company's overall strategic position is viewed as highly desirable.

Invest in plant equipment and new technologies to produce new products and to maintain our production facilities to remain competitive.

Be comfortable with change. We will pursue change as a strategic weapon. There is no safety in standing still, nor is there any advantage in abiding by the rules set by our competitors. Change will not be pursued for its own sake, but neither will change be avoided because it is uncomfortable or because of the risks associated with change.

Be market and service driven. We will develop systems and processes to facilitate this strategy.

Questions for Discussion

1.   Who are the customers of Stroh's?
2.   What aspects of Stroh's vision, mission, values, and strategy support the fundamental principles of TQ described in chapter 1?

The Parable of the Green Lawn[30]

A new housing development has lots of packed earth and weeds but no grass. Two neighbors make a wager on who will be the first to have a lush lawn. Mr. Fast N. Furious knows that a lawn will not grow without grass seed, so he immediately buys the most expensive seed he can find because everyone knows that quality improves with price. Besides, he'll recover the cost of the seed through his wager. Next, he stands knee deep in his weeds and tosses the seed around his yard. Confident that he has a head start on his neighbor, who is not making much visible progress, he begins his next project.

Ms. Slo N. Steady, having grown up in the country, proceeds to clear the lot, till the soil, and even alter the slope of the terrain to provide better drainage. She checks the soil's pH, applies weed killer and fertilizer, and then distributes the grass seed evenly with a spreader. She applies a mulch cover and waters the lawn appropriately. She finishes several days after her neighbor, who asks if she would like to concede defeat. After all, he does have some blades of grass poking up already.

Mr. Furious is encouraged by the few clumps of grass that sprout. While these small, green islands are better developed than Ms. Steady's fledgling lawn, they are surrounded by bare spots and weeds. If he maintains these footholds, he reasons, they should spread to the rest of the yard.

He notices that his neighbor's lawn is more uniform and is really starting to grow. He attributes this to the Steady children, who water the lawn each evening. Not wanting to appear to be imitating his neighbor, Mr. Furious instructs his children to water his lawn at noon.

The noon watering proves to be detrimental, so he decides to fertilize the remaining patches of grass. Since he wants to make up for the losses the noon watering caused, he applies the fertilizer at twice the recommended application rate. Most of the patches of grass that escape being burned by the fertilizer, however, are eventually choked out by the weeds.

After winning the wager with Mr. Furious, Ms. Steady lounges on the deck enjoying her new grill, which she paid for with the money from the wager. Her lawn requires minimal maintenance, so she is free to attend to the landscaping. The combination of the lawn and landscaping also results in an award from a neighborhood committee that determines that her lawn is a true showplace.

Mr. Furious still labors on his lawn. He blames the poor performance on his children's inability to properly water the lawn, nonconforming grass seed, insufficient sunlight, and poor soil. He claims that his neighbor has an unfair advantage and her success is based on conditions unique to her plot of land. He views the loss as grossly unfair; after all, he spends more time and money on his lawn than Ms. Steady does.

He continues to complain about how expensive the seed is and how much time he spends moving the sprinkler around to the few remaining clumps of grass that continue to grow. But Mr. Furious thinks that things will be better for him next year, because he plans to install an automatic sprinkler system and make a double-or-nothing wager with Ms. Steady.

© 1994 American Society for Quality. Reprinted with permission.

Discussion Questions

1. Within the context of the continual struggles to create a "world-class" lawn and "world-class" business, draw analogies between the events when total quality is implemented.
2. Specifically, translate the problems described here into business language. What are the implementation barriers to achieving total quality?

ENDNOTES

1. James Brian Quinn, *Strategies for Change: Logical Incrementalism*, Homewood, Ill.: Richard D. Irwin, 1980.
2. Richard J. Leo, "Xerox 2000: From Survival to Opportunity," *Quality Progress*, Vol. 30, No. 3, March 1996, pp. 65–71.
3. Malcolm Baldrige National Quality Award Criteria For Performance Excellence, 1999, p. 30.
4. Matthew W. Ford and James R. Evans, "Conceptual Foundations of Strategic Planning in the Malcolm Baldrige Criteria for Performance Excellence," Working Paper, College of Business Administration, University of Cincinnati, 1998.
5. J.M. Juran, *Juran on Planning for Quality*. The Free Press, New York, 1988; and J.M. Juran, *Juran on Leadership for Quality*. The Free Press, New York, 1989.
6. Ronald E. Purser and Steven Cabana, "Involve Employees at Every Level of Strategic Planning," *Quality Progress*, May 1997, pp. 66–71.
7. Bob King, *Hoshin Planning: The Developmental Approach*, Methuen, Mass.: GOAL/QPC, 1989, pp. 2–3.
8. The Ernst & Young Quality Improvement Consulting Group, *Total Quality: An Executive's Guide for the 1990s*, Homewood, Ill.: Dow Jones-Irwin, 1990.
9. M. Imai, *Kaizen: The Key to Japan's Competitive Success*, New York: McGraw-Hill, 1986, pp. 144–145. Reproduced with permission of McGraw-Hill.
10. Adapted with permission from "TQM," The Stroh Brewing Company.
11. Corning Telecommunications Products Division Malcolm Baldrige National Quality Award 1995 Winner Application Summary.
12. Solectron Malcolm Baldrige National Quality Award Application Summary, 1997.
13. Based on Ford and Evans, op. cit.
14. R.N. Anthony, "Planning and Control Systems: A Framework for Analysis," Boston: Division of Research, Graduate School of Business Administration, Harvard University.

15. Henry A. Bradshaw, "From Leadership to Customer Satisfaction: The Total Quality Management System," Presentation Material from the 1996 Regional Malcolm Baldrige Award Conference, Boston, June 6, 1996; and Doug Keare, "Lessons Learned and Quality Journey," Presentation Notes, 1997 Quest for Excellence Conference, Washington, D.C.

16. Richard C. Whiteley, *The Customer-Driven Company: Moving from Talk to Action*, New York: Addison-Wesley, 1991.

17. Arthur R. Tenner and Irving J. DeToro, *Total Quality Management: Three Steps to Continuous Improvement*, Reading, Mass.: Addison Wesley, 1992.

18. Mark Samuel, "Catalysts for Change," *TQM Magazine*, 1992.

19. Samuel, "Catalysts for Change."

20. James H. Davis, "Who Owns Your Quality Program? Lessons from the Baldrige Award Winners," College of Business Administration, University of Notre Dame (n.d.).

21. John Persico, Jr., Betty L. Bednarczyk, and David P. Negus, "Three Routes to the Same Destination: TQM, Part 1," *Quality Progress*, January 1990, pp. 29–33.

22. *Business Week*, "Where Did They Go Wrong?" October 25, 1991.

23. Leadership Steering Committee, *A Report of The Total Quality Leadership Steering Committee and Working Councils*, Procter & Gamble Total Quality Forum, November 1992.

24. Thomas H. Patten, Jr., "Beyond Systems—The Politics of Managing in a TQM Environment," *National Productivity Review*, 1991/1992.

25. George H. Labovitz and Y.S. Chang "Learn from the Best," *Quality Progress*, 1990, pp. 81–85; J.M. Juran, "Strategies for World Class Quality," *Quality Progress*, March 1991, pp. 81–85.

26. Davis, "Who Owns Your Quality Program?"

27. American Quality Foundation and Ernst & Young, International Quality Study Best Practices Report, 1992; *Business Week*, "Quality," November 30, 1992.

28. Cyndee Miller, "TQM's Value Criticized in New Report," *Marketing News*, 1992.

29. "TQM," The Stroh Brewing Company.

30. Adapted from James A. Alloway, Jr., "Laying Groundwork for Total Quality," *Quality Progress*, Vol. 27, No. 1, January 1994, pp. 65–67. © 1994 American Society for Quality, reprinted with permission.

Bibliography

This bibliography is a sampling of the hundreds of books that have been published in response to the quality revolution. They are arranged in the following categories:

1. Malcolm Baldrige National Quality Award
2. Deming philosophy
3. Employee involvement/human resources
4. General reference
5. Management
6. Case studies of quality practices
7. Service organizations
8. Tools

Malcolm Baldrige National Quality Award

Brown, M.G. *Baldrige Award Winning Quality: How to Interpret the Malcolm Baldridge Award Criteria* (8th ed.). White Plains, N.Y.: Quality Resources and ASQC Quality Press, 1998.

Haavind, R. *The Road to the Baldrige Award*. Boston: Butterworth-Heinemann, 1992.

Ross, J.E . *Total Quality Management: Text, Cases and Readings*. Delray Beach, Fla.: St. Lucie Press, 1993.

Steeples, M.M. *The Corporate Guide to the Malcolm Baldrige National Quality Award: Proven Strategies for Building Quality into Your Organization*. Milwaukee: ASQC Quality Press and Business One Irwin, 1992.

Deming Philosophy

Aguayo, R. *Dr. Deming: The American Who Taught the Japanese About Quality*. New York: Simon & Schuster, 1990.

Deming, W.E. *Out of the Crisis*. Cambridge, Mass.: Massachusetts Institute of Technology Center of Advanced Engineering Study, 1982.

Gabor, A. *The Man Who Discovered Quality: How W. Edwards Deming Brought the Quality Revolution to America—The Stories of Ford, Xerox, and GM.* New York: Times Books, 1990.

Joiner, Brian L. *Fourth Generation Management.* New York: McGraw-Hill, 1994.

Killian, C.S. *The World of W. Edwards Deming.* Washington, D.C.: CEEPress Books, 1988.

Mann, N.R. *The Keys to Excellence: The Story of the Deming Philosophy.* Los Angeles: Prestwick Books, 1989.

Neave, H.R. *The Deming Dimension.* Knoxville: SPC Press, 1990.

Scherkenbach, *William W. Deming's Road to Continual Improvement.* Knoxville, Tenn.: SPC Press, 1991.

Walton, M. *Deming Management at Work.* New York: G.P. Putnam's Sons, 1990.

Employee Invovement/Human Resources

Cooksey, Clifton, Richard Beans, and Debra Eshelman. *Process Improvement: A Guide for Teams.* Arlington, Va.: Coopers & Lybrand, 1993.

Grazier, P.B. *Before It's Too Late: Employee Involvement . . . An Idea Whose Time Has Come.* Chadds Ford, Pa.: Teambuilding, Inc., 1989.

Kinlaw, Dennis C. *Developing Superior Work Teams.* Lexington, Mass.: Lexington Books, 1991.

Kohn, A. *No Contest: The Case Against Competition.* Boston: Houghton Mifflin, 1986.

Ryan, K.D., and D.K. Oestreich. *Driving Fear Out of the Workplace: How to Overcome the Barriers to Quality, Productivity, and Innovation.* San Francisco: Jossey-Bass Publishers, 1991.

Scholtes, P.R. *The Team Handbook.* Madison, Wisc.: Joiner and Associates, 1988.

Wellins, Richard S., William C. Byham, and Jeanne M. Wilson. *Empowered Teams.* San Francisco: Jossey-Bass, 1991.

General Reference

Evans, J.R., and W.M. Lindsay. *The Management and Control of Quality* (4th ed.). Cincinnati: South-Western Publishing Company, 1999.

Feigenbaum, A.V. *Total Quality Control* (3rd ed., revised). New York: McGraw-Hill Book Company, 1991.

Forsha, H.I. *The Pursuit of Quality Through Personal Change.* Milwaukee: ASQC Quality Press, 1992.

Johnson, R.S., and L.E. Kazense. *TQM: The Mechanics of Quality Processes.* Milwaukee: ASQC Quality Press, 1993.

Juran, J.M., and F.M. Gryna. *Juran's Quality Control Handbook* (4th ed.). New York: McGraw-Hill Book Company, 1988.

Juran, J.M. *Juran on Planning for Quality.* New York: The Free Press, 1988.

Juran, J.M. *Juran on Quality by Design,* New York: The Free Press, 1992.

Juran, J.M. *A History of Managing for Quality,* Milwaukee: ASQC Quality Press, 1995.

Shetty, Y.K., and V.M. Buehler. *The Quest for Competitiveness*. New York: Quorum Books, 1991.

Tenner, A.R., and I.J. DeToro. *Total Quality Management: Three Steps to Continuous Improvement*. Reading, Mass.: Addison Wesley, 1992.

Townsend, P.L., and J.E. Gebhardt. *Quality in Action: 93 Lessons in Leadership, Participation, and Measurement*. New York: John Wiley & Sons, 1992.

Walsh, L., R. Wurster, and R.J. Kimber, eds. *Quality Management Handbook*. New York: Marcel Dekker, Inc., and ASQC Quality Press, 1986.

Management

Berry, T.H. *Managing the Total Quality Transformation*. New York: McGraw-Hill, 1991.

Bowles, J., and J. Hammond. *Beyond Quality: How 50 Winning Companies Use Continuous Improvement*. New York: G.P. Putnam's Sons, 1991.

Brocka, B., and M.S. Brocka. *Quality Management: Implementing the Best Ideas of the Masters*. Homewood, Ill.: Irwin, 1992.

Chawla, Sarita, and John Renesch, eds. *Learning Organizations: Developing Cultures for Tomorrow's Workplace*, Portland, Oreg.: Productivity Press, 1995.

Dixon, G., and J. Swiler. *Total Quality Handbook: The Executive Guide to the New American Way of Doing Business*. Minneapolis, Minn.: Lakewood Books, 1990.

Dobyns, L., and C. Crawford-Mason. *Quality or Else: The Revolution in World Business*. Boston: Houghton Mifflin Company, 1991.

Eureka, W.E., and N.E. Ryan. *The Customer-Driven Company: Managerial Perspectives on QFD*. Dearborn, Mich.: ASI Press, 1988.

Garvin, D.A. *Managing Quality: The Strategic and Competitive Edge*. New York: The Free Press, 1988.

Hradesky, J.L. *Productivity and Quality Improvement: A Practical Guide to Implementing Statistical Process Control*. New York: McGraw-Hill Book Company, 1988.

Hudiburg, J.J. *Winning with Quality: The FPL Story*. White Plains, N.Y.: Quality Resources, 1991.

Imai, M. Kaizen: *The Key to Japan's Competitive Success*. New York: McGraw-Hill Publishing Company, 1986.

King, B. *Hoshin Planning: The Developmental Approach*. Methuen, Mass.: GOAL/QPC, 1989.

Schmidt, Warren H., and Jerome P. Finnigan. *The Race Without a Finish Line*. San Francisco: Jossey-Bass, 1992.

Senge, P.M. *The Fifth Discipline: The Art and Practice of the Learning Organization*. New York: Doubleday Currency, 1990.

Shecter, E.S. *Managing for World-Class Quality: A Primer for Executives and Managers*. New York: Marcel Dekker, Inc., and ASQC Quality Press, 1992.

Whiteley, R.C. *The Customer-Driven Company: Moving from Talk to Action*. New York: Addison-Wesley Publishing Company, Inc., 1991.

Case Studies of Quality Practices

American National Standard: Guide for Quality Control Charts, Control Chart Method of Analyzing Data, Control Chart Method of Controlling Quality during Production. Milwaukee: American Society for Quality Control, 1985.

Hiam, A. *Closing the Quality Gap: Lessons from America's Leading Companies.* Englewood Cliffs, N.J.: Prentice-Hall, 1992.

International Quality Study: A Definitive Report on International Industry-Specific Quality Management Practices (Automotive Industry Report). Cleveland, Ohio: Ernst & Young and American Quality Foundation, 1992.

International Quality Study: A Definitive Report on International Industry-Specific Quality Management Practices (Banking Industry Report). Cleveland, Ohio: Ernst & Young and American Quality Foundation, 1992.

International Quality Study: A Definitive Report on International Industry-Specific Quality Management Practices (Computer Industry Report). Cleveland, Ohio: Ernst & Young and American Quality Foundation, 1992.

International Quality Study: A Definitive Report on International Industry-Specific Quality Management Practices (Health Care Industry Report). Cleveland, Ohio: Ernst & Young and American Quality Foundation, 1992.

Lefevre, H. *Government Quality and Productivity—Success Stories.* Milwaukee: ASQC Quality Press, 1990.

Peters, T., and N. Austin. *A Passion for Excellence: The Leadership Difference.* New York: Random House, 1985.

Peters, T.J., and R.H. Waterman, Jr. *In Search of Excellence: Lessons from America's Best-Run Companies.* New York: Harper & Row Publishers, 1982.

Service Organizations

Baker, R.H. *Serve Yourself: Customer Service from the Inside Out.* Amherst, Mass.: Human Resource Development Press, Inc., 1992.

DiPrimio, A. *Quality Assurance in Service Organizations.* Radnor, Pa.: Chilton Book Company, 1987.

Drewes, W.F. *Quality Dynamics for the Service Industry.* Milwaukee: ASQC Quality Press, 1991.

Heskett, J.L., W.E. Sasser, Jr., and C.W.L. Hart. *Service Breakthroughs: Changing the Rules of the Game.* New York: The Free Press, 1990.

Lash, L.M. *The Complete Guide to Customer Service.* New York: John Wiley & Sons, 1989.

Lefevre, H.L. *Quality Service Pays: Six Keys to Success.* Milwaukee: ASQC Quality Press and Quality Resources, 1989.

Lele, M.M., and J.N. Sheth. *The Customer Is Key: Gaining an Unbeatable Advantage Through Customer Satisfaction.* New York: John Wiley & Sons, Inc., 1987.

Rosander, A.C. *The Quest for Quality in Services.* Milwaukee: ASQC Quality Press and Quality Resources, 1989.

Rosander, A.C. *Deming's 14 Points Applied to Services.* New York: Marcel Dekker, Inc., and ASQC Quality Press, 1991.

Spechler, J.W. *When America Does It Right: Case Studies in Service Quality*. Norcross, Ga.: Industrial Engineering and Management Press, 1988.

Tschohl, J. *Achieving Excellence Through Customer Service*. New York: Prentice-Hall, 1991.

Zeithaml, V.A., A. Parasuraman, and L.L. Berry. *Delivering Quality Service: Balancing Customer Perceptions and Expectations*. New York: The Free Press, 1990.

Tools

Automotive Division: Statistical Process Control Manual. Milwaukee: American Society for Quality Control, 1986.

Basic Training in TQM Analysis Techniques. Springfield, Va.: U.S. Department of Commerce, National Technical Information Service, 1989.

Brassard, Michael. *The Memory Jogger Plus+*. Methuen, Mass.: GOAL/QPC, 1989.

Clements, R.B. *Handbook of Statistical Methods in Manufacturing*. Englewood Cliffs, N.J.: Prentice-Hall, 1991.

DataMyte Handbook: A Practical Guide to Computerized Data Collection for Statistical Process Control (3d ed.). Minnetonka, Minn.: DataMyte Corporation, 1987.

Evans, James R. *Statistical Process Control for Quality Improvement: A Training Guide to Learning SPC*. Englewood Cliffs, N.J.: Prentice-Hall, 1991.

Gitlow, H., S. Gitlow, A. Oppenheim, and R. Oppenheim. *Tools and Methods for the Improvement of Quality*. Homewood, Ill.: Irwin, 1989.

Harrington, H.J. *The Improvement Process: How America's Leading Companies Improve Quality*. New York: McGraw-Hill Book Company, 1987.

Ishikawa, K. *Guide to Quality Control*. Tokyo: Asian Productivity Organization, 1982.

Leebov, W., and C.J. Ersoz. *The Health Care Manager's Guide to Continuous Quality Improvement*. American Hospital Association, 1991.

Marsh, S., J.W. Moran, S. Nakui, and G. Hoffherr. *Facilitating and Training in Quality Function Deployment*. Methuen, Mass.: GOAL/QPC, 1991.

Mazur, G., J.B. ReVelle, and S. Nakui. *Quality Function Deployment: Advanced QFD Application Articles*. Methuen, Mass.: GOAL/QPC, 1991.

Mears, Peter. *Quality Improvement Tools and Techniques*. New York: McGraw-Hill, 1995.

Miller, G.L., and L.L. Krumm. *The Whats, Whys, and Hows of Quality Improvement*. Milwaukee: ASQC Quality Press, 1992.

Mizuno, S., ed. *Management for Quality Improvement: The Seven New QC Tools*. Cambridge, Mass.: Productivity Press, 1988.

Moran, J.W., R.P. Talbot, and R.M. Benson. *A Guide to Graphical Problem-Solving Processes*. Milwaukee: ASQC Quality Press, 1990.

Morse, W.J., H.P. Roth, and K.M. Poston. *Measuring, Planning, and Controlling Quality Costs*. Montvale, N.J.: National Association of Accountants, 1987.

Nikkan Kogyo Shimbun, Ltd./Factory Magazine, ed. *Poka-Yoke: Improving Product Quality by Preventing Defects*. Cambridge, Mass.: Productivity Press, 1988.

Ott, E.R. *Process Quality Control: Troubleshooting and Interpretation of Data.* New York: McGraw-Hill Book Company, 1975.

Participant Guide for Total Quality Management (TQM) Quantitative Methods Workshop. Springfield, Va.: U.S. Department of Commerce, National Technical Information Service, May 1990.

Pyzdek, T. *Pyzdek's Guide to SPC: Volume One /Fundamentals.* Tucson: Quality Publishing, Inc., and ASQC Quality Press, 1990.

Pyzdek, T. *Pyzdek's Guide to SPC: Volume One /Fundamentals (Workbook).* Tucson: Quality Publishing, Inc. and ASQC Quality Press, 1989.

Pyzdek, T. *Pyzdek's Guide to SPC: Volume One/Fundamentals (Workbook for Services).* Tucson: Quality Publishing, Inc., and ASQC Quality Press, 1992.

Pyzdek, T. *An SPC Primer: Programmed Learning Guide to Statistical Process Control Techniques.* Tucson: Quality America, Inc., 1987.

Swanson, Roger. *The Quality Improvement Handbook.* Delray Beach, Fla.: St. Lucie Press, 1995.

Wilson, P.F., L.D. Dell, and G.F. Anderson. *Root Cause Analysis.* Milwaukee: ASQC Quality Press, 1993.

Index